THE COMPLETE IDIOT'S GUIDE TO

Slam Poetry

by Marc Kelly Smith with Joe Kraynak

ALPHA

A member of Penguin Group (USA) Inc.

This book is dedicated to the slam family and the folks who have performed at, organized, attended, embraced, and believed in the slam across America and around the world.

Publisher: *Marie Butler-Knight*
Product Manager: *Phil Kitchel*
Senior Managing Editor: *Jennifer Chisholm*
Acquisitions Editor: *Mikal E. Belicove*
Development Editor: *Ginny Bess Munroe*
Production Editor: *Megan Douglass*
Copy Editor: *Molly Schaller*
Illustrator: *Jody Schaeffer*
Cover/Book Designer: *Trina Wurst*
Indexer: *Tonya Heard*
Layout/Proofreading: *Angela Calvert, Donna Martin*

Contents at a Glance

Part 1:   **What Is the Poetry Slam?**   1

1   Digging the Roots of Spoken Word Poetry   3
Learn the history of spoken word poetry, starting with the Greek poets and dramatists.

2   Soaking In the Spirit of Slam   19
Take a peek at the community, the spirit of the slam movement, and the people who carry on its tradition.

3   Slam Competition—Rules, Regulations, and Other Formalities   29
Take a brief primer on the rules and regulations that govern most poetry slam competitions and the way those rules are bent and broken.

Part 2:   **Becoming a Performance Poet**   45

4   Penning the Powerful Slam Poem   47
Pick up a truckload of tips and tricks for composing powerful performance poems.

5   From Page to Stage   63
Try out some professional techniques for overcoming stage fright, establishing an effective rehearsal regime, and delivering a powerful performance.

6   Honing Your Performance Technique   75
Graduate from absolute beginner to star-status thespian by practicing the techniques and exercises in this chapter.

7   Building a Performance and a Few More Skills   91
Structure a complete performance from opener to closer and pick up a few more skills along the way.

8   Where and How to Gig Around   105
From open-mike night at neighborhood venues to paid professional gigs at the hottest nightclubs, this chapter shows you the where and how of slam poetry.

Part 3   **Going Poet Professional**   115

9   Packaging and Promoting Your Performance   117
Assemble a killer press pack complete with your resumé, poetry action photos, audio recordings, video clips, and sample poems, and learn how to promote yourself.

10 Taking Your Show on the Road   131

*Everything you need to know to plan a successful tour,
schmooze club owners and slam organizers, and make sure
you get paid.*

11 Old-School Advice: Act Professional   143

*Take your bohemian poet status seriously and learn how
to follow proper etiquette at a slam poetry competition.*

Part 4:   Setting the Stage for Yourself and Others   155

12 Should I Become A Slammaster?   157

*Ask the right soul-searching questions to find out if you have
what it takes to become a slammaster. Do you really want to
do it?*

13 Scoping Out the Right Venue   171

*Go bar-hopping and find the right place to stage your poetry
slam. Here you learn what to look for in the ideal venue.*

14 All the Slam's a Stage   185

*Learn the conditions and platforms on which you will be
performing and how they will affect your show.*

15 Let's Get Technical   195

*Lights, sound, camera, action! Making sure everything works
the way it's supposed to before the curtain rises on that really
big show.*

16 Choosing Your Crew   207

*Don't try this alone. Learn how to draft the right people and
assemble an effective, efficient, and enjoyable volunteer staff.*

17 Taking Ownership of *Your* Show   217

*Infuse your show with your personality, and let your vision
be the driving force. Here's how.*

18 Get the Word Out: Publicizing Your Show   229

*Grab your flyers, your megaphone, and half a dozen friends,
and start spreading the word. If you promote it, they will
come.*

19 It's Showtime!   243

*Opening night, a packed house, and sparks are flying ...
now what? Here you learn everything you need to know
to put on a brilliant show.*

20 Expanding Your Market: Special Shows   259
    Broaden your slam vision with ideas for special shows,
    road trips, and other intriguing slam offerings.

Part 5:   **We Are Slamily: The Slam Family**   **273**

21 Take It from the Top: PSI, the National Organization   275
    Join the ever-expanding slam family by becoming a member,
    volunteering, and attending a few meetings.

22 NPS-IWPS: The National Competitions   287
    Bone up on everything from the history of the Nationals to
    the steps you must take to officially enter your team into the
    competition.

23 More Eventful Events (and How to Get Involved)   303
    Learn about and take advantage of other important, official
    slam events around the country.

24 Slam the World Over: The Global Community   315
    Take a world tour of slam from the United States to Canada,
    Germany, Switzerland, France, and even Singapore!

Appendixes

A Reference Material   327
    Still hungry for slam? Then check out these additional
    books and articles.

B Slammin' Websites   331
    Many poetry slams and individual slam poets across the
    country and around the world have their own websites.
    Here are some of the best.

C SlamSlang   339
    When you encounter a cryptic term or phrase, turn to this
    SlamSlang glossary to learn what it means. It doesn't cover
    all the terms, but it comes pretty close.

    Index   347

    CD Track List   374

Contents

Part 1: What Is the Poetry Slam?   **1**

1 Digging the Roots of Spoken Word Poetry   **3**

Spoken Word Poetry's Long Tradition 4
  Battling Bards *5*
  Beat, Hip-Hop, Rap, and Other Genres *6*
Slam Takes Center Stage 7
  Sowing the Seeds of Slam *7*
  The Big Definition of Slam Poetry *8*
  Poetry and Performance *9*
  Conflicts and Synergies *9*
  Staged Bouts for Audience Appeal *9*
  Family, Feuds, and Friendships *10*
Who Inspired This Madness? and Why? 11
  The Chicago Poetry Ensemble *11*
  The Fires Rage *12*
Poetry Of, By, and For the People 13
Wherefore Art Thou, Slam? 13
Slam Poetry Goes National 14
  Marc's Blow-by-Blow Account of the First NPS *14*
  To Balance the Account—Gary Glazer's Recollections *15*
  The One-Two Punch: The Second and Third NPS *16*
Slam Poetry Goes Global 16
Slam Poetry Here and Now 17

2 Soaking In the Spirit of Slam   **19**

"The Points Are Not the Point" 20
Relearning the Art of Listening 21
Performance Poet as Audience Servant 22
Boo! Hiss! Audience with Attitude 23
Breaking Down the Color (and Collar) Barriers 23
Competition and Camaraderie 25
The Culture of Democracy 26

3 Slam Competition—Rules, Regulations, and Other Formalities   29

It's a Game, Stupid! 30

The First Slam Competition 31

Following the Rules 32

  Perform Your Own Work 33

  Three Minutes Is All We Can Stand 33

  No Props, Costumes, Trombones, or Other Carry-on Luggage 33

  Scoring: 0 to 10 (or Down to Minus Infinity) 34

Famous Slam Disclaimers 35

  We Begin Each Slam with a Disclaimer—Bob Holman
    at the Nuyorican Café 35

  The Mean Chicago Rules—Marc (So What!) Smith 36

  The Official Emcee Spiel Used at the National Poetry Slams 37

The Many Flavors of Slam 37

  Unseen Slam 37

  Theme Slams 38

  Cover Slam 39

  Relay Slam 39

  Prop Slam 40

  Pong Jam Slam—Music to the Poetic Ear 40

Local Slams—Laws and Bye-Laws 41

Heading for the Nationals—Get Serious! 42

Part 2:   Becoming a Performance Poet   45

4 Penning the Powerful Slam Poem   47

Seeing Is Believing—Concrete Vs. Abstract Language 48

  Slam Examples of Concrete Language 49

  Abstract Language 49

  Flaccid Phrasing 50

  Too Smart for Your Performance 51

Rock to the Rhythm 51

It's Gotta Sound Good, Too 53

Guess the Rhyme 54

No Sermons, But If You Must Preach ... .55

Once Upon a Slam—Storytelling 57

What's Your Point—Oratory, Poetics, or a Laundry
  List of Love? 59
    Pop Ideas and Newspaper Politics 60
    Write About Yourself 60
All Forms Can Slam 61

5 From Page to Stage   63

Confronting Stage Fright—Overcoming the Fear 63
    Slay the Confidence Busters 64
    Is That Text Well-Prepared? 65
    Visualize Success 66
    Practice, Practice, Practice 66
    Shift Your Focus 66
    Please Release Me 67
    Tricks (or No-Brainers) of the Trade 68
    Not Recommended 68
Celebrating Your Slam Virginity, and Then Losing It 69
Accumulate Stage Time 70
Rehearse, Rehearse, Rehearse 71
From Closet to Mirror to Tape Recorder to Friendly Ears 72
    Through the Looking Glass 72
    Replay 73
    Recruiting a Critique 73
    Let It Out in Workshops 73

6 Honing Your Performance Technique   75

Performance as an Art Form 76
    Engage 76
    Entertain 77
    Affect 77
Entertaining Fundamentals 78
    Vary the Volume 78
    Tweak the Tempo 80
    Articulate 81
    Breathe Deep and Pause 82
Shake, Gesture, and Move 83
    Walk the Talk 84
    Imagine the Stone 84

Paint the Reading Room Red 85

Shake It Out 85

Look 'Em in the Eye 85

Mood, Persona, and Where You Be 87

7 Building a Performance and a Few More Skills   91

Mastering the Art of Seductive Revelation 92

Enter and Open with Flair 92

Hold 'Em 94

Mixing It Up 95

Something Up Your Sleeve 95

From Knee-Slappers to Side-Splitters 95

Spectacle and Visual Accessories 96

Musical Accompaniment and Sound Effects 96

The Edge 96

Cohesive and Corrosive Patter 97

Closers 97

Be Genuine in Content and Style 98

All Forms Can Slam—Take Two 99

Avoiding Common Performance Clichés 99

Memorization 100

How We Make Memory Deposits 100

Bringing It Back 101

The Memorization Curve 101

Performing in the Zone 102

8 Where and How to Gig Around   105

Happy Days Are Here Again 106

Open Mike Search 106

Getting on Track with Weekly or Monthly Shows 108

All the Gigs You Can Do 108

Bookstore Readings 109

Nightclubs, Saloons, and Other Informal Venues 109

Late-Night Theater 110

Performance Venues 110

Schools Can Do It, Too (Educational Outreach) 110

Don't Forget the Slams 110

Do-It-Yourself Venues (Create Your Own Show) 111
Performance Poetry Etiquette 101 111
　Proper Etiquette for Poets and Performers *111*
　Audience Etiquette *113*

Part 3:　Going Poet Professional　　　　　　　115

9　Packaging and Promoting Your Performance　　117
Thinking Like a Marketing Mogul 118
Slapping Together a Press Pack 118
　Get It in Print *119*
　Get It on Tape *120*
　Roll 'Em: Filming Your Act *123*
　Low-Budget or All-Out Glitz? *124*
Establishing Yourself on the Web 124
　Structuring Your Website *125*
　Promoting Your Website *126*
Generating Stories, Interviews, and Media Attention 126
　Step 1: Write a Press Release *127*
　Step 2: Send the Press Release *127*
　Step 3: Call 'Em *127*
　Work Your Angle *128*
　Hit the Airwaves *129*
　Press the Flesh *129*

10　Taking Your Show on the Road　　　　　131
Tour Planning 101 132
　Step 1: Route Your Tour *132*
　Step 2: Score Some Gigs *133*
　Step 3: Get a Ride *134*
　Step 4: Find a Place to Sleep and Shower *134*
　Step 5: Marketing Your Tour *135*
Schmoozing the Bookers, the Waiters, the Ticket Takers 136
　Slams and Their Masters *136*
　Nightclub Owners and Their Managers *136*
　Buttering Up the Booking Agents *137*
　Concert Halls—Performing in the Big House *138*

Don't Get Set Up to Fail 139
Getting Paid 140

11 Old-School Advice: Act Professional   143

Oh, Behave! 144
Keep It Down During a Performance 145
Don't Pull Focus While Others Are Performing 145
Don't Glower 145
No Hoot-and-Holler Cheerleading 145
Keep Conspicuous Negative Opinions to Yourself 146
It's Not Your House 146
Would You Talk That Way to Grandma? 147
Be Prepared 148
Have a Plan 148
Practice Your Performance 149
Offstage Preparation: Getting the Nerves Out 149
Hitting Your Mark 150
Use Your Nervous Condition to Your Advantage 150
Make the Right Approach 150
Take the Mike 151
Respect Your Audience 151
Primping for the Stage 151
Hawking Your Wares 152

Part 4: Setting the Stage for Yourself and Others   155

12 Should I Become a Slammaster?   157

Do You Have the Itch? 158
Taking Inventory—Do You Have What It Takes? 159
Are You Doing This for Yourself? 159
Do You Have a Vision? 160
Do You Have a Support Network? 160
Do You Have the Time and Energy? 161
Are You a Show Maker? 162
Are You As Crazy As the Rest of Us? 163
Tallying Your Talents and Resources 163
Been There, Seen That 163
Been There, Done That 164

The Obstacles Ahead 164

The Hoity-Toity Establishment *164*

Cash Flow Problems *165*

Shifting Sands—Unforeseen Changes *165*

Pettiness and Social Hostility *166*

Sharpening Your Vision 167

Look Inside: Personal Needs *167*

Look Around: Community Needs *167*

Slam Spin-Offs—An Ever-Evolving Art *168*

13 Scoping Out the Right Venue   **171**

Composing a Venue Wish List 172

Think Small—Small Enough to Create a Happening *172*

Ambience Is Everything *173*

Frame the Picture 175

The Necessary Services *176*

Location, Location, Location *176*

Now Write It Down 177

Say Ohhmmm and Begin the Search 177

The Finger Walking List *178*

Foot Walking List *178*

Get Connected *179*

Pick a Night 179

Judgment Day 180

Closing the Deal 181

Money Talk *181*

Who Does What? *182*

Hey! I Can't Find a Venue! 183

Hooray! You Did It! Now Make It Yours 183

14 All the Slam's a Stage   **185**

Rising Above the Rabble—Stage Focus 185

Poet-in-a-Box: The Black Box 186

Above the Crowd on the Bandstand 187

The Spartan Stage: Cleared Space 188

The Great Hall 188

The Big-Time Stage: The Proscenium 189
   Bring on the Bells and Whistles *189*
   Bigger's Not Always Better *189*
The Outdoor Stage: Help! 190
   Speak Up, They Can't Hear Ya! *190*
   Think Big *191*
The Rickety Rent-A-Stage 191
What? No Stage?! No Cleared Space?! 192
Worse Than Nothing: Bad Scenes 192

15 Let's Get Technical   **195**

Tuning In to Sound Systems—Can You Hear Me Now? 196
   "Testing ... One ... Two ... Three ..." *196*
Light 'Em if They Got 'Em 198
   Lights Up, Lights Down *198*
   Homespun Lighting Systems *199*
   Top-Shelf Lighting *199*
Adding Some Glitz 200
   Dressing for Performance *200*
   Spicing It Up with a Little Music *202*
   Slide Shows *202*
   Props and Drops *205*

16 Choosing Your Crew   **207**

Flying Solo—the Self-Made Slam 208
Organizing by Committee 208
The Duties to Delegate 209
   Marketing *209*
   Scouting for Talented Performers *210*
   Trustworthy and Reliable Assistants *210*
Emcees Wanted—Charisma Required 211
   Auditioning Emcees *212*
   Relief Pitchers—Back-Up Emcees Need Charisma, Too *213*
   Mixing It Up with Different Personalities *213*
Offstage Support 214
   Sound and Light *214*
   Doorperson *214*

Scorekeepers/Timers 215

Merchandise Sellers 215

Judges 215

In-House Ensembles 216

17 Taking Ownership of *Your* Show   217

Acting as Gracious Host 218

Greeting Your Guests 218

Introducing Your Guests 219

Acting as the Maitre d' 219

Setting a Stage, Not a Pedestal 219

Watch the Clock—Starting on Time 221

Fueling Audience Frenzy 221

Making the Most of a $lam $ituation 222

Preserving the History 222

Creating Anthologies 223

Compilation CDs 224

T-Shirts and Souvenirs 225

Establishing Profitable Partnerships 226

Absurd Ambitions and Other Worldly Temptations 226

18 Get the Word Out: Publicizing Your Show   229

Know What You're Promoting 230

Angles and Selling Points 230

Marketing Materials: Forms That Fit 231

Making a Name (and Logo) for Yourself 231

Cheap, but Effective: Flyers and Postcards 232

Not as Cheap, but Very Effective: Posters 233

Garnering Some Free Press 233

Managing Mailing (and E-Mailing) Lists 234

Paid Ads 234

Cool Calls 235

Website Appeal 235

Radio and TV 236

Never Underestimate Word-of-Mouth 237

To Whom Are You Promoting? 237
   How Many People Do You Need to Reach? 237
   Calculating the Break-Even Point 238
Motivating Yourself with Deadlines 239
The Push 239
Thank You and Goodnight 240

19 It's Showtime!   **243**

Finding Form in Your Vision 244
Drawing Up a Slam Itinerary 244
The Main Station Stops 246
   Greetings 246
   Open Mike 246
   Special Acts and Guest Performers 247
   The Competition 248
Detailing Your Trip Tick 249
   Adding Ceremony and Ritual 249
   Bring It On—Heckles, Jekylls, and Hydes 251
   Jacks in the Box 251
Competition as a Theatrical Device 253
   Signing 'Em Up 253
   Picking the Judges 253
   Alternative Styles of Judging 255
To Spin or Not to Spin? 256
Pace 256
Leave 'Em Wanting More Effect 257

20 Expanding Your Market: Special Shows   **259**

Courting the Institutions 260
   Types of Institutions 260
   Getting Your Foot in the Door 261
Book Fairs and Festivals 262
Corporate Conventions and Corporate Programming 262
Benefits and Their Paybacks 263
Shaping Your Show for a Special Gig 263
   Motorcycle Slam 263
   Celebrity Slam 264
   Slam Dunk Poetry Day 265

Other Twists 266

The Youth Slam 266

The Music + Poetry + Slam Slam 267

Bah! Humbug! The Holiday Slam 267

From Nothing Something Slams 268

Fat Tuesday Celebration of the Seven Deadly Sins 268

Chi Town Classic 268

Slammin' Across America 269

Your Overall Strategy 270

Part 5:   We Are Slamily: The Slam Family   273

21   Take It from the Top: PSI, the National Organization   275

Incorporation—A Necessary Evil 276

Connecting to the National Scene 277

Becoming a PSI Member 277

Help Wanted: Volunteers 279

Staying in the Loop with the Listserv 280

Open Lines of Communication 280

PSI's Noncorporate, Nonprofit Structure 281

The Slam Family 281

The SlamMasters' Council 282

How to Register and Certify Your Slam 283

Certification and Registration—What's the Difference? 283

What Is Certification "Evidence"? 284

How Long Does Certification or Registration Last? 284

The Closest Thing to a Corporate Structure:
The Executive Council 284

Professional and Volunteer Staff 285

Subcommittees 286

22   NPS-IWPS: The National Competitions   287

A Brief History Lesson 288

Tournament Rites and Rituals 288

Preshow Tuesday 288

Opening Day 289

It's All About Bouts 289

Sideshows and Other Roadside Attractions 290

Meetings and Other Formalities 290

Hey, We Have Fun, Too 292

It's Official—The PSI Rule Book 292

Three Basic Rules 293

The Three-Minute Rule 294

Team Pieces 295

Scoring 296

Judges 296

Sending a Team 297

Team Selection Process 298

Who Gets To Go? 298

Competing as an Individual 299

Storm Poets at NPS 299

Flying Solo at IWPS 299

Attending as a Volunteer 300

Hosting a National Competition 300

23 More Eventful Events (and How to Get Involved)   303

PSI Educational and Outreach Programs 304

Slam Graduates: ACUI College Slam 304

Slam Summer Camp 305

*Pumping Poetic Iron at the United States Scholar-
Athlete Games* 306

Slammin' @ Your Library 306

New York SCORES Annual Poetry 306

Sowing the Seeds of Slam 307

Closer to Home: Regional Slams 307

Southern Fried Poetry Slam 307

Rust Belt Slam 308

Western Regional Slam at Big Sur 309

Slam Spin-Offs 310

Midwest Poetry Slam League 310

The New Word Series 311

Battle of the Bay 312

Taos Poetry Circus 312

The Canadian Spoken Word Olympics 313

Russell Simmons's Def Poetry Jam 313

24 Slam the World Over: The Global Community   **315**

Exploring Slam's Growth Pattern 316

Slam in Germany 317

Slammin' at the Substanz *318*

The History of the German International Poetry Slam *318*

Poetry Slam in Denmark 321

Slam in Switzerland 321

Slam in France 322

Slam in Singapore 324

Other Slam Importers 325

Appendixes

A Reference Material   **327**

B Slammin' Websites   **331**

C SlamSlang   **339**

Index   **347**

CD Track List   **374**

Foreword

I can't tell you how many people I've met whose lives were changed by the poetry slam. In Chicago there are dozens of writers and performers who found their voices onstage at the Green Mill. Lots of them have moved on and now do other kinds of writing, for bigger audiences. But the slam lives on in most of their work, and I'd describe its presence this way: They're writers who never forget they're writing for an audience. They entertain. They know what it means to get booed off a stage.

When I was a reporter working in the public schools, I hooked up with some high school students who competed in teen slams. For them it was anything but a lark. It was about getting people to hear their thoughts and hear their writing and take them seriously. It was about getting honest feedback from a real, live audience, which, of course, is what any writer needs most of all, especially when he or she is starting out, and what so few get. Slam poetry also created this amazing community, where sensitive, smart kids from the south side and west side and north side of the city, kids of different races and backgrounds, kids who were often seen as loners and oddballs in their own schools, all got to know each other. They had a nice little scene. For many of these kids, I think it was the first time they had real peers, and there were moments where you could feel their excitement at that: The world was just opening up to them and everything was new and giddy and very, very fun.

What Marc Smith invented when he created the slam was so deeply, intuitively perfect, it's kind of breathtaking. The slam is a game. The slam is a fun night out. The slam is an artistic form, with different rules and different pleasures than other artistic forms. The slam is powerful enough to change your life. That's a crazy combination of things, when you think about it.

And the book you're holding in your hand is his tell-all. The guy who invented basketball isn't here to give you advice on how to master the game, but the guy who invented the slam took the time to jot down some pointers, all the way down to how to overcome your stage fright and how to breathe.

Chances are, if you've read even this far into the book, you think you might want to try the slam, but you've never put yourself on stage like that with your own work before. The introverted part of yourself—which is a big part of most people who write—is standing sternly on guard over the other part of you, the hammier part. My advice is to give in to the hammier part. Being onstage can be really fun.

If you think this book might help you get over the hump, chances are it will. The unpretentious, DIY, let's-have-fun spirit of the slam is the same spirit behind the *Idiot's Guides*. Marc takes you through everything you need to know to get onstage to read your work, and—anticipating the possibility that you'll love it—he explains how to go pro, how to run your own slam events, how to do what he does. It's a generous book. Marc wants to help. Marc wants to keep the movement going. Marc thinks he just might be able to change your life.

—Ira Glass

Ira Glass is the host and producer of *This American Life*. The show is heard each week by over 1.6 million people on 470 public radio stations. It's produced by Chicago Public Radio and distributed by Public Radio International. *Time* magazine has named him "America's Best Radio Host." For more information, please visit www. thisamericanlife.org.

Introduction

Chicago. 1984. The Get Me High Jazz Club.

One fall night, in this place, poetry did something it hadn't done for decades. It rose off the page and wafted into the lungs of its passionate creators. It jumped up on the bar, right alongside beer bottles and half-empty glasses. It embodied itself in the very poet-performers who created it. And it screamed. It whispered. It pranced and danced. It cried and laughed. Most importantly, it engaged the audience, entertained it, and deeply affected it. And it hasn't stopped since.

Back in 1984, slam poetry ripped its way out of its artistic womb and resurrected the spoken word literary tradition. And the movement continues to grow. At bars and coffeehouses, church basements and nightclubs, in schools and meeting rooms, and even in the streets, poets are composing soul-searing poetry and performing it with the passionate intensity of actors on a stage. And the audience loves it.

Sound intriguing? You betcha. But slam poetry is more than that. It's poetry, performance, competition, community, business, spirituality, camaraderie, a social movement, and so much more. And now you want to be a part of it. But how do you get started? How do you write poetry that's conducive to an onstage performance? How do you find a place to perform it? How do you hone your acting skills to dazzle the audience? And how do you start your own poetry slam competitions? Well, that's what this book is all about.

Welcome to *The Complete Idiot's Guide to Slam Poetry*

Maybe you've penned a little verse on your own. Or you read some poetry in high school or college and really didn't like it. Maybe you just hunger for some more enlightening nightlife options than head-banger bands, wet t-shirt contests, and big-screen sports. Whatever the motivation, this book is devoted to welcoming you back to the world of poetry, proving that poetry can be fun and engaging, and showing you how to get involved in slam poetry by performing onstage, organizing slam shows, or even just becoming a more informed member of the audience. This book also provides plenty of sample poems, both in print and as audio recordings on the CDs, to show you some of the best of what slam has to offer.

What You Will Learn in This Book

This book includes information for all levels of poetry slam, from youngster to retiree, from novice to Pulitzer Prize–winning poet. It presents a brief history of the slam poetry movement along with the vision that inspired its beginning and fuels its development. It shows you what you need to know to compose and perform effective poetry at everything from open-mike night at your local coffee shop to paid performances at professional theatres. And if you don't have a slam show in your area, this book shows you how to start your own show. As an added bonus, this book takes you beyond the city limits to the National Poetry Slam and introduces you to the national and international community.

To provide some structure for this hodgepodge of topics and techniques, this book divides the material into the following easily digestible parts:

Part 1, "What Is the Poetry Slam?" provides a brief history of literature's oral tradition from the ancient Greeks to the present, reveals the vision that drives the slam poetry movement, and explains the rules and regulations that govern slam poetry competitions.

Part 2, "Becoming a Performance Poet," shows you how to compose and perform your own original poems. In this part, you learn techniques for composing poetry that's conducive to a live performance, exercises for rehearsing your poem and honing your acting skills, and how to sniff out places where they'll let you onstage.

Part 3, "Going Poet Professional," is for the more seasoned slam poet—when you feel confident enough in your craft to start making some money at it. This part starts by showing you how to market yourself and your performance, organize and manage a tour, and act like a professional, so people will take you seriously. It finishes by giving you some ideas for how to make money outside your performances.

Part 4, "Setting the Stage for Yourself and Others," moves you backstage and center stage, making you the puppet master of your very own slam show. First you learn if you're cut out for the job and want the aggravation. The remaining chapters go on to show you how to locate and evaluate prospective venues, assemble a team of volunteers, take control of your show, and deal with critics.

Part 5, "We Are Slamily: The Slam Family," takes you beyond your local slam to the national and international community. In this part, you learn how the organization operates and how you can get involved. You even learn how (and when) to fill out the essential paperwork for entering your team into the national competition. This part also helps you to understand more fully the competitive nature of slam and see it at work in the international scene.

Appendixes. At no additional charge, we included three valuable appendixes. Appendix A provides a list of additional books and articles about slam. Appendix B presents addresses and brief reviews of various slam websites. And Appendix C defines the most common slam jargon and details about key slam rules and regulations.

Notes, Tips, Cautions, and Other Extras

As you read through this book, you'll begin to notice that the pages are sprinkled with little boxes of text. Think of these as jewelry boxes—they contain some gems that were just too important to blend in with the other text. Be sure to check them out.

Backstage Skinny

When you've spent as many years as I have performing at and organizing poetry slams, you learn tricks and techniques from the best (and the worst) slam poets and organizers. These Backstage Skinny boxes take you behind the scenes to let you in on some of the secrets to success.

SlamSlang

Every discipline has its own shorthand and jargon, and slam poetry is no different. To keep you from feeling like an outsider, these SlamSlang boxes highlight and define any terms and phrases that you might find unfamiliar. Don't miss the glossary at the back of this book, either.

SlamSpeak

Poets have composed poetry to deal with every imaginable emotion, experience, and topic. When a poem is particularly pertinent to a topic or a seasoned slam poet was able to offer a unique insight, I dropped it in inside one of these little (and sometimes big) boxes.

Whoa!

Take my advice and learn from my mistakes—I've made plenty. To avoid some of the bonehead blunders made by most beginning slammers and organizers, scan the book for these Whoa! boxes and glean some sage advice.

Dig This!

As I was writing this book, ideas popped into my head that didn't quite fit into the standard text but were too important to leave out. I stuck them in these Dig This! boxes so you wouldn't feel cheated.

What's on the CD

The CDs at the back of this book contain some magnificent poetry and commentary. If a track on a CD is relevant to the current discussion, this CD Track icon tells you which track to play.

Acknowledgments

Several people had to don hard hats and get their hands dirty to build a better book. I owe special thanks to Mikal Belicove for choosing me to author this book, for handling the assorted details to get this book in gear, and for teaming me up with Joe Kraynak, one of the best wordsmiths in the business. Thanks to Ginny Munroe and Molly Schaller for guiding the content of this book, keeping it focused on novice slam poets, ferreting out all our typos, and fine-tuning our sentences. Megan Douglass deserves a free trip to Bora Bora for shepherding the manuscript (and art) through production. And the Alpha Books production team merits a round of applause for transforming a collection of electronic files into such an attractive book.

Special thanks to Mary Fons, my press secretary and pal on this journey; my good friends Mark Eleveld, Steve Marsh, and Gary Glazner; and the host of other slam family members who contributed their hard work, valuable insights, and unique voices to this book.

Trademarks

All terms mentioned in this book that are known to be or are suspected of being trademarks or service marks have been appropriately capitalized. Alpha Books and Penguin Group (USA) Inc. cannot attest to the accuracy of this information. Use of a term in this book should not be regarded as affecting the validity of any trademark or service mark.

Part 1

What Is the Poetry Slam?

Poetry slam blends poetry, performance, and competition to spawn a captivating event in which poets compete in front of an animated, electrified audience. It's a festival, a carnival act, an interactive class, a town meeting, a con game, and a poetic boxing match, all rolled into one.

This part introduces you to the world of poetry slam from its birth cries at the Get Me High Jazz Club in Chicago to its current international success. These chapters reveal slam's key philosophies, describe the social activist movement that fuels slam's growth, and provide details on the rules and regulations that govern poetry slam competitions.

Digging the Roots of Spoken Word Poetry

In This Chapter

- Understanding slam as the rebirth and extension of ancient oral traditions

- Tracing the chronicle of spoken word poetry prior to slam's emergence in the early 1980s

- Moving beyond the merely competitive nature of slam

- Zooming in on a definition of a slammer: Who? What? When? Where? Why?

- Scanning slam's over-15-year history on the national and international level

Slam poetry is a style of poetry that's composed for the purpose of being performed in front of a live audience and in a competitive arena. Slam poets battle against one another like wrestlers vying for a championship belt. Each poet takes his or her turn onstage to perform original poetry and prove superiority as both poet and performer. The audience typically gets involved, and crowds have been known to become a little unruly. As you'll learn later in this chapter, the competition itself isn't the core of slam poetry, but it does stimulate the poet/performers and the audience in an effort to raise the level of the art.

If you've ever attended a standard poetry reading, where poets read their works to stoic, well-behaved audiences, slam poetry might sound new and exhilarating—a cross between a poetry reading, a revival meeting, and a barroom brawl. However, poetry has a long tradition of being both loud and competitive. This chapter explores a bit of the history of spoken word poetry that gave rise to slam poetry and reveals the basic ideas that fuel slam's evolution.

Spoken Word Poetry's Long Tradition

Throughout human history the spoken word and poetry have been vital to communicating all aspects of the human condition. Every culture, every group of people, has had its poets and historians speak to them about love, hate, politics, family, neighbors, war, gods, and everything else that human beings typically care about. These poet/performers have proclaimed the joys of victory, the anguish of defeat, and all emotions in between. And many have passed on their stories and wisdom through verse recited aloud to the common people.

To this day, nestled in northern Michigan is a place called Stone Circle. Folks have been gathering there around an open fire for over a decade to preserve their oral tradition by telling stories and reciting poems as the red sparks fly into the starry summer nights. In West Africa, griots carry news from village to village singing their verse celebrations just as their ancestors did over eight hundred years ago. In Jamaica, dub poets deliver the political news in much the same manner, and in Irish pubs, poets turn their backs on their audiences as an act of humility when rhyming out the lyrics and ballads that relate the tests and toils of their Gaelic culture.

SlamSlang

Slam poetry is a term that describes a style of spoken word poetry composed to be performed in front of a live audience and quite often in a competitive arena. A **poetry slam** is the actual performance poetry event that usually culminates in figurative battle between slam poets.

Guru Nanak, the sage of the Sikh religion, gathered his flock by reciting divinely inspired poems outside city gates to the plucking of his rabab's strings. Western civilization reckons back to the blind poet Homer whose epics were composed to be recited aloud, as evidenced by oft-repeated "formulas" like "fleet-footed Achilles" and "when rosy-fingered Dawn appeared." Other famous Western works have roots in oral tradition, as well, including *Beowulf* and even the Bible.

Slam poetry carries on this oral literary tradition, encouraging today's poets and performance artists to address the modern human condition; deal with current personal, political, spiritual, and social issues; and knock the socks off the audience. And slam encourages poets to do all this not only through their written words, but also through the art of performance.

Battling Bards

In the elitist halls of colleges and universities, some literature professors scoff at the notion of performance poetry competitions. They seem to ignore the fact that literary competitions have a long and honorable history. Dionysus, the ancient Greek god of fertility (also believed to be the inventor of wine), was believed to watch over his ecstatic worshippers as they drank the blood of animals and danced in an orgiastic frenzy during which poet/dramatists, Euripides and Sophocles to name a famous pair, competed for first prize in the local drama competition.

Many cultures have used competitive literary events to pique their listeners' interest and improve the quality of their art. In fifteenth-century Japan, Samurai-turned-poet Basho wandered the countryside judging haiku contests. Long before that, his predecessors in the poetic arts engaged in contests to collectively compose lengthy poems called *renga*, each poet adding a verse until the renga was complete. The trick was to compose an exquisite verse that would awe the other poets and challenge the next one to top it with superior verse.

In the early 1600s, Cervantes mentions poetry contests in his famous work, *Don Quixote*:

> ... tell me, what verses are those which you have now in hand, and which your father tells me keep you somewhat restless and absorbed? If it be some gloss, I know something about glosses, and I should like to hear them; and if they are for a poetical tournament, contrive to carry off the second prize ...

At this same time in Mexico, no doubt influenced by their fellow poets in Spain, hundreds of poets would gather to compete in public poetic jousts (called *Justas Literarias* in Spanish) to win awards and fame.

Poetry competition was popular in Chicago in the early 1980s, when Al Simmons formed the WPA (World Poetry Association) and staged poetry boxing matches complete with ring girls

Backstage Skinny

For information about the current goings on at the Taos Poetry Circus, check out the World Poetry Bout Association website at www.poetrycircus.org.

dressed in bikinis who carried cards to announce the round numbers. These poetry bouts eventually migrated southwest to New Mexico to become the Taos Heavyweight Poetry Championships, which still take place today under the big top at the Taos Poetry Circus.

Even in the hallowed halls of modern mainstream poetry, competition is often vicious, though not carried out in a public forum. Instead of competing for audience approval, poets throughout modern times have submitted their poems to poetry contests and to publishers, vying for the approval of critics and publishers. If you think that's not a competitive arena, think again.

Beat, Hip-Hop, Rap, and Other Genres

Poetry's oral tradition has never come close to drawing a last breath, but it certainly was neglected in America and most of Western Europe during the twentieth century. Some attribute this to *New Criticism*'s grip on literary sensibilities. Others say that mass media and TV drew audiences away from live poetry performances and other performance arts. (Of course, a good portion of social critics blame all of our social ills on TV and mass media.)

In the '50s and '60s the beatniks and hippies rekindled interest in spoken-word poetry by reacting to the icy political restrictions of the Cold War era. Allen Ginsburg recited *Howl* at Gallery Six in 1956 long before it appeared in print, and even after *Howl* was published, Ginsburg continued his passionate recitation of it time and time again. (Just how many times did Ginsburg read that poem?!) The stereotypical images of beatnik poetry readings are stamped on the public psyche to this day. Goatees, bongos, and the swirl of reefer in the air still permeate our collective mindset. Most of us remember news clips of flower children reading poems to National Guard troops while slipping daisies into rifle barrels, and we associate these images with free love and free verse. The poems of Amiri Baraka, Lawrence Ferlinghetti, and even Muhammad Ali, were at the vanguard of a nation in flux during the radical sixties.

SlamSlang

New Criticism is a formal way of interpreting literature that focuses mainly on the structure and content of the text, ignoring any outside influences, such as the historical and social climate in which the text was written and events in the author's life. New Criticism fostered a more elitist view of poetry and other forms of literature by attempting to make "good taste" objective.

In the '70s the raging howl of the '60s was traded in for a disco beat and leisure suits. The poetry boomers born out of the beats and hippies grew up, got jobs, and put their kids into good schools. But in less fortunate neighborhoods another revolution was re-mixing music and language, stuffing it with new meaning. The culture of that revolution is Hip Hop—underprivileged kids break-dancing on street corners and laying down lyrics in a circle, rapping. Cops came and kicked them off the corners, so they started parties, spun records, scratched the grooves, blended the music, and rapped over it. What began with a few hundred black and Latino kids in neglected neighborhoods of New York City has become a worldwide entertainment industry. It was a music thing, but words fueled it.

Slam Takes Center Stage

By the early 1980s traditional poetry events had diminished to sporadic, self-absorbed, non-adventures cramped uncomfortably in bookstore aisles and attended by a handful of insular followers. Even the most prominent poets could hardly attract more than a few dozen devotees who politely, and dispassionately, applauded each poem in a series of monotone presentations that barely shifted in style from one muttering to the next even when the subject changed dramatically from God to war to heartbreak. In those days open mikes, the come-one-come-all poetic forums, had no legitimate audience whatsoever. They were self-indulgent displays of poets reading to poets. Each of the participants were eager to hear only themselves and quickly left after they uttered their last line.

This ineffective approach to the presentation of poetry is what the early slammers in Chicago reacted to, sought to change, and did change.

Sowing the Seeds of Slam

The seeds of slam were sown in the womb of the Monday Night Poetry Readings held at the Get Me High Jazz Club on the near-northwest side of Chicago: Nelson Algren's and Mike Royco's hood, a beat-down section of the city that is now, decades later, one of the hippest places to see and be seen in.

The ill-bred poets of the Get Me High Jazz Club adopted and lived by the following principles:

◆ The poet on the stage is no more important than the listening audience.

◆ Performing is an art, as much an art as crafting the text itself.

◆ If you're speaking onstage you have an obligation to do it well; after all, you're competing with all other forms of entertainment.

◆ As Wendell Berry instructs us, poetry is not to glorify the poet, but rather to celebrate the community around the poet.

Dig This!

Wendell Berry is a poet/philosopher who lives and works on a small family farm in the Kentucky River region of Henry County, Kentucky. Berry's poetry and essays encourage readers to get back to the land and connect with one another in order to re-stitch the moral fabric that holds our society together. Find out more about him at www.ncteamericancollection.org/litmap/berry_wendell_ky.htm

---

These principles do not seem outrageous now, but at the time they were radical. The "establishment poets" thought performing cheapened the art of poetry, but in practice, it strengthened it. Performing forced the early slammers to scrutinize their texts and red-pencil out the "fluff" to be sure that the ideas and emotions they contained were genuine, precise, and powerfully expressed. Their goal was to communicate, and if the response was poor, they reworked the text, polished the performance, and gave it another go. Sometimes they produced sparkling gems, but many times they tossed poem and/or performance into the circular file because it was just plain crap. They learned the art and style of performance poetry by trial and error.

Above all, performance poets acted as servants to their audience. Not mystics, not scholarly snobs, not preachers or saints more perfect than the masses they stood before. Slammers were, and are, just part of the crowd. As another Chicago poet, Carl Sandburg, put it:

> Poetry is the heart of the people, and the people is everyone, you and I and all the others; what everybody says is what we all say.

The Big Definition of Slam Poetry

Stumble into any bar or coffee shop during a poetry slam, and you'll witness poets performing their poetry (out loud) to win the adulation of the crowd and the high scores of the judges. At least, that's the first impression you might have. In fact, slam poetry isn't just a poetry reading, and it certainly doesn't focus exclusively on competition.

So if it isn't just a poetry reading and it isn't just a competition, what is it?

Slam poetry is a word circus, a school, a town meeting, a playground, a sports arena, a temple, a burlesque show, a revelation, a mass guffaw, holy ground, and possibly all of these at once. Slam poetry is performance poetry, the marriage of text and the artful presentation of spoken words onstage to an audience that has permission to talk back and let the poet performer know whether he or she is communicating effectively. You hardly ever miss the point at a poetry slam, and if you do, just stand up and holler "Huh?!"

Poetry *and* Performance

When you say "poetry" to most people, they think of the printed word, the text. After all, for the past 200 or so years, the printed word was everything. Poets in print could win the Pulitzer Prize or the Nobel Prize; a poet screaming better poetry on a street corner in New York could maybe win a night in the slammer. However, if you went to hear that Pulitzer Prize–winning poet recite one of your favorite poems, you might walk away a little disappointed. Oftentimes, the poet had no desire to perform the poem or even add a little inflection to liven it up. The poetry would drone on like a ceiling fan.

Slam poetry attempts to invigorate poetry by giving equal weight to the poetry and the performance of it. In a poetry slam, a mediocre poem performed passionately can (and should) beat out a superior poem recited by a poet who barely exhibits any signs of life. Slam poets strive to achieve their best in both text and performance—to compose superior poems and perform them passionately and exquisitely.

Conflicts and Synergies

If one word sums up the philosophy of slam, it is "integrity." Slam pulls no punches—in the poetry, in the performance, in the poet-audience interaction, or even in the organizational meetings. Though poets and audience members are expected to exhibit a certain level of respect for one another and a tolerance for their inherent differences, they are encouraged to express themselves honestly and to confront one another on important issues.

The illustrious Greek philosopher, Socrates, taught dynamically through his dialogues, posing a series of questions to his students to raise their awareness of unchanging truth. In much the same way, slam encourages healthy debate and competition in order to raise the level of slam poetry as an art form and continue its dynamic evolution.

Staged Bouts for Audience Appeal

When you witness your first poetry slam, you might begin to think that slam poets take the competition seriously, and you would be right. But the competition itself is not the be all and end all of slam poetry. It's window dressing. The competition, the battles, the bouts are merely, yet importantly, a theatrical device intended to stoke the competitive fires of the performing poets, encourage audience participation, and pump some fuel into an entertaining evening of poetry, friendship, and camaraderie. When the poetry is great, when the performances are inspired, no matter who nabs the top prize, all involved—the poet/performers, the organizers, and the audience—walk away winners.

Family, Feuds, and Friendships

Although the poet/performers take center stage at any poetry slam, slam reaches far beyond those in the spotlight. It reaches beyond the walls of a particular venue. It encompasses all those involved in pulling off the show, including the emcee, the host, the ticket-takers, the volunteers who organized and promoted the event, and all those who work on the national and international levels to serve the slam community. More important than any individual performer or event, slam is a community of organizers who have discovered a vital way of presenting poetry aloud onstage in public, enabling its passion, wisdom, and beauty to be experienced with full impact.

Flyer from one of the first poetry readings at the Get Me High Jazz Club.

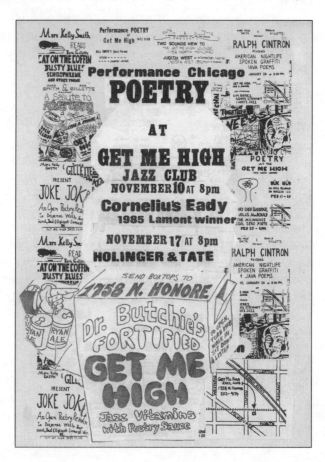

Who Inspired This Madness? and Why?

Slam poetry is the brainchild of Marc Smith (*So What!*) and the blue-collar intellectual eccentrics who crammed into the Get Me High Jazz Club on Monday nights from November 1984 to September 1986 for a wide-open poetry experience. Finger-poppin' hipster Butchie (James Dukaris) owned the place and allowed anything to happen, and it usually did. The experimenters in this new style of poetry presentation gyrated, rotated, spewed, and stepped their words along the bar top, dancing between the bottles, bellowing out the backdoor, standing on the street or on their stools, turning the west side of Chicago into a rainforest of dripping whispers or a blast furnace of fiery elongated syllables, phrases, snatches of scripts, and verse that electrified the night.

SlamSlang

Marc's **So What!** handle came from the early days at the Get Me High Jazz Club when it was important to remind everybody taking the stage, including Marc himself, that they were on an equal footing with everyone else. The people onstage were not big shots just because they had the microphone in hand and the limelight shining on their faces. To this day, whenever Marc introduces himself to an audience, it responds with a thunderous "SO WHAT!"

The Chicago Poetry Ensemble

The Chicago Poetry Ensemble (a handful of dedicated poets) was the foundation of slam's early experimentation. The courage of their work to some minds has been unmatched by those who have followed them. They were on point in a hostile environment. They were criticized and scoffed at by the academic insiders and the hipper-than-thou outsiders for daring to perform poetry like actors or clowns or singers. Maybe, they were just too naïve to know that they were doing what they shouldn't be doing: what the establishment found distasteful and what the nouveau rebels thought too entertaining. All that matters now is that they did it and formed the roots of what became slam.

The poets who formed the Chicago Poetry Ensemble and who were the initial pylons of the slam structure are rarely mentioned in the current accounts of slam history. They have all gone on to other careers. To preserve their names and provide a sense of what a motley mob they truly were, the following list gives their names and occupations:

John Sheehan—ex–Roman Catholic priest

Rob Van Tuyle—high school teacher

Anna Brown—performance artist

Jean Howard—model

Ron Gillette—editor for a floral magazine

Dave Cooper—paralegal

Karen Nystrom—student who sold ties at Marshall Field's

Mike Barrett—copywriter for the *Chicago Tribune*

The Fires Rage

The success of Monday nights at the Get Me High led to the creation of a poetry vaudevillian cabaret show called the Uptown Poetry Slam, the original slam. The first show was held on July 20, 1986, at the Green Mill Cocktail Lounge on Chicago's north side. It's where the term "poetry slam" was first coined and stamped on the face of performance poetry and later competitive poetry. The success of the Get Me High readings and the Chicago Poetry Ensemble necessitated finding a larger venue with a real stage, stage lighting, a quality sound system, and more room for bodies to listen. The Ensemble had been performing one-night stands around Chicago and needed a home bigger than the Get Me High Jazz Club. They had had a couple successful outings at club owner Dave Jemilo's nightspot, the Deja Vu, and when he purchased the Green Mill in the summer of 1986 he gave them the go on Sunday nights to experiment with a new type of poetry show.

History can be made as easy as that.

The first years of the Uptown Poetry Slam included music, short plays, slide shows, dance, and just about any form of entertainment that incorporated a strong element of words. As an afterthought, a competition was added to the third and final set. It was the show closer and everyone hushed up to hear who would win the $10 or the Twinkies.

Dig This!
The Twinkie prize was held in high esteem. No, it wasn't a booby prize, it was for the winner!
Another coveted slam prize was a box of Macaroni & Cheese autographed by the judges. And for many years Big John, the doorman at the Green Mill, offered the Sunday night slam winner Lotto tickets as an alternative to taking the $10. It was called the Big John Scam. In the ten years that Big John ran his scam, nobody ever scratched off more than another free ticket.

Poetry Of, By, and For the People

Of course, many slammers from the early years are remembered and revered within the slam community. Every movement has its celebrated leaders and heroes. In the world of slam, Patricia Smith, Lisa Buscani, Cin Salach, Larry Francis, Danny Solis, Pat Storm, Gary Glazner, Bob Holman, Michael Brown, Deb and Steve Marsh, and Alan Wolfe are among the many who have been elevated to the high status of "slam elder."

But slam is not about making stars. It's about everybody all together in a room with their hair down and feet up. From its beginning, slam has been an art form and entertainment open to all people from all walks of life—young and old, rich and poor, blue collar and white collar, gays and straights, priests and prostitutes, biologists and belly-dancers—a multi-colored, multi-cultural gathering of people who love to hear and perform poetry.

That's right, any and all are welcome at a slam. Walk through the doorway, find the host, introduce yourself, sit down and listen, or ask if there's room on the list for you to recite your masterpiece. If you've never addressed a public audience before, you might get the handle *virgin virgin* hung on you for a couple hours until you break your poetic hymen and throw down a few syllables. If you've performed all around town and people know your work too well, you might get greeted by an alarming groan of recognition.

> **SlamSlang**
>
> In the world of slam, a **virgin virgin** is a person who has never performed a poem in front of a public audience in his or her life. You might have read your limericks to your tropical fish and tapped the tank to get a reaction, but that doesn't count.

Wherefore Art Thou, Slam?

You can find poetry slams at nearly any location—in schools, at the office, at festivals, in bars, at wedding celebrations, at museums, in cultural centers, and even in laundromats. Performance poets perform anywhere. They have trained themselves to succeed wherever and in whatever context they're called on to emote—bowling alleys, churches, temples, pool halls, street fairs, commuter trains, discotheques, you

> **Backstage Skinny**
>
> Go to www.poetryslam.com and click **Slam Venues** to find local slams across the country and around the world.

name it. The slam's mission has been to throw off the shackles of how and where poetry should be presented. "Try anything and go anywhere" has been the creed. Seek out an audience and compel them to listen. If you can stop bowling balls with a line of verse, you're slammin'.

Slam Poetry Goes National

In 1990, the first National Poetry Slam (NPS) competition was held in San Francisco as part of the third Annual National Poetry Week Festival. Gary Glazner, the inspired promoter of this first inter-city slam, greeted the Chicago poets and the San Francisco audience with the verve of a hot dog vendor barking the relish they were about to devour. Lois Weisburg, the commissioner of Chicago's Department of Cultural Affairs, was instrumental in making this premiere NPS happen. Under her suggestion, and with the city's financial help, Chicago sent a team of four poets (rather than just a solo poet, as had been originally proposed) to challenge teams from San Francisco and New York City. Gary recruited a San Francisco team, and Bob Holman, who had just started the slam at the Nuyorican Café in New York, arranged for Paul Beatty to be the sole New York representative. The following section provides my first-hand account of that first-ever National Poetry Slam.

Marc's Blow-by-Blow Account of the First NPS

About three hundred people showed up at Fort Mason, quite a crowd for a poetry reading in those days, even in San Francisco, the mecca of the beats. Plopped down in the first rows with their arms crossed over their chests were more than a few sour faces ready to dismiss this "slam thing" as just another desperate gimmick to con people into attending a reading by a group of aspiring nobodies. I shared the emcee duties with Gary Glazner, who graciously allowed me to do so. I was concerned that the evening would turn into a carnival event. The coin was tossed and Chicago chose to go first. The team was comprised of Patricia Smith, Dean Hacker, Cin Salach, and me. I was doing double duty as emcee and performer, but that's what had to be. Patricia stepped to the microphone and by the time she finished, the audience was on its feet roaring applause. Not a sour face could be seen anywhere. Standing ovations cheered on the Chicago team for the rest of the evening. And the San Francisco team got their due, as well. The fire had been brought down from the mountain, and that room knew something important had just happened.

> **Dig This!**
>
> This is a tenet of slam philosophy: What we do, what we know, what we discover gets passed on from poet to poet, from city to city, from slam to slam, even to our rivals … our competitive enemies.

Rather than strut our stuff, the Chicago team consciously imparted to the audience, and the other poets, that what we had uncovered in Chicago and developed into this powerful performance style was a craft and a technique they, too, could learn and apply to their performances and shows. Poetry no longer needed to be treated like a museum piece or school lesson. It was as dynamic and exciting as any of the other performing arts.

We came back home from San Francisco and started planning for the second National Poetry Slam. The movement had gone national.

To Balance the Account—Gary Glazer's Recollections

Herman Berlandt and Jack Mueller were running the festival [The third Annual National Poetry Week Festival 1990]. Herman had asked me to come up with an event in response to Rumors Cafe in North Beach wanting poetry programming. I remembered [Chicago's] Poetry Slam and suggested we do a slam at Rumors where the winner would appear at the festival. The idea grew to inviting Chicago and New York to participate. Jack called [Marc Smith] to issue the invite, while my wife Margaret and I were in Bali.

Because bringing the poetry slam to San Francisco was my idea, I hosted and produced the Poetry Slam series at Rumors. It was hard to get poets to participate, not the academic poets but anyone at all. You had to explain what a poetry slam was; you had to convince them that the competition was a way to get the audience involved. That first series of poetry slams in San Francisco I spent a lot of time just calling people and asking them to be a part of it, breaking down the barriers. The slams were getting a lot of media coverage; radio and even CNN picked it up and that of course stepped on the toes of the local poetry bigwigs. Herman and Jack hired me to produce the big event with Chicago and New York at Fort Mason. As was common with the festival, they were unable to pay me, so I broke with them and told Jack that if he was ever able to pay me what we had agreed upon that we could talk about the poetry slam again being part of the festival.

I worked very hard to make sure we had an audience. Because the opening night of the festival had Lawrence Ferlinghetti and Maya Angelou—and only drew an audience of about 100 people (I counted), half of whom were bused in from Glide Memorial Church—I was right to be worried.

I got a loudspeaker permit and cruised the city with a carload of poets hyping the event. I spent one afternoon calling over 200 people in the National Poetry Week Festival Rolodex, putting over 100 people on the guest list. I hired Whitman McGowan to be a barker to stand out in front of the venue and call people in carnival-style. I asked Fritz (from the Toad Venom poem) to sell hot dogs like at a ballpark to the audience. I photographed Kate Proper, the manager of the Lusty Lady Theater, in a spiked sexy boot on a stack of poetry books, and that became the Slam logo for the next few years and the model for the early trophies.

Then in the most genius move of all, when Smith and I were walking he said, "I don't want to steal your thunder, but I would like to put this event on next year,"…

… I said, "Yes."

Thus began the comradely concept of passing the National Poetry Slam from city to city that continues to this day. That idea drove the early growth of the slam. It was that spirit that shot the slam past the Taos [Poetry Circus] event which remains a small regional event. Although the slam has grown to a worldwide movement, it has against all odds changed and continues to change the way the world views poetry.

The One-Two Punch: The Second and Third NPS

Held in Chicago, the second National Poetry Slam invited eight cities to participate. This four-day tournament attracted more than one thousand spectators to a half dozen nightclubs around the city. Seven hundred and fifty fans crammed into one of Chicago's most popular rock clubs to watch the New York, St. Louis, Cleveland, Ann Arbor, San Francisco, Milwaukee, Boston, and Chicago teams battle it out. Lisa Buscani and Patricia Smith became the divas of the slam as they went toe to toe in the individual championship, Patrica emerging the winner by a fraction of a point.

From Chicago the NPS was passed on to Boston where the basic four-day tournament structure (still in use today) was repeated. That year, 12 teams participated and solidified the tradition of this annual event that in 2003 attracted 63 competing teams and several thousand audience members. Each year the tournament is passed from one city to the next, like an Olympic torch—a gift from one city to another, as well as an organizational headache. Ask anybody who has done it.

Slam Poetry Goes Global

The first person to envision an international slam scene was Michael Brown, originally from Chicago and now based in Boston. Michael contacted Erkki Lappalainen and sought to create an Olympic-style slam match. It never materialized, but through Michael's missionary work, slam spread to Sweden, London, and Germany.

Closer to home, Canada started its own regular slams in Montreal, Vancouver, Toronto, Winnipeg, and Ottawa and has participated in the U.S. national slams since

1992. But by far the strongest slam community outside the United States is in Germany. Several slam zealots are responsible for this missionary work, including Boris Preckwitz, Ko Bylanzky, and Rayl Patzak. Chapter 24 provides an overview of the slam movement in Germany and reveals how a few hard-working devotees can inspire a country.

At Roma Poesia the first truly International Poetry Slam was held in 2002 with poets from Spain, France, Russia, Germany, England, Italy, and the United States. The slammers performed in their native tongues with translations projected on a huge video screen behind them. It was the best answer so far to the problem of judging a multi-lingual slam competition, and it was a complete success. The Italian audiences witnessed and enjoyed the physical performance and the verbal music of various foreign languages without losing the meaning of what was being said.

The worldwide growth of slam spread east to Asia thanks to Chris Mooney Singe. This Australian-born Sikh saw similarities between the evolution of slam and how the divine Guru Nanak spread the Sikh religion. He has created in Singapore a Slam Cabaret that mixes music, dance, drama, poetics, and competition into a night designed to gather and celebrate Singapore's multi-cultural treasures. He and his wife, Savinder, have visions of passing the gift of slam on to Malaysia, Australia, and beyond.

> **What's on the CD**
>
> CD #1 track #1:
> Chris Mooney Singe performing at the Singapore Slam

> **Dig This!**
>
> Sikhs view Guru Nanak as a directly God-inspired being in the same way that Jews relate to their inspired Prophets, Christians to their Messiah or Christ, or Hindus to their Avatars (Brahma, Vishnu, Shiva, etc.). Likewise, Sikhs view Guru Nanak as having received the same direct inspiration from the Divine without any human intermediary.

Slam Poetry Here and Now

By some estimates the slam is the largest and most influential literary arts movement of our age. Its principles and formats are used by educators at every grade level to stir student interest in poetry and break down the misconception that the poetic arts are for high brows only. College curriculums have included slam as a new literary genre to be studied as both a historical force and performing art. Theatergoers on the Great White Way have witnessed slammers rock the house at the Tony Award–winning production *Def Jam Poetry on Broadway*. Festivals around the world include slam events in their programs.

Only time can reveal what true and lasting influence slam will have on the world's literary legacy. But what we do know is that there are over 500 slams operating around the globe attended by thousands and thousands of people. And you don't have to play bongos, don a beret, or hide behind your dark glasses to be part of it.

The Least You Need to Know

- The slam is more than just a competition; it's a global social/literary movement.

- Slam merges the art of performance with the art of writing poetry.

- The slam movement was started at the Get Me High Jazz Club in Chicago by Marc Smith and members of the Chicago Poetry Ensemble.

- The first slam show began on July 20, 1986, at the Green Mill Cocktail Lounge when club owner Dave Jemilo gave Marc and the Ensemble the opportunity to stage a weekly experimental poetry show on Sunday nights called the Uptown Poetry Slam.

- Slams are held anywhere and attended by people from all walks of life and all cultures.

- Slams have gone worldwide and continue to spread as a gift passed on from poet to poet, venue to venue, and culture to culture.

Chapter 2

Soaking In the Spirit of Slam

In This Chapter

♦ Examining the true nature of slam competition: "The points are not the point"

♦ Making the audience an integral part of the show

♦ Using slam to foster an environment of mutual respect in the midst of heated competition

♦ Bonding through trials, turmoil, and brutal battles

♦ Understanding the democratic nature of the slam family

Slam poetry transcends the poet-performers, organizers, audience, and even the competition itself. It rises to a level that encompasses slam poetry as a social movement, as a way of life, and as an art form. But some people just don't get it. As with any discipline, some rogue participants and organizers—as well as misguided, misinformed miscreants—misconstrue the higher goal of slam poetry or use it for their own self-serving purposes. They lose the proper perspective, wander off the path of enlightenment, and end up missing out on the best that slam has to offer—the honing of one's skills as poet and performer, the dynamic interaction with the audience, healthy relationships with friends and fellow slammers, and participation in a truly democratic community.

To help you avoid the pitfalls of missing the spirit that steers slam, this chapter introduces you to the most important aspects and tenets of the movement. Here, you learn that competition is secondary to poetry and performance, that "points are not the point," that connecting to the audience is what it's all about, and that slam has no hierarchical structure designed to lock people out. After absorbing the information in this chapter, you will have a clear understanding of the dynamic culture and community that slam is intended to foster.

"The Points Are Not the Point"

The points are not the point … the point is poetry.

This adage, coined by slam poet and organizer Allan Wolf of Asheville, North Carolina, is often repeated at the commencement of slam competitions around the world to remind us of what the movement is all about. Competing in a poetry slam is not about getting the highest score, walking away with a pocketful of cash, or trying to fill a trophy case. The true goal is to inspire people from all walks of life to listen to poetry, appreciate and respect its power, and ultimately to take the stage to perform their own original works. And the competitive aspect of slam poetry has succeeded at achieving this goal. Slam has attracted droves of people, some of whom swore off poetry in high school and college and are surprised to discover that they actually like it, or at least like some of it.

> **Dig This!**
>
> PSI (Poetry Slam, Inc.), the nonprofit association that represents slammers and slam venues, was first incorporated in 1997 to legally represent the slam family and protect its reputation against outside entities seeking to exploit this flourishing grassroots movement.

I'm not trying to negate the role of competition in slam poetry. Competition is an integral part of any poetry slam. It inspires slam poets to write their best poetry and hone their performance skills. It fires up the audience and encourages them to interact with the poets and emcees. And it provides a structure for the poetry slam that holds the whole crazy show together, energizing all those involved, including the audience.

PSI acknowledges this goal of slam poetry in its mission statement, which makes no mention of "competition." Its mission is to promote the awareness of and interest in *performance* poetry, not *competitive* poetry. Slam competitions, from their onset, have been viewed as theatrical devices geared toward grabbing and holding an audience's attention. Even if the poetry and performances suck, the competition and the audience reactions should be enough to save the show … theoretically, at least.

Another way of looking at the competition is captured in a quip from the Nuyorican Café, the home of New York City's premier slam club: "The best poet always loses."

This maxim emphasizes the fact that slam competitions are not true tests of whose poem and performance is best. Those of us who have watched competitions over the years can attest to the veracity of this statement. We can also attest to the fact that audiences of a size hitherto unheard of are listening to and enjoying poetry at slam competitions. The audience might not remember who won the battle but they do remember the words, lines, and stanzas that rocked their minds and touched their hearts.

> **Dig This!**
>
> As the evening wears on, the judges' scores naturally tend to drift higher. This universal phenomenon known as "score creep" makes it clear that the judges' scores are not entirely objective. Performing last often is enough to tip the scales in favor of a particular performer.

Relearning the Art of Listening

When is the last time you listened to a poem or a story or even a song? I mean really listened to the point at which you clearly understood the lines?

Most of us have forgotten how to listen. We've become visual, video-based, text-based, bar-code-reading junkies. We read the paper for our news, watch TV and play video games for entertainment, and increasingly communicate with brief typed messages via e-mail and instant-messaging programs. Gone are the days when we listened to the radio for news or to hear Radio Mystery Theater. Gone are the days when students were expected to listen and take notes in class. Few of us tell stories anymore, and most of us have a tough time remembering even the funniest of jokes. We might as well have lopped off our ears.

> **Dig This!**
>
> In ancient Greece, Medieval England, and in many other countries and times, people relied on spoken language for their news, entertainment, and schooling. As people began to write stuff down, they became increasingly dependent on written text to a point at which the appearance of the printed text became important in the interpretation of it. Fully appreciating the poetry of e. e. cummings, for instance, would be impossible if you couldn't see it in print. Slam moves poetry back toward the oral tradition, forcing the audience to listen as well as watch.

One of the benefits of performance poetry, including slam, is that it retrains our ears and helps us relearn the fine art of listening. It also encourages the performers to write comprehensible verse and speak their poems clearly. At a poetry slam, you don't sit at a table with the text of a poem in front of you, following along as the poet performs it. In most cases, you don't have a screen that displays the text during each performance. You need to focus on the poet and tune in to what the poet is saying, what you're hearing. As you attend more poetry slams and practice the art of listening, you begin to really hear and understand more of each poet's performance. You might even notice that you hear more of what everyone has to say in all areas of your life.

Performance Poet as Audience Servant

Throughout history, societies have placed their best artists on pedestals. They might have starved those artists, but they glorified them during their lives or at least after they died. Placing artists and performers on pedestals is not all that bad—assuming every artist has the opportunity to compete for those honors. Problems arise, however, when a particular group of artists or critics monopolize the art and agree on a set of rules that prevents other gifted artists from having a shot at the prize. As Five Man Electrical Band sang in the 1970s in their hit song *Signs*, "Sign said you got to have a membership card to get inside. Uh!"

Upon receiving the membership card and the accompanying notoriety, many establishment poets decided that the audience consisted of a bunch of ignorant low-lifes and that the more cryptic and incomprehensible they could make their verse, the better it was. This only served to further alienate audiences and turn poetry into a caviar that only the most elite intellectuals could swallow. Unless you were a card-carrying elitist, attempting to get your poems in print was futile.

> ## Dig This!
>
> The best slam poets know that they are audience servants, not sycophants. One of the most disgusting sights at a poetry slam is a poet who knowingly grovels for high scores or audience approval. The poet should serve the audience not only by entertaining its members but also by challenging them. The line is very thin, but performance poets who successfully straddle that line turn in brilliant performances.

Slam poetry attempts to dissolve the barriers by knocking the poets off their perches and making them recognize their true role—as servants to the audience. Slam poets learned early on that they had better please the audience if they wanted to have any hopes of surviving, let alone winning, a competition. In the poet-audience relationship, the audience is the standoffish mate that the poet must woo. The role of the audience is to listen carefully and provide the feedback that the poet needs in order to sharpen his or her skills as poet and performer. Sometimes this feedback is encouraging. Other times, it lets the performer know in no uncertain terms that he or she had better polish the poetry and practice a little more before trying this again.

Boo! Hiss! Audience with Attitude

Key to the success of slam is audience participation. It took some time to convince the patrons at the Green Mill slam that it was okay to talk back and get a little rowdy. The death toll of any poetry reading is the droning monotone of the pedantic and often pompous poet who bores the audience with endless meanderings of obscure allusions or self-indulgent confessions from his or her morning journal.

At most slams such poets had better wear their thickest skin. Slam audiences are allowed and often encouraged to react to what they like and dislike. And they're not stupid. At the Green Mill the first sign of trouble is finger-snapping. No, that's not dig-me-daddy-o finger snapping, it's more akin to whistling at a bull fight or the rattle of a snake that's about to strike. If the snapping doesn't stop 'em, folks start stomping their feet. When all else fails, they groan like grislies—a low, nasty, threatening groan.

Experienced slam audiences have mastered some specialized reactions, as well. One of the most telling is the feminist hiss, which traditionally was used to gently slap a male poet who just recited a sexist line. Some audiences use the feminist hiss for just about anything a man does as soon as he steps onstage. Guess-the-rhyme is another popular reaction at the Green Mill. If a particular poet's rhymes are all too predictable, someone in the audience chimes in by announcing the rhyming word just as it trickles out of the poet's mouth.

Around the world there are slam rituals that give the audience a voice and permission to use that voice in reaction to the performances they experience. For example, in Jerusalem, after slammers present their poems onstage, the audience has an open discussion about the merits of the poem. Then the slammer presents the poem a second time and receives a score from the judges who have heard poem and discussion. In Wiesbaden, Germany, the entire audience scores the performances on ballots passed out at the beginning of the evening: one to five for content, one to five for performance. Included at the bottom of the ballot is a space for comments and criticisms. Honest and immediate feedback has enabled slammers to grow as performers and polish their art into highly effective modes of communication.

Breaking Down the Color (and Collar) Barriers

At about the same time as another famous Chicagoan, Reverend Jesse Jackson, was forming his Rainbow Coalition, the slam community was forming its own rainbow coalition, even though it wasn't consciously trying to do so. Visit any National Poetry Slam competition, and you'll see what I mean. At these events, men and women of all ages, all races and nationalities, all socio-economic brackets, and a wide range of occupations gather to share their poetry, their performances, and the joy of creating and being part of the slam family.

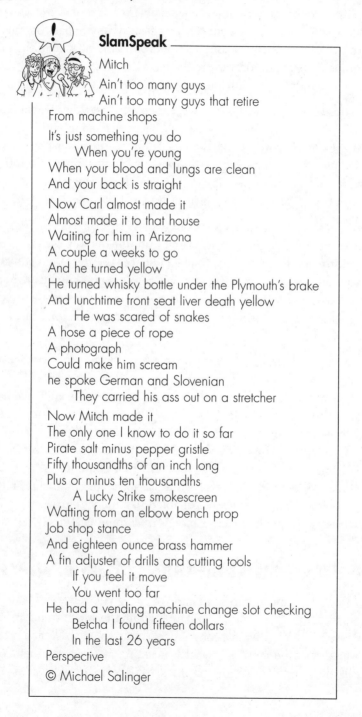

SlamSpeak

Mitch
Ain't too many guys
Ain't too many guys that retire
From machine shops

It's just something you do
        When you're young
When your blood and lungs are clean
And your back is straight

Now Carl almost made it
Almost made it to that house
Waiting for him in Arizona
A couple a weeks to go
And he turned yellow
He turned whisky bottle under the Plymouth's brake
And lunchtime front seat liver death yellow
        He was scared of snakes
A hose a piece of rope
A photograph
Could make him scream
he spoke German and Slovenian
        They carried his ass out on a stretcher

Now Mitch made it
The only one I know to do it so far
Pirate salt minus pepper gristle
Fifty thousandths of an inch long
Plus or minus ten thousandths
        A Lucky Strike smokescreen
Wafting from an elbow bench prop
Job shop stance
And eighteen ounce brass hammer
A fin adjuster of drills and cutting tools
        If you feel it move
        You went too far
He had a vending machine change slot checking
        Betcha I found fifteen dollars
        In the last 26 years
Perspective

© Michael Salinger

Sure, you'll see some healthy competition and some passionate arguments. You might even see a scuffle or an all-out brawl—every crowd has a couple of people who like to fight, especially if alcohol or drugs are involved. For the most part, however, you will see people from all walks of life getting along and sharing in the excitement—aging hippies, young Goths, burly construction workers, leather-clad bikers, button-down office types, you name it.

The only prerequisite for belonging to the slam family is a sincere desire to enjoy and promote performance poetry. You don't even need to write or perform.

SlamSpeak

Eddy Two Rivers had just arrived back in Chicago after a stay at a certain state institution. While he was away he had a lot time on his hands. He wrote poetry. To celebrate his return to Chi-town he decided to stop in at an old "Indian" bar, the Green Mill. What he didn't know was that the ownership had changed during his absence and when he walked through the door he wondered, "What the hell happen' here?" There was some guy climbing on the bar reciting poetry:

"Once you were the hog butcher of the world,

…

Once the tools were made here

…

Now union stooges walk the yards pushin' buttons now and then
Robots both mechanical and in the flesh

…"

"Wait a minute." thought Eddy, "I write poetry, too."

From that experience, sticking his nose into the Green Mill slam, Eddy Two Rivers has gone on to publish several books, win national literary awards, produce plays, and teach poetry in schools around the country.

Eddy's story has been repeated a hundred times throughout the slam community. The slam believes that poetry is the voice of all peoples and all walks of life.

Competition and Camaraderie

The slam world is not without conflict. I have witnessed (and been involved in a few) heated arguments about biased scores, wrongheaded judges, rigged teams, and other infractions of the rules and code of honor. Sometimes these manifestations of the competitive spirit are ugly and have on a few occasions come to petty physical violence—Alpha males beating their chests, Alpha females ripping off their blouses to show that they have chests, too, protest meetings that have extended deep into the early morning hours during the national tournaments, and other nasty scenes. But there have also been great moments of camaraderie and compromise.

Conflict is not necessarily evil, and in the case of slam, it's downright unavoidable. Slam intentionally stuffs a community of artistic, passionate individuals into an intense arena of competition, entertainment, and service. And whenever you place a bunch of intelligent, passionate people in close contact, sparks naturally begin to fly. This is slam's prime energy source—the electricity that powers the movement. The human drama that plays out and life lessons learned and ignored are as much a part of the experience as listening to the poems.

The Culture of Democracy

The slam community has no grand, high, exalted mystic ruler, no dictator, nobody handing down fixed mandates on how to run local competitions, write poetry, or structure a performance. Each poetry slam and slammaster is autonomous, free to call her own shots. Each show maker decides how she wishes to run her slam. Each slam follows its own rules, rituals, and regulations. Most adhere to the majority of the principles mentioned earlier in this chapter and throughout this book, but only by choice, not because they are compelled to do so by some higher authority.

Dig This!

Slam, particularly the National Poetry Slam, has rules that govern the events and ensure a fair competition, but the rules are relatively lax and are riddled with loopholes. The spirit of the rules is what is most important. Everyone knows that gray areas exist in the interpretation of the rules, but the slam community encourages participants not to exploit the gray areas for their own personal gain.

Poetry Slam, Inc. is structured like a small democratic country. All members belong to the slam family and can vote on the general principles and policies of slam's evolution and direction. The slammasters, those individuals who organize regular slam events, comprise the main governing body of the movement. They create and approve by vote the specific projects that PSI originates and brings to fruition. The Executive Council and the professionals under its supervision are responsible for the business end of getting things done in a timely and efficient manner and within budget.

> **Dig This!**
>
> PSI is an anomaly in the realm of national non-profit arts organizations. Until a few years ago, it had received no major outside funding. It conducted all its business and staged all its events by the sweat and effort of its volunteer force and the money folks paid to see the shows. That's changed. In 2003 the NEA awarded PSI $20,000 to help stage NPS 2003. PSI is now actively seeking funding to expand its outreach programming and events. There's just so long you can fly by the seat of your pants without crashing. To learn more about PSI and its programs, check out its website at www. poetryslam.com.

The Least You Need to Know

- Forget about the points—they don't matter.

- When you're in the audience, listen carefully, and be ready to react to the performer to show your approval or disdain.

- Slam poets should serve the audience without groveling for high scores or approval.

- The slam organization is democratic, and the community welcomes people from all walks of life.

- PSI (Poetry Slam, Inc.) is the nonprofit membership association representing the worldwide slam community. Its three main bodies are the Slam Family, the SlamMasters Council, and the Executive Council.

Slam Competition—Rules, Regulations, and Other Formalities

In This Chapter

- ◆ Understanding the rationale behind slam competition
- ◆ Revisiting the first slam event—where it all began
- ◆ Boning up on the four main rules that govern traditional poetry slams
- ◆ Undercutting the seriousness of it all with slam disclaimers
- ◆ Examining some interesting deviations from traditional poetry slams

When you witness your first poetry slam, you might begin to wonder, "What the heck is going on here?" There's a carnival barker onstage who revs up the audience and introduces the performers; a bunch of poets, some of whom act as though they ought to be gagged and chained up somewhere; an audience that's way out of hand; and a few knuckleheads scattered among them who score the performances but apparently adhere to no clear set of criteria. Does anybody in the room know what's going on?

This chapter explains the basic structure of slam poetry competitions and analyzes the rules and regulations that govern the various types of slams. Of course, you don't need to be a certified slam judge to enjoy a poetry slam (assuming there is such a thing as a certified slam judge), but knowing what's going on helps you get more out of the show. Besides, if you decide to compete or to host your own shows, you'll need to know this stuff.

It's a Game, Stupid!

Whereas the competition didn't begin the slam movement, competition surely has been a major factor in its spread. That's easy to explain. Competition is basic to the human spirit and an integral part of the human experience. It identifies ability and celebrates achievement. And it's fun to watch. Who doesn't enjoy booing a judge, cheering a victorious hero, or sympathizing with an unjustly defeated friend?

However, the competition is only a means to an end—a way to get people excited about poetry, encourage poet/performers to write well and perform brilliantly, and foster a community of people who love performance poetry.

Many slam poets forget in the fervor of competition that the slam is not a serious determination of who's the best poet or performer. When they react furiously to a low score or bask too long in the glory of a perfect 10, they forget that most of a slam competition is arbitrary—a subjective concoction with unavoidable biases. By what objective criteria can you compare a sonnet to a rant or a seventeen-syllable haiku to a full three minutes of rap laced with pop images and slick jokes? How can judges, picked randomly from a rowdy unlettered crowd, be seen as an authentic testimony to a poet's value?

The competition is a theatrical device; it's not meant to be the litmus test of a performance or text. It's a natural drama. Everybody in the moment of the drama wonders who will win, who will get the high score, and who will walk away ten bucks richer. A half hour later, most have forgotten the numbers, but hopefully not the words.

People listen more intently during a slam competition because it follows a format everyone recognizes—the slammer's up, the pitch comes, a swing, a strike, a stolen simile, a homerun, a diving metaphor that saves the game. When a slammer steps up to the microphone, it's batter up. When he speaks, it's the pitch and swing. When the scores go up, it's the formal acknowledgement of what the audience might have already decided. "This dude didn't know what he was saying or how to say it." Strike 3. Or "She was sensational! I wanna buy her book." Grand slam! Like most sporting events, everybody has an opinion about what should have happened and who should have done what when. That keeps them involved up until the last syllable is uttered.

The First Slam Competition

The very first slam competition occurred at the Green Mill on the third (or was it the fourth?) week of the Uptown Poetry Slam's opening run. (No one can remember for sure.) It was an afterthought, a secondary element of the show, filler for the final act.

Al MacDougal, a merchant marine working on the ore boats that navigate the Great Lakes, was the first slam champion. Mary Shen Barnidge, a freelance theater critic, was his last challenger in a king-of-the-hill contest that lasted (I think) nine rounds. Al had successfully defended the hill from eight other opponents, but Mary knocked him off his pile of eight wins with her Dionysus poem.

What's on the CD

CD #2 track #12:
Mary Shen Barnidge performing "Dionysia"

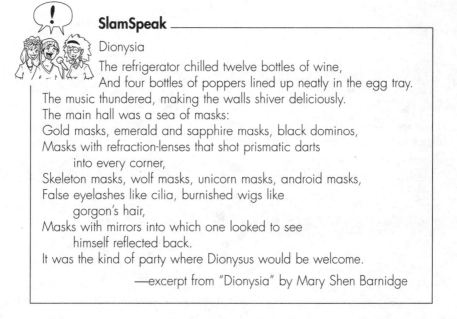

SlamSpeak

Dionysia
The refrigerator chilled twelve bottles of wine,
    And four bottles of poppers lined up neatly in the egg tray.
The music thundered, making the walls shiver deliciously.
The main hall was a sea of masks:
Gold masks, emerald and sapphire masks, black dominos,
Masks with refraction-lenses that shot prismatic darts
        into every corner,
Skeleton masks, wolf masks, unicorn masks, android masks,
False eyelashes like cilia, burnished wigs like
        gorgon's hair,
Masks with mirrors into which one looked to see
        himself reflected back.
It was the kind of party where Dionysus would be welcome.

—excerpt from "Dionysia" by Mary Shen Barnidge

But the audience raged against the imbalance of awarding Mary the $10 prize for a single winning poem when Al had won the first eight. In the end, Al got the money and bought Mary's drinks for the rest of the evening.

Whoa!

Mary doesn't remember it that way. She swears she wasn't slated to take on Al until weeks after his first slam victory, and then he didn't show up to defend his title. If we knew back then that we were making history, we might have downed less beer and recorded the details of these early events. Ah well.

That competition was determined by audience applause. It took a few months of haphazard experimentation—slams judged by holding up hands, by screaming and not clapping, by clapping without screaming, by stomping of feet—to arrive at the general rule that *competitions should be judged on a point system by judges selected randomly from the audience.* It's still an arbitrary system, but this method elicits less commotion and focuses the boos on the hapless judges rather than on the emcee and organizers.

Following the Rules

Rules are important to the structure of any competition. Baseball has nine innings; basketball, two timed halves; and yachting, one long sail. Regulations on structure and procedure frame an event into a digestible dramatic experience. Individual behavior is controlled by parameters set for the benefit of those who play and those who watch the play—no spitballs, no cork bats, no clipping, and no plagiarism. They promote sportsmanlike behavior, keep down the fistfights, and give everybody something to complain about. Rules are meant to create a fair playing field for all who participate. And in the slam the rules are also created to be questioned; after all, it's a passionate arena of free speech.

Rules vary from slam to slam, and they should. Each locale needs to adopt the regulations that are most agreeable and entertaining for their specific audience. It's art, not robotics. Be creative. Following are some basic rules to get you started. Feel free to modify or scrap whatever doesn't work for your particular show.

Dig This!

When you play on someone else's field you have to play according to the home team's program. That's just common courtesy. Don't try imposing your rules on someone else's show, and don't let anybody do it to you.

- Perform your own work.

- Perform in three minutes or less.

- No props or costumes.

- Scores range from 0 to 10 or down to minus infinity.

The following sections examine each of these rules in agonizing detail.

Perform Your Own Work

Most slams encourage and require poets to perform their own work. The rule's intent is obvious: to discourage plagiarism and maintain a level playing field. It simply wouldn't be fair for a novice to pit her first poetic creation against someone reading the great works of Gwendolyn Brooks or Langston Hughes. This rule also encourages young writers to test their ideas and writing skills, opens the doors for poetic innovation, and gives each performer a sounding board for his or her free voice and unfettered emotions. Performers break this rule all the time—sometimes deceitfully, sometimes with the permission of the audience, and sometimes because a particular poetry slam focuses on the works of famous poets.

Three Minutes Is All We Can Stand

Prior to the slam it was not unusual for a poet to tax an audience's patience with a fifteen-minute poem of questionable aesthetic value. Stage hogs who cared little about the people they inflicted their words upon, or the other poets lined up waiting to read, would drain every ounce of patience from an audience and kill any chance for those who followed to succeed. The Three-Minute rule put a limit on how much bad verse a poet could spew before the hook appeared in the wings to yank him out of the spotlight. It also became the basic time unit of the competition itself. It's the "at bat"—you get three minutes to make your hit happen. And for most poets that's more than enough time to score big or crawl back to the dugout.

No Props, Costumes, Trombones, or Other Carry-on Luggage

Here's another rule that is often broken for the sheer fun of breaking it. The No Props rule originally was initiated during the planning of the 1990 National Poetry Slam. Most of the shows mounted at the Green Mill by the Chicago Poetry Ensemble employed props, music, and costumes. The Uptown Poetry Slam gained a reputation as a cabaret of multi-media poetic arts that stretched the boundaries of the acceptable at a poetry event. But when discussing what might happen at our first major national competition, we decided to rule out the use of props and music. I remember saying, "What if someone brings a ten-piece orchestra onstage? Or poodles? How will we get them on- and off-stage without messing up the rhythm of the show? How can you judge an orchestra against a solo poet reciting a villanelle?" It was somewhat of a tourniquet on the creative juices, but it has saved many an organizer the nightmare of exploding cabbages, bath tubs, and six-foot submarine sandwiches, all of which have found their way into poetry performances at special slam competitions staged for the pure joy of breaking the rules.

Scoring: 0 to 10 (or Down to Minus Infinity)

Few slams play by the "mean" Chicago rules that allow the judges to score into the minus numbers. That's a shame, because the audience loves it when "bad" gets its due and good gets a 10. The 0 to 10 scoring system is fairly universal. At the National Poetry Slam, five judges score each performance, the top and bottom scores are dropped, and the sum of the remaining three scores represents the "score." In other words, a perfect score would be 30 points.

Audience score card for 2003 NPS.

BOUT #1 7:00					
TEAM 1		**TEAM 2**		**TEAM 3**	
POET	**PTS**	**POET**	**PTS**	**POET**	**PTS**
1		1		1	
2		2		2	
3		3		3	
4		4		4	
TOTAL		TOTAL		TOTAL	
BOUT 1 STORM POET:				**SCORE:**	

BOUT #2 8:30					
TEAM 1		**TEAM 2**		**TEAM 3**	
POET	**PTS**	**POET**	**PTS**	**POET**	**PTS**
1		1		1	
2		2		2	
3		3		3	
4		4		4	
TOTAL		TOTAL		TOTAL	
BOUT 2 STORM POET:				**SCORE:**	

BOUT #3 10:00					
TEAM 1		**TEAM 2**		**TEAM 3**	
POET	**PTS**	**POET**	**PTS**	**POET**	**PTS**
1		1		1	
2		2		2	
3		3		3	
4		4		4	
TOTAL		TOTAL		TOTAL	
BOUT 3 STORM POET:				**SCORE:**	

Some slams require the judges to score the poetry and the performance separately: 1 to 5 for performance and 1 to 5 for text. Some score by holding up roses. Some determine the winner by audience applause, which can sound different depending on where you sit. Some have secret ballots. The more involved an audience is in the judging, the more entertaining the show.

Famous Slam Disclaimers

Slam organizers from early on have tried to express to newcomers that "all's not fair" at the slam—that it's entertainment. Trying to determine whose poem and performance is truly the best through a slam competition is absurd. Remember, "points are not the point." To drive this point about points home, many slammasters have created rituals and liturgies that announce these facts of life at the beginning of their shows. This ensures that the audience approaches the event with the proper perspective. The following sections demonstrate some sample opening comments. Note how they succeed in presenting the slam as a competition and then undercut the importance of the competition.

We Begin Each Slam with a Disclaimer–Bob Holman at the Nuyorican Café

Bob Holman introduces every slam competition at the Nuyorican Café with the following preamble, versified, of course:

As Dr. Willie used to say,
We are gathered here today
because we are not gathered
somewhere else today, and
we don't know what we're doing
so you do—the Purpose of SLAM!
being to fill your hungry ears
with Nutritious Sound/Meaning Constructs,
Space Shots into Consciousness
known hereafter as Poems; and
not to provide a Last Toehold
for Dying Free Enterprise F@#* 'em
for a Buck'em Capitalism'em. We disdain
competition and its ally war
and are fighting for our lives
and the spinning

What's on the CD

CD #1 track #2: Bob Holman's "Disclaimer"

of poetry cocoon of action
in your dailiness. We refuse
to meld the contradictions but
will always walk the razor
for your love. "The best poet
always loses" is no truism of SLAM!
but is something for you
to take home with you like an image
of a giant condor leering over
a salty rock. Yes, we must destroy
ourselves in the constant
reformation that is this very moment,
and propel you to write the poems
as poets read them, urge you
to rate the judges as they trudge
to their solitary and lonely numbers,
and bid you dance or die between sets.

The Mean Chicago Rules—Marc (So What!) Smith

At the Green Mill Cocktail Lounge in Chicago, I begin every Sunday night slam with the following disclaimer:

At the slam you, the audience, are always in control. If you like something cheer madly. [The audience cheers.] But if you don't like what you hear you may also express yourselves in one of several manners. If you don't like it a little bit, you snap your fingers. [The audience snaps.] That's not dig-me-daddy-o, those guys are dead and gone. This is a new regime. If you don't like it a little bit more, stomp your feet. [They stomp.] If it's god awful bad, you groan. [Grooooooooooaaaaaaaaaaaaaaaaan!] There's also the feminist hiss. [Hisssssssssssssssssssss] It used to be for when a man got sexist in his poem, but now it's for just about anything as soon as he steps up onto the stage. [They cheer.] After years of being hissed at, the men finally came up with the masculine grunt. [a whimper] That says it all about the masculine grunt. There's also Guess the Rhyme: If there should happen to be a rhyming poet up here on the stage and you, the audience, can guess the rhyming word before it arrives, you may in unison with the poet say the word and watch his or her face—it's great fun. Finally we have instituted the Amen. [Amen!] Because a lot of this slam poetry has gotten very rhetorical over the years, and sometimes we like that rhetoric and sometimes we don't, we say Amen to both. [Amen!] What's great about the Amen [Amen!] is that the poet doesn't know for sure whether it's a positive Amen or a negative Amen. Could I have an Amen please? [AMEN!]

And just before the competition begins, I review the rules, as follows:

Here are the rules. Rule number one: No poem may go over three minutes. You are all timers. If it even feels like three minutes start snapping. Rule number two: Listen to the poem. Then, judges, rate the poem 1 to 10, 10 being high. However, you may go into the minus numbers, but you can only tie the lowest score ever scored at a poetry slam which is [everyone together] MINUS INFINITY!

The Official Emcee Spiel Used at the National Poetry Slams

The official emcee spiel used at the nationals is much more succinct and sounds much more … official. Before the start of any national slam competition, this is what you hear:

"The [National] Slam is a performed poetry competition judged by five members of the audience. Poets have three minutes to present their original work and may choose to do so accompanied by members of their team. The judges will then score the piece anywhere from 0 to 10, evaluating both the poet's performance and the contents of the poem. Points will be deducted for violating the time limit. The highest combined team score wins the bout. We encourage the audience to let the judges know how you feel about the job that they are doing. We exhort the judges to remain unswayed by crowd pressure. We are sure that the poetry will be worth your attention."

The Many Flavors of Slam

Slam was meant to be a liberating experience, a creative mix, a door opening to new ways of presenting poetry onstage. Challenging and reformulating the rules has become almost as important as creating them. The most accepted way of challenging how things are done is to create alternative competitions. They keep the doors open and the slam minds fresh, and provide models for a new approach. The following sections describe some of the more interesting spin-offs.

Unseen Slam

In the UK, slammers have created an event they call the Unseen Slam. It consists of three rounds, or "heats" as they call them over there. The first takes place before anybody sits down, while people are still milling about in the lobby or on the street. A hat filled with the first lines of well-known and not-so-well-known poems is passed around. Those poets who want to jump into the fray, pull out a line, and spend the next half hour scribbling away creating a new work inspired by the words drawn from the hat. At the end of that half hour the audience sits down and the show begins. The contestants perform their freshly written treasures on stage. When all have been heard, the judges present their scores by holding up cards with numbers on them. Low scores get dropped, and the lucky performers move on to the second heat, which is another impromptu writing exercise.

This time the audience shouts out suggestions of words that all the remaining poets have to use in a poem they create over the next fifteen minutes. And once again, at the end of the writing time, the audience listens to the contestants present their poems, witnesses the scoring, and consoles those low-scoring poets who get knocked out.

In the final heat, two poets remain onstage, each having to write yet another poem with the whole audience looking on … in just fifteen minutes! Talk about pressure! This time, the host or audience provides a theme that the poets must address. The poet who turns out the best poem and best performance (in the eyes of the audience) is declared the winner.

A similar type of impromptu slam occurs in the states: The Dumb Rhyming Word Game. The audience is asked to shout out three words that the poet contestants must employ in a text they write during the early portion of the show. The catch is they must not only use the words but also rhyme them in the context of the poem.

Theme Slams

A theme slam is a wonderful way to get poets off of the same old topics. How many times does an audience want to hear "war is bad" or "love is good"? A theme slam can take the slammers to new places and challenge and expose new beliefs. "The Ad Man Slam," "The Topless Slam," "The Dog Walk Slam," and "The What Santa Didn't Bring Me For Xmas Slam" have inspired some far-out poetic creations. It's important not to interpret the theme too narrowly. It's meant to inspire, not restrict. So when a poet barely mentions toothpaste in the "Brush Your Teeth Slam" don't disqualify him. On the other hand, if someone performs their experimental verse about modern dance motifs at the "Mother's Day Slam" they might deserve to be booed off stage.

What's on the CD

CD #1 track #4:
Ron Gillette performing "Adman"

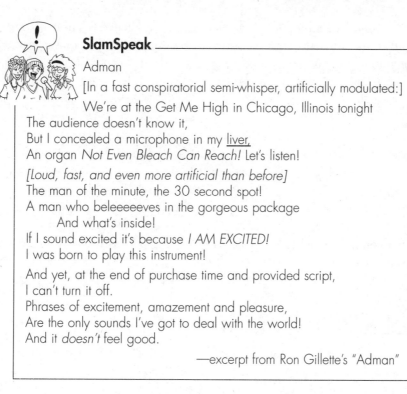

SlamSpeak

Adman

[In a fast conspiratorial semi-whisper, artificially modulated:]
We're at the Get Me High in Chicago, Illinois tonight
The audience doesn't know it,
But I concealed a microphone in my <u>liver,</u>
An organ *Not Even Bleach Can Reach!* Let's listen!

[*Loud, fast, and even more artificial than before*]
The man of the minute, the 30 second spot!
A man who beleeeeeves in the gorgeous package
 And what's inside!
If I sound excited it's because *I AM EXCITED!*
I was born to play this instrument!

And yet, at the end of purchase time and provided script,
I can't turn it off.
Phrases of excitement, amazement and pleasure,
Are the only sounds I've got to deal with the world!
And it *doesn't* feel good.

—excerpt from Ron Gillette's "Adman"

Cover Slam

To celebrate all the great poems of the past and present, many slams hold "cover" slams. The rule requiring original work is discarded, and performers pay a nod to their favorite poets or poems, performing works that are not their own. The authors they cover can be from centuries ago such as Rumi or Petrarch, or contemporaries such as former poet laureate Billy Collins or Pulitzer Prize winner Mary Oliver. Many times slammers pay tribute to their heroes in the slam community and to each other. The Cover Slam is another way of reminding slammers that slamming is not supposed to be about "I … I … I … I." It's about a "we" that goes back to the dawn of the word.

Relay Slam

Another format from the UK is a freestyle event called the "relay" slam. Groups of poets take the stage and the audience calls out words. A poet grabs one of those words like it's a jumpball in basketball and begins to dribble, creating poetic lines for as long as he can. When he's empty he passes it onto another poet. The host monitors the event, keeping the action going by prompting the audience to chime in with new words, themes, and ideas until the poets start to sputter. Often music is added to keep a pulse going while the verses are being invented. At the end of the relay, the audience decides by applause who was their favorite Slam Relay word dribbler.

Prop Slam

As a reaction to the "no prop rule," and to have some outrageous fun, most NPS tournaments include a Prop Slam as a side event to the official proceedings. The most memorable of these can't be described herein because they stepped far beyond the PG rating. But other spectacles have included wheeling performers in on hospital gurneys to accentuate a poem about sloth, a six-foot submarine sandwich torn apart onstage to emphasize gluttony, and a mesmerizing performance by a man and woman duet using heavy chains and garbage can lids to create a jangling rhythm behind a multi-voiced poem about roaming the alleys of Chicago.

Pong Jam Slam—Music to the Poetic Ear

Every first Sunday of the month at the Green Mill, poets are invited to perform to the musical accompaniment of the Pong Unit Band. It can be magical. The poets ask for any type of music they wish—"Super Comic Hero Music," "Russian Folk mixed with Salsa," "Low Down Muddy Water Blues"—and the band provides it. If the poet finds the groove, a whole new level of experience enriches the night.

This is ancient history. Poetry and musical instrumentation have been partners since Pan tooted his flute and Homer plucked the lyre. Our most recent poetic ancestors did the same. Carl Sandburg traveled throughout the Midwest reciting poems to the strums of his guitar, usually out of tune. Jack Kerouac's spontaneous style of writing was deeply influenced by the phrasings of bebop he performed them to. And in the slam world this tradition continues. Former slam champion Cin Salach combines her poems with the music of the Loofah Methode. Vancouver slammer CR Avery is his own one-poet band, creating complementary rhythms on harmonica and piano to meld with his words.

What's on the CD

CD #1 Track #6: Performance poet C.R. Avery

CD #1 Track #7: Cin Salach and the Loofah Methode performing "Blind Spots"

Throughout the slam community you can find evenings similar to the Pong Jam Slam. Musicians find it to be a refreshing alternative to their pure musical commitments—surely better than their wedding gigs.

Local Slams—Laws and Bye-Laws

The organizer at the local level who takes on the burden of creating a slam has every right to construct that show in a manner that best suits the community it serves. The time, the energy (and don't forget the dough) organizers expend to achieve liftoff deserves devotion and respect. They will initially wonder if the payoff is worth the effort. All of them encounter resistance and criticism from friends and foes alike. At this very moment there are slammasters sitting in the darkest corners of bedrooms with their hands gripping their heads mumbling "Why, why, why?"

So if you've started a slam, keep in mind that it's your show. If folks think it's bogus, let 'em start their own. If they start one and begin drawing audience away from yours, maybe it's time for a little slam examination. If not, you're on the right track. Often-times, two competing slams in the same area or city both thrive. After all, poetry is a big house with many rooms.

However, slam does have a handful of sacred traditions that define the essential nature of slam. Slams that break with these traditions usually become something other than slams. Here are the main traditions that define a slam:

♦ **Slams are open to all.** Slam was a reaction against elitism and exclusivity and therefore is open to any and all who walk through the doors. Of course, nobody welcomes a jerk who's bent on using the stage to impose wickedness on the audience. Slam provides everyone with an equal first chance (and often a second, third, and fourth chance) to find a place in the community and on a slam stage. If a particular slam works for you, great. If it doesn't, try someplace else, even another slam, or create your own slam. Slams can be as different as night and day, but all slams should be open to all poet performers.

♦ **All styles, forms, and subject matter are welcome.** Sonnets, haiku, *pantoums*, villanelles, raps, rants, ballads, limericks … you name it, and it's been performed on a slam stage. Love, religion, politics, body odors, taxes, dog poo—it's been done. Anything and everything is game, but remember, the audience can give it right back. And there are more of them than there are of you.

SlamSlang

Pantoum is a Malayan form of accentual-syllabic verse that consists of an indefinite number of quatrain stanzas with the specific restriction that lines two and four of each stanza be repeated in lines one and three of the following stanza.

- **The all-important audience should always be in control.** Let them actively express themselves, not abusively but honestly. Announce the ground rules, and they'll do the rest. If you give them a say, they'll be back to listen again and again. At the first printing of this book, the Green Mill Uptown Poetry Slam was in its seventeenth year playing to standing-room-only crowds. Over fifty thousand different people have seen that show. That should be proof enough.

Heading for the Nationals—Get Serious!

Every year, slam teams and individual performers from across the United States and even outside the United States gather to perform and celebrate at the National Poetry Slam. In 2003, poets representing 60 cities in the United States and three cities in Canada descended on my hood, Chicago, to join in the extravaganza, and many more wanted to come. To give the National Poetry Slam some semblance of order and prevent it from becoming a logistic nightmare, the Nationals have set some criteria that teams and individuals must meet in order to be selected:

- **Only certified slam teams may compete.** The national tournaments were created to encourage the development of local slams. To support that end, all the teams and individuals competing at national events must come from certified local slams, shows that are ongoing and serving a specific community.

- **Each local slam must conduct an open competition to select its team members.** This policy prevents some unscrupulous person from recruiting the top performance poets from around the country and engineering a team of ringers. Don't laugh; it's been done.

- **Individuals may qualify.** In some cases it's possible to compete at NPS as an individual. If no regular slam is in your area or if the local slam just started and can't get it together to send a team, you may qualify. And even if you don't get into the official competition, you can participate in the many fringe events at the nationals.

- **Participants must be members of PSI.** Poetry Slam, Inc. (PSI) manages the national tournament and requires that all competitors be members of its non-profit association. Membership levels range from $15 per year to $1,000 for the big shot donors.

Dig This!

If you and/or your team are selected to perform at the nationals, be prepared to raise some money for travel, lodging, and entry fees. It's well worth the costs and the hassles. The national events are attended each year by hundreds of poets who praise it as the best experience they've ever had, inside and outside of poetry.

Chapter 22 fully explains National Poetry Slam competitions. Skip ahead if you want, and get all the dope.

The Least You Need to Know

- The competitive component of slam poetry is a theatrical tool intended to liven up the show and inspire the poet/performers to do their best.

- At the National Poetry Slam, poets are required to perform their own work, in three minutes or less, wearing no costumes and using no props, and are scored on a scale from 0 to 10.

- At the beginning of each slam event, the emcee typically recites a disclaimer that undercuts the seriousness of the competition and sets a tone for the show.

- Organizers experiment with the standard slam format to create variations, such as Unseen Slam, Prop Slam, Theme Slam, and Relay Slam.

- To remain true to slam, follow the traditions that define it: Open it to anyone, allow all styles of poetry, and give the audience control.

Part 2

Becoming a Performance Poet

Poetry slam is seductive. Sitting in the audience at a competition, you almost spring out of your chair with desire to seize the mike and perform your own poems. And the cool thing about slam is that you can … anyone can.

This part shows you how to make a successful transition from the printed word to performance poetry—from page to stage. Here you learn how to pen poetry that's conducive to a stage performance, overcome stage fright and other vicious inhibitions, and master the performance techniques that entice and engage an audience. With these skills and techniques (and a little practice), you'll be well primed for your first (or next) performance.

Chapter 4

Penning the Powerful Slam Poem

In This Chapter

- ◆ Painting vivid imagery using concrete language and precise diction
- ◆ Making your verse dance and flow to the right rhythm
- ◆ Rhyming without making your poems sound like bad Mother Goose
- ◆ Knowing your point and expressing it vividly in verse
- ◆ Spinning a yarn—slam storytelling

Unless you're a *free-styler*, an improv artist, or a South African *praise poet*, what you say onstage starts with what you scribble on the page; therefore, garbage in, garbage out. If you start with flatulent verse, the performance will surely stink up the joint. Your verse needs to engage and entertain the audience, and to do so it must follow time-tested poetic principles. Ignoring these principles generates text that conjures a sea of blank faces, an undercurrent of snickers, or the dreadful communal "huh?" Adhering to these principles and making proper use of poetic devices ensures that the verse you craft is powerful, crystal clear, and can dazzle the most dispassionate audience.

SlamSlang _____

South African **praise poets** (Imbongi) have influenced their local politics for time immemorial by creating and maintaining the reputation of tribal chiefs. To this day, praise poets declaim the political climate and social injustices around them through oral poetry.

Free-stylers are improv rappers who duel poetically onstage or in circled groups on street corners over vocally or instrumentally produced rhythms called *backbeats*. Free-styling has extended into the slam world and even into more traditional poetry realms.

SlamSlang _____

Sounds produced by the human voice to provide a basic 4-beat rhythmic pattern behind verses laid down by rappers is **backbeat**.

This chapter doesn't teach the basics of composing poetry; for that, grab a copy of *The Complete Idiot's Guide to Writing Poetry*, by Nikki Moustaki (Alpha Books, 2001) or another book about composing verse. Nor does this chapter reveal the secrets of writing the perfect slam poem (as if there were such a thing). Instead, this chapter focuses on the poetic devices and techniques that you, as performance poet, must employ to compose poetry that's compelling when performed live, onstage.

Seeing Is Believing—Concrete Vs. Abstract Language

Basic to all good writing is concrete language, or words and phrases that project on the minds of the audience vivid images, sounds, actions, and other sensations. If your text is rich with imagery (piles of gold doubloons) your audience will see, smell, and taste (eyeball sniffin' slobber) what you're telling (squawk twitter howl) them. They'll hold it in their mind's eye, ear, and nose, savoring it as long as it takes to sink its (saber) point into their (valentine) hearts. They'll handcuff together (associate) the birds, sunspots, and stones (ideas) skipping over your poem into their minds and actually link them with things (ravens, inkblots, and smooth pebbles) they've seen (a brain photograph), heard (marbles bouncing on a snare drum), tasted (sticky cotton candy lips), and touched like cold silver fish flapping in their hands. They'll smell the wild onions crying in your words.

Dig This!

Always choose the right word for the right job. For example, you can run in many different ways—sprint, jog, lope, scamper, dash, scurry, trot, bustle, skedaddle, and so on. Use your word processor's thesaurus, buy a thesaurus, or use an online thesaurus like the one at www.thesaurus.com.

Slam Examples of Concrete Language

Over the years I have noticed that almost all the great slammers fill their poems with concrete language. I've also noticed the impact of concrete language on the audience. They almost always comment on an image or sensual experience that blistered, boiled, or positively charged their brain cells as if it really happened to them.

Here are a couple excerpts from slam poets who are adept at using concrete language and who have been very effective onstage. Both are National Slam champions.

What's on the CD

CD #1 track #9: Lisa Buscani performing "Sirens of the Mill"

CD #1 track #10: Shane Koyczan performing "Beethoven"

> as they let the music
> invade their nervous system
> like an armada marching through
> firing cannonballs
> detonating every molecule in their bodies

> —from "Beethoven," by Shane Koyczan

> And I thought of my brother down at the Popsicle
> factory,
> put his hand on a guardrail as a two-ton punch
> press
> whistled millimeters from his fingers.

> —from "Sirens at the Mill," by Lisa Buscani

Abstract Language

Abstract language goes the other way. It's the stuff humans have concocted in their brains to generalize the world and human behavior. Words like "greed," "intelligence," "universal," and "thinking" are abstract words. We know what they mean, sort of, but can you smell intelligence? Can you touch thinking? When was the last time you tried to taste greed?

Abstract language sticks like marbles to Teflon. The audience might be able to grasp it, but they can't hold it. If their collective mind wanders, brain chatter takes over and all you receive at the end of your performance is polite applause, if that. Here is a revision of Lisa Buscani's verse written in more abstract language:

And I thought of industrialization,
subjecting its workers to possible disfigurement
as they worked near machines on the assembly line.

Exercises

Find concrete language to bring to life the following generalized abstract phrases:

♦ Hunger affects the population of many minor countries.

♦ Some creatures entered into her dreams.

♦ Attaining one's goals brings happiness.

Take one of your poems and go through it, circling all the abstract language. Rewrite the poem, replacing the abstract words and phrases with concrete language.

Flaccid Phrasing

Both prose and poetry are stronger when they're active. A phrase shouldn't lie lifeless like a corpse. It should punch the audience in the gut, grab it by the collar, or whisper seductively into its ear. To compose dynamic poetry, follow these two basic rules of good writing: Avoid the passive voice and avoid feeble verbs.

Passive voice places no one in charge of the action: "The apple was shot off Johnny's head." Who did the shooting? Active voice fingers the perpetrator: "Susie blasted the apple off Johnny's head."

Feeble verbs such as "is" and "are" lay on the beach like pale weaklings waiting for Mr. Universe to kick sand in their faces. You want verbs with muscle. "There are thirteen ghosts in the house." Yeah, so? What are they doing, just floating there namby-pamby? "Thirteen ghosts pillaged the house like an L.A. mob." Now we're getting somewhere.

Exercises

Which of these stanzas are in the active voice and which are passive? Rewrite the passive stanzas to make them active:

♦ It is time that takes hope from us
And turns the face of tomorrow dark.

♦ There are negative experiences that
will not let my mind rest.

♦ Blow North Wind! Fury foul the tide
   And wrap the shore with froth and brine.

♦ Many are the uncertain folk who wander
   Pondering the past, defeated by regret.
   Their voices huddle in their brains
   Blamed and shamed by themselves
   Reframing what they didn't do.

Read through one of your poems and circle all the passive constructions and weak verbs. Rewrite them in the active voice.

Too Smart for Your Performance

Difficult allusions, obscure references, and antiquated language are ill-suited for the stage. The audience won't be holding an unabridged dictionary on their laps, and the distractions that are ever-present in a public setting make it difficult to access the memory banks quickly enough to recover the connection between oblique literary references and the fabric of the poem. Attention gets diverted to the handsome face in the back row, the annoying mope pulling up a chair in front of you, or the sirens singing on the ribbon of pavement outside. Give your audience something clear and concrete to hold on to.

> **Whoa!**
>
> Don't dumb down your work. Know your audience and the ideas and diction you can use to communicate effectively to them. Avoid being too highfalutin' or overly simple-minded with your language.

Rock to the Rhythm

One characteristic that sets poetry apart from other forms of writing is rhythm, or patterns formed by the almighty line and other poetic devices. We hear and recognize rhythmic patterns through the use of various line lengths, meter, *syntax*, sense, and recurring imagery.

Traditional line forms and meter are uncommon in the slam world. You hear echoes of the hearty *iambic pentameter*, the light-hearted *tetrameter*, and the staccato *dimeter* lines mixed

> **SlamSlang**
>
> **Syntax** is the arrangement of words to construct phrases and sentences. By manipulating syntax, you can change the rhythm of a sentence and control which words and phrases are stressed.

inside the phrasing of many performance poems, but always above or below an implied beat accentuated by the various performance techniques described in Chapter 6. The strength of performance poetry lies in its willingness to layer a variety of line lengths, meters, and rhythmic patterns into one piece. Like a jazz trumpeter who creates astonishing new variations on a tired melody, performance poets break form to create new form.

However, slammers have not completely abandoned all traditional rhythmic forms; in fact, one of the strongest and most common rhythmic constructions employed in the slam world is also one of the oldest: the repetition of parallel constructions. Here are a few examples:

> Out of the cradle endlessly rocking,
> Out of the mocking-bird's throat, the musical shuttle,
> Out of the Ninth-month midnight,
> Over the sterile sands and the fields beyond …

> —from "Sea Drift," by Walt Whitman

> throw the briefcase in the back seat,
> loosen the tie,
> roll down the window,
> pull on the shades,
> pull on the racing gloves,
> push some tunes into the tape deck
> …
> I don't have time to be a Sunday driver,
> I don't have time to be cruising flowers,
> I don't have time to be sight-seeing.

> —from "Motor Red, Motor White, Motor Blue,"
> by Austin Slam champion, Phil West

The repetition of parallel constructions causes stressed and unstressed syllables to occur at approximately the same place and time from line to line, setting up a distinct rhythm on the page that the performer can reinforce through various techniques: pause, breath, and articulation. By repeating a phrase, the performer can often build suspense, increase the dramatic tone of the poem, and even undercut the previous lines with a surprise at the end.

Exercise

Recurring imagery, parallel phrasing, repeated words and sounds, accented syllables, and themes reintroduced over and over create the rhythms that give poetry its musical quality. Read through a favorite poem by a great author and circle all such rhythmic patterns. Do the same for one of your poems. Do you hear the music in your work?

> **Whoa!**
>
> Break form only when you know what you're breaking. The most accomplished slammers dig deep into past poetic traditions to learn and acquire poetic writing skills that give them an abundance of choices to make and remake into forms of their own.

It's Gotta Sound Good, Too

Sound is to poetry as color is to visual art. Poetry must be compelling to the human ear; that is, the language must be sonically rich. To make your words bing, ting, zip, grip, rattle, and bong, employ a variety of sonic devices. Following are definitions of some sonic devices that can strengthen your poems and produce the *euphony* and *cacophony* you want to ripple and crash off your text and onto the stage. If you ignore these, you're probably not writing poetry.

◆ **Alliteration** is the repetition of the initial sounds of two or more words in a line or series of lines, such as "singing songs of silence."

◆ **Hidden alliteration** is the repetition of sounds *within* two or more words in a line or series of lines, such as "Long ago re*gal gl*ory re*gal*ed at tab*l*es set by the poor."

◆ **Assonance** is the repetition of two or more identical vowel sounds preceded and followed by differing consonant sounds that are close enough together in the poem to create an echoing effect. "Ping" and "thing" are rhymes (which are assonantal, too), but "ping" and "teen" are assonantal (without rhyming).

◆ **Consonance** is like hidden alliteration, the repetition of two or more identical consonant sounds and differing vowel sounds close together in a poem, such as "the brigh*t* li*tt*le Bri*t*ish boy." The "b" sounds are alliterative and "t" sounds are consonantal.

◆ **Onomatopoeia** is the use of words that mimic or suggest the sounds they describe, such as "buzz" or "bellow."

> **SlamSlang**
>
> **Euphony** is the pleasant combination of sounds and sonic devices. **Cacophony** is the mixture of sounds and sonic devices that clash and create harsh, discordant effects. Both have their purpose and place in well-crafted poetry.

Guess the Rhyme

Sometimes slammers must rhyme, but if they do it too much, they're committing a crime. When slammers get loose and start sounding like Seuss, the audience boos and readies the noose. Annoyed yet? Although rhyme is the best-known sonic device, predictable and relentless end rhyme is too easy and cheesy and not at all pleasy. The following list describes the various types of rhyme that can offer more surprising and appealing sonic color than tedious end rhyme:

- **Cross Rhyme** rhymes a line ending word with a word in the middle of a preceding or following line.

  *Love finds ways to **mask***

  *The bitter **task** when it says,*

  Good-bye.

- **Interlaced Rhyme** rhymes words in the middle of one line with words in the middle of another line.

  *Hapless rode the **headless** horsemen*

  *Like a **bedless** husband in the night*

- **Internal Rhyme** rhymes the end of a line with a word in the middle of the line:

  *Like worms in his **eyes** twisted his **lies***

- **Linked Rhyme** rhymes the last sound of a line with the first sound of the next lines:

  *Sling your sizzling muck across the **room***
  Fume** at me from **afar
  ***Tar** and feather my position,*
  I shall not alter a single word.

- **Slant Rhyme, Off-Rhyme,** or **Near Rhyme** allow sounds that aren't quite identical to masquerade as rhyme:

  He picked up the wrench
  And went to the hedge
  *To find his **neighbor***
  *And return the **favor**.*

♦ **Wrenched Rhyme** twists unmercifully the spelling, sense, and sound of words to make them fit into a rhyme scheme:

Those stogied folk across the bar
Believe themselves to be
*Patriotic **illumanies,***
***Epiphanies** of a new age dawning.*

Rhyming is as ancient as language itself. It can enrich your poems and performance if used with skill, surprise, and moderation. But when it degenerates into mindless, arbitrary *rhymation*, you're exposing yourself and the slam reputation to just criticism from the scholars who know the precision it takes to write high-quality verse.

SlamSlang

Rhymation describes the tedious and sometimes nonsensical practice of rhyming a long, long series of -tion and -sion words. It also applies to common word endings of -ize, -ism, -ary, -etic, -ation, and a dozen others.

No Sermons, But If You Must Preach ...

Over the years, many, indeed most, performance poets have written political poems. They are highly effective, especially in front of large audiences. Slammers can create the same frenzy that evangelistic preachers do when they supercharge their flock with emotional hyperbole. The line between *rhetoric* and poetry has become blurred in the slam world. To some, the pop political ideas expressed on slam stages lack the depth for which fine poetry has always been noted. To others, it is vital news being heralded to the masses.

The rhetorical devices identified and defined in the following list have been used for centuries to manipulate emotions and drive home particular points of view. They are highly effective (and potentially dangerous) forms of communication, commonly used in religious and political propaganda. Although they're effective, an educated audience can recognize immediately when a poet is barking his own dogma and will let the poet know pretty quickly that he's barking up the wrong tree. Use these devices in moderation or avoid them completely:

SlamSlang

The term **rhetoric**, as used here, describes the use of powerful, sometimes misleading language intended to persuade an audience to take a particular stand on an issue or stir the emotions of the audience simply to obtain more applause and a higher score.

◆ **Antanagoge** starts out really mean and then pulls the punch. You let fly some really harsh stuff, and then get yourself off the hook (of looking like a real jerk or appearing too bitterly ironic) by softening your first statement with a second qualifying statement.

"His head brought to mind
The bobbing countenance of a kangaroo,
But the steady gleam of his big new teeth
Charmed us as an unpouched baby's should."

—from "My Brother's Child" by Pete LaFete

◆ **Antiphrasis** is the use of a word or phrase in the opposite sense of its literal meaning, often as a form of name-calling. Calling a guy who's six-foot-seven, 300 pounds "Tiny" is antiphrasis.

◆ **Aporia** is the questioning of an issue to lead the audience to form an opinion about it without directly stating a stand on the issue:

"Have you ever wondered
why politicians who promote public education
send their kids to private schools?"

The statement does not say that politicians are immoral elitists, but it sure implies it.

◆ **Apostrophe** is speaking to someone or some personified thing that is not there:

Hear O' Israel
the star belongs to no one
for not David would believe
his child has become Goliath
spitting imperialist warheads
at children holding slingshots …

—from "Hear O' Israel," by Kevin Coval

◆ **Bombast** is rant speech that goes overboard and is too inflated for the situation.

◆ **Ecphonesis** is an emotional exclamation or outcry:

Backstage Skinny

Slam poets are masters of rhetoric, using it effectively to rile up an audience and implant their beliefs and ideas. Listen to Taylor Mali's slam classic "How to Write a Political Poem" on **CD #2 track #5.**

What's on the CD

CD #2 track #5: Taylor Mali performing "How to Write a Political Poem"

Oh god how I long to be wrapped in golden singles of
American cheese
Drizzled with its salty goodness.
Oh god put me in the sauna so the cheese will melt …

Oh god
Take me
Take me and dip me like fondue into your vat
of silken American cheese food products …

—from "America (It's Gotta be the Cheese)," by Eitan Kadosh

♦ **Epiphonema** is a climatic summation at the conclusion of a poem:

The hydrogen bomb the neutron bomb engineered death and pantyhose
Mom the flag and apple pie
It's gotta be the cheese.

—from "America (It's Gotta be the Cheese)," by Eitan Kadosh

Once Upon a Slam—Storytelling

Slam champions Lisa Buscani, Patricia Smith, Shane Koyczan, and others have developed their own particular styles of storytelling that have enormous audience appeal. Storytelling has been around since the first prattling of human speech. Myths, legends, folk tales, and the excited exaggerations of first graders stand as testimonies to the fact that we love a good story and enjoy inserting ourselves into those storylines.

The primary function of any kind of narrative is to relate an incident or a series of incidents, telling a tale about something that happened, might happen, or that we imagine happening. The main components of these narratives are the basic beginning, middle, and ending, but other ingredients contribute to making stories memorable, especially at a slam:

♦ **Character.** Often a persona of the poet herself speaks in the first person, but the character can be anybody or anything from a dog to a prizefighter to a rock rolling down a hill. Pick a character that's colorful and intriguing.

Whoa!

Should you choose only one character? Sometimes; sometimes not. Like any narrative, slam stories can mix a variety of characters into the action, even within the basic three-minute limit. Sometimes multi-character slam poems turn into group pieces that give voice to a variety of characters and attitudes.

◆ **Time and place.** Stories occur somewhere, at some time, even if that some-where or sometime is just a mood or state of mind. Time and place frame the characters and the story itself:

Downtown bound
Grab for the dollar
Get out of my way
Five o'clock rush!

—from "Bicycle Jockey" by Marc Smith

◆ **Action.** Action covers movement, the purpose and direction, and the target that becomes clearer and clearer as the story poem unfolds. The audience needs to know why the character is struggling, where the character is headed, or what the character wants early on:

Man,
I gotta get this package
Up to Mister Never Seen
A bad day dirty room
Snot crack ceiling in his life.

—from "Bicycle Jockey" by Marc Smith

◆ **Obstacles and conflict.** No story exists unless the heroine struggles against some psychological dilemma or social injustice. She must slay a dragon, zigzag through opponents to score a goal, or find her Romeo.

MOVE IT!
You are an obstacle
I will not wait for.
Home to the broad lawns with you
Home to the taxes.
Home to TV makes your life go bye bye
Lickity split zip bam boom
Varoom into tomorrow.
MOVE IT!

—from "Bicycle Jockey" by Marc Smith

◆ **Point of view.** Point of view often determines a poem's style and diction as well as its stage presentation. Is the speaker observing the story from a distance or is he passionately involved? Pissed off? Stoned?

I'm that Nobody nobody knows
Who could make a difference
In your status quo.

—from "Bicycle Jockey" by Marc Smith

◆ **Crisis.** A crisis is a point of no return, the fulcrum that changes everything for the character and energizes the poem, raising the stakes, raising its level of importance. A crisis begs to be resolved, and that keeps the audience engaged.

◆ **A bulls-eye.** The story has to finally hit a target and fulfill the audience's expectations or cut those expectations off at the knees with a surprise. Nothing is more disappointing or frustrating than listening to a tale that has little or no payoff or a joke without a punch line.

It helps to have humor along the way. And when it's over, don't spend another five stanzas pulling the arrow out of the carcass. No one cares. After you pop the balloon, the suspense is over.

Listen to "Bicycle Jockey" on the CD and try to identify the obstacles he encounters, the crisis, and the desire he rides away with on his handlebars.

What's on the CD

CD #2 track #15:
Marc Smith and the Pong Unit
Band performing "Bicycle Jockey"

What's Your Point—Oratory, Poetics, or a Laundry List of Love?

One of the most wonderful things about poetry performance is that thousands of choices are available. If you ask slammers where they get their ideas, you'll hear a million answers. Writers are observers first, and the world is full of observable reality—from snakes to space, emotions to eggplants, from love to death and back—anything is game for a poem.

Of course, all types of topics are available for speeches, editorials, TV commercials, and simple conversations. The same qualities that make slam accessible and attractive to all kinds of people—openness to all styles and subject matter—cause it (as loose as it is) to become really twisted.

Dig This!

If you keep going to slams, eventually you'll hear a poem that makes you turn to your tablemate and ask, "Is this a poem or a grocery list?" And it might just be a grocery list, or a speech, or a journal entry. If it's a *good* grocery list, maybe one could say that it has poetic merit, but most of the time these forms are just masquerading as poetry and taking advantage of slam's freedom.

So how do you make sure you're taking risks with your poetry but not bending the rules so far that they break? Ask for some honest feedback from your fellow slammers and astute audience members. Analyze your poems and identify their poetic devices. If they're bountiful, you're on the right track.

Pop Ideas and Newspaper Politics

Commenting on society, celebrities, politics, and anything else we find interesting or controversial is something we all do everyday, and it's most certainly something every poet eventually weaves into a poem, intentionally or not. It's natural to want to make sense of an often-disturbing world; that's probably why you're writing poetry in the first place.

Whoa!

When you sit down to pen an angry poem about "war" and "suffering" and "the White House" along with words like "children" and "oppression," make sure it's coming from as personal a place as your toenail fungus. You can try to be the voice for a generation of squished grasshoppers, but you'd better be speaking from underneath the sole of *the man's* shoe.

Many political poems do well (if they're written and delivered well) because, by their nature, most political poems have an aura of importance and give the poet/performer an aura of serious artist. It's difficult to give a low score to a poet who performs a poem lambasting an unjust war, especially if the poet speaks honestly from personal experience. It's even tougher to score the next performer higher when his poem is about something relatively trivial, such as toenail fungus. "Toenail Fungus" might have been the better poem and the performance might have been superior, but when it comes to significance, war trumps foot fungus.

Write About Yourself

One of the first lessons writers learn is to "write what you know." The purpose of saying such a thing is not to limit your imagination—what kind of poet has no imagination? The idea behind this age-old advice comes down to specificity, details. God and the devil are both in the details. Because you know only what you feel, see, taste, or touch along with a little bit of what you hear, you can be specific about your experiences. Generalities are phony fluff. Real details paint a sharp image on the canvas of the mind and speak truth. Even the composition of a successful persona poem requires you to draw on personal experience to fill in the details in order to communicate your vision honestly and vividly.

What's on the CD

CD #1 track #12:
Patricia Smith accompanied by percussionist Michael Zerang performing "Medusa."

SlamSpeak

A superb example of a persona poem is Patricia Smith's "Medusa." Here's an excerpt from it, but you can listen to the entire poem on **CD #1 track #12.**

> Dammit, Athena, take away my father's gold. Send me away
> to live with lepers. Give me a pimple or two.
> But my face. To have men never again be able to gaze
> at my face, growing stupid in anticipation
> of that first touch, how can any woman live like that?
> How will I be able to watch their warm bodies
> turn to rock when their only sin was desiring me?
>
> All they want is to see me sweat. They just want
> to touch my face and run their fingers through my ...
>
> my hair
>
> is it moving?

—From "Medusa," by Patricia Smith

All Forms Can Slam

Many people who have spent little time within the slam world have a misconception that only a certain type of pop poem succeeds on a slam stage. In my career, I performed a spectrum of classical works ranging from Shakespearean sonnets to the very formal works of Wallace Stevens and Robert Frost; from translations of Baudelaire to the page-conscious works of e. e. cummings—all to abounding applause. Poets performing at the Green Mill have written and presented villanelles, haiku, sestinas, and even *concrete poems* drawn on canvas hanging onstage as the poet/poem delivered the words.

SlamSlang

Concrete Poems are
  p   o   e   m   s
Constructed   on   the   page
To   form   visual   images
That   connect   with   some-
Thing   in   the   poem   like   a
C O N C R E T E B L O C K

The guiding principle has always been that all forms are welcome on a slam stage and can succeed if the poet learns the art of performance and applies that art to the poems he presents. Some poems are more difficult to perform than others, just as some music—a Mozart concerto, for instance—is more difficult to play than "Chopsticks." But no matter how difficult the work, if it was crafted with the intention of being heard aloud, a slammer's voice will bring its sound to life.

The Least You Need to Know

- Use concrete language to paint vivid images on your audience's brain cells.

- Use dynamic verbs to re-create movements and gestures in your poetry.

- Achieve rhythm in your verse through word choice, syntax, various sonic devices, and the intelligent use of rhyme.

- Slam is a nearly perfect medium for sermonizing and pontificating onstage—just make sure that you're genuine, you speak from experience, and you have plenty of rhetorical tools at your disposal.

- One of the best ways to generate ideas for poems and learn how to craft poems based on your personal experience is to collaborate with other poets and analyze audience feedback.

Chapter 5

From Page to Stage

In This Chapter

- Taking the stage with confidence and panache
- Performing your poetry like you know what you're doing
- Losing your slam virginity … welcome to the family!
- Preparing, practicing, rehearsing, and other pre-performance workouts
- Mixing it up in rehearsals to keep them interesting and to polish various aspects of your performance

All right, you've pulled out all the poems you've penned and reworked them for the stage. You've jumped ahead to Chapter 8 to get an idea of where to go to find poets and slammers spouting off. You've checked out a number of places, sat in the back, and struggled with the voices in your head that keep flip flopping, "I can do that." "No, you can't." "Yes, you can." "No, you can't." Well, guess what, one of those voices is right. You can and you will, and this chapter will get you through the trauma.

Confronting Stage Fright—Overcoming the Fear

Tonight's the night! You're there—at the Big Little Slam ready to wow the world with your lyrical lassos. You've auditioned to the wall, to your roommate, and over the phone to your grandmother in Tucson. You've put on your lucky jeans and had a well-balanced breakfast first thing this morning. Doorman Bob signed you up for the open-mike competition and gave you the number three position. You've assessed the other poets before you and you're thinking, "No contest!" Slammaster Macado calls your name and proclaims you to be a slammin' virgin virgin. The crowd cheers. You hop up onstage and feel …

… like diving right back off.

Whoa!

Do I need to compete during my virgin virgin performance? No. Most slams have an open-mike session for first-timers so they can acclimatize to the slam atmosphere. But many virgin virgins do dive in mouth-first as slam competitors.

Dig This!

Scared? I often tell audiences that performance poetry ala Marc (So What!) Smith started because the first time I read a poem at an open mike I had so much adrenaline racing through my arteries that my arms started flapping.

Your mouth is a sheet of fabric softener, your knees wobble as you walk, and when did you develop this uncontrollable shaking-hand affliction?

You're not dying. You've just got a bad case of stage fright. It happens to everyone, and it's a very scary feeling. Symptoms of stage fright may include dizziness, headache, upset stomach, the immediate and total absence of saliva, the immediate and total absence of memory, shaking limbs, nervous laughter, fidgeting, blushing, a racing heart, shortness of breath, and an overwhelming desire to use the restroom even though you just used it five minutes ago!

Stage fright afflicts us because we humans know that we're not perfect. Excuse me, maybe you're a saint, maybe you're a despicable desperado—no matter who you are, when you go onstage you're allowing yourself to be seen, heard, and, in a slam, judged. You're under the lights and under the gun. But take heart—stage fright is just part of the performance package and can actually benefit you in many ways. If you can develop techniques to curb your stage fright, you can begin to harness its positive effects.

Slay the Confidence Busters

The first step in dealing with stage fright is to get to the root of the problem. Are you trembling with nervousness because you didn't rehearse your piece enough (shame on you) or because of some deep-seated fear of failure? We won't attempt to help you resolve ancient issues with your parents or curb your anger with the playground bully, but we can point out the following common archetypes and help you overcome their foibles:

- **Total Avoider:** At all costs, the Total Avoiders use every strategy in their quick brains to avoid, evade, and escape situations that require them to speak in front of three or more people they do not know. Heck, they won't even speak in front of three or more friends or family members! Total avoiders are typically afraid—afraid of stumbling over words, being laughed at, or being heckled. To overcome the Total Avoider in you, just do it—take the microphone and let 'er rip.

- **Reluctant Martyr:** The Reluctant Martyr steps forward, confronts the situation, and buries the fear behind a stoic mask, while negotiating foxhole deals with God and the Universe. The Reluctant Martyr doesn't enjoy the performance, and it shows. If you can perform in public, but it pains you, you're probably performing only for the benefit of the audience. Perform for yourself, too, for the joy it brings *you*.

- **Jobber:** The Jobber is similar to the Reluctant Martyr, in that she can take the stage and deliver, but finds little enjoyment in it. Performing is just another unsavory task that must be done. If you're a jobber, loosen up, have fun, play.

- **Shy Guy or Girl:** Shy Guy or Girl is another Marc Smith who was so shy he couldn't order a pizza over the telephone, but who deep inside wanted to be heard … and would be after overcoming the cowardly child inside. Shyness is a symptom of a lack of confidence, and two treatments are available: Take the stage and succeed, and take the stage and fail. Success proves you can do it. Failure reveals that the Universe won't crumble if you stumble.

Speaking in front of people is an art, a skill you've already mastered to a certain degree. You do talk to people, don't you? Every day. And as far as not being good enough, think about it: The human race is definitely flawed, but we've put rocket ships into space, composed brilliant sonatas, built skyscrapers, and even developed places like Dollywood. The people who create great things aren't anywhere near perfect and neither are you. It shouldn't stop you from trying—not trying is the only real failure.

Is That Text Well-Prepared?

Having confidence in your text increases your confidence onstage. If a poet introduces a performance with "Well, I just wrote this one this morning but here goes …," you're probably about to witness a forgettable performance. If you're insecure about your text, that insecurity will eat into your confidence performing it. Recalling the hours of hard work you put into preparing your text (and your performance) has the opposite effect, helping you develop an aura of the poised performance poet.

Visualize Success

Long before Michael Jordan ever flew through the air with that amazing hang time and body control, he imagined himself doing it. If he never thought he could, he never would have tried. The same goes for any play, show, film, book, recording, or bubble gum you chew and enjoy. Someone visualized the end of the journey before they took the first step. Imagine your name being called. Imagine yourself walking briskly and resolutely to the stage. See the faces watching you; smile at them, tell them, "I'm scared. Wish me luck." Step up to the microphone, take a deep breath, smile again, say, "Here goes." Lay down the words like gems of your soul on a smooth beach or like thrashing winds on a stormy night. Return to your seat bowing to the applause, cheers, and looks of admiration. Mentally rehearse your victory and believe it. When the real moment comes, your vision will eclipse your stage fright—after all, you've been here before … in your mind.

Practice, Practice, Practice

Envisioning a stellar performance is an important first step, but if you don't back it up with time and effort, your actual performance likely will flop. After you have played out the performance in your mind, stand up and live the scenario in your apartment or backyard. Walk through it, speak it, feel it, visualize it, and pretend … like a kid at the playground imagining a future as a major league baseball player.

Shift Your Focus

Your brain can cause you all sorts of trouble, especially if it's overactive and spins out negativity. If your thoughts turn inward and you start thinking, "Oh my God; I can't do this. I'm going to make a fool of myself. Hear that pounding? My heart's exploding. I'm about to cry," you had better shut down the negativity factory. Shift your focus to relaxation. Breathe in "I am …" breathe out "relaxed." Keep doing it. When the negative thinking starts swirling you down, go positive, or calm. Try any of the following relaxation exercises:

- Breathe in deeply and s-l-o-w-l-y from your belly. Then breathe out s-l-o-w-l-y and completely.

- Shift your focus to a point outside yourself. Think about that point and nothing else. You are that point.

- Think of something pleasant or funny or beautiful.

◆ Go physical. Do some push-ups, pace, tighten and relax your muscles. (Of course, you probably don't want to be doing jumping jacks during your performance, but a little physical exercise before your performance can decrease anxiety.)

Backstage Skinny _____

Try this exercise used by singers and musicians to expand their lung capacity, and use it to keep your mind off your fears and release tension:

1. Breathe in a steady count for 8 counts.

2. Hold your breath for the next 8 counts

3. Breathe out at a steady rate for 8 counts.

4. Repeat.

Start with the tempo of your 8 count at a comfortable rate and then slow it down or increase the count from 8 to 16 to 24. In addition to becoming more relaxed, you will begin to understand time and tempo as musicians do.

Please Release Me

Okay, you didn't do any of the relaxation exercises, and that nervous anxiety has penetrated your muscles and limbs and is all locked up. You haven't solved the problem. This pent-up energy is going to come out agitated and inappropriately, causing twitching eyelids, shaking limbs, and cracks in your vocal chords.

Dig This!

Years after I had already gained much success performing onstage as a poet chalking up hundreds of appearances, I ventured onto the theatrical stage to play the role of Mac, the dock boss, in a theater production of *On the Waterfront*. At the audition, all of us hopefuls were asked to do a cold reading of one of the scenes. My first lines were something like "Shut up and get back to work." The tension built as I waited for my cue. The other actors were calmly reading their lines and playing their parts as well as they could in the laid-back audition, when I blasted out "SHUT the F___ UP AND GET BACK TO WORK!" with such force that the casting director nearly fell off her seat. The other actors stared at me like I was a freak. I got the part anyway. They felt sorry for me.

An effective and inconspicuous way to release pre-performance tension is to do some isometric exercises. Squeeze your toes together in your shoes (you should feel your leg muscles tighten) and then release the tension while taking a deep breath. Then, with your elbows against your sides, put your fists out like a prizefighter and squeeze, pressing your elbows and upper arms against your body (you should feel your stomach muscles tighten) and then release the tension, taking a deep breath. You can do this with your neck and shoulders, too. You can even push against a wall. Push and release and breathe until the tension is unlocked.

Tricks (or No-Brainers) of the Trade

Even seasoned veterans who have mastered all the relaxation techniques can get the pre-show jitters, but they have a few fairly obvious tricks up their sleeves to deal with the unavoidable:

◆ If your stomach gets violently upset before you go onstage, don't eat a spaghetti dinner before you walk out the door.

Backstage Skinny

Just as you rehearse your lines, choreograph and rehearse your gestures and movements. Planned movement might seem a little forced at first, so make a dance of it and have some fun. Even if you move differently during your performance, the practice provides you with the confidence of knowing how your body moves.

◆ If you get "cotton-mouth," drink plenty of water before you go up there and take some onstage with you—who cares if you have to stop and take a swig? You're thirsty.

◆ If your hands tend to tremble, memorize your lines instead of reading off a page. It's usually hard to see hands shaking unless a poet is holding a page. Memorize your piece and voilà! Invisible hands.

◆ If you're a sweaty performer, wear dark colors. It's a little distracting to see huge wet spots forming on your shirt when you're reading a haiku about a cool, placid lake.

Not Recommended

"Liquid courage," a.k.a. alcohol, coffee, and/or other elixirs, are not advisable (though often abused) for performers trying to cope with public performance anxiety. Liquor and coffee are big dehydrators and most of the time will jack you up with more nervous energy, unless you're really loaded, in which case you shouldn't be performing at all. Drugs are obviously a bad career move in many ways, and if you've ever been in the unfortunate position of watching a drug-addled person onstage, you know it's a bad choice for performance, too. Alcohol, pints of coffee, and/or a couple tokes might seem like a miracle solution to your thundering fears, but take it from me and a thousand other performers who've been there and done that: They eventually betray you and push you—ahhhhhhhh!—off a scary cliff.

Celebrating Your Slam Virginity, and Then Losing It

It happens only once, that day when you finally open your mouth in front of strangers. You hear your words, your creations, crack the silence, and it could be the beginning of a fantastic new romp and gallop through life. Most of us, if we're close to sober when we do it, remember the day, the place, the poem, and the response. The absolute best way to approach your first time is to gather support from friends and family, bring them with you as witnesses, and make a party of it. But going solo can have its reward, too, a rite of passage, a proof of the truth within you. Go for it. Seize your dreams.

> ### Dig This!
>
> One virgin's goal had nothing to do with a performance career. He kneeled at the edge of the Green Mill stage, pulled out a small box and a poem, and proposed in verse to his very surprised and happy lover in the first row.

SlamSpeak

Confessions of a Virgin Virgin

"I had been writing poetry for a long time, but when I heard about the slam, I was very foggy on what to expect. My friend Derrick Brown slammed, but his writing was superior to mine, so I never thought I'd be good enough to compete. When I found out that he was one of the best in the country, I figured that maybe my stuff was worth spewing. In the summer of 1998, I finally decided to give slam a try and headed to the storied Green Mill. I brought along three friends and was convinced that at least two of them would clap for me. We got there early and sat in the middle of the room, and since there were only 40 people there, I signed up. By the time the slam rolled around, the place was packed and I was getting cold feet. This had much to do with the air-conditioning, but I was definitely scared that my poems would fall on deaf ears. I had memorized the pieces because I thought that was important. I had written humorous pieces and deduced that if the lines weren't going over well, I'd cuss a bunch and tell momma jokes. I'd even practiced movements that I thought were 'poetic.'

When I got called up, I forgot about everything I was afraid of and let loose. It was mostly a blur; my sober friends told me that the audience laughed at all the right lines and that I smiled the whole time. I do recall that it was an amazing rush and that I hammed up my performance. So by the time I got called to do my second piece, I had a boat-load of confidence and played with the words more and really made it a point to enjoy the moment. I ended up winning and was immediately hooked on performing poetry. Since then, I've totally bombed on some occasions, but I've always had confidence in the potential of my poetry because of that initial response from the Green Mill crowd."

Joel Chmara has been slamming since 1999, was a member of the 2000 Normal, Illinois slam team, and as slammaster founded an off-campus collegiate slam at Illinois State University.

What's your goal? Not for life, just for today. Perhaps it's to win the slam. Perhaps it's to have a good time or impress some cutie in the audience, which, by the way is a common and legitimate (if often futile) goal. Whatever your goal is, when you step up to that stage for the first time, hold that goal out in front of you. Peek past the horizon. Visualize it. If you keep your eye on the prize, you won't have time to think about shaking limbs, thick tongue, or sweaty palms. If you're super-focused, it'll be over too quickly and you'll be thirsty to do it again. You will have taken the first step toward achieving a long-range goal. Hell, just being up there is success. And if you hit the wall and crash the train (at some point you will, so be ready) peel yourself off the wall, fix the engine, lay some new track, and steam around the other way. Believe it or not, the failures, the flops, and the bombs can build as much inner confidence as the victories.

What's on the CD

CD #1 track #18: Joel Chmara performing "For My Itchy Brother"

Accumulate Stage Time

If you baked a cake every day for 10 years, you'd probably know how to make a darn good cake. Over that time, you probably would have acquired dozens of different recipes, substituted ingredients, adjusted the butter in the frosting, and so on. And in your 10 years of cake baking, you'd probably make a few cakes that didn't rise, that imploded, or that just plain didn't taste good. But because you've been baking cakes so long, you know a thing or two about how to fix problems and what works every time (sugar) and what never does (tuna fish).

A professional is not someone who is good all the time. If you see someone perform numerous times and they're amazing every time, chances are very good that they've been doing it for a while. *Professional performers have failed as many times as they've succeeded.* That's the difference between professionals and amateurs. A true professional learns from his or her mistakes, fixes them, and gets back on the horse. Professional performance poets can't make mistakes and fix them or achieve riotous success without tallying hours and hours of stage time.

The more time you spend onstage, the more …

◆ Familiar and confident you'll become with your text and performance.

◆ Attuned you'll be to how an audience reacts to you.

◆ Aware you'll be of your strengths and weaknesses.

Whoa!

"I ain't no professional. I'm just reading this book to …." Whether you are a professional, semi-professional, or hobbyist, accumulating stage time and experience enables you to relax and enjoy your time onstage. And even if you never make a dime performing your poems, you'll bring bliss to yourself and the people who hear you.

And if you drop a line or blank out completely, you'll find a way to cover it or use it to your advantage. Seasoned performers make mistakes, but they know how to deal with them. The more time you spend onstage, the more mistakes you'll make, and the more capable you'll become at handling them.

Rehearse, Rehearse, Rehearse

Spending years studying a performing art is not enough. You need to put what you learn into practice, lots of practice. This means not only performing, but rehearsing. In the early years of slamming it was a chore to get poets to even consider rehearsing, let alone do it. To this day some celebrated poets approach a forty-minute reading engagement with little or no preparation. Their idea of rehearsal is paging through their volumes and choosing which random collection of poems they intend to read, and then deciding upon a vague order in which to present them. They lumber ponderously up to the podium clutching a stack of *chapbook*s flapping with colored tabs that mark the pages they intend to vocalize. Their devoted followers excuse this ill-prepared approach and politely pat their palms together after each blandly delivered poem. The general public reacts otherwise. They regard it as schlock, especially if they paid a good price to witness it.

Serious performance poets rehearse. It's a discovery process. Each run-through uncovers accidents of choice and insight into new choices. No two rehearsals (or performances) are alike. And it's work—real work, good work—that can be exhilarating and, at times, demoralizing. To overcome the tedium and despair that surfaces during the rehearsal process, try the following:

> **SlamSlang**
>
> A **chapbook** is a small, typically self-published book of poems, ballads, or stories.

> **Dig This!**
>
> For the first eight months of shows at the Green Mill, the Chicago Poetry Ensemble would rehearse one or two evenings during the week and for four hours straight on Saturday and Sunday to put up one twenty- to thirty-minute segment on Sunday night. That's about 15 hours of rehearsal for one half-hour performance.

- **Set a rehearsal schedule.** Most serious writers develop a daily writing discipline. They set aside a portion of the day exclusively for writing, usually the same hours at the same place. You should develop a similar discipline for rehearsing. Set aside a specific amount of time, say a half hour or an hour every day for three to five days a week. Something regular.

- **Rehearse in layers.** Don't try to polish a piece to perfection in a single day.

For instance, on Day One just read through your poems five or six times, making mental or written notes about your delivery. On Day Two stand in front of a mirror and work out facial expressions and gestures as you read each poem, stopping occasionally to jot down notes. On Day Three combine the poems into a series and casually read through them. On Day Four do your first official run-through, trying not to stop but noting where you've stumbled. On Day Five do another run-through. On Day Six speed-read through your performance until you can do it lightening fast without a flaw. Keep rehearsing daily until your performance is as natural to you as blinking your eyelids.

◆ **Spice it up with some variations.** Change things up as you move through the process, play mind games with yourself to make the process entertaining. For instance, perform your poems as if you're an old man, a pirate, a super hero, a mad scientist. Go through them standing on one foot, crawling on the floor, shouting, whispering, as if playing tennis with Robert Frost. Through playful rehearsal a performer can discover new choices, new twists, new turns.

Practice should become a daily part of your art. Football players do it. Actors do it. Musicians do it. As a performance poet, you should do it, too.

From Closet to Mirror to Tape Recorder to Friendly Ears

Athletes commonly vary their workouts to strengthen different muscle groups, improve their agility, and avoid becoming bored silly. As a performer, you should vary your rehearsals to inspire your desire to rehearse and to strengthen various aspects of your performance. Practice in the park, on your rooftop, in the car on your way to work, in the shower or before you fall asleep as a supplement to your daily rehearsal routine. The following sections describe a few additional rehearsal options and techniques in greater detail.

Through the Looking Glass

Quit trying to pull rabbits out of the hat in the closet; you've been in there too long. Besides, everyone in the house can hear you. Go to the bedroom, Alice, and look into the big mirror above mama's dresser, or go buy a full-length mirror at the hardware store—it's a good investment. That's you in the mirror. Smile at yourself. Say, "Hey I like you." And then pick up your poem and spray the reflection. If you're like me, your mind will go bopping back and forth from noticing facial expressions and body movement to being caught up in the passion of the words. That's good. When you see something goofy, like your eyebrows bouncing up and down (or a Cheshire smile where it shouldn't be), try to amend it. If you see something brilliant, duplicate it on the next go 'round. You're your own audience in the mirror; study yourself and learn to groom your onstage appearance.

Replay

Another method of rehearsing that works well for some people (but not all) is speaking into a tape recorder and playing it back. At first, the sound of your own voice might make you crawl into a hole and shudder. Climb back out. Most everybody has the same reaction the first time they hear themselves. Just keep in mind that what you're hearing is different, not bad. For those who overcome the urge to gag at the sound of their own syllables, tape recording is very effective. Not only will you start picking up on and correcting obvious glitches in enunciation, volume, and tempo, but you'll begin memorizing by osmosis. Think about those songs and jingles you hear on the radio over and over. They stick in your head without your even trying. Same goes for your poem. If you listen to it over and over again, it'll tattoo itself on your neurons.

Backstage Skinny

If you have a camcorder (or can borrow one), set it up on a tripod or on a table and perform in front of it. Play back the video and jot down some notes on things you'd like to improve.

Recruiting a Critique

You have performed to your mirror, tape recorder, camcorder, and every other inanimate object in your house or apartment. Now it's time to phone a friend—or a few friends or a friendly director or an accomplished performance poet—and do a run-through in front of a live audience. Don't burden them with an ill-prepared performance, and don't go into this activity expecting strokes. Have specific questions you'd like feedback on, such as "Am I gesturing enough or too much?" "How's my volume?" "Am I speaking too fast?" Asking specific questions discourages general reactions that serve no purpose or, worse, kill your confidence. Your friend says, "I don't know that much about poetry, but I guess you're doing it alright," and you're back down in that hole again. If you set up your live rehearsal properly, obtain specific constructive criticism, and do it often, this exercise can be one of the most productive.

Let It Out in Workshops

Writing workshops can be another performance preparation opportunity. But be careful, in the workshop atmosphere it's sometimes more a preview performance than a rehearsal or coaching. All the writing workshops I've ever attended had a good dose of peer pressure and underlying competitive edge. If you want to keep your confidence high, be sure you're in a nurturing group, or be so damned good going in that you blow 'em out of the water.

The Least You Need to Know

- ◆ To overcome stage fright, be prepared—polish your verse, memorize your poems, rehearse till you drop, and don't forget to breathe.

- ◆ To become more comfortable onstage, lose your slam virginity at an early age and accumulate as much stage time as possible.

- ◆ Don't rely on alcohol, coffee, or drugs to help you overcome stage fright; they usually intensify it and leave you with a host of other problems.

- ◆ Treat rehearsals as a discovery process in which you focus on various aspects of your poem and performance in layers.

- ◆ Obtain feedback during a rehearsal by performing in front of a mirror, recording and playing back an audio or video clip of yourself, or performing in front of some close friends or colleagues.

Chapter 6

Honing Your Performance Technique

In This Chapter

- Mastering the performance techniques you need to engage, entertain, and affect your audience

- Tuning in to variations in volume, tempo, and articulation

- Learning to look your audience straight in the eye and make them see your visionary scene

- Pumping your thespian muscles with some physical exercises

- Injecting your performance with mood, attitude, and persona

Most of us have suffered through poetry readings during which the poets were about as animated as roadkill. No facial expression. No gestures. No intonation. No sign of life, whatsoever. Even their skin appeared ashy, as if they had just stepped off the set of *Night of the Living Dead*. They were zombies who threatened to kill us, not by eating our flesh but by droning on, monotone, until they had completely sucked out our will to live.

Don't be one of these soul-sucking zombie poets. Reach deep inside, pull out your pulsing heart, and fling it on the stage. Make the audience listen.

Grab it by the throat … figuratively, of course. Use your voice, your eyes, your body, your heart, and your soul. Make faces, stomp, gesture, whisper, yell. Do whatever it takes to capture your audience's attention, keep it entertained, and communicate your poetry through your impeccable performance of it. As a slammer you have stepped into the arena of the spoken word, and now you need to speak it well. This chapter shows you how.

Performance as an Art Form

Watching a portrait artist sketch the outline of a face, and with a quick stroke of a brush or line of a pencil produce a nose, then eyes and mouth, we recognize the skills she must have acquired to deftly render the likeness with confidence and apparent ease. Great performers also display skills that make their performances seem natural and precise. Performance is an art, an art that slammers take very seriously. It has its own brush strokes and shading and color—its own technique.

To be successful in rendering their art form, all performers must accomplish three goals; they must engage, entertain, and affect the audience. From Shakespeare to Sesame Street, all valued art grabs people, holds onto them, and shakes them up in some way.

Engage

A poet rushes up to the lectern, and without so much as a hello or even a glance at the audience he speed-reads through pages of poetry about the untimely death of a loved one. His nose points down and his voice blathers a rapid mutter that barely rises above the shuffle of papers in his grip.

Who cares?

No one. Mr. Nose Down is telling a tale of deep sorrow to a room full of people who can hardly wait for him to finish. Why? Because they weren't listening in the first place. They weren't engaged.

If you want an audience to listen, you must first capture their attention. It's a courtesy "Hello." It acknowledges them. It says, "We're in this together." And there are many ways to do it. Shout at them. Whisper to them. Turn out the lights and flash them back on. Hop into the spotlight grinning. Or slowly blow up a balloon and when it gets soooo soooo big, pop it! Or try staring at them for a long time. Do something … anything! … anything that says you know that they're there and that they matter.

SlamSpeak

"… the basic task of anyone concerned with presenting any kind of drama [performance] to any audience consists in capturing their attention and holding it as long as required. Only when this fundamental objective has been achieved can the more lofty and ambitious intentions be fulfilled: the imparting of wisdom and insight, poetry and beauty, amusement and relaxation, illumination and purging of emotions."

—*An Anatomy of Drama*, Martin Esslin

Entertain

And after you've engaged them, entertain them—make your words tap dance in their heads. You might be thinking "Oh my God, I'm a poet. I'm not supposed to be entertaining—I'm supposed to be deep, metaphysical, and profound, but not entertaining." Wrong. All great art is entertaining, and yours had better be, too.

To be entertaining means simply to hold an audience's attention. And the key to doing that is having choices: choices to achieve variety in the structure and execution of your performance, choices that allow you to turn a tight corner and surprise them, to tickle their senses, to spin them off into a new orbit.

Affect

Television is entertaining, too. So is it art?

Yes. No. Well, sometimes, but not often. TV holds our attention. And so does a pinball machine or a computer game or the hot bod in your aerobics class. But these forms of entertainment lack one essential element of art, the third and most important element in the triage of performance dictum: the ability to *affect* the audience. After you've engaged an audience and are holding their attention, then, if you are a serious artist, you must move them, change their perspective, shift their emotions, enlighten them with those "lofty and ambitious intentions."

What's on the CD

CD #1 track #13: Todd Alcott performing "Television"

Backstage Skinny

How do you affect an audience? You dig deep into the most private corners of your experience and exhume your humanity—those viewpoints, fears, desires, victories, and sorrows that make you uniquely you.

Entertaining Fundamentals

The secret to becoming an outstanding performer is to assemble a toolbox full of performance techniques—techniques that enable you to vary mood and point of view, manipulate the volume and pace of your performance, and use your body as an effective communication tool. Having a robust collection of performance techniques at your fingertips always comes in handy.

The following sections teach you the most basic techniques—from adjusting the volume and pace of your performance to establishing eye contact and using your body to communicate. These sections include *exercises* you can practice by yourself and *classroom activities* that you can incorporate into a school curriculum. By mastering these basic techniques, you'll have the performance skills you need to engage, entertain, and affect your audience … assuming, of course, that your poetry is as good as your performance.

Vary the Volume

Know the first rule of public speaking: *Be sure they hear you! EVEN IN THE BACK ROW!* That's simple enough, but you probably don't want to shout through your entire performance; variations in volume can help you hold the audience's attention. What if I say "Mary had a little LAMB."? Does that have the same meaning as "Mary had a LITTLE lamb."? What if I screamed, "MARY! MARY! MARY! HAD a little lamb."? I probably wouldn't be invited to recite my poems to Miss Mary's first-grade class, but I certainly would get her attention.

The volume at which we speak words, lines, stanzas, and entire poems naturally fluctuates, and these fluctuations can influence the meaning and significance of those words, lines, stanzas, and poems—sometimes slightly and sometimes very considerably. Your decibel level can also convey emotions that underlie the text. Loudness can convey anger, alarm, distress, and hatred. Softer volumes convey timidity, tenderness, secrecy, and intimacy. In addition, speaking loudly or softly enables you to EMPHASIZE a particular word or phrase.

The range in volume we allow ourselves when speaking in front of an audience is usually quite narrow—until we give ourselves permission to stretch it. And when we stretch, we acquire more choices. And MORE CHOICES is the KEY to being entertaining.

Exercises

Write down all the emotions you associate with being loud, and all the emotions you associate with a soft-spoken person. Say loudly words usually associated with soft volume. Do the same for soft words. Notice how the meanings change. Are there some emotions that are expressed in both loud and soft voices?

Try whispering loudly. That's right, whisper so the neighbors can hear you. This is an important skill you need to master so that your audience can still hear you when you're whispering to achieve a dramatic effect. You do this by using the same muscles (lower abdominal muscles) we all use to push stuff out, but instead of pushing down you push up. When you whisper your lines, use a lot of air.

Classroom Activities

Ask the class for a line of poetry, a familiar phrase, or a song lyric. Have one ready in case the class gives you the silent treatment. Start at one end of a row and have each person say the same line getting louder and louder with each new person down the row. By the time you reach the last person, you should need to plug your ears, and your students will have noticed a distinct range in volume from the first person to the last. Ask the class if they thought the row got as loud as they could. The response (in a loud mass voice) will probably be "NO!"

Ask for five volunteers to jump up to the front of the class to see who can be the loudest. Offer a prize of $1.00. This is your first slam competition. Use it to crack the ice and get the students over their inhibitions of performing before their peers. Ask for another line of poetry, phrase, or song lyric. Do warm-up rounds to give the contestants two stabs at shouting in school. Hope that one of them screams their lungs out, because more ice will shatter. Do the real round and have the audience applaud for who they think should get the money. If all goes well, your class will now be ready to do anything you ask. If the principal or the security guard looks in, you've really done your job and have instantly become cool in the eyes of your students. You can probably start signing autographs.

Backstage Skinny

The exercises are designed not only to teach performance fundamentals, but also to subtly and gradually break down the inhibitions many students have about performing.

In the other direction go down a row, getting softer and softer, repeating a line. After about seven or eight students speak the line so softly it's inaudible, ask the class what happened. Usually someone will say, "You can't hear them." This gives you an opening to introduce the fine art of whispering loudly, as discussed in the previous section.

Spread your students around the room against the walls and have them all at once push the air out of their lungs and create a whisper that carries a hundred feet or so. Keep feeding them lines to repeat in a loud whisper. Do all the lines of a short poem. It doesn't take much for them to master the loud whisper.

(This is also the second sneaky trick to get your students relaxed and ready to stand alone in front of the others and recite words.)

Tweak the Tempo

Just as you can vary your volume for dramatic effect, you can vary the tempo or pace of your performance. The speed at which we say things conveys a meaning all its own. Name the emotions for slow and fast. Stretch your self-imposed limits on how fast you can speak lines. Listen to some hip-hop artists and see how rapid-fire they can pop out lines. If you're an old jazz buff, think of bebop and the speed at which some of those solos flew. Do the same with your words. Practice like a musician practices complicated riffs, taking a few measures (lines) at a time until you nail that down and can move on to the next "measures."

Backstage Skinny

Stretching your tempo range is a little tougher than extending your volume. The muscles in your mouth need to get used to enunciating properly at high speeds. Don't get discouraged. It's like lifting weights. Increase the speed little by little. Keep the enunciation clear and crisp. You can do it.

Dig This!

Nearly every class has at least one student who has great, almost sadistic, fun slowing things down to a crawl. Encourage this playful experimentation to help your students test their limits.

After you become a certified fast-talker, slow it down. Imagine your mouth in slow motion, the words and lines creeping ever so slowly out of your mouth as if you are giving directions to a foreign tourist. Pause between words, stretch the syllables, and breathe. In many cases, if you begin to lose an audience with a rapid-fire performance, you can bring it back; re-engage the audience by suddenly downshifting and slowing your pace.

Classroom Activities

Call for a line from the class and then ask a particular row to recite the line increasing the speed with each student. Have fun with it. Don't worry if the words get jumbled up—that's part of the game. Then have the next row slow the line down. Ask the class to note how the meaning (or the nuance of the meaning) changes as the tempo changes. When the line starts to get really, reeeeeaaaaaallllllly slow, ask the class how they achieved the slower phrasing: by pausing between words, stretching the syllables, taking more breaths.

Articulate

As you slow down your speech, you should discover another fundamental technique for varying your expression: *articulation*—the time value we assign to each syllable. When we stretch those syllables, the words and the line slow down. When the articulation changes, the inflection (the pitch at which we sound out the syllables) also tends to change. When articulation and inflection change, so does the meaning. Repeat the word "execution" a dozen times, changing the time value and pitch of the various syllables. Can there be a happy execution? A quick one? A slow one? A clean one? A dull one?

The choice a performer makes in regard to the articulation (and inflection) is all her own. A poetic text almost never indicates how the lines are to be articulated. Each reader discovers an articulation that's suitable to his or her understanding of the poem. Other than by asking the poet directly, no one ever knows just by reading a poem how its author intended it to be interpreted, and it doesn't matter. As a performer you have a responsibility not to mess with another poet's work (unless your intention is to mess with another poet's work); you're to perform interpretations that honor the poet's intent as best you can. When performing your own work, you're responsible only to yourself and your poetry. Slammers often breathe fresh life into old poems by changing the articulation, tempo, and volume from performance to performance, in the moment, in the now. Just listen to one of your favorite rock stars sing an "unplugged" version of one of their hits, and you'll understand perfectly.

SlamSlang

The precise dictionary definition of **articulation** is "the act or manner of producing utterance or expression." But we're talkin' slam here, and we change the rules (as well as the definitions), don't we?

Backstage Skinny

A major distinction between performance poetry and oral interpretation is the liberties slammers take in phrasing a text, whether it's their own or someone else's. Oral interpreters objectively examine a text and try to present it as they believe the author intended it to be heard. They are like skilled classical musicians playing each note exactly as scored. Slammers are more akin to jazz musicians who make a text their own through creative performance. They do not seek to distort or disrespect the meaning, but they do mix their minds with the minds of other authors when performing other artists' works. Both approaches have their place and purpose, and many classical works are being given new life through creative interpretations by performance poets.

Exercise

Put on some instrumental music and try reading or reciting a familiar poem to the beat of the music. Match as best you can the rhythm of the poem to the rhythm of the recording. Now put on a different musical selection and recite the same text to it. Note how the articulation changes. Note how the nuanced meaning of the poem might change.

Dig This!

Here's another articulation exercise. Stand before the class and be their conductor in stretching words. Hold your hands up and control how long they hold the syllables. "Buttt Terrrrrrrrrr Flyyyyyyyyyyyyyyyyyyyy. But Ter Fly!" You conduct a few words and then have a student or two take over as maestro.

Classroom Activity

Form several circles of about eight students each. Have one student in each circle think of a line of poetry. Instruct the students in each group to take turns reciting the line in a different way by modifying the articulation, inflection, volume, and tempo as they please. Tell them to have fun and GO TOO FAR! Stretch the boundaries of what they think is cool and acceptable. After each student in the circle has had a turn, have each student offer up his or her rendition of the line and have the group repeat it. At the end of this exercise nearly all of the class's inhibitions will have been vaporized.

Breathe Deep and Pause

Poetry is constructed from patterns. Patterns are rhythms. To speak we must breathe. Without a lungful of air, speech is silent, so during your performance, you need to breathe. Obvious, huh? What might not be so obvious is that the places in your poems where you take breaths create patterns. Part of the craft of creating a poetic text is to control—via line, syntax, diction, and meter—where you take your breaths. As performers we can create a subtext of a poem by phrasing the language of the poem with our own choices as to where we breathe. Think of the breaths you take in speaking as the rests in music.

Backstage Skinny

Listen to different musicians play the same melody and notice how each makes different choices in their phrasing. This is achieved in part by where the musician chooses to take rests. As you write, rehearse, and perform, be conscious of where you take your breaths.

Different from the spaces created by breaths are dra … mat … ic … pauses. You can keep an audience …

… hanging …

for a long …

... time, just by adding the silence of a dramatic pause. It creates space. It can re-engage an audience's attention. It can make a turning point in a poem a major event. It can emphasize an important moment. Unlike breaths, a dramatic pause breaks the rhythm, rinses the sonic palette, and builds suspense. And when the rhythm returns, it's a joy to hear it with fresh ears.

Exercise

Next time you're in a conversation with friends (make sure they're friends), for the fun of it and as an educational demonstration to yourself, stop mid-sentence at the gripping point of the story you're telling and count in your head how long you can hold them gaping until they say, "Well, what happened?" or until you let them off the hook yourself. Notice their eyes; are they glued to you with that waiting look? If so, you're successfully using the dramatic pause. If nobody feels the void, either they're not really your friends or you need a more suspenseful story to tell.

Find a poem that has a formal meter, a Shakespearean sonnet or a nursery rhyme would work. *Scan* the poem and mark out its *feet*. Read it through and notice where to naturally take breaths. Now mark down an arbitrary pattern of where you take breaths. Read the poem again using the new pattern. Notice how it changes the music—and maybe the meaning—of the poem.

SlamSlang

There are many poetic **feet**: iambs, trochee, anapest, dactyl, spondee, etc. They are the basic units of measure in a line of poetry and are determined by different combinations of stressed and unstressed syllables. To **scan** a poem is to determine the kind and number of feet in each poetic line. If you're a slammer and unfamiliar with scansion and poetic feet, get to the library quick and find a basic poetry guide before you hit the stage again.

Shake, Gesture, and Move

Are you a walking stiff, stuck in the closet of your self-imposed limits? Then stand up! And shake it out! Bend over, clasp your hands together, and swing your arms like an elephant's trunk.

Scholars tell us that ninety percent of human communication is nonverbal and that nonverbal communication is often more effective and revealing than the words themselves. Why they had to tell us rather than just acting it out, I don't know. But think about it, how many times

Dig This!

You probably have noticed that when some people stand in front of an audience to speak, their bodies say something very different than what their mouths say. Usually their bodies are saying *"I'm nervous! I'm scared! Why am I up here? Please like me!"*

Backstage Skinny

When onstage, avoid purposeless motion—swinging arms, shifting feet, sticking your hand in your pocket, pulling it out, nodding your head, pacing, or rocking. Remember, all movement onstage is communication, and it's heightened communication because you're in a conspicuous position watched by all eyes. The spotlight shows everything. In the best performances each and every movement flows naturally along with the words being spoken.

have you seen someone fidget, and you knew you weren't getting the total scoop about something? How many times did you know exactly what someone was going to say before the first word tripped off their tongue?

As performers we need to train our bodies to be in sync with the words we're saying. This can happen quite naturally once we get comfortable onstage in a public setting. We're usually comfortable with our bodies in private or in the presence of people we know well, when we're not afraid of being judged, our bodies are usually in total agreement with our words, unless we're trying pull something over on the ones we love and trust. We just need to carry this physical self-confidence over to the public setting. The following exercises should help.

Walk the Talk

Remain standing. Simon didn't tell you to sit down. Start walking around the room, not like an elephant. Walk like you think a policeman walks. Walk like a hooker. A priest. A jock. A diva. Walk like the floor is hot, very hot. Ouch! Walk like you're moving through thick pudding. Be goofy. If you're with friends or in a classroom doing this madness, look at how crazy everyone's expressions are. Make some sounds that express what your body is doing. Do this all day if you want, it's great fun. Do it at work and see what happens.

Imagine the Stone

In front of you is a rock, a very heavy rock made of the densest matter in the universe. You, however, have some superstrength and can lift the rock with great effort. Bend down, lift the rock, carry it a few feet, and set it down in its new position. As you do so, recite a favorite line of poetry.

Now move the rock, but this time it's papier-mâché, and you're just plain you, no superpower—light rock, normal you. Pick up the rock and move it saying the same line.

Dig This!

Sometimes I have classes imagine they're catching fluttering butterflies and putting them in a basket. They recite lines of poetry as they do so, noticing the pauses and rhythm changes when they catch one.

Did the way you said the line match the exertion of your body? Did the meaning of the line change with the weight of the rock? Was there really a rock there?

Paint the Reading Room Red

There's a can of paint at your feet. Look into it and give it a color, any color. Imagine that the paint can has been standing open for a very long time and the paint has become very thick. Reach down into the can, scoop out a handful of this very heavy paint, and fling it across the room pronouncing its color. Blue! Orange! Purple! Throw some at your classmates. Duck!

Now the paint is watery. What happens to your body pulling the watery paint out of the can? What happens when you fling it? How does its color sound now?

Shake It Out

Several body movement exercises not only help you tune your body's communication skills, but they also help release performance tension and anxiety. Try the following exercises:

◆ Bend over and start to groan. Slowly raise your torso, increasing the pitch and volume of your groan into a shrill sound like a siren. Then slowly drop your torso down, slowly lowering the volume and pitch. Repeat this five or six times. Try it while shaking your arms and hands like a preacher crying "Hallelujah!"

◆ Roll an imaginary ball across the floor. Do this with a friend or classmate. Start with a small ball and let the ball increase in size and weight as you roll it back and forth. Say a line of poetry as you do it and see how the tempo, volume, and articulation change. Notice what your body does. Try bouncing the ball off the wall.

◆ Create a dance movement to recite lines to: a waltz 1 2 3, a funky chicken, a ballet, an electric slide, anything, making it goofy. Say the lines as you dance. Then change the tempo and change the dance step. Notice again what your body does and how the words sound.

Look 'Em in the Eye

If you're trying to avoid a person you don't like, someone you're afraid of, or someone you've been gossiping about, look at their shoes … or your own shoes. If you look in their eyes, you might just reveal the truth. Onstage, however, when you're performing your poems, revealing your honest insights and your innermost feelings, you want to connect with your audience. You want to look them in the eye and invite them to witness the inner workings of your soul. Or you might want to create an illusionary drama for them.

You can use your eyes in at least four ways during a performance to achieve very different results:

♦ **The Speechmaker's Shift** Shifting your glance around the room in an effort to keep everyone engaged is what speechmakers, preachers, and narrators do. It gives a general feel to what you say, a proclamation. If you pause a second and really look into each person's eyes as you scan, you'll deepen your connection to the audience.

Backstage Skinny

If you haven't overcome that shyness to a degree that allows you to comfortably focus on someone's eyes, try the old trick of focusing on their foreheads. Start there but don't stay there. Don't deny yourself the soul connection you can experience with full, intimate eye contact.

♦ **The Direct Approach** Performance poets, singers, and stand-up comedians can get away with this. Actors inside the reality of a play cannot. If a politician does it, it turns into a scandal. Singling out an individual in the audience and focusing on that person creates an illusion of intimacy that the audience immediately believes. Picture a sexy lounge singer strolling over to a patron, looking into his eyes, and singing a song dripping with sensual innuendo. It creates an impromptu drama between you and the person you address. The audience sees in isolation a world separate from its own. It's intimate, and it's compelling. Use it for the most intimate sections of your poems.

♦ **The Wall Focus Technique** Another way to establish intimacy is to fix your stare on the wall behind the audience and recite your poem as if you're watching the scene unfold. The people in the audience feel transported into your mind. They're enraptured, as if you're revealing ancient mysteries from a trance. The spot on the wall can represent anything—a place you see, a person you're speaking to, or the vision itself. The important thing is to believe you see it. If you see it, the audience sees it, even though it isn't there.

♦ **The Imaginary Friend Routine** This is similar to focusing on a spot on the wall, but in this case you zoom in on an imaginary person onstage. Do it with conviction. Make yourself believe that you're interacting with a real, live person, and the audience just might buy a drink for your fantasy friend.

If you've been staring down so long that the vertebrae in your neck are permanently fused into a downward curve, try the following exercises.

Exercise

Turn off that TV and go for a walk. Look up. When a car passes by, try to establish eye contact with the driver or a passenger in the car. When someone approaches, greet the person … remember, no mumbling. Look the person in the eye and speak your greeting loud enough so that the person can hear you. Go to the corner store or newsstand. Establish eye contact with the person working the counter. Walk over to the local café and order a cup of coffee. Say something to your server—connect. Try to make this exercise a part of your life. You'll not only become much more comfortable onstage, but you'll also enhance your life and the lives of those around you.

> **Dig This!**
>
> Slamming is not acting. Performance poets bring to life very heightened language, peak moments, and strongly expressed emotions. Actors stay closer to the complete reality of a character, not just the brief moments of high passion.

Mood, Persona, and Where You Be

You've mastered the basic techniques, but something seems to be missing. You can shout your poem, whisper lines, articulate, enunciate, extrapolate, and postulate. And you can do it all while looking your audience straight in the eye. But something's missing … you.

Without you, that poem lying on the page is little more than a dry wind blowing across desert sands. It needs a trumpet to blow through, a voice to sing its song. You're the instrument, the voice, the embodiment of that poem. When you take the stage, you surrender yourself—body, mind, and soul—to the poem. And to do that poem justice, you need to use everything at your disposal to bring it to life—your mood, your attitude, your persona.

Rehearsing a poem and performing it requires you to get in character, just as if you had the starring role in a movie or play. You need to understand the poem—its spirit, tone, and voice—and then allow that poem to manifest itself in you and play itself through you. This is what really gives a performance its punch.

> **Whoa!**
>
> That persona isn't always you. The greatest mistake a poet/performer can make is to assume that he or she need always be the Poet communicating the Poem. Poems are not just poems; they're sensual and passionate expressions of a multitude of specific ideas, emotions, and experiences of a poet's life. And as a performer, you need to personify those specifics, be the poem more than the poet, be life itself.

Classroom Activity

Ask for a volunteer to read his or her poem in front of the class. If you've done the preceding exercises, there should be at least one student eager for more attention; hopefully he has a poem with him, a short one. After the student reads the poem through, don't let him sit back down. Tell him he's your guinea pig for the next exercise. Explain to him that his rendition of the poem was fine but that now the class is going to help him find some new choices. Ask the class to shout out suggestions giving him ...

- **A new persona.** Some type of person other than himself. For instance, a carpenter or a bag lady, an animal, or even an inanimate object.

- **An emotion.** Any kind of emotional state—angry, sorrowful, tipsy. Don't worry about matching it to the poem you've heard. It's better if it's off the wall. This is an exercise, not the final performance.

- **A setting.** In a church, at school, swimming in a bowl of cereal.

You should end up with something like: "An ecstatic but timid ballet dancer auditioning at a bowling alley." Of course, the assignment is ludicrous and can never be achieved, but just giving the students permission to expand their choices will catapult them into new dimensions ... usually. Sometimes they just freeze up at the challenge and you need to go back to body language exercises and being an elephant to loosen them up again.

However, most of the time it does work, and when the students see themselves and others transform, they all want to get into the game. They begin to appreciate and understand the freedom and magic of the stage, how much fun it is, and how by entertaining their fellow students with poetry they release themselves from the limitations of their everyday selves.

Backstage Skinny

Poems and performances might have one general mood and voice but can shift to a number of moods and voices. The shift can occur in a line, a word, or a stanza. You can go back and forth throughout a poem and performance creating a rhythm that complements metrical and/or sonic rhythms of the poem.

The Least You Need to Know

- Your function as a performance poet is to engage the audience, keep it entertained, and affect it in a meaningful way.

- Variations in volume, tempo, articulation, and other aspects of your performance keep the audience from dozing off and provide you with ways to subtly change the meaning and significance of selected words and phrases.

♦ Performance exercises should exaggerate your movements, volume, tempo, facial expressions, and other aspects of your performance to help you stretch the limits and explore your range.

♦ Establishing eye contact with your audience demonstrates your sincerity and connects you with the audience.

♦ You're not always you performing; the mood, persona, and setting of each poem is different. Let the poem morph you into the character required to perform it.

Chapter 7

Building a Performance and a Few More Skills

In This Chapter

- Transforming a loose collection of poems into a tight, dynamic set
- Smoothing the transitions between poems with some lively patter
- Opening with a bang and closing with a boom
- Turning the audience against you—surefire techniques you want to avoid
- Memorizing your poems … not just learning your lines

People attend slams to have their brains stimulated, their hearts massaged, and their funny bones tickled. Your job as performance poet is to do at least one of these things (preferably all three) in your allotted time slot. Whether you're performing a twenty-minute set or an hour-long solo tour de force, you must select poems and arrange them in such a way that keeps the audience engaged and entertained while their hearts, minds, and souls rise and fall to the rhythms and substance of your verse.

Forty minutes of non-stop, rapid-fire rant can be as unbearable as forty minutes of ponderous plodding, dreary gloom, or I I I "aye-yie-yie" self-absorption. You need to mix it up, vary your mood and voice, don a persona, add a dash of humor, demonstrate your range. This chapter shows you how. Here you learn how to structure a set that starts with a bang, ends with a boom, and keeps the audience enthusiastically engaged from start to finish. In addition, this chapter reveals tips and tricks for memorizing your material so you can do something more interesting with your hands than clutch a sheet of paper.

Mastering the Art of Seductive Revelation

Your performance set should be like an exquisite mansion, with each room having its own purpose and décor, but tastefully linked together by an overall aesthetic. Open the front door and invite your guests in with a gripping show opener; then take them on a well-planned tour of your multi-faceted verse. Don't go rushing up to the attic and then stumbling down to the cellar pushing them past the parlor's glistening antiques. Don't unlock the secret passageways as if they were routine entrances and exits. Don't hit the high point of the tour—the view of the magnificent gardens from the second story baroque balcony or the art deco swimming pool under the sliding floor—until the lesser rooms have been examined. And don't turn out the lights in the haunted bedroom until you've built the suspense into heart-pounding agony. Then, just as the screams and shivers begin to fade, hustle them out yearning for more.

Enter and Open with Flair

By the time the emcee finishes uttering the last word of your introduction, you had better be ready to vault onto the stage and deliver a captivating opener. The first three minutes of your performance can mean the difference between a raging romp and a desperate crawl to the finish line. You'll eventually discover through trial and error which poems in your repertoire most effectively lay down the desired mood and expectation for each set. Until then, try some of the following:

◆ Funny poems are almost always a good starting point. They let the audience members know it's okay to enjoy themselves and that your performance is going to be fun, not a dreary poetic exercise. However, if you open with humor, deliver some funny stuff later; otherwise, you end up disappointing an audience by failing to deliver what you made them expect.

◆ Self-effacing patter at the top of your performance can remove an audience's "show-me-something-big-time-slammer" attitude. Humbling yourself before an audience is always a good tactic. "Hi, I'm Marc Smith." "So What!" You lock arms with them. And when you do deliver the goods, they're not only cheering you—they're backslapping one of their own.

◆ A series of very short poems, each of a different theme and/or mood, can tune you in to your audience's mental and emotional whereabouts, to what its political bent is, to its moral disposition, to its mood. If you don't get a big yuck from your dead dog limerick or your "I love your waddle" poem, but the sonnet about your mother evoked a collective sigh, lay off the roadkill and stick with mom.

◆ Take the sly approach. It's gutsy, but if you do it right, it works. Make yourself your own opening act and purposely hold back or even downplay your performance power. You get the audience thinking, "This dude's no better than an open miker. He's just one step above a virgin virgin." And then *bam!* You kick it up full force and blow their minds. In essence, you use a mediocre performance as a foil to accentuate your virtuosity.

Whoa!

We're not advocating that slammers pander to the whims and biases of an audience. The strategy is to open the door and be accepted into its consciousness. Then, when everyone feels comfortable, start unfolding the origami, peeling the onion, and exposing the inner layers of your soul.

◆ Try a participation poem. Nothing can crack open the guarded shell of an audience faster than participation. It'll seem awkward at first, but after you get your audience talking back, they'll want to keep talking. Make the audience's role simple, a few one-word responses, noises, and hand gestures. Make it loud and silly. And give them the instructions with clarity and confidence. Don't ask—command in a nice way.

◆ Shift into high energy. Medium-length, fast-tempo poems filled with exuberance can be a good way to start a show when the audience seems especially lethargic. You pull out all the stops and say, "We're going for it! Jump on the train or jump off." If they don't jump off, you're on your way to a fine performance. If they do, well, there's always plan B. You do have a plan B, don't you?

Exercise

Make a list of all the poems in your repertoire. Circle the humorous ones with one color, the high-energy ones with another, and the audience participatory ones with yet another. Now arrange them according to length, placing the shortest at the top of the list. Try the most-colorfully circled poem closest to the top of your list as the opener at your next performance. See if it works. If not, try the next most-colorful one. Note why it might have worked and why not. If a poem is sort of—but not quite—working as an opener, rewrite it to refine what's working and eliminate what's not.

Hold 'Em

The heart of your performance has to be entertaining. It has to hold the audience's attention. It should be well thought-out and segue effortlessly from one poem to the next. There should be logic to its movement and variation in its tempo, pace, volume, and tone. Too much of one thing becomes a drag. Too little of another can leave dissatisfied stomachs growling. The following five qualities are key elements of a top-notch performance:

♦ **Balance**   Make sure the poems and your arrangement of them establish a feeling of balance. Loading the front end with high-speed diatribes will make the slow-moving story poems in the middle seem unbearably long. Ten minutes of Haiku, followed by ten minutes of sonnets followed by ten minutes of sports poems is going to seem like three different performances weighing down the audience like a lead blanket.

 Backstage Skinny

Counterpoint can act as a cohesive element in your performance when the audience recognizes what's happening. You interlace one set of poems, for example, sonnets about death, with a contrasting set, raps about the joy of living in the moment. The audience understands the relationship and reasoning behind it and accepts the link.

♦ **Cohesion**   Cohesion is the glue connecting one poem to the next. Sometimes a little patter can bond seemingly disparate poems to one another. "After I wrote that poem about eating a half gallon of double Dutch chocolate ice cream, I looked out the window and wrote this poem about a red wheelbarrow." A stronger way to link poems is by theme—one perspective on fatherhood followed by another—or by mood, style, or tempo.

♦ **Pace**   A performance should build to a climax, not rush there; peak and plateau, peak and plateau, rising steadily and never slowing to a stop or racing too fast.

♦ **Unity**   You act as the prime element unifying your performance. You wrote the poems, you are performing the poems, and the poems reflect your personality, convictions, and tastes. Don't ruin the unity with sudden shifts in style, subject matter, or mood. Steaming ahead with an anti-war theme in the first three poems and then shifting to a mix of sex poems and romantic fantasies about life on the moon will quickly derail your train.

♦ **Variety**   Mix it up, as explained previously and in the following section.

Mixing It Up

To build variety into your performances, pay close attention to the selection and order of your poems. A long series of short poems drains an audience's enthusiasm. "How many more of these is he going to read?" A five-minute poem followed by an eight-minute poem on the same subject will have people sneaking out the side exits. If the tempo and mood of every poem in your set is the same, you'll hypnotize your audience into a stupefying trance. Of course, you don't always want some stream-of-consciousness-frenetic-Robin-Williams-stand-up-routine back-flipping across the stage either. Your goal is to infuse your performance with enough variety to keep it energized and keep the audience interested.

Something Up Your Sleeve

Suspense and surprise add joy and juice to your performance and can re-engage the audience's interest if it starts to wane. An unexpected laugh, a serious turn, a story poem building to a climax, or a complete character shift can be like the rush of a roller coaster sliding over the peak tracks and diving down at high speed. Wheee!

From Knee-Slappers to Side-Splitters

An unexpected funny poem in the middle of a deadly serious performance can often garner more laughter than it would in a comedy routine. The audience is thirsty for relief. Toss a bucket of poetic confetti into the audience at the right moment and they'll roar. And sometimes you can keep the laughter rolling with a series of short, funny stanzas that play off the first joke. Lacing an entire performance with periodic humor can create an enjoyable rhythm that makes your serious message enticingly delicious rather than hard to swallow.

Backstage Skinny

A criticism leveled at the slam world has been that many of the poems that win slam competitions are comedic. But there's a reason for that. The slam world is mostly an amateur arena, and beginning writers find it easier to succeed with humor than with deeply serious material. An audience will laugh at something even if it's not that funny, because it's fun to laugh. But an audience will not accept hackneyed accounts of serious subject matter. If you want an audience to empathize with pain, sorrow, or any other serious emotion, then you need to be genuine about it and communicate those feelings and ideas artfully.

Spectacle and Visual Accessories

You've been traveling through the mansion, and all the rooms have been breathtakingly beautiful, so much opulence. One more elegant room might burn out the audience. Just how many polished pieces of furniture can you admire in one afternoon? The next door opens and a red-nosed, shrill-laughing horse hoofs your head as a roomful of evil clowns jiggle with screams and a live monkey screeches from a cage overhead. The old Victorian mansion just took on a new color.

When done well, spectacle, costumes, and audio/visual tricks can jolt your audience into a new dimension. They can also provide much-needed comic relief to clear the palate for the next episode of your performance. But be careful not to clutter up your performance with too many spectacles or stunts, or be too timid to give the ones you use full impact. Ten minutes of clumsy visual accoutrements could turn your performance into a farce. Failing to fully exaggerate a stunt will leave folks wondering, "What was that?"

Musical Accompaniment and Sound Effects

Adding music and sound to your performance heightens its entertainment value. A forty-minute set of music and poetry can be an absolute thrill. It's important to include several a cappella moments within a musical set to remind the audience of the joy of a solo poetic voice. And be sure to mix up the instrumentation that accompanies your performance—bass, drums, and poet; piano and poet; full band and poet. Music offers infinite variations, so does poetry—together, they offer infinite variations squared.

Backstage Skinny

If you're going to use music once or twice in your performance, it's best to use it somewhere in the middle or in the grand finale. Opening with music and never returning to it might leave your audience waiting for more that never arrives.

Many poets have used sound effects to accent and comment on the moods and ideas of their poems. Experimental slammers have laced whistles, rattling chains, clinking plates, bells, and barking dogs into performances. This form of audio spectacle can be very effective. I've watched and listened to slammers carry on poetic dialogues with themselves via tape-recorders manipulated onstage as if the mechanism was a character itself.

The Edge

It's another Tuesday night at the Silver Spoke Slamorama. The regulars are seated at their favorite tables stage left laughing and joking, reading their latest creations to one another. Newcomers are scattered about on stools and at the two-tops skirting the stage. Friends who have already experienced the Silver Spoke are filling them in on what to expect.

The open mike begins and it's as entertaining and pleasant as usual. Everyone is comfortable, jovial, in the groove (the rut) when the side door bangs open and a homeless bag of rags comes crashing in, bumping against the doorframe ranting and flinging his fists around about in the air.

"Oh my god!"

Heartbeats accelerate. Every eye in the room beams a bead on this tornado when, bam! Another human storm crashes through, and another, and another, all ranting and whirling their soiled garments in the faces of a stunned audience.

The Edge (a preplanned, interactive poeic invasion) has entered and done its job. Everybody's nerve endings are exposed. Everyone, for at least a moment, slipped between reality and unreality, safe and threatening, understanding and unknown, and for the rest of the evening they'll be raw, on the alert for the next blast through the side door. The Edge is whatever puts the audience on edge, changes the rules, challenges the status quo, and kicks comfort in the seat of its pants.

Cohesive and Corrosive Patter

In the early years of the slam at the Green Mill I would not allow any patter at the show. "When you're performing here," I'd tell the poets, "No blah-blah between the poems. Let the poems speak for themselves." It was a reaction against the current poetic conventions that allowed dull and self-indulgent dribble to spew between each poem. Nothing kills an evening's performance faster than impertinent patter presented in an artless fashion. If you have interesting and critical information that can enhance the enjoyment of a poem or light its fuse, use it. If it adds nothing, "Nix the blah blah and read the darn poem!"

Closers

Always plan to end your act with an effective closer. A good closer wraps up a fine performance, acts as your last word, and gives people in the audience something to stuff into their pockets and take home with them. Like openers, you'll find the best closers through trial and error. Until you do, try these options:

- Use something short that touches on the strongest theme presented in your performance, sentimentally connects to the audience, or gives the audience one last goodnight laugh.

♦ A fast-moving rocker that blows the top off their heads one last time, isn't too long, and doesn't open up new thematic territory is effective. Don't try to top the previous high point of your performance set.

Whoa! _____

Never use an untested poem for an opener or closer, and never close with something lengthy or something that introduces a new topic or style.

♦ Use a sentimental ending for a mostly comedic show, or a comic ending for a serious one.

♦ A medley of poems that moves from the last portion of your performance into the closing poem without announcement is a good bet. It builds and builds, and the closer comes and takes it out. Done powerfully, a medley closer almost always evokes an encore—and even if it doesn't, it puts a fine end on a fine performance.

Backstage Skinny _____

After some success as a slammer you'll probably find your reputation attached to a *signature piece*, a poem and performance that represents the essence of some part of you. Your signature piece becomes an easy and natural closer. The audience is waiting for it from your first word, and when it finally comes, it guarantees applause.

Be Genuine in Content and Style

Slam has always been open to all kinds of subject matter—even the coarse and politically incorrect. The control lies with the audience. They have ultimate veto power. At the Green Mill, an offensive performer can be booed, stomped, and snapped off the stage, but not solely because of the topic. Most people get the hook because they presented offensive material in an inarticulate manner or because the poem or performance (or both) are phony.

If you are not writing from your own experience, you're usually spewing propaganda. If you're evoking false emotions in yourself and spouting principles you do not follow or information that's been fed to you by media machinations, you're as dishonest as the most despicable politician. The function of art is not to peddle ideas like products or agendas, it is to offer a unique and truthful experience that expands humankind's understanding of itself and the universe around it. It is sacred. And if we as a people sell art down the road of commercial and political expediency, we will have lost the most important source for keeping ourselves free from the tyranny of those who would control our destinies to enhance their own.

All Forms Can Slam—Take Two

Coloring your performance with many different poetic forms is one way of adding an elegant variety to it. A limerick here, a sonnet there, a string of haikus, and a sestina by the poet who inspired you to write can adorn your performance with the same grace and surprise that a piano concerto brings to a swinging jazz quartet or a heavy rock concert. Including classical forms in your set tells your audience that you know your art in depth and you respect its traditions. As we've said before, all great poetry based in the oral tradition is slammable.

Avoiding Common Performance Clichés

High-quality performances can carry a lot of fluff. This is true for all the performing arts, and slammers are no exception. If you're serious about your art you should try to avoid, or at least not fully depend on, the following cheap tricks:

- ◆ Promoting pop ideas borrowed from the newspapers, magazines, TV, and radio. The crowds might cheer you enthusiastically because you're voicing their beliefs, but you're really just preaching to the choir.

- ◆ Shocking an audience for the sake of shocking them. Hey, if you want to shout obscenities on the stage a thousand times or pronounce the N word until your lungs expire, fine, but you're not breaking new ground. Lenny Bruce did it fifty years ago when you could have been beaten to pulp and put in jail for doing so. It's not novel or daring anymore. It's just ignorant and rude.

- ◆ Playing to the audience with overdone, imitation hip-hop. Hip-hop has added a highly imaginative lexicon to all the spoken arts. Some of its innovative language will be with us for centuries. Unfortunately, commercial rap has turned thousands of stage poets into pseudo emcees with affected hand gestures and monotonous rhymations, rhythms, thinking that they can hide behind easy political ideas and overused backbeats. If you're from the ghetto, go for it, but if you're from a nice middle-class family, why not write a *quatrain* or two about your mother?

Whoa!

Affected styles of presentation spring from many sources, not just pop culture. The slam has created its own share of mannerisms that young poets copy to emulate their heroes. That's okay, but when you hear yourself performing every poem in your notebook at the same tempo, volume, articulation, and mood, ask yourself if that's you onstage or somebody else inside your mind and body.

Memorization

Dancers memorize dance steps; singers memorize lyrics and notes; musicians memorize fingerings, tones, scales, chords, and melodies; actors memorize speeches, dialogues, entrances, body movements, cues and responses, and curtain calls. Slammers who wish to compete on the same stages as these professionals should also memorize their poems and their performances. The benefits of having your poems memorized are that it …

♦ Frees your mind and body to focus on the physical communication of your poem in performance.

♦ Projects an image of professionalism and accomplishment to the audience.

♦ Enables you to be more spontaneous in your performance. Rather than shuffling through manuscript pages for that perfect poem for that perfect moment, you instantly pull it from your mental filing cabinet and deliver.

♦ Gives you a deeper understanding of your text.

♦ Keeps your mind young and flexible.

Think of your memory as a muscle and the stanzas of your poems as weights. The more you lift, the stronger your muscle. You lift one line and then add another, and then a stanza and another stanza until the entire poem feels like feathers on your brain.

How We Make Memory Deposits

You can make deposits into your memory account in any number of ways. Memory experts call this process *encoding*, and it consists of a number of mental tasks:

Backstage Skinny

Memorize through an active rehearsal to experience your poems rather than just reciting them. Your physical movements will help you remember the words, and the words and images will help you remember your movements.

♦ **Focus Your Attention.** Really listen to—or watch, smell, feel, or sense—your perceptions. Tune into what's going on.

♦ **Reason.** Understand the logic (or lack of it) behind what you're doing, listening to, watching, smelling, feeling, and so on.

♦ **Associate.** Link new perceptions or information with something you've previously experienced and stored in your long-term memory.

♦ **Elaborate.** Gather or create an abundance of information to support what you wish to remember. For instance, create in your mind's eye a whole seascape of sand, surf, and old wooden boats stranded on a reef to support the line: "I must go down to the sea again/To the lonely sea and the sky."

Bringing It Back

Storing something in long-term memory is only half the battle. Onstage you have to retrieve those lines you've banked away—you have to bring them back into your conscious mind. You do this in one of two ways:

- **Recall.** Search your long-term memory, find the desired chunk of data, and move it to the top of the stack.

- **Recognition.** Perceive sensory information that triggers an immediate retrieval.

Information in long-term memory often gets buried under a heap of similar information acquired more recently; this makes it nearly impossible to retrieve the original material. If you read through a stanza ten times, slightly changing wording each time: "That night I saw you," "That evening I watch you," "This twilight I studied you," you're reinforcing trouble. When in the learning stage, be careful to repeat lines exactly.

Information for which you have few associations and little background knowledge is more difficult to store and recall than language that paints vivid images in your mind. Know that this isn't your inability or failure; it's just naturally a more difficult task.

As you get more comfortable with the memorization and recall process, you'll notice key phrases and words that become cues linking line to line and stanza to stanza. Train yourself to be more conscious of these links. These key words and phrases act as life preservers that float all around you as you try to stay afloat.

The Memorization Curve

I've found that when I memorize a poem or a series of poems, the process takes me over the peaks and valleys of what I call the "memorization curve":

- The journey starts on a Peak. Everything is a bright, sunny sky. I'm excited about the prospect of having another poem in my repertoire. I read the entire poem through five or six times as I slide down the slope into …

- The Valley of Blah Blah Blah. "Oh, man. This is work. The same lines over and over again. I'm bored." And now I'm headed up a steep mountainside. Tramp.

Tramp. Tramp. Line. Line. Line. My mind must constantly refocus—"Refocus, darn it!" I go stanza by stanza, reading them each 5 or 6 times. And just when I begin to think that I'm climbing an endless slope, I emerge at …

◆ Peak Number Two, and my poem sails off my lips and into the air like an eagle soaring above the rocky mountains of my dreams. I want to jump up and down, wave a flag, and proclaim to myself, "Got it!" The job's finished, but I'm not done. I've gone blank onstage enough to know that reaching peak number two only ensures that you can retrieve your lines in the quiet and comfort of your own living room, and that's much different than pulling them up amidst the distractions of a slam audience. So I travel on and dip down into …

◆ The Forget-It-Not Valley, where I recite the lines I think I've thoroughly memorized and discover that even the smallest distraction can trip me up. So I work them with the radio on or as I wash the dishes, passing through a jungle of noises and climbing up another switchback. Line. Stanza. Poem. The trail's not as tedious this time. I see my eagle words circling along my trek and I know from experience that I'll reach a peak if I just keep tramping on, and soon I'm standing at …

◆ The Top of the World. I have reached the third peak and have become the eagle, the sky, and the poem itself, and the landscape below is applauding.

Exercises in Flexing the Memory Muscle

Select a poem you want branded on your brain cells, and then perform the following exercises:

◆ Listen to your voice as you read the poem aloud.

◆ Record yourself reading the poem aloud and then play back the recording and listen carefully.

◆ Rehearse the poem, blocking your movement and testing gestures as you recite.

◆ Final test: Perform an unrelated task as you recite the memorized lines. Wash the dishes, take a walk, mow the lawn, whatever.

Performing in the Zone

Most professional performing artists, those who have been on the stage in the spotlight for more time than they can remember, will tell you that the greatest moments onstage come when they lose themselves in their performance—when they enter the zone, the field, the transcendent place where dancer and dance, singer and song, poet and poem blend in with the audience and become one in a communal merging of art, performer, and witness. The ego, the this and that, the us and them, the me and you, is gone, merged into a single soul. The performer forgets that there's an audience out there judging. The audience stops judging and analyzing the veracity of the performer. They witness the performance itself. And the performance affects them deeply.

To all performing poets, the zone is (or should be) the ultimate goal. And for the audience, it's what they hope for and remember long afterward.

The Least You Need to Know

- ◆ Your performance should open with a strong piece that engages the audience, followed by several pieces that hold their attention, and finishing with a closer that wraps up the set and delivers a knockout punch.

- ◆ Your set should be varied but balanced, using humor, spectacle, musical accompaniment, and other techniques to keep the audience engaged and entertained.

- ◆ To smooth transitions between poems, arrange the poems in a logical order and use patter sparingly to lead from one poem to the next.

- ◆ Your performance can include all forms of poetry, but avoid getting in the rut of mimicking pop performance styles.

- ◆ To commit something to long-term memory, associate it with a vivid image, a strong sensory perception, or an experience.

Chapter 8

Where and How to Gig Around

In This Chapter

- Sniffing out venues where you can do your slam—from open-mike to weekly shows

- Giving yourself a chance to be discovered and hit the big time

- Knocking on doors: bookstores, dance clubs, theaters, libraries, schools, and more

- Reaping the benefits of following proper etiquette, both as performer and audience member

- Creating opportunities with a slam show of your very own—dreams of an aspiring slammaster

You've been performing to yourself in the mirror, to the neighborhood cats and dogs, and to any friends and relatives who owed you a favor. But the cardboard cutout crowd is beginning to feel a little flat. You're ready for a 3-D performance. You're dying to parade your performance onstage, to pour out your vibrant verse to a live, enthusiastic audience.

Now what?

Before you can perform onstage, you need to find a stage to perform on. Fortunately, slam's popularity has made it fairly easy to find a place to slam whether you live in a major metropolitan area or in Teensytown, USA. You just need to keep your eyes and ears open and do a little detective work. This chapter shows you how to begin your investigation and provides you with some valuable leads.

Happy Days Are Here Again

In the early 1980s, before the slam began, finding opportunities to air your poetry in public—even in big cities like Chicago and Peoria—was a monumental task. That has changed. Across the country, poetry, spoken word, and slams are hot commodities. Club and coffee house owners, librarians and schoolteachers, program directors and artistic committees are ambitiously seeking out and creating reading series and performance events to feed the growing hunger for spoken word performance. As an aspiring performance poet, your task is to hunt down performance opportunities and seize them. After you've opened a door or two, more opportunities will start popping up as naturally as daisies over the graves of dead poets and cowboys. Step one, of course, is knowing where to look.

Open Mike Search

From the very first second of your search for open mikes you're going to be building an arsenal of information that will stay with you and aid you for years to come. There was a time in my early career when I knew, firsthand, every poetry group, club, open mike, event, and workshop in the greater Chicago metropolitan area. One resource led to another, and soon I was an authority on poetry events in my city and a few other cities, too. Here are some ways of finding your first open mike opportunity:

◆ Pick up the weekend edition of your local daily newspaper, open it to the arts and entertainment section, and scan through the notices and listings of events—find anything? These days you can check the display ads, too, for major and weekly poetry events, something that was unheard of before slam became popular.

◆ Flip through a copy of your town's alternative newspaper (if it has one). The alternative press typically covers arts and entertainment venues more thoroughly than the standard dailies. Chicago has the *Reader*; New York City has the *Village Voice*; San Francisco has *Poetry Flash*; and Indianapolis has *Nuvo*. Get a copy of the alternative paper and scan the notices and event listings. Have a paper and pen handy, because you *will* find opportunities here ... unless, of course, you're living in the upper Yukon.

◆ Find the flyers. You can bet they're posted somewhere in your neighborhood or in a neighboring hood. Adjacent to the automatic entrance doors of supermarkets, on the walls of coffee shops, tacked onto the bulletin board in the church basement, in music clubs, on light poles, in shop windows, you name it. Somewhere in your city there's at least one flat surface covered with posters, post cards, leaflets, and flyers of all sizes and colors and styles, and in that montage of graphic art and fonts you're going to see poetry announcements of one sort or another.

>
>
> **Whoa!**
>
> One of the first radio interviews I did was for a poetry show in the Hudson Bay area. Wherever human beings settle, you'll find poetry. And wherever there's poetry, someone wants it or is reading it aloud to someone else.

◆ Check out the public library. First look at the library's bulletin board and then ask. Yes, ask. Practice talking to people, as instructed in Chapter 5. Chances are the librarian is as shy as you. "Hi, do you know of any poetry readings in the area?" "No, but I can tell you who would." That's how it works. Peruse the poetry section while you're there and see if you can find the works of any of the slammers mentioned in this book. If not, ask the librarian to order their books. You'll be doing your part to help the movement.

◆ Visit your local cultural arts center (most cities have them), and check out their programming literature and announcement board. Talk to people there, too. Ask them what they know. Ask them if they know of any local poets whom you could call to get some friendly poetic advice. Be personable and polite—these people might soon be an important part of your performance poetry future.

◆ Call the English departments of your local community college or the state university. Get past the student secretary if he doesn't know anything about poetry, and speak to a professor or, better yet, the department head. No luck there? Call the theater department and do the same. Go down to the university and roam the halls. You'll see walls full of flyers and posters announcing everything from soccer games to beer blasts. Find the poetry, man!

> **Backstage Skinny**
>
> The slam community is open to assisting poet folk in finding their way. Contact the slammaster nearest you, even if she's in the next state, and ask her for suggestions of where to perform. You'll get help or my name's not So What!

◆ Go online. Of course! Go online and punch in "poetry" on that search engine. Whoa!!!!!!!! Too much info! Overload!

Narrow it down to your locale. Go to www.poetryslam.com and see where the nearest registered slam is. The net search might strain your eyeballs, but it's worth the surfing if it finds a campfire on the beach where folks share poems under the midnight moon.

If you live in a fairly large city, try to pinpoint the locations of the artsy neighborhoods. Every city has one or two neighborhoods that are more artistically inclined and offer a livelier nightlife. In these neighborhoods, you're more likely to find staple-riddled telephone poles packed with flyers for poetry readings, band concerts, plays, and other artistic offerings.

Getting on Track with Weekly or Monthly Shows

It's my personal guarantee that if you thoroughly explore all the options mentioned previously, you'll find some kind of poetry reading and/or open mike to attend. And after you do, get to work. There's no need to lose your virginity on the very first night. If you're lucky enough to track down a weekly show, check it out for a month of Mondays. Be an interested audience member. Become a regular. See how things work. What's the protocol? Is there a sign-up sheet at the door or does the host carry it around with him? How early do you have to get there to sign up? How many poems do you get to read? What kind of poems and subject matter do the poets normally present? Take notes or at least jot down some particulars when you get home.

Backstage Skinny _____

Slams are open to all styles and subject matter, but many other poetry readings have unspoken taboos. You probably won't get arrested or thrown out by the poet police, but you could end up with an invisible albatross around your neck. Reading Death Metal verse to the Christian Society for Higher Learning, or preaching the gospel to the atheists might charge you up in a way, but will it expand your audience base? Knowing your audience is a prerequisite for all successful writing and performing.

All the Gigs You Can Do

Performance careers do not grow in isolation. True, a few writers have entered the halls of greatness as solitary figures, but only a few and usually after they're dead and gone. For performance poets, success is nearly impossible without connecting and working with audiences and other performers. The following sections describe the places and situations in which you can expect to perform. Be open to them all, and seize every opportunity in every spotlight they offer.

Bookstore Readings

Independent bookstores host many poetry readings and open mikes. Sometimes they combine the appearance of a fairly well-known poet with an open mike to attract an audience for their guest. These readings can be fairly formal and sometimes cramped between the bookshelves; however, many of them are expertly organized by store owners who cherish fine literature and love the spoken word.

> ### Whoa!
>
> The big franchise bookstores (the ones selling this book—oops!) have jumped on the bandwagon of creating "readings" and sometimes slams. They are often sad and disheartening affairs for both author and audience. The managers of these megaplex bookstores are often burdened with too many responsibilities to devote the passion and care required to stage a focused and effective event. The invited author speaks into a sub-quality microphone slapped up next to a tiny table and chair surrounded by a cluster of devotees who wait for a signed copy of the author's latest while the inattentive masses ramble through the aisles shopping for cookbooks and birthday cards. These are not great opportunities for pro or amateur.

Nightclubs, Saloons, and Other Informal Venues

Nightclubs, taverns, music clubs, and other venues that don't feature a formal "Slam Night" do often include spoken-word performances in their acts. They might lack the structure of a professional slam show or the formality of a bookstore poetry reading, but they spill over in the joy and excitement of electrifying entertainment. If the club shows have been running successfully for a long period of time, that's a good sign that the management is behind them and the organizers are doing their job. Secure a spot in the show, and you can count on a steady gig and a solid springboard for your slam career.

> ### Whoa!
>
> Beware of new shows in saloons and nightclubs. The owner or organizer might be using the slam or spoken word as a gimmick to belly up customers to the bar and could not care less about treating the poets with respect. Remember, as a performance poet you're an artist, not background music.

Late-Night Theater

During the nineties, theater companies began to notice that poetry slams were racking up enviable audience numbers that matched and usually exceeded the numbers most theater companies drew for anything less than a big hit. And the crowds were young, diverse, and intelligent. Theater managers immediately started to tap into the slam's audience base by creating poetry-related theater events. These were hardly ever open-mike situations, but they did rely heavily upon local talent and usually fit into their off-night and late-night programming. When you're ready to graduate from being strictly an open miker, check out the late-night/off-night theater scene.

Performance Venues

Dance companies, art galleries, improv troupes, comedy shows, and other performance venues all have recruited performance poets and slammers to add a spoken word spark to their artistic visions. After all, performers in all genres share a common spirit—we love an audience and live to serve it. Dance or paint your poems. Tell a joke; make the audience laugh. Dress up and prance your poems across the stage. Adapt your poetry and performance to whatever situation you face, whatever the audience needs, and, in the process, expand and strengthen your own artistic vision.

> **Dig This!**
>
> Under the direction of faculty members Gary Anderson and Tony Romano, Fremd High School in Palatine, Illinois, has included slammers in their annual Writers Week's program for over ten years.

 What's on the CD

CD #2 track #2: Tye-himba Jess performing "Black Poets on Death's Corner"

Schools Can Do It, Too (Educational Outreach)

In Chapter 23, you'll learn how PSI (Poetry Slam, Inc.) and the slam family have moved into the educational realm. When starting out, remember to keep your eyes open for opportunities that arise at the local library or at your alma mater to recite poems at some seasonal event, or as a special attraction at the schools for National Poetry Month. Later, when you've honed your skills, you'll be teaching workshops to the kiddies, but that's in a future chapter of your career. For now, settle on any opportunity that arises and keep your eyes open for future openings.

Don't Forget the Slams

No other poetry event is as open to beginners as a slam. One of the guiding principles of all slams is to offer an open platform for all people of all talent levels and experience, and usually the new bloods get special attention. It can be a little scary, especially at slams that allow full audience feedback, but a slam is absolutely the most open atmosphere you'll encounter when starting out, and it will nourish you if you give it a chance.

Slams, as you're beginning to learn from reading this book, occur anywhere from bookstores to brothels, from the steps of a library to the special purpose rooms of state penitentiaries. Find one, saddle it up, and your career as a performance poet will begin to gallop.

Do-It-Yourself Venues (Create Your Own Show)

Can't find an open mike or a weekly show with an open slot? Then create your own show and give yourself a little stage time. In Part 4, you'll learn all about starting your own show to give yourself and others an opportunity to perform. Of course, it requires a great deal of work, generosity, and sacrifice, but the benefits far outweigh the costs. I started my first show at the Get Me High Jazz Club because I was shut out from the establishment poetry scene and frustrated by the long wait-to-read lists at the open mikes around town, which were few and far between. The labor of creating your own show pays off by giving you a guaranteed opportunity to present two or three or more of your poems every week or every month. It also brings you the satisfaction of helping other performance artists, and it helps you establish contacts with other poet/ performers and create an amazing new world in which to live.

Performance Poetry Etiquette 101

In *The Complete Idiot's Guide to Writing Poetry* (Alpha Books, 2001), Nikki Moustaki offers some excellent etiquette suggestions for poetry readers and audience members at open mikes. In the following sections I've expanded on that advice and added some slam qualifiers to it.

Proper Etiquette for Poets and Performers

How you behave at a slam or open mike is going to affect your future opportunities. If you're a jerk at a slam, the audience is going to snap, stomp, and groan you off stage. The slam emcee might be eager to sign you up for a repeat performance—but only to feed you to an audience that's thirsty to have at you again. At an open reading the host and audience might not fully show its disdain for your behavior, but it will definitely make them think twice about asking you to attend other events. Here are some do's and don'ts from Nikki's book with additions from my notebook on slam etiquette:

- **"If you have time, begin your reading with another poet's work."** Nikki's advice here is right on, but don't feel compelled to open with a classic—you can work it into the middle or end of your performance. Keeping the great poetic works alive or honoring your contemporaries should be part of every poet's mission.

- **"Thank your audience … before you begin."** Thanking the audience is acceptable at some slams some of the time, but don't be phony about it and don't over-do it. In the slam world, many poets have gotten too slick in this department. We've heard too many, "How are you all doing out there? I said, *how are you all doing out there?*" almost demanding that the audience acknowledge them. That's not a thank-you. That's intimidation.

> **Dig This!**
>
> At the Green Mill there's an audience tradition that squelches poets who go on too long with some pre-poem blather. Folks shout, "Read the frickin' poem!" Only they shout it with a word change here and there.

- **"Read to your time limit … and don't go over."** Say that again a hundred times! Nothing is more selfish and arrogant than assuming that you should be heard for a longer time than the other poets in the open mike. What makes you more important than them? The slam has set a standard that most open mikes in the general poetry world now follow: poems of a reasonable length (around three minutes) and no more than two or three poems unless the crowd screams for more.

- **"Don't explain your poems."** The meaning of your poem should be clear and accessible to your audience, and your performance should communicate the text effectively. If you have to explain it, you're doing something wrong.

- **"Don't apologize for your work."** A healthy aura of humility is good. Self-deprecation gets old real fast. Write your best verse, perform it as best you can, and let the audience decide if it likes it or not. Don't knock yourself or your work—plenty of people out there will be happy to do that for you.

- **"When you're done, thank the audience again."** Show your thanks with a bow or a nod or a smile. You'll find that the more you humble yourself to the audience, the more they'll give back praise and admiration. Try it, you'll see.

Here are a couple additional rules of slam etiquette:

- **Don't bore the audience with your life story.** No one wants to hear your detailed biography or how your day went. We all have biographies and we've all had days of our own. The audience came to witness performance poetry, not to hear a eulogy.

- ◆ **Never stop in the middle of a poem and start over.** It's gonna happen once or twice, but that should teach you a lesson that ends it forever. Nothing is more tedious than listening to the rerun of a mediocre poem because the poet messed up the first time around. And sometimes it gets messed up the second time around, too. Ugh!

Audience Etiquette

The slam world asks the audience to loosen up and be vocal, some slams more so than others. In Chicago, the Green Mill encourages positive and negative feedback in the form of cheering, snapping, stomping, groaning, and the famous feminist hiss. Other slams pride themselves on being gentle—no booing or heckling allowed. Whatever the situation, most open mikes abide by the following audience rules and regulations, as explained in *The Complete Idiot's Guide to Writing Poetry*:

- ◆ **"Don't talk while another poet is reading."** This applies to performers as well as patrons. Nothing annoys me more than a fellow performer chattering through someone else's performance. It's professional courtesy to shut up and listen, and I make it a habit to inform the offending poets of this. When it comes to straight audience members, different standards come into play. Of course, the audience members should stop chatting when a performer takes the mike, but the audience has every right—in fact, an obligation—to respond honestly (and sometimes vocally) to a performance. If the poet onstage isn't communicating effectively and loses the audience, no one should gag the audience just to indulge the performer.

Whoa!

So does some drunk at a slam get to stand up and heckle a virgin virgin during the open mike? No. Inappropriate chatter and obnoxious outbursts should never be tolerated, and an emcee can recruit the audience to control it. If there's a big mouth disrupting the show, ask your audience to shush him with you. One hundred people telling him to SHUT UP! should get through to the densest philistine.

- ◆ **"If you like the poet's work, tell her."** Tell her how it moved you. Tell her how it connected to something that happened to you. Tell her what worked. And if asked, tell her what didn't. Be gentle with your criticism, but be truthful. The slam is an incubator for lots of young poets, and one of the ways they'll learn their craft is through clear and honest feedback.

Following are a couple additional slam etiquette rules:

◆ **Don't walk in front of the stage or stand by it, drawing audience focus from the performer.** And if you do, get yourself to a counselor and find out why your inner child is demanding so much attention.

◆ **Limit your human and inhuman audio emissions.** If you must eat, don't slurp and gulp like a Hoosier hog grunting and slopping in the mud. Don't crumble the wrappers. Do turn off your pager, cell phone, or other bleeping device. Slam emcees are sure to shame you if you make a racket during a performance.

◆ **Show your appreciation through applause.** At slams the poem is the important factor, not the poet's reputation and personality. And slam poems usually get thunderous applause. It might be the tradition in some circles to reserve applause for only the best performances, but in the realm of performance poetry, encouraging applause is a proper part of the appeal.

The Least You Need to Know

◆ When you're first starting out, look for open-mike opportunities in your town or city.

◆ Many venues that feature weekly shows with bands, stand-up comedians, and other performers plug slam poets into their shows.

◆ In addition to slam events, bookstores, nightclubs, theaters, schools, and other institutions seek out slammers for special events.

◆ When you perform, be humble and appreciative, be considerate to the other performers, and don't knock your own poetry or performance.

◆ As an audience member, don't make noise during a performance, don't walk in front of or stand by the stage, and support the performers with your applause and honest feedback.

Part 3

Going Poet Professional

After a few performances, you've come to realize that poetry slam is in your blood. You go to bed thinking about your next performance and wake up early to jot down some punchy lines. Maybe you even perform your latest composition in the shower or in the car on your way to work.

You decide that you have only two options: get counseling or quit your day job and become a professional performance poet. Can you make a living at it? Maybe, but not until you read the chapters in this part. Here you learn various ways to make a few bucks as a performance poet and possibly even eke out a decent living at it.

Chapter 9

Packaging and Promoting Your Performance

In This Chapter

- ◆ Convincing yourself that it's not only okay but essential to market your work

- ◆ Developing a savvy and successful marketing strategy

- ◆ Creating a press pack—from low-budget to top-of-the-line

- ◆ Marketing yourself, your poetry, and your performance on the web

- ◆ Planning and publicizing your first (or next) slam poetry tour

As a slam poet, you are a product. A lot of poets find that idea a little too corporate, too "establishment." It does sound a little cold, but if you don't think of yourself that way when it comes to snagging gigs and selling your book(s), your CD(s), and your one-person show, your fan base is going to consist of your mom and maybe one or two of her closest friends. If you're satisfied with life as a hobby poet, you can afford to avoid the drudgery of marketing. But if you have a passionate desire to have people experience your work or you want to make a little money slamming, you need to market yourself, and this chapter will show you how.

Thinking Like a Marketing Mogul

The best way to start developing a marketing strategy is to put yourself in the other gal's shoes. If you were a regular Jane sitting in a café someplace, what poster or flyer for a poetry performance would catch *your* eye? Probably something POW! HELLO! WOW! LOOK AT ME! with colors splashed on it, a design that beats all other designs with plenty of pertinent information printed clearly, boldly, so that you don't have to squint to read it.

If you're a busy slammaster or bar owner with 10 promo packs stuffed in your mailbox every day, what would make *you* take the time to read one and not the others? Probably something unique, professional, and direct; absolutely under five pages (you're a busy person) with plenty of whitespace—telling you immediately who, what, and when. You'd want something that's quick to read, convincing, and shows you that this act will make your audiences go wild. And you don't want it giving you, the boss, any new problems.

Look around the landscape, flip through magazines, check out the billboards—what advertising strategies work? The most successful individuals and companies (for better or worse) know their customers; they know the strengths of their products or services; and they push, push, push until everyone and her dog knows who they are and what they do. If you believe in your poetry, in your performance, and in yourself, and you want to reach as many people as possible, start thinking like some fat cat corporate marketer. What does your audience need? What does it want? What is it about you, your poetry, and your performance that delivers? When you realize what you have to offer and why your audience can't live without it, you'll be ready to push, push, push ….

Slapping Together a Press Pack

Begin by pulling together all your credentials into one place and creating the essential performance poet press pack. You'll be sending it out for big gigs and small across the borders to Anytown, USA. It will serve both as a general overview and as a detailed insight into who you are, what you do, how you do it, and what people have said about you after you've done it—a name, a face, and a reason why.

You can assemble the marketing materials in any of several ways, but your packet should include items from three essential categories:

- Printed stuff (such as a biography, sample poems, press clippings, and so on)

- Audio recordings (tape or CD)

- Visuals (a VHS tape or DVD recording of a solid performance)

The following sections cover these categories in greater detail.

Backstage Skinny

On rare occasions organizers contract an act solely because they love it and could give two hoots if anybody pays the cover charge to see it. But those are indeed very rare occasions. Organizers usually book acts because they anticipate people lining up out the door and around the corner to see and listen to the entertainment.

Get It in Print

The easiest stuff to gather consists of the paper products. The ultimate goal is to create a folder or bound booklet, so the papers are easy for the recipient to handle and tough to misplace. This folder/booklet should contain the following items:

- **A one-page biography.** Keep your biography short and punchy. Consider writing it in the third person; for example, "Tennessee Mary is an actress and a performance poet living in Chicago and dedicates all her performances to her cat, Toonses." A biography written in the third person sounds more objective, as though somebody else is blowing your own horn for you.

- **One or two action photos of yourself.** These photos should capture vividly who you are and what you do. They should show the flavor of your performance style and (if possible) show people listening intently to your words. Headshots are okay, but they don't say much more than "Oooh, she's cute." Think of this photo as a visual sound bite—one look and they get the idea. Put your name, or the name of your act, on it in big bold type.

- **A resumé highlighting your top performances.** Your resumé should highlight where you've played and when; it should be a record of your past performances. Create two or three versions gearing each toward a different type of engagement. For example, one might focus on festivals and writing conferences and another one might list mostly nightclub work. Put your best foot forward, but don't overstate your experience.

- **Reviews, news clippings, magazine articles.** If you've paid enough dues to acquire any magazine or newspaper coverage, photos showing you in action on stage pleasing the crowds, or reviews of your excellent chapbook (short, typically self-published book), clip them out, blow them up, polish them pretty, and stick them into the paper section of your kit. They are the hard-fact evidence that supports your claims. Don't include every article ever written about you, just the most current and most prestigious ones.

Whoa!

Proofread any printed materials carefully before sending them out. This includes your biography, resumé, cover letter, and any press releases you compose. Ask a friend or relative, preferably someone who's fairly literate, to proofread the page(s), as well.

♦ **A couple sample poems (two or three, max).** Even though your mettle will ultimately be tested by your onstage performance, your marketing target might want a taste of the page without the stage. This doesn't mean that you should stuff an envelope full of poems and ship it to a slammaster or an artistic director. A few of your very best poems (two or three, not twenty) will be enough for them to decide if your style and content is something they want on their stage.

Get It on Tape

The paper has set the scene, now the slammaster wants some proof. Increasingly, booking agents and presenters, especially those who work for well-known cultural institutions, will not even consider applicants who do not submit audio and video samples of their performances. It's the fastest and easiest way for them to make a first or second pruning of the pile of wannabes stacked on their desk, or solidify a final decision. In less than thirty seconds they'll know if they want to explore, book, or pitch.

The Do-It-Yourself Audio Method

Audio recordings, of course, are less involved than video. If you've got a decent audio recorder, try to rope a friend into working the recorder for you. That way, you can focus on your performance rather than on pushing the buttons, setting the volume, and watching out for the person who walks by the table and knocks over the recorder. If you have no friends (I'm sorry), take the recorder to your next performance anyway, set it up in a place where the sound is pretty good and where someone won't pilfer it, test it once or twice, and then, before you go onstage to rock the masses, press the Record button.

Presto! By the end of your performance, you have your very own live recording and, if you're lucky, some of the cuts will be good enough for your promo package.

Getting a Little Sound Advice

You've tried the solo do-it-yourself method three times and something always goes wrong. It's time for another approach. Hunt down some musician friends, or friends who know musicians, and ask their advice. These days most musicians record their music in basement studios or on-site "live" with their own equipment, either for product or for the purpose of reviewing their performances. They have more than a little expertise in getting it right. Their ears are tuned for high-quality results. They might be willing and able to set you up with some better recording equipment—microphones that capture the natural tone of your voice or mixing boards that tweak the EQ to perfection—or, at least, they might point you in the right direction to find what you need. They might even invite you over to their home studio and in less than a few hours … Eureka! A cassette or CD filled with your finest words. If they're your good buddies, buy 'em dinner. If it's a friendly business exchange, slip them a few bucks. In either case, get your butt to their next gig and applaud loudly.

Get the Wallet Out

If all your musician friends are busy and you're too anxious to wait for their schedules to clear, track down a professional recording studio. Look in the yellow pages or in the local performing arts newsletter. You might be surprised to find that the cost isn't too crazy. Studio time required for the relatively easy setup and session that spoken word takes could be as little as a couple hours at a cost of $80 to $100 per hour. That's just a couple hundred bucks! And you might even be able to get the editing and *mixing* done, and burn a few CD samples, too.

The Clock's Ticking

Whatever approach you take, be it the complete do-it-yourself method, the professional studio session, or something in between, the more you prepare in advance, the less time and money you'll spend on the recording process. The following list explains what you need to do to prepare:

SlamSlang

Mixing is the process of combining and layering audio clips to produce a final recording.

Dig This!

A promo CD can be a basic homespun recording of your act. It doesn't have to be some slick studio album. That comes later after you've signed your Warner Brothers contract. Your promo CD is just a sample of what you do. But remember, quality production makes a difference. Kids screaming, "Daddy! Mommy!" in the background won't help.

◆ Select the poems you wish to record far in advance of the recording date, and rehearse them until they're second nature. (Review Chapter 5 on memorization and rehearsal.)

◆ Time out your pieces and decide on the order.

◆ If you plan on adding any special effects—clanking sounds overlaid with ghostly whispers or just plain background music—know exactly what they are and how you want to incorporate them before the tape starts running.

◆ If you've got some musical accompaniment, be sure you've rehearsed several times prior to the studio session.

Each tick tock of the studio clock is a dollar sign flying out the window. Nothing is dumber than wasting studio time on basic rehearsal business. And don't expect the sound engineers to tell you how to run your recording session; they just push the buttons and shift the levers. Have a plan in your head and lead the session.

Aftersounds—Editing and Production

Sometimes the recording session accomplishes only that, getting down a few tracks on a cassette tape or a CD. Back home you listen to it and love lots of it, but oh, no! the sound is too low on that stanza and the front end of this poem has no passion, and the whole thing is a little dry. Don't get out the razor blades, and don't go back to square one. Editing and mixing can get you closer to the finish line. After all, it's a demo recording, not Radio City Musical Hall.

Whoa!

Most club owners and slam organizers don't sit around with a pot of tea, listening to and loving all the CDs they get in the mail. Put the best of the best tracks on your promo CD or the one(s) you think will grab the attention of your audience. If you're lucky, they'll listen to the first thirty seconds or so of each track. You know you're brilliant—they just want to know if you're good enough.

Cut out the sections you don't like and splice in the intro to the next poem or fade music in and out over the glitches. Or insert a narrative about yourself to disguise the blunders. Find yet another friend who likes to get creative with audio mixing and ask him to make it pretty. If the audio sample can hold the listener's attention for three minutes, it won't matter if it's a pure and perfect nonstop performance. It will have convinced the booker that you have the juice to entertain.

After you have one or more satisfying tracks, it's best to burn them to a CD … assuming, of course, that you have a CD burner. If you don't, call a friend or relative who has a computer with a CD-R or CD-RW drive to help. Because the procedure for burning a

CD varies depending on the equipment and software you're using, I don't include step-by-step instructions here. If you have no idea what to do, get some junior-high kid to help you. Most kids learn how to burn CDs shortly after they learn to speak.

Roll 'Em: Filming Your Act

In a perfect world, you would beam yourself over to your dream venue, audition for the appropriate people, and land the ultimate gig through your astounding perform- ance and water-tight writing. Over time, scouts would see you in the flesh and book you on the spot for the Dodge Festival—this is ideal, of course. Until then, if you can provide a video of your performance, it can only help.

Again, be resourceful. Unless you're living in a cave, you or someone you know owns a cam- corder. Buy your buddy a cup of coffee and pay his cover charge in return for a few minutes of filming. Heck, most people will jump at the chance to do something with their camcorder other than filming their sleeping cat.

> **Dig This!**
>
> The Dodge Poetry Festival, held biennially in Waterloo Village in northern New Jersey, is the largest poetry event in North America.

Built-In Opportunities

Many performance spaces have a habit of video-recording the talent that passes through for their archives. If you see a camera in a room you're playing, ask if you can copy a clip of your performance. You might get lucky and acquire a sample with no more effort and expense than it takes to dupe a tape.

> **Backstage Skinny**
>
> If you perform at the National Poetry Slam, you might be able to purchase (for a small price) footage of your performance. At nationals, PSI provides a video- recording service to its members to aid them in their careers.

Call the Pros

If all else fails, grab your yellow pages, look up the number for a video recording stu- dio, and hire a professional to tape a performance. Remember to go into the studio well prepared. Cover all the preparation tips listed earlier in this chapter for an audio recording, plus the visual stuff: how you look, how you move, the background, the lighting, what you wear, did you cut your hair? You can spend a lot of time and effort for naught if your toupee is leaning or a cat is walking along the fake fireplace mantel behind your head. On a shoot, every visual detail matters. You'll never hit perfection, and you don't have to, but you should at least be sure that your nose hairs are clipped.

The Final Product

After you have one or more video clips, it's best to transfer your clip(s) to DVD. Five minutes of performance is all you need for your demo. You can add a longer version and even include the print portion of your press pack on it. You can pack a lot of material on a DVD.

If you don't have a DVD burner and you don't know anyone who owns one, take your tape to a DVD transfer service and have it done professionally. You can usually get two hours or more of film transferred to DVD for about fifty bucks. Just make sure the service doesn't copy-protect the disc. You can find plenty of these services on the web. Just open your browser and use your favorite search engine to look for "transfer video to DVD."

Low-Budget or All-Out Glitz?

If you just won the lottery or scored your first lead role in a slam movie, you can afford to spring for a glitzy press pack, complete with three 8-by-10 glossies of yourself, fancy covers for your CD and DVD, and key chains that play haikus. You could drop a good chunk of cash to have your booklet professionally bound with a laminated cover and buy some slick envelopes to mail out your packet. If you want to go low-budget, though, it's fine to staple the papers together and send in a cassette recording of yourself. What matters most is that it's not slapped together carelessly and that it has personality, something that stands out in a crowd, that entertains. The questions you must answer are simple: What would grab your attention in a press pack? How best can you show the world in two dimensions who you are and what you do on the three-dimensional stage? If you stick to what you find to be interesting and work hard to present yourself in the best possible light, your press pack is guaranteed to hit the mark.

SlamSlang

A **blog** (short for "web log") is a publicly accessible personal journal that enables an individual to voice his or her opinions and insights or just keep an online record of experiences. People also use blogs to share photos with friends and family and to foster online communities.

Establishing Yourself on the Web

The Internet has been essential to the growth of the slam movement. Through chat rooms, personal websites, *blogs*, and venue homepages, word about slam and poetry performance has spread far and wide.

Just about everybody who writes poetry eventually finds him or herself in front of a computer screen, and just about every computer screen is hooked up to the net. So get wired and create your own personal web page. Here's why:

◆ **It's fast**—Say you get a gig in Taos a week from Monday. You can update your website immediately with all the info. All your fans in Taos see you're coming to their neck of the woods, and hopefully they'll come to check out your set.

◆ **It's effective**—A website is another way for you to present yourself to your public and prospective employers. Hoards of people prowl the web for information. A website gives you a shot at reaching these people.

◆ **It's relatively inexpensive**—Some services actually allow you to set up a free site, but they're usually loaded with pop-ups and give you little artistic leeway. Your best bet is to pay the fee for registering your own unique domain name (typically less than 50 bucks) and go buck wild. If you don't know how to design and maintain a website, check out *The Complete Idiot's Guide to Creating a Web Page*, by Paul McFedries.

◆ **It's hot, it's hip**—A lot, and I do mean a *lot*, of poets lurk around online. Whether they're updating their own sites, chatting in chat rooms or in online poetry forums, or checking scores from the latest bout at Nationals, any poet who's interested in following what's happening in the world of poetry is online. You can connect with these people, make new friends, score gigs and, maybe most important, score places to stay in the towns where you land gigs.

> **Dig This!**
>
> Think carefully about your web page background and overall design. If you use images of Aztec pyramids as your page background, that says something about you. If you use images of dancing cats as your background, that says something entirely different. Either one is fine—just recognize who you're trying to appeal to and why.

Structuring Your Website

You can use the material in your press pack to structure your site. Your opening page should include one or two photos of you, a brief biography, and links to some sample poems, audio clips, press clippings, and maybe even a video clip of one of your best performances. If you have any future performances lined up, be sure to include dates and times and the addresses of the venues. Consider including a link for your e-mail address, so fans and organizers can easily contact you.

> **Backstage Skinny**
>
> Maintain your website and add to it regularly to keep 'em coming back for more. If your site remains stagnant, your fans will have no reason to revisit.

Shortly after posting your site, visit it yourself to make sure it looks as good as it did when you created it and to ensure that all the links work. Fix any problems immediately; otherwise, visitors might become so frustrated trying to navigate the site that they never get to the good stuff.

Backstage Skinny

Be generous. If you respect another poet's work or are impressed by a particular venue, add a link to that poet or venue's website to show your appreciation. As other poets experience your generosity, they will begin to return the favor and help promote your site.

Dig This!

The media gets quite a kick out of the slam, and that won't change any time soon. Remember: If you want to be a professional poet, you'd better be sticking your mug in front of that camera as much as possible—this is no time to shun the paparazzi. For some strange reason, people think a photographed poet is more intriguing than an unphotographed one.

Promoting Your Website

Just as you must get the word out about yourself and your performances, you need to spread the word about your site. Mention your website in your press packet, so slammasters and club owners can check it out. Include your website address on *all* of your promotional materials, as well—flyers, posters, CDs, press releases, whatever. Add it to all your e-mail correspondence, paint it on the side of your car, airbrush it on your t-shirts, tattoo it on your forehead. Okay, I'm getting a little carried away, but you get the idea—promote your website, so it can promote your work.

If you know other performance poets who have websites, ask them to include links on their sites that point to your site. In addition, some search sites, such as Yahoo!, allow users to recommend sites to be included in their database. (Check the bottom of the opening Yahoo! page for a link that pulls up a page telling you what to do.) By adding your site to the database, it's more likely that a link for your site will pop up when someone searches for your name or for a general phrase such as "slam poetry."

Generating Stories, Interviews, and Media Attention

You've gotten your press pack together, you've set up a few gigs, and you have a super website so all your fans (current and future) can access up-to-the-minute information about you. The next step? Publicity.

Contrary to popular belief, news cameras and journalists don't possess some innate skill that allows them to find the Next Big Thing. They need to be coaxed and reminded about it constantly. Part of your job as the Next Big Thing is to alert them to your presence and sell yourself to them, just as you sold yourself to the proprietor of the place where you scored your latest gig.

Why do you want the press at your gig? Because they produce pictures and copy that a lot of people see—a lot more people than are going to fit into Bessie's Bean House. Articles, pictures, and interviews give you street credibility and some valuable materials to stuff in your press pack. And you get to feel like a star, which is always good for morale. The formula for press attention is simple: Write a press release, send it out, and follow up with a phone call. The following sections provide the details.

Step 1: Write a Press Release

This, above all else, should be short and sweet. It's your bio, a bit about what you're doing in town, and the location of the gig. Never write a press release that's longer than a single page—they won't read it. If they want more information, they'll call you. Just make sure you include your contact information on the press release.

Step 2: Send the Press Release

The obvious step to take after writing your press release is to send it out. The most difficult aspect of this step is deciding when to send it. If you send a press release too early (a month before you appear somewhere), the newsroom/features editor might lose it or junk it because it's not relevant at that second. Wait a week or two weeks before the performance, and be sure to send it to the right person. Poetry slam press releases are certainly more suited to the Arts & Entertainment editor than to the Classifieds editor. (If you're sending the press release to a magazine, they might need a little more lead time.) Check the newspaper or magazine's website for a fax number, mailing address, or e-mail address of the department or editor you want to target, or call the office to obtain the information.

Step 3: Call 'Em

You don't want to be a nuisance, but a few days before your gig, call the newspaper office and remind them about your gig. Invite the journalist to come, and provide her with some enticement—that's a fancy word for "bribe" (free cover charge?). The worst she can do is hang up on you. The best she can do is come to the show, enjoy your performance, and generate positive press about you and the show. The venue owner and the slammaster will be happy because they got some media attention and free advertising. The journalist will be happy because she's got a cool story. And you'll be happy because you're famous. Well, kind of.

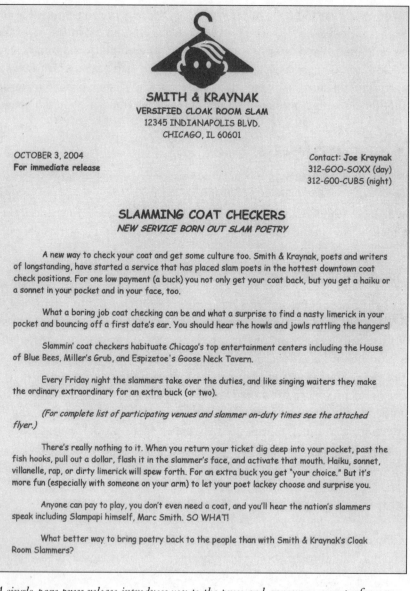

SMITH & KRAYNAK
VERSIFIED CLOAK ROOM SLAM
12345 INDIANAPOLIS BLVD.
CHICAGO, IL 60601

OCTOBER 3, 2004
For immediate release

Contact: **Joe Kraynak**
312-GOO-SOXX (day)
312-GOO-CUBS (night)

SLAMMING COAT CHECKERS
NEW SERVICE BORN OUT SLAM POETRY

A new way to check your coat and get some culture too. Smith & Kraynak, poets and writers of longstanding, have started a service that has placed slam poets in the hottest downtown coat check positions. For one low payment (a buck) you not only get your coat back, but you get a haiku or a sonnet in your pocket and in your face, too.

What a boring job coat checking can be and what a surprise to find a nasty limerick in your pocket and bouncing off a first date's ear. You should hear the howls and jowls rattling the hangers!

Slammin' coat checkers habituate Chicago's top entertainment centers including the House of Blue Bees, Miller's Grub, and Espizetoe's Goose Neck Tavern.

Every Friday night the slammers take over the duties, and like singing waiters they make the ordinary extraordinary for an extra buck (or two).

(For complete list of participating venues and slammer on-duty times see the attached flyer.)

There's really nothing to it. When you return your ticket dig deep into your pocket, past the fish hooks, pull out a dollar, flash it in the slammer's face, and activate that mouth. Haiku, sonnet, villanelle, rap, or dirty limerick will spew forth. For an extra buck you get "your choice." But it's more fun (especially with someone on your arm) to let your poet lackey choose and surprise you.

Anyone can pay to play, you don't even need a coat, and you'll hear the nation's slammers speak including Slampapi himself, Marc Smith. SO WHAT!

What better way to bring poetry back to the people than with Smith & Kraynak's Cloak Room Slammers?

A single-page press release introduces you to the press and announces your performance and the location of the gig.

Work Your Angle

Just as every city poet needs a city poem, every journalist needs an angle. How should a reporter from the *Blandsville Bugle* write about a poetry slam when he's usually writing up the minutes from the City Council meeting on street cleaning? He has to make his story relevant to his audience, put an intriguing spin on it. In your press release, or in your phone conversation with the reporter, you should think about what angle he could take in his story. If he's any good, he'll figure this out, but it never hurts to point the reporter in the desired direction. Maybe your poems are representative of a place nothing like Blandsville and you're bringing a new voice to town. Maybe you grew up in a town like Blandsville and you feel as though you're coming home. Think about what your audience would be interested in—again, remember the secret rule of marketing: Put yourself in the other gal's shoes.

> **Dig This!**
>
> For years journalists have used the angle of Marc Smith, a construction-worker-turned-poet, as the lead-in to articles about his creation, the slam. It's a hook, this juxtaposition of contrasting images, that piques a person's interest.

Hit the Airwaves

When you're looking for press coverage, don't lock your focus on the printed word; send your press release to radio and TV stations as well. Consider including an audio recording (for radio stations) or a video clip (for TV stations). If you can land a brief spot on radio or TV (and you can make it to the studio), you have a great opportunity to reach a potentially large audience. Short of that, the station might play one of your clips or at least announce the date, time, and location of your performance.

If you're at a venue where a TV crew or radio broadcasting team is swarming about anyway, talk to them. If your best friend works at the Public Access station in town, make an appearance. Even if no one watches, you can record your bit and add it to your library of promotional materials.

Press the Flesh

You've flashed the press. Now it's time to press the flesh—hit the streets and start meeting fans, press, venue owners, and slam organizers face to face. A super way to promote your work in person is to attend special events. If a big poetry or arts fair is coming to town, you'd better be there passing out fliers, promoting your website, talking up your latest project, and so on. Events like the Taos Poetry Circus and the National Poetry Slam are two events where poets and fans swarm like bees to honey. What better place to meet people and introduce yourself to the press? Getting media attention is relatively easy, assuming you're relentless in your pursuit; if you push your product enough and in the right way, they'll start coming to you.

The Least You Need to Know

- ◆ Whether you want to inspire and entertain people with your poetry or make a buck as a performance poet, you must advertise and market yourself.

- ◆ To develop a successful marketing strategy, put yourself in the other gal's shoes.

- ◆ Your press pack should include your biography, one or two action photos of yourself, a resumé of your past performances, two to three sample poems, a cassette or CD with three or so audio recordings of your performance, and a VHS tape or DVD with at least one video clip of your performance.

- ◆ Because most slam poets and enthusiasts hang out on the web, you should create and maintain a website that focuses on your poetry and skills as a performer.

- ◆ A couple weeks before your gig, type up a one-page press release and send it to every media source in that town or city, including newspapers, radio stations, and TV stations.

Chapter 10

Taking Your Show on the Road

In This Chapter

- ◆ Planning your very own slam poetry tour

- ◆ Advertising your tour to attract hordes hungry for poetry

- ◆ Honing your people skills to deal effectively with club owners, slammasters, and stage crews

- ◆ Avoiding common pitfalls that can undercut the success of even the most dynamic performance

- ◆ Getting your fair share of the proceeds

Most performance poets sleep on couches or on mildewed futons in the backs of vans while touring from coast to coast. Very few of us are lucky enough to travel the world and stay in four-star hotels with silk sheets and linen napkins, performing in front of sold-out concert halls, and coming home with more dough in our pockets than when we left.

A handful of slammers have gone on to careers in the movies and on television, achieving legitimate star status. But for most slammers, 99 percent of them, the world they perform in is a semi-professional arena that reaches heights unheard of in other amateur forums, but which doesn't qualify as the celebrity pro bowl. Still, slammers gig around; and like most fledgling entertainers, they need to know the biz as well as everyone else. This section gives you what you need to know, whether you are a troubadour slammer on the steps of a library or a budding poet laureate jostling the podium at the Lincoln Center.

Tour Planning 101

You have a press pack and a website. Reporters know your face, your name, and your work. You've been performing your act more often than you call your mother (go call your mother). You have a healthy stack of killer poems. And you've polished your act through tireless, torturous rehearsals. You can take center stage at any venue, perform unshaken in front of the most unruly audience … and knock 'em dead. You're so confident, in fact, that you're beginning to lose your taste for the local fare. Now might be the right time for you to take your show on the road—set up a tour for yourself. The following sections lead you through the basics of setting up your tour and marketing it to ensure its success.

Whoa!

Should you go on tour? The answer to this question should be pretty easy. If you know plenty of slammasters and plenty of poets in various towns, if you have a chapbook or other merchandise to sell, if you can afford to take off work for the duration of your tour, and if you can stand performing your poetry every night for several weeks straight, then go for it. If you answered "no" to any of those questions, stay home and get some more practice under your belt.

Step 1: Route Your Tour

The first step in planning your tour is to pick a general geographical location. Do you want to do a mini East Coast Tour? West Coast? Midwest, maybe? The area should be one where you know at least a few venues and you won't have to drive halfway across the country to get from one venue to the next. Do you know any club owners or slam organizers in this area who book featured performers? Whom do they know? Talk to the club owners and slam organizers and start networking to find out what's available in the area. If they mention slams you've never heard of, go ahead and write those down and get some contact information.

Next, plot the most sensible date-to-date path you might take if you scored features in every slam on your list. How long does it take to get from one venue to the next? It would be a shame to schedule a slam in San Francisco and then have to leave in the middle of the night to drive to ~~~~ Mexico the following evening. Think ~~~~ sting.

Plot an efficient route from one venue to the next.

Step 2: Score Some Gigs

Lining up gigs takes time. If it's April and you want to go on tour in May, you're probably too late. Give yourself and the venue time to book the gigs and time to line up backup performers. If this is your first contact with a particular club owner or slam organizer, send the person your press pack and give the person some time to review it. Club owners and slam organizers also need time to incorporate your information into their promotional materials.

Be gracious and thankful to the people who know and love you and book you on the spot. Above all, follow up with these venues the week before you're scheduled to perform. Provide them with a detailed itinerary, including the dates, times, and locations of your performances and contact information (cell phone or phone numbers of places where you'll be staying). Don't let a miscommunication or a scheduling snafu undermine a valuable opportunity to perform—you're a poor poet and can't afford to miss a chance to shine, or to sell your act, books, and CDs, right? Right. If you're driving, get a good map of the area(s), and make sure to pack clean underwear. You never know who you'll meet on the road.

Step 3: Get a Ride

Unless you're planning on doing a walking tour, you need some mode of transportation to get where you're going. If you have a *reliable* car, great. If you have a magical pass that lets you ride free on airplanes, even better. Short of that, all sorts of options are available: Greyhound busses, trains, rental cars, even hitchhiking. I'm not about to recommend riding the boxcars, but that's certainly another way of getting around the country. Touring poets have used all of these travel modes at some time or another.

Backstage Skinny

Most organizers want to see their feature in the flesh at least an hour before that feature goes on. They want to know that you arrived safely, that you're well, and that you still plan on performing. Calculate that one-hour grace period into your travel time. If you perform at 9:00 P.M. at the Nuyorican, plan on being there at 8:00 P.M. or earlier, or you might lose the gig and tarnish your reputation.

Transportation will be your biggest expense, so consider all the options. Trains are certainly romantic and appeal to many poets, but buses are cheaper and can provide you with more than enough material to write about (that is, if you can tune out the guy snoring in the seat next to you). Of course, if you take a plane, train, or bus, you'll need a ride from the station to the venue, as well. Be sure to line up something well in advance. It helps if you have friends or relatives in the towns where you'll be performing.

Step 4: Find a Place to Sleep and Shower

Vagrancy is no fun. The police hassle you, the locals avoid you, and unless you can find a place to wash up, after a few days you start to smell funny … and that's no way to impress people. Before you set out on your tour, arrange accommodations for each night you'll be on tour. Motels can get expensive, campgrounds (with showers) can be scarce and located far from the venues, and sleeping in your car gets old really fast.

This is one of those times when nice guys come in first. If you've been nice and sweet to every poet, club owner, slammaster, and patron you've ever met,

Backstage Skinny

You might be a bohemian poet, but that doesn't make you a barbarian. Bring your host(s) a bottle of wine or offer to pay for the pizza. Use good manners, don't trash the place, and be sure to thank your host(s) for their hospitality.

chances are much better that someone you know will let you crash on their couch when you're in town for a performance. E-mail your friends and acquaintances, call them, call the venue. Many slammasters are incredibly generous and kind people and often offer housing suggestions (or their own couch) right away to incoming performers. Although these accommodations might not be the most comfortable, they're usually free, and they offer the added bonus of enabling you to spend quality time with fellow slammers.

Step 5: Marketing Your Tour

After you've got your 6-date, 20-date, or year-long tour booked, you need to market it, just like you marketed yourself to kick-start your slam career in the first place. Send out your handy-dandy press release. Announce your tour plans on poet *listservs*.

Work with the promoters and the owners of the venue to make sure they're working as hard as you are to get the word out. Several weeks before your tour, you should print flyers (ones you think will get people's attention) with the specific dates you'll be appearing at the different venues. Mail the flyers to the owners of the venues and ask them to post the flyers a week before you arrive. It'll show them you're serious about all this and it will generate buzz for you and the show.

SlamSlang

A **listserv** is an automated mailing list on the Internet. Poetry listservs contain the names and e-mail addresses of people who want to receive up-to-date news, announcements, and information about poetry and poetry events. When you send an announcement to a listserv, the listserv automatically broadcasts it, via e-mail, to everyone on the list.

Contact radio stations in the area and sell yourself as a good story for them, too. The slammasters can probably help you with this and steer you toward local stations that show an interest in slam.

Let people know you're coming. Market your tour like a maniac. You worked diligently to establish yourself and your act. You invested loads of time in planning your tour, scoring gigs, and lining up transportation and accommodations. When you hit the road, you'll be paying out some serious cash in travel expenses. So don't undercut the success of your tour by failing to let people know about it. Attract as many patrons as possible. Pack the seats. Give the venue's proprietor a standing-room-only crowd. The proprietor will beam with joy, and you'll have plenty of customers lined up to purchase your merchandise. Everybody wins.

Schmoozing the Bookers, the Waiters, the Ticket Takers

Well, you did it. You got your proverbial foot in the door. Now, you need to develop a velvet tongue and a generous demeanor in order to make all those people who booked you delighted to have you perform in their town. You need to know how to treat these people and their volunteers and employees with the respect they deserve. In short, you need to work on your people skills. The following sections describe the various roles people play, from the slammaster to the club owner to the service worker, in order to help you develop genuine people skills.

Slams and Their Masters

Local slams are organized and staged by what we call slammasters. These are the people who have convinced venue owners that poetry is good for business (not an easy thing to do) and good for their souls. They check to be sure that the lights are on and the doors are open. They arrange for some kind of stage and sound system. They design, print, and pass out a million flyers without passing out themselves. They recruit emcees and volunteers and persuade newspaper and radio reporters to cover their events. They find lodging for visitors, beers for boozers, pop for the youngsters, and coffees all around. They listen to everybody complain.

They are the barons and baronesses of their fiefdoms, and some keep tight control on what goes down at their show. Treat them with great respect and show your appreciation. Most have been in your shoes and know all about the perils of performing better than you. They know how to run their shows. A good slammaster does everything she can to give you the best opportunity to succeed. It serves her self-interest to do so. Some get personal and show you around town. Some pay for dinner and give you a bed. They are, or should be, your best ally. They care deeply about performance poetry and the poetry slam movement. You can form long-lasting friendships with slammasters. Bow and kiss their feet if you have to.

> **Dig This!**
>
> Most slammasters have a fixed format into which they plug their performers like a homily in a church service or the best man's toast at a wedding. One of the best ways to demonstrate your respect is to show up early and be prepared.

Nightclub Owners and Their Managers

Most club owners and managers do not have the same enthusiasm for slam as the slammasters do. They often greet new prospects with gruff indifference. Don't take it personally. Club owners have seen and heard it all before. In one year, a major club owner books over 300 different acts. He handles crowds from 50 to 500, sometimes 1,000 … weekly. They're constantly worried about people stealing their stuff, breaking their stuff, breaking each other's heads, and (if it's a bar) losing their liquor licenses. They have little patience for irresponsible behavior, careless mistakes, and self-important people. They've heard every lame excuse ten times over. Don't try to manipulate a club owner. Deal with them straight up. Most of them have gotten into the business for the same reason you're slammin'. It's their passion, and they don't want anything or anyone messin' it up.

Club managers are another story. They're middle management. To most of them, especially new hires, it's a job. And they do as middle-management does in any industry—they put in their time and cover their ass. They are used to dealing with bands, not poets, and won't understand the specific requirements of a performance poetry show. You look like a big headache to them. For the most part, they're concerned with getting a good ring on the cash register and sailing through the evening with no disasters. Often they wonder how their boss could be so dumb as to book a poetry act.

Of course, that's too general a view. There are some club managers who are golden. They have had pleasurable experiences with slammers, appreciate the professionalism of performance poets, and lay out the red carpet. Compared to bad rock and roll, even bad spoken word can be a relief. In either case, give the club managers what they need—first and foremost, an outstanding performance. Be good to their employees, don't cause problems, don't incite a riot, and do show appreciation for anything the manager does to make your performance more enjoyable and successful.

Backstage Skinny _____

When working in clubs, make friends with the servers immediately. Learn their names. Buy your first drink. Tip them heavy. The success or failure of your engagement could very well be held in balance by their attitude toward you. Nothing can kill a spoken-word performance quicker than the repeated bang of a cash register drawer or a waitress taking an order in a VERY LOUD VOICE. An audience gets a subtle cue from the servers; if they're interested and respectful, it tells the audience, "This is a good act." If they're rolling their eyes and flinging empties into the bottle shoot, you might want to finish up your set and scoot.

Buttering Up the Booking Agents

Fifteen years ago the notion of having booking agents for performance poets was unheard of. Not now. Increasingly slammers find a good chunk of work through independent agents who book literary speakers/entertainers for universities, secondary schools, cultural centers, and festivals.

As with every profession, you have competent and incompetent booking agents. Horror stories of incompetent booking agents abound. There's the one about the middle-man booking agent collecting fees for major engagements and then never passing the money onto the artist. Another common true story has the incompetent agent booking engagements on the wrong day in the wrong town for the wrong event. You showed up in drag for the Erotic Slam on August 15 only to find out that you were booked for the Haiku Slam on August 14! Boy, was that organizer pissed when you showed up at her office a day late looking like Barbara Streisand.

On the other hand, experienced agents, the good ones, can make your dream come true. Some performance poets work throughout the year chalking up five, ten, even fifteen well-paying gigs in a single month. What you should keep foremost in your mind about agents is that to them you're a commodity. If you sell, they'll work hard for you. If you don't, it's see ya later. Very few agents are altruistic art lovers who want to help keep the starving artist from returning to his day job. Always check the reputation and the details of the work an agent does for you. Don't assume he's going to handle details like making sure the sound equipment is working and that a table is available for your merchandise. Most would only feign sympathy while listening to you complain that the program listed you as the now deceased performance poet Mac Smoth (So Was) or that the hotel lodging consisted of a cabin with an outhouse.

Concert Halls—Performing in the Big House

Your career is galloping along and your friendly professional agent has booked you a dream engagement at the Eagle Mount Art Center or the Alexander Hamilton Opera House, with seating for 1,000 plus. Your contracts are signed and you've secured some comfortable lodgings. You're flying first class, cross continental, exhilarated to have finally made it as a real performing artist. Brace yourself. You're about to fly through some turbulent skies and find out how insignificant you really are.

Major concert halls are managed by staffs that have catered to some of the world's top entertainers—Elton John, Willie Nelson, Pearl Jam. Your gig is filler to them. No performance poets (as yet) have come close to the star power that the big houses deal with. You're a lightning bug to them. They will treat you with courtesy and general respect, but your stature in the slam world or the literary awards you've won won't impress them. While you're bubbling with anticipation, they're watching the clock. And if you don't tell them specifically what you need, the curtain will rise and you'll look like a deer in the headlights.

As with clubs, it's important to make friends and treat everyone from the queen bee on down to the worker bees with dignity, but it's more important to do your homework and communicate your needs clearly. Do some research before climbing aboard that jet plane. Most big houses have lengthy contracts packed with technical information. Read the contract. Talk personally with the stage manager about lighting and sound requirements. If you're on the program with other acts, find out about their setups. Can you modify your needs to simplify the transition between performances?

After you know what you need, you must communicate your needs clearly to the technical crew. The people you deal with at concert halls are professionals. They're busy, they know their stuff, and they're literal. Tell them exactly where you want that microphone placed onstage. Tell them precisely where you want the spotlight to shine. Don't be bossy about it, but communicate clearly and directly, and carefully consider their suggestions. If they tell you that an idea of yours won't work, it probably won't work. If you insist on having it your way, they're likely to clam up, do it exactly as you instructed, and then have a good laugh backstage when your act bombs because you didn't listen to them.

Your main contact will most likely be the program director. This person typically is the one person who cares if the show goes well; the rest are just doing their jobs. If you're having trouble communicating with the technical crew, track down the program director and try working through her.

By the time your career propels you to a big stage it most certainly will involve more than just you going solo in front of a microphone. Your act might contain music, slide shows, dancers, and who knows what. All this requires coordination, and if you're the leader, you're the one who has to develop a plan and relate the plan clearly to the tech people, usually in a two-hour, pre-show rehearsal. Be nice, be clear, and listen to their recommendations. The big house staff can make you or break you.

SlamSlang

Call time is a theater term that designates the hour and minute when you're expected to arrive at the theater for the night's performance. You either sign in or inform the stage manager that you're there. After you're there, remain available. You're under the stage manager's charge and direction.

If you're scheduled to perform at a theater or concert hall, expect a *call time* or sound check several hours prior to your performance.

Don't Get Set Up to Fail

Whether you perform at Radio City Music Hall or Smoky Jane's Bar and Grill, follow one simple rule: *Don't get set up to fail.* Don't let anything or anybody for any reason screw up your performance. It's difficult enough to succeed onstage without having to battle screeching sound-system feedback or lighting that makes you look like Bela Lugosi. This is your performance, so it's your responsibility to make sure it works. To ensure the success of your performance, you need to do two things: deal with any personality quirks you might encounter and anticipate any potential problems that might arise. You're not going to do it perfectly. Don't even expect anything close to perfection. The best you can hope for is that you'll keep most of the monkeys in the closet and catch a few of the wretches that fly by. To avoid some of the more common pitfalls, check the following:

- Does the owner know you're coming? Check a couple weeks before the gig and then once again a day before your performance.

- Has the show been advertised properly; is your name printed correctly?

- Are the doors open? You might be surprised.

- Has someone prepared the stage, cleaned it, cleared it? Is there a stage? What happened to it?

- Is the stage lighting working? Is there someone there to turn it on and run it?

- Is the sound system working? (This is a biggie, the area that always gets mangled.) Has the sound system been set at the proper levels? Has someone done a sound check?

- Is there an opening act? What kind of act is it? Do the poems you selected provide a proper follow-up for the opening act? When do you take the stage? Find out who's performing before you and who's performing after you. Check the schedule.

- Is there an open mike before your show? If there is, how long is it scheduled to last? If an open mike is scheduled before your performance, ask the slammaster or promoter to adhere to a reasonable time limit. If you get an inkling that the open mike is going to be a drawn-out free-for-all, or that the organizer considers it more important than your performance, prepare for the worst. Unregulated open mikes can drain the last drop of interest out of an audience, and even a brilliant performance will not refresh it.

Getting Paid

You just gave the performance of your life to a packed house of cheering fans. The patrons' hard-earned cash is flowing into the club owner's coffers, and the club owner is beaming. You delivered. Now it's time to collect.

In most cases, the person who booked you conscientiously seeks you out and pays you on the spot. Sometimes they seem to be more concerned about your getting paid than you are. I've done more than 2,000 performances over 18 years and have been stiffed only a handful of times, but when it does happen, it stings.

Backstage Skinny _____

Get payment details up front, before you show up for your engagement. How much will they pay you? How will they pay you? Cash or check? When will they pay you? Immediately after you perform? A week later? Two months later? Having specific payment details up front makes it much easier to confront someone when he fails to pay you the agreed-upon amount on time in the form you expected.

To avoid the pain, keep in mind that this is business. The club owner got her cut; now it's time for you to get your share. You don't have to be a jerk about it, but don't be shy or avoid a confrontation just because it's a little awkward. People don't pay for one of two reasons: Either they forgot or they planned all along to pimp you. In either case, you should approach him and politely ask for your money. If he forgot to pay you, he'll appreciate the fact that you reminded him instead of complaining behind his back or launching a negative campaign against him on the Internet. If he knowingly avoided paying you, then you have every right (almost a duty to yourself and your fellow performing artists) to confront him and get your money.

When you find yourself standing around, unpaid, for an hour after your engagement and see the money man laughingly hitting on some beautiful fan of yours downing cocktails, it's time to walk over, notion him aside, and ask, "Are you the person that takes care of the money?" or "I thought I was supposed to be paid right after I finished?" He should jump to it. And if he doesn't, climb the ladder up to the top dog. Don't leave a club engagement without pursuing every avenue. After you're out the door it gets tougher and tougher to secure your dough. If the person knowingly tried to stiff you, it's easier to shame the person face-to-face than by e-mail.

SlamSpeak _____

MONEY

Workers earn it.
Spendthrifts burn it.
Bankers lend it.
Women spend it.
Forgers fake it.
Taxes take it.
The dying leave it.
The heirs receive it.
The thrifty save it.
Misers crave it.
Bartenders ring it.
Waitresses bring it.
I could use it!
I could use a little money.

—Anonymous

What's on the CD

CD #1 track #8: Marc Smith and the Pong Unit Band performing "Money"

Dig This!

Slammers typically get paid $50 to $200 for club work or $500 to $2,000 for institutional work. It all depends on the venue that engages you. Local musicians can give you a good idea of what to expect. The trials and terrors of making it as a local musician is very much akin to what the semi-professional slam poet faces.

Some larger organizers pay by check after the fact, usually a week to a couple months later. Most of the time they tell you this in advance, but not always. If the check doesn't arrive when it was promised, call and bug the organizer. Big institutions hardly ever screw a performer out of money, but they do at times drag their feet.

If you're contracted to do a performance that involves travel and lodging expenses, get all this settled in writing beforehand. If there's a mix-up at the hotel and the clerk doesn't have a record of your room being billed directly to the promoter, don't pull out the credit card and plan to clear it up later. Have the clerk call your contact person and settle it then and there, before you check in.

Getting paid as a performer involves the same common sense practiced in all matters of life. It's tempting to suppose that artistic people are somehow nobler than the rest of the world; they're not. Be watchful and get paid every penny you deserve.

The Least You Need to Know

♦ To plan your tour, determine a route, score some gigs, get a ride, line up places to stay, and then fire up your marketing machine.

♦ When dealing with club owners, slammasters, ticket takers, servers, and others on the road, be genuinely nice by understanding where they're coming from and by delivering what they need.

♦ When performing at a large venue, such as a concert hall, clearly communicate your needs to the stage crew and other technical staff.

♦ To avoid common pitfalls that can ruin your performance, learn to deal properly with people and anticipate any potential catastrophes.

♦ Find out ahead of time who's going to pay you, how much, when, and in what form (cash or check), and then don't leave a venue until you are paid the agreed-upon amount.

Chapter 11

Old-School Advice: Act Professional

In This Chapter

- Debunking the negative connotations surrounding the term "professional"
- Learning proper poetry slam etiquette
- Achieving professionalism through careful planning and preparation
- Acquiring the confidence of a professional performing artist
- Selling your chapbooks, CDs, and t-shirts without stepping on someone's toes

The term "professional" carries some serious negative connotations with the bohemian poet crowd. "Professional" conjures up images of corporate America, suit-and-tie society, button-down, right-wing conservatives—*The establishment!* "Professional" implies a eunuch who blindly follows orders and willingly and daily sacrifices his imagination and vision for the greater good of capitalism. Call a poet "professional," and you're liable to get punched in the face.

This chapter attempts to strip away those negative connotations and present the professional performance poet as the model for all slam poets. This model poet hasn't traded imagination for a suit and tie. She doesn't kiss up to the establishment. She hasn't "sold out." On the contrary, the model poet achieves a meaningful coolness by demonstrating daily, in all her actions, dignity, integrity, honesty, generosity, diplomacy, and a host of other admirable qualities. She makes a promise; she keeps it. She borrows money; she pays it back promptly. She says she's going to meet you at eight o'clock; she's there at seven fifty-five waiting for you. She rocks the house with her performance, gets a lousy score from the judges, and shrugs it off instead of storming offstage.

Of course, even the most professional poet can slip, but if you follow the guidelines in this chapter, you can develop an aura of professionalism that will help you succeed in slam poetry and in all of your other endeavors.

Oh, Behave!

At a poetry slam, the way you behave as an open-mike poet, audience member, slammaster, featured performer, or competitor forms the impression people have of you. If you throw down the mike after receiving a low score, the club owner and slam organizer will never invite you back, the audience will shut you out, and word of mouth might end an otherwise promising slam career. If you heckle another poet who's performing onstage, you come off looking like a jerk and invite the same treatment when you take the stage.

> **Dig This!**
>
> Most slams specify their own socially acceptable ways to criticize a performance, such as finger-snapping at the Green Mill. When you visit an unfamiliar venue, learn its customs as if you were visiting a foreign country. Don't assume that what's acceptable at one venue is okay at another.

Of course, this doesn't mean that you should sit still, hands folded neatly in your lap, and remain perfectly quiet during a performance. That would go against everything slam stands for. Slam was built on the concept that sharing poetry is important, and sharing one's opinion about poetry is important, too. But common decency overrides your freedom of speech. Express your opinion tastefully and respectfully. Don't be obnoxious and do not do or say anything that's demeaning to the performing poet. The following sections provide specific guidelines on how to behave properly at a poetry slam.

Keep It Down During a Performance

Nothing exposes the rank amateur faster than loud talking during someone else's performance. The audience has to strain to hear the performance over the vocal commotion at the end of the bar or pouring in from the lobby. The pros are guilty of this, too, but they usually catch themselves and shut up. The self-centered amateur keeps on no matter how many glares come his way or how many people shush him. In short, keep it down.

Backstage Skinny

If you have a cell phone, turn it off during the performances or put it in vibration mode (assuming your cell phone has a vibration mode).

Don't Pull Focus While Others Are Performing

It doesn't take noise to disrupt a performance. Sometimes amateurs (and a few mean-spirited pros) hamper a performance without spilling a word. Instead, they draw audience attention silently, like ill-mannered mimes. They do the equivalent of arriving late at a wedding wearing a gorgeous white dress and scooting down the aisle just as the processional music begins. Don't swagger into a poetry slam with great fanfare and flourish when others are onstage. It's just plain rude. And don't stand conspicuously adjacent to the stage smoking your pipe or adopting some other pose while someone else is trying to deliver the goods. Take your place quietly and draw no notice. Be wallpaper until your moment comes.

Don't Glower

Certain slam circles employ an obnoxious strategy designed to diminish another slammer's chance of obtaining a fair score from the judges. A team of competitors and their friends sit in front of their opponent and no matter how good the performance is, even if it's mind-blowing and house-rocking, they sit with their arms crossed over their chests and scowl. To the performers it's like having a sea of disapproving English professors placed before them. It dampens their spirit. It confuses the audience's intuitive response to what they've experienced and it deprives everyone of the communal transcendence that a great performance can generate. It's cheap and dishonest. Don't do it.

No Hoot-and-Holler Cheerleading

Speaking of cheap and dishonest, some slammers have adopted another sinister tactic that's the flip side of the glower—cheerleading. Cheerleading is not (on its surface) damaging to the performer; it's damaging to the show. It's premeditated group canned laughter that distorts the picture to gain undeserved praise and high scores. Most veteran audience members sense the distortion, but new folks and the judges sometimes buckle under the peer pressure and join in with the false applause. We've all been to theatrical performances where the house has been papered with friends to impress the critics. The cheerleaders in these situations laugh at all the jokes, good and bad. Nobody's fooled. In fact, most are annoyed. They won't be back. They get enough dishonesty at the office.

Keep Conspicuous Negative Opinions to Yourself

When you're in a position of power as a poet or organizer, your actions and voice are magnified sevenfold by your status and reputation … whether you like it or not. Even if you try to be self-deprecating, your opinion carries more weight than the opinion of someone who is not actively involved in the slam. The poet you boo or bad-mouth can be irrevocably hurt and damaged by any indiscreet and overly negative pronouncements. You might not like the poem or the performance of it, but don't crucify the poet over it. Even the most spectacular performance poet occasionally bombs, and amateurs who fail in their early attempts often go on to become exceptional poets and performers.

SlamSpeak

The Scholars
Bald heads forgetful
of their sins,
Old learned, respectable bald
heads
Edit and annotate the lines
That young men, tossing on their
beds,
Rhymed out in love's despair
To flatter beauty's ignorant ear.

—William Butler Yeats

Being vocally critical of an amateur performer is like scolding a child for not reading perfectly the first time. The slam family is not about discouraging others; it's about encouraging and empowering its poets and performers.

If that's not convincing enough, think of yourself. One day the poet you criticized so boldly in public could be holding the strings to your next performance. If you gain a reputation for pompously slinging mud at whomever you opine to be inferior, you'll acquire an army of enemies that will stand guard against your entrance to the circles they control. You can dislike someone's work—that's human—but try to separate the poem and the performance from the poet whenever possible. Don't let it get personal.

It's Not Your House

You're the organizer of a very successful poetry event, the slam everyone loves. Each week more and more people bring new friends to witness the fabulous offbeat entertainment they've discovered. All the preshow tasks are attended to in a timely fashion—the sound is set, the lights are set, the backdrop showing your logo is hung and illuminated, the props for the closing ritual and the table holding the t-shirts and funky prizes are in place. Another magnificent slam is about to begin … You glance up from your well-deserved preshow cocktail to see the guest performer you booked on faith shoving the t-shirt table to the side, plugging a recording device into the sound board, pasting his poster face next to the logo, pushing aside the closing props, and setting a pile of his CDs in their place. Then, three of his friends join him onstage for a photo session. He hasn't even introduced himself to you yet.

Sound like exaggerated fiction? It's not. It has happened. (And that poet will never work at the Green Mill again.)

When playing a venue that's not your own, first check with the organizer before doing anything, no matter how simple the action. (You can use the toilet without asking permission, sometimes.) This is standard practice throughout the performing arts world. In the big houses and concert halls the stage manager fields all requests no matter how trivial they might seem. The organizer's the boss. In clubs it's the manager or the owner. At slams it's the slammaster. The motto is: Ask first and heed the answers you get.

Would You Talk That Way to Grandma?

Many spoken word artists (usually the ones still shockingly wet behind the ears) feel that it's their devil-driven duty as heroic, unheard-of artists to be uncompromisingly explicit in their use of four-letter language and violently sexual subject matter. After all, they are self-appointed defenders of everyone's freedom of speech and would be hypocrites if they were to even slightly bend to the sensibilities of their audience. They won't find much work.

When you're in someone else's living room, club, coffeehouse, or concert center, act accordingly. It is not hypocritical to respect sensibilities. It's mature. It's professional. And if the day comes when your career has taken you to great heights and you wish to risk it all by assuming a stance drastically counter to the status quo—do it. That's courage, to risk all for the sake of a passionate belief. But if a relative nobody with nothing to lose starts flinging four-letter, hate-filled diatribes at an audience merely to test the limits of free speech, get the hook. Better yet, go hook yourself.

Whoa!

Nobody's saying you must put an iron clamp on the foul language. Slammers use quite a frickin' lot of it. But most of the time it reflects the vernacular of their experience, and is part of the message they're trying to convey. Slam would not be slam if all the doors to language were not open.

Be Prepared

You are a professional poet—or you want to be. You want people to take you seriously. But getting taken seriously as a poet is tough. It's much more difficult to accomplish than gaining respect as, say, a brain surgeon. Well, why are brain surgeons regarded as professionals? Probably because they put a lot of time and effort into learning how to do something that not everyone can do and then doing it very well. They weren't born brain surgeons—they worked hard to get into that smock.

If you want people to regard you as a professional poet, you must behave professionally. A brain surgeon wouldn't walk into the operating room twenty minutes late, asking the nurse where to make the first incision. (At least, I hope not.) Likewise, you shouldn't bust into a gig late without the slightest idea what you're going to perform. You plan your set, rehearse your material, prepare for your performance, and then execute flawlessly. Follow these simple rules, as explained in the following sections, and people will see you as you see yourself—as a professional.

Backstage Skinny

When planning your set, pay particular attention to your show opener; it can make or break you. For years I've used "Nightbound" as my ice-breaker. Listen to it on the CD.

What's on the CD

CD #1 track #14: Marc Smith and the Pong Unit Band performing "Nightbound"

SlamSlang

Block is a theater term for mapping out the various actors' positions and movements onstage during a scene.

Have a Plan

A few slam poets wing it at every performance. Some old pros have done their bit so often they don't need a plan anymore. But those who are starting out should lay out their set before arriving at the venue.

If you're a featured poet, the guest performer, you've got a lot to work out before the gig. Most feature sets run from twenty to thirty minutes. If the average poem is three minutes long, that allows you to do between six and ten poems. Prepare them all. *Block* your movements, memorize your lines, and decide on a set order. If you feel too locked in by having a single plan, concoct several. Think about the desired effect on the audience. Do you want to rev 'em up with a spicy love poem at the beginning or save that for the big finale? When will you need to inject some humor into the mix? How many encore poems should you have ready? Before the gig, switch your set around a little to try out different formats. When you arrive at the venue, feel out the crowd. You might have to change your entire set based on the vibe you're picking up from the venue's ambience and the crowd's mood. That's something a professional is ready to do.

Practice Your Performance

We've all forgotten lines—it's inevitable. Heck, most of us have probably forgotten our own names at some point in time. What counts is your ability to recover, and you increase your recovery chances through practice. The difference between a poet who rehearsed his or her butt off and one that mumbled through a few lines while driving to the venue is usually crystal clear: The prepared poet recovers and finishes out the performance. If you mess up a line or forget a word, go on. If you've rehearsed enough, you can usually ad lib without calling attention to your blunder.

You should rehearse every day as instructed in Chapter 6, but especially on the day of a performance. Do it while you're dressing. Do it while you're frying up some eggs. Do it in the shower. Run through your lines at least twice. This will increase your confidence and it will please your audience when they see how smooth you are. It isn't over-doing it to run lines twice in the morning, once in the afternoon, and then one more time a couple hours before an important performance.

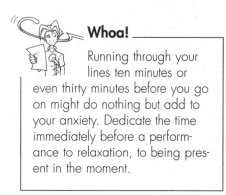

Whoa!

Running through your lines ten minutes or even thirty minutes before you go on might do nothing but add to your anxiety. Dedicate the time immediately before a performance to relaxation, to being present in the moment.

Offstage Preparation: Getting the Nerves Out

All the pros I know have rituals they go through prior to a performance. For years I've been arriving at the Green Mill two hours early to do the most menial tasks. I'm there because if I stayed home I'd get antsy. Some performers take long walks. Some watch TV. Some pace. Some rehearse. Some do relaxation exercises. Find a way to keep your mind off the upcoming performance—some way to calm your nerves.

Any method of meditation can work to relax you. They all have the desired effect of shifting your focus to the moment you're in rather than thinking about the past or, in your case, the future performance. Try the following:

◆ **Physical exercise.** Shake your limbs. Do isometrics—muscle against muscle. Jump up and down. Any physical action stimulates the chemicals in your body that counter anxiety. Even a brisk walk can help.

◆ **Vocal exercises.** Try vocal exercises similar to those singers use. Reciting throw-away lines (something fun but not intended for the performance) will ready your vocal chords and help relieve the stress.

◆ **Be goofy.** Walk like a duck. Swing your arms like a baboon. Run in place. Assume a nutty persona. Sing "Mary Had a Little Lamb." If you've ever spent time backstage of a theater production, you've probably witnessed some bizarre behavior before the curtain went up. It's all about releasing the tension.

Hitting Your Mark

Slammaster Moe has tapped you on the shoulder and cued you that you're going on after the next song plays out on the jukebox. A river of adrenaline courses through your veins. You suddenly realize that the house is packed with people you don't know. They all seem to be frowning. "Oh my God. What am I doing here? I'm a fraud. I never wanted to be a performer in the first place. I just wanted someone to like me." You're not going to hit your mark in this state. You'll probably just trip over the furniture and stammer out an "Uh uh uh uh."

Those minutes and seconds before you utter your first word can be a frightening eternity. You'll most likely recover, but it might take its toll on your emotional well-being. The good news is that this pause before a performance doesn't need to be so traumatic. Get in character, and take control. The following sections offer some tips.

Use Your Nervous Condition to Your Advantage

Are you nervous? You bet you are. Even after a thousand performances, you'll still be nervous. If you're not, you're dead. Just know that you will be nervous no matter what you do to counter it, and use that nervous energy to blast off. Let those nerves take your first words out to the back row, or whisper them to an imagined lover in the first row.

Backstage Skinny

Many slammers don't wait to get to the stage. They begin their performance right in the audience and work their way up to the microphone reciting their opening poem. This can be electric, especially at more traditional poetry events. But be careful, you've just set a high standard for the rest of your performance to live up to. Be sure you can hold that note.

Make the Right Approach

Your performance begins as soon as the emcee announces your name, so the manner in which you approach the stage matters. Approaching too slowly might whither the audience's attention or generate expectations too high for your planned first lines to fulfill. A hasty approach might look ridiculous or make you look like a kook. Your approach should be tuned to the performance that follows. To achieve this, get in character as soon as your name is announced and stay in character until you utter the very last word.

Take the Mike

You're in character. The audience is ready and waiting. Now it's time to take that mike and do your thing. You crafted a great poem, rehearsed it, and became it. Now deliver it.

But not so fast.

When you're standing at the mike you have the power to heighten the suspense or diffuse it. Seize this opportunity. Take a brief moment to assess your surroundings—the lighting, the microphone, the sight lines, and any obstacles (such as posts) standing between you and the audience. Wait until your careful silence quiets the rabble. And then … unleash that poem.

> **Dig This!**
>
> A lot of poets will tell you that the best thing about slams and open mikes are the people they have met in their adventures onstage and off. Slams big and small foster life-long friendships and loving relationships, and those connections should be at the heart of the whole thing.

Respect Your Audience

It's easy to see by now that the audience is your intimate other. If you're not winning them over in some way, at some time, you're doing something wrong. Does that mean you're not brilliant? No, sweetheart, you're just misunderstood and under-appreciated.

That said, if Judge #3 didn't "get" your epic-rhyming-tone-poem about the meaning of life as seen through the eyes of a tadpole, don't take it personally. He didn't like it. Someone else probably did. Well, maybe. The point is, the judge isn't saying *you* are a 2.3 or that *you* are a -.09. He simply didn't get it or didn't like it and judged it according to his knowledge and tastes. Let it go. Don't give him dirty looks, and don't hassle him after the slam. Next week, that same judge might love your performance, so don't burn any bridges. Some slammers get very upset by scores and see wins as big deals and losses as crushing defeats. Scores are just scores. It's just a slam. Everyone wants to have fun, especially the audience, and they paid to get in. If you act like a brat and give others flack for their right to an opinion, you're taking away from their good time—and nobody wants that. Don't let the night turn ugly.

Primping for the Stage

When it comes to the way you dress for a slam poetry performance, the term "professional" drops its highbrow connotations. You don't need to dress in a suit, polish your shoes, straighten your tie, or slip on a pair of panty hose. But you don't want to take the stage looking like an unkempt slob, either. You want to dress appropriately for the venue but in a way that's uniquely you. Do your homework. Check out what the other performers are wearing, do a little soul searching, and come up with a tasteful outfit that's you. And check out the following list of do's and don'ts for specific suggestions:

- If the no-costume rule is in effect, don't wear anything that might be ruled as a costume or prop—a beaver hat, gaudy jewelry, lingerie.

- Don't wear a hat that shades your eyes. You want to make eye contact with your audience.

- Don't wear dark sunglasses. They obscure your eyes, too.

- Fix your hair. That doesn't necessarily mean combing it, but your hair should look like you did something intentional to it.

- Practice basic hygiene. You know what I mean.

- Wash your clothes, and iron them if you need to. Ironing is a good way to calm down before a performance.

Hawking Your Wares

Selling product is a big part of a performance poet's life. Sales help finance your tour and get the word out about your art. They also give your loyal fans a way to experience your work when they're not watching you live. Keep in mind, however, that most people don't enjoy having merchandise shoved down their throats. And many people won't see you as God's gift to slam, no matter how popular you are.

Backstage Skinny

Go to the PSI online store at www. poetryslam.com and take a gander at the variety of products from t-shirts to videos sold by poets in the slam community.

When selling your stuff in clubs take a casual approach. Before you set up your personal slam poetry kiosk in the lobby, check with the management; it's professional courtesy. If you get the okay to lay out some merchandise, ask where and how you should lay out the goods. Don't just grab a table and start packing it full of chapbooks, CDs, t-shirts, and other paraphernalia. And if you're sharing the shelf space with other performers, don't monopolize the space. They need to hawk their wares, too.

The Least You Need to Know

♦ Acting professional does not require you to trade in your soul for a three-piece suit or register as a Republican before the next election.

♦ When another poet is performing, pay attention and don't do anything to detract from the poet's performance.

♦ Planning and preparing thoroughly and well in advance places you in a much better position to confidently deliver a high-quality performance.

♦ Professionalism requires that you treat all those you meet with candor and respect, even if you don't particularly like someone.

♦ Before setting out your chapbooks, CDs, t-shirts, and other paraphernalia for sale, check with the management.

Part 4

Setting the Stage for Yourself and Others

To provide performance poets with a stage, or at least keep them off the streets, volunteers contribute their time and talents to organize and host poetry slams. Though their efforts may earn them no monetary reward, these hard-working folks receive the gratitude of the performers and the satisfaction of having created their own performance art—the show itself.

This part teaches you how to host a poetry slam in your neighborhood. Here you learn everything you need to know to put together a killer show: how to scope out potential venues, organize volunteers, line up performers, plan your show, publicize, rig audio and lighting equipment, and much more.

A typical Slam Master
in action

Chapter 12

Should I Become a Slammaster?

In This Chapter

- ◆ Finding out if you have the desire and determination to make it as a slammaster

- ◆ Assessing the costs, both in time and money

- ◆ Counting heads—can you muster up a reliable support network?

- ◆ Taking inventory to determine how much you already know about organizing a show

- ◆ Anticipating common problems and spirit-busting obstacles

You live in Dullsville, where people go to ice cream socials on Friday nights and stay home on Saturday nights to watch TV. Nobody does anything fun. And the few "fun" things can't possibly be considered intellectually stimulating—ball games, car races, movies. You have to drive 60 miles to see a live band. The arts community has no leadership. The only accessible slam show is 30 miles away and is torturously dreary. You may as well be living in a basement at the local cemetery.

Whaaaa! Whaaaa! Whaaaa!

Stop your whining. Drop that remote. Spring out of that recliner and put together your own slam show. But wait a minute. Can you do it? Do you have what it takes? If you were to start your own show, what would you be getting yourself into? Well, this chapter will help you answer those questions and decide if being a slammaster is the life for you.

Do You Have the Itch?

If you've got the itch, you'll know it as sure as if a Mississippi mosquito were sucking on your face. If you attend a slam, and you can't hear the poems over your own thoughts of, "This would be a whole lot more interesting if ...," you have the itch. If you commonly walk into telephone poles because you are preoccupied with ideas for various slam scenarios, you have the itch. If you're sitting at the Clyde Clip Clop Word Fair and can't help but think, "Gee, those cowboys with the hats and bolos are a nice touch, but I'd add a yodeling competition," you have the itch.

And when you have the itch, you'd better scratch it, baby, because it ain't goin' away. Is this a bad thing? Should you be afraid? Heck no, you'll survive. You're going to run full-speed into glass doors, fall off your horse more than a few times, and kick yourself for being such a damn fool. But none of this matters; if the slam bug has its incisors in your flank, it's hopeless. You're going to make a difference whether you like it or not.

SlamSpeak

Confessions of a Virgin Slammaster

I attended my first slam at the Cantab Lounge in Cambridge, MA, in the fall of 1996. I was infected on the first night and continued going weekly (the slam replaced my spiritual needs and became my Sunday Mass), until I accepted a university job and moved to Fargo, ND. I took a job working in the college union organizing events, volunteer services, and a variety of student activity programs on campus at North Dakota State University. I felt a great need to establish a slam in Fargo. After all, in my eyes, the slam was the ultimate multicultural program. Where else could you amass an audience of such variety—so many different people who wouldn't ordinarily share the same space listening to poetry? I started moonlighting as a waiter at Luigi's, an Italian restaurant in Fargo, to pursue a slam venue. I had my eye on the nightclub downstairs, which was owned by the same restaurateur. After five months, and after establishing a positive relationship, I approached the owner with the idea of letting me have the last Monday of the month to run a poetry slam. He was right on board. Six weeks later, September 27, 1997, we held the first "Slam on the Plains" and drew 125 people. We were on to something.

—Fargo's first slammaster, Robb Thibault, has gone on to create ACUI National College Slam (see Chapter 23).

Taking Inventory—Do You Have What It Takes?

Before you set out on any journey, you take inventory. Do you have your money, keys, medicine, plane tickets, and toothbrush? The same is true when you decide to embark on any important venture, such as getting married, starting a business, or buying a home. You need to take a personal inventory to determine if you really want to accept a new responsibility, and then take an external inventory to ensure that you have the requisite resources to succeed, or at least survive. To decide whether you have the desire and resources you need to make your slam show a success, answer the following questions:

◆ Are you doing this for yourself?

◆ Do you have a vision?

◆ Do you have a support network?

◆ Do you have the time and energy?

◆ Are you a show maker?

◆ Are you as crazy as the rest of us?

The following sections explore these questions in greater detail.

Are You Doing This for Yourself?

Few of us are completely selfless, altruistic individuals. We do what we do because our actions reward us in some way. Maybe they bring us money, give us pleasure, or make us feel appreciated by those we love. There's nothing wrong with that, so don't beat yourself up if you're creating a slam show primarily because you think it'll be a blast, give you more artistic freedom, and increase your visibility in the slam community.

However, if you're setting out to completely use people for your own benefit, you're in the wrong division of the entertainment industry. The slam has been adamantly opposed to exploitative personalities and organizations wishing to exploit its name, reputation, and collective energies merely for their own financial gain. The movement stands upon the shoulders of thousands of dedicated, service-minded people who have received

> **Whoa!**
>
> We're not saying that the slam community doesn't have its share of self-serving people. It does. We've all acted on selfish motives. And many of us have experienced great public shame when we realized our true intentions.

little or no material return on their unbelievable personal investments of time, money, energy, and emotion. By becoming a slammaster you're joining an extremely passionate group of self-sacrificing idealists.

But you need not be Mother Theresa—unless you really want to be. There's nothing wrong with a dog wagging its own tail. A spot in your slam to do your own work? An opportunity to stretch your performance horizon? A chance to earn a little money and get some respect and attention? Nothing's wrong with that. The conflicts arise when people start getting waaaaaaaaaay more than they give back and when they consider themselves to be waaaaaaaaaay more important than they really are—when the tail starts wagging the dog.

Do You Have a Vision?

Starting a slam affords you the opportunity to create, not just pour your soul into some slam mold. Take the basic form and explore. Twist it, turn it, hold it up to the sun and moon. Roll it down the byways of your brain and see what sticks to it. The strength of the slam movement is that it is constantly evolving, rediscovering itself, developing new and effective ways of attracting audiences, and making words onstage an enjoyable and profound experience.

> **Dig This!**
>
> Chris Mooney Singh, the creator of the Singapore Slam mentioned in Chapter 1, brought his vision to life as a cabaret of poems, songs, and dance. The competition fits in at the end as a capper to his show. Other artists in Singapore are already spinning off his vision, creating their own spoken word shows.

To take advantage of this valuable artistic opportunity, you need to have a vision, a picture in your mind of what an ideal slam show would be. Would your show be a classic competition—no props, no costumes, no musical accompaniment, no performances over three minutes? Would it include other performance arts, such as dancing? Would you try to work in a live band? Would you use the 0 to 10 point system or rig up some cheesy Applause-O-Meter? How 'bout some farm animals? Of course, your vision is going to get skewed in its execution. That's natural. But if you start without a clear vision, the show will dissolve quickly into chaos and spin completely beyond your control.

Do You Have a Support Network?

Organizing a slam event isn't something you do alone. By its very nature it's communal, a collaboration. It takes time, money, devotion, and sacrifice—not only from you but from an army of dedicated volunteers. You need help from other people—performers, owners, bartenders, designers, ticket-takers, PR people (to advertise), and an emcee or two. If you have a rich uncle to bankroll your venture, you can hire a staff, but if you're working two jobs just to pay the bills, you're going to be asking favor upon favor.

If you're fidgeting right now, you should be. Collaborating on a shoestring can often be frustrating. But it can also be extremely liberating and rewarding, a soul-expanding experience. Slam has drawn writers and poets out of the loneliness of their dreary, spare writing rooms to the joy of creating and performing together.

Backstage Skinny

If you're a control freak and think that you need to do everything yourself to have it done right, one of two things is going to happen; either you will change or you will fail. Learning to delegate and rely on other people will free you to focus on more important issues and help you carry the burden of being a leader.

Do You Have the Time and Energy?

Unreasonable expectations can doom your efforts even before you get started. If you approach the task of organizing a program thinking that you can slap together something on Tuesday for a Wednesday night show, you're going to be sorely disappointed when Wednesday night rolls around. To improve your chances of success, go in knowing that the job is tough. Let's add up the time a slammaster will devote to his or her new show over a period of time, say the first six months:

- **Upfront tasks:** Formulating a vision, sketching a show format, scoping out and contracting a venue, lining up talent, *reading this book*, and so on can easily require a minimum investment of ten hours a week for four weeks.

- **Marketing and advertising:** Designing and producing flyers, press releases, and other marketing materials on a regular basis can demand five to ten hours a week, every week. Add another five hours for distribution.

- **Following up:** Calling people, lining up acts, checking your message machine, making sure your performers arrive on time, and writing your newsletter (or updating your website) tacks on another four hours a week, at least.

- **Hiring and training:** Hunting down and hiring door people and sound technicians, interviewing and auditioning hosts and emcees, and replacing staff that quits takes more time and money. Add another five to ten hours, plus a good chunk of aggravation.

- **Running the show:** Plan on starting early in the afternoon. You need to check all those last-minute details. Do you have the markers, scorecards, prizes, and extra chairs? Has someone hung the lights and delivered the sound system?

After the show, you'll be lucky if you're packed and ready to head home by midnight. So let's see, that's four to five shows a month times six months times ten hours per show equals *two hundred and forty hours*, plus or minus a few.

At this point, you might be thinking, "Wait a minute, that's over *eight hundred hours*! More than one hundred and thirty hours a month. Close to thirty hours a week. Hey, that's more time than I put in at my day job!" It gets easier over time—as your show gets established and gains a rockin' reputation, and you get more people to help you, but at the beginning it's (ugh) real work.

Are You a Show Maker?

You have located a great venue and convinced the owner to let your poets do their thing under her roof. You have some great prospects for open-mike performances. You lined up some big-name slam poets. You put together an excellent volunteer staff and spent all week distributing flyers. The chairs are in place, the lights are on, the sound system is perfect, and all the right folks, young and old, are lining up to pay their cover charge. Now what?

YYYYYAAAAAAAAAAAWWWWWWWWWWWWNNNNNNNNNNNNNNNNN

Your show bombs. All those enthusiastic spectators leave bleary-eyed and brain-dead, ready for bed, an apathetic "so so" echoing in their heads. You did everything right, so what happened to make it go so wrong?

SlamSpeak

Bill Veeck (1914–1986) is a baseball legend and hustler who worked in various capacities for the Chicago Cubs and owned several baseball teams, including the Cleveland Indians, St. Louis Browns, and the Chicago White Sox. He introduced several attractions to liven up the game of baseball, including printing the names of the players on the backs of their uniforms, setting off fireworks after home team homeruns, and giving away merchandise to fans.

Your slam can be well executed technically and still lack the most essential ingredients: flare, spark, drama. The P.T. Barnum, Florenz Ziegfeld, Bill Veeck effect. The nuts and bolts are very important, but the fireworks, the whammy, the zing is what makes people chatter about what rattled their saddles last night. The lively attractions are what burns your show into the collective memory of your audience and inspires them to advertise your show by word of mouth days after it's over. Don't let your zany creative soul get lost in the business of taking care of business. Show makers are creative animals, risk-takers, fun-builders. And if you don't have a zany, creative side, find someone who does and turn them loose on your plans. Sometimes you need to sacrifice yourself for the good of the show.

Are You As Crazy As the Rest of Us?

Starting a slam is like having a kid. Nobody would be insane enough to attempt it if they realized beforehand how much work and heartache were involved. You just need to approach it with a little faith, blind faith. Most of us who started our own slams did it in blissful ignorance—we honestly didn't consider how much sweat and sacrifice it would demand. We were crazy with the itch (I still am—look at this goofy book I'm writing). The glorious part of this adventure on which you are about to embark (Hey, you've got the itch, right?) is that when you get that green gushing monster growing out of the seedling you planted, it spits out fruit in a thousand ways you never, in four millenniums, could have anticipated.

Tallying Your Talents and Resources

People like to talk themselves out of trying new things by convincing themselves that they don't have the knowledge or talent required. In some cases, they're right, but most of the time, these people are just victims of a critical confidence shortage. If you've been to a few slam poetry events, dabbled in poetry, created your own greeting cards on a computer (or by hand), counted money, set the dinner table, or had a productive argument with a friend, relative, or co-worker, you have at least some of the skills and experiences required to run your own show. You just need to apply those skills in a new way. The following sections help you realize just how much you already know.

Been There, Seen That

You should have attended at least one poetry slam before you even think about creating your own. Better yet, see as many as you can. Go to www.poetryslam.com and find the slam nearest you. Visit it, talk to the slammaster, volunteer to be a judge, and mingle with the slammers. Plan your vacation around slam visits to Texas, Boston, New York, Chicago, and the Bay Area. Take a road journal along, jot down impressions, ask advice. You'll be surprised at how much you absorb just by acting like a sponge.

While you're in the car or on the plane, or throttling your cycle over the Blue Ridge Parkway, think about all the theatrical events you've been to: concerts, plays, puppet shows, bar mitzvahs, holy communions, football games, commencement ceremonies, political rallies, you name it. These are all dramas with rituals you can draw from when creating your slam vision. And if you've been involved with any of these events, even in the smallest capacity, you have valuable practical experience to tap into. Don't discount any of it.

Been There, Done That

At work, at home, at play, wherever you are actively doing something, you're acquiring or sharpening practical skills that you'll use when organizing and running your show. I gained experience dealing with people on construction sites, battling with architects, and soliciting estimates from subcontractors. All that experience of interacting with fellow humans and dealing with diverse personalities transferred to my work as slammaster. It helped me deal with crotchety club owners, egocentric poets, and other headstrong slammasters. (It did. I swear to concrete heaven it did.)

If you're married or have a roommate or two, you're picking up valuable negotiating skills. Call on these skills when you need to negotiate with a venue owner or performance poet. If you pay your bills, you have the necessary money-management skills. Apply those skills to make sure your expenses don't outstrip your income. If you ever made a cool poster for a science fair, you have what it takes to put together a flyer or a press release. Have you ever hooked up a stereo system or set up a computer? Then you probably have the basic knowledge you need to figure out how to set up and turn on a basic sound system. And if you ever served in a leadership role—as a manager, coach, team leader, or director—you probably have the organizational skills you need to run a slam.

And if you don't … just chalk up another one for on-the-job training.

The Obstacles Ahead

As you know from earlier chapters, slam is not about negativity and discouragement, but before you make the big leap and decide to organize a slam, you should be aware of the inevitable obstacles you will encounter. Oh yes, they're out there—big and small, significant and petty, genuine and political.

If you know what to expect, you'll have a better chance of warding off the blows, tolerating the pain, and recovering when the unavoidable is unavoidable. The following sections reveal some of what goes with the territory.

The Hoity-Toity Establishment

Expect the literary elitists to be jealous. They're going to be critical. After all, they're protecting their lonely citadels. You have several strategies at your disposal to

counteract their attacks: fight them, make fun of them, welcome them into the mix, or ignore them. Pick the strategy that you're best at. If you're great at debate, go toe-to-toe. Are you funny? Then poke fun at them and at yourself to undercut their seriousness. Are you more of a diplomat? Then welcome them into your house and demonstrate your magnanimity as a host. Whatever happens, don't let the establishment change your vision or, even worse, abandon your slam. They're yesterday. You're the future.

Cash Flow Problems

Finances can severely limit your vision. You envision a beautiful open stage with top-of-the-line lighting and crystal-clear audio, a glitzy full-color advertising campaign, and top-dollar feature poets. Your wallet, on the other hand, dictates reality: a decent stage that most of the audience can see, a microphone with an amp and a single speaker, black-and-white flyers, and a couple up-and-coming poets who agreed to do you a favor if you'd let them sleep on your couch.

It could get more dismal before it improves. Plan on forking over a chunk of change for advertising, a feature performer, and other expenses without a dime coming back. It's best to set aside a pool of dough to draw on. Money obstacles are always gonna be there. It's the Arts, my friend. But if you have a little nest egg on the side, you'll be better able to ride out the tough times.

Dig This!

Back in 1984, when I started the Get Me High Monday night show, I put $500 out in the first few months without seeing a nickel come back. Seven years later, when Chicago hosted the 1991 NPS, pauper poet Marc had $8,000 on the line. Thankfully we sold out the final night championship bout and the money poured in. But costs have escalated. In 1999, Henry Sampson, the NPS tournament director that year, and I each staked $20,000 of our savings in reserve to pay the NPS bills if the event flopped. Of course, it didn't. Whew!

Shifting Sands—Unforeseen Changes

The high profile venue you chose worked out to be the greatest! The shows you envisioned are a perfect match! News has reached your ears that National Geographic is going to do a story on your efforts to bring poetry alive in Paw Maw, Indiana ... and what?! ... the owner's getting divorced?! He's sold the place?! It's closing down next week?! It's going to be a Lackluster Video Store?! Oh no!

The unexpected is the worst. It blindsides you. The highway department decides to tear up the street and install a new sewer system outside the front door. They block off the street. The plumbers strike. A two-month project takes almost a year to finish. Someone forgets to put the sidewalk back.

Whoa!

You might think that the appearance of an outlaw biker club at your slam is an "unexpected" that could prove disastrous. Not necessarily so. Jean Howard and Rob Van Tuyle turned just such a situation into a shiny hubcap. For several years they assisted the Chicago Outlaws in staging a series of biker slams at Outlaw headquarters. The scantily clad mamas always seemed to win. Be ready for the unforeseen obstacles and have faith that you'll overcome them when they come over you.

Pettiness and Social Hostility

Dealing with the public can be torturous. Prepare for the worst: whining, complaining, attempts to undermine your efforts, back stabbing, power grabbing, and just about every other negative human characteristic you can imagine. When people are miserable, they take some strange delight in having other people join them. Following is a list of some of the comments you're sure to hear:

"Put me at the top of the open-mike list. I have to leave early."

"Don't put me first."

"I'm reading a poem, why do I have to pay?"

"Why did she get to read three poems, when you only let me read one?"

"I'm sorry to tell you this, but nothing I've heard at your slam is poetry. It's just a bunch of people having group therapy."

"The drinks are too expensive here."

"The food here is pretty bad."

"The judges' scoring was biased toward … Republicans … Democrats … feminists … Cubans … race car drivers."

"You think you're quite a big shot, don't you?"

Be ready to smile, and once in a while politely ask the folks who complain to find someplace else: There's the door. It swings both ways.

Sharpening Your Vision

Despite the warnings and your own reservations, you want to organize your own show. You have the itch, and you probably have the resources to pull it off. Congratulations! Welcome to the club. Your next step is to start focusing your vision. Maybe you have some ideas for how you want your slam structured, but you need to tweak that vision to ensure that it delivers what you want and serves your community's needs. If you don't do that, your show will disappoint you and/or the audience, and nobody wants that to happen. The following sections lead you through this soul-searching, vision-focusing process.

Backstage Skinny _____

The original slam had three main goals:

1. To give the Chicago Poetry Ensemble and the audience more room.
2. To have a weekly spotlight for exploring the concept of a poetry cabaret.
3. To see if it could be done.

There was no serious thought of making money, just a hope not to lose too much.

Look Inside: Personal Needs

To ensure that your slam will meet your needs and be a rewarding experience for you, ask yourself what you hope to get out of the experience. Do you want an audience for yourself? To create something bigger than a solo performance? To serve your community? To provide an opportunity for all the wonderful poets you know? Are you hoping to send a team to the nationals?

Use your answers to adjust your vision. If you're hosting a slam because you want a chance to perform your own poems, work your performance into the show. If you're hoping to recruit members for a slam team, be sure your show has an opportunity for open-mike performances. If you want to give your poet pals a stage, work them into the act. And then move on to the next section to tailor your show to your audience.

Look Around: Community Needs

Although it's quite acceptable and common for a slammaster to envision a show without considering the needs of the audience and the local poets, it's a little risky. Unless you feed the needs of your community, they're probably not going to be very supportive. So ask yourself what you hope your slam will accomplish and how it will serve the community: Will your slam be a platform for young people to express rebellion, for seniors to mix with teens, for minorities to gain a voice, for closet poets to emerge? Should it be a forum for teaching poetry? A place to go to escape the fashion culture of TV and mass media? A place to have a good time? All of these? None of these? What does your community need? And how do these factors affect your vision?

Slam Spin-Offs—An Ever-Evolving Art

Think of the slam movement as a wild mythological beast that keeps growing and changing. What makes it evolve into some new, wondrous creature? You do. Your vision gives it another eye, another leg, new organs. Sometimes it doesn't look pretty, but it keeps creeping along. Others before you have changed its course, others after you will, too. Here are a few spin-offs of note:

♦ **"Chick" Slams**   Girls, girls, girls! Chick slams go by all sorts of pseudonyms from "Estrofest!" to "Labia Poetica," but they all have one thing in common: these slams are for ladies only. All-female poetry nights have gained a great deal of popularity among college-age women, especially, but certainly aren't limited to college campuses. Many organizers of all-female poetry events find that the shows garner great work from female poets who feel intimidated by the often male-dominated world of slam. In an all-girl environment, the ladies are more comfortable baring their souls and sharing their work with a crowd.

♦ **Improv Slams**   An improvisational theater group in Florida used slam poets to inspire a new improv theater game. One or two slam poets kick out poems that act as a springboard for the improv group to create scenes based on the imagery, cadence, subject matter, and/or the characters found in the poem. Scoring is optional. The game expands the landscape of the poem and interlaces drama and poetry in an exciting new way.

♦ **Drama Slam**   Another theater group in Chicago created a drama slam. Short scenes were presented by several competing ensembles to judges who scored the scenes with thumbs-up/thumbs-down ballots. The thespians used the event as a benefit for their next season's subscription series.

♦ **Music and Dance Slams**   Musicians and tap dancers have put their own twist on the standard slam. Band slams and tap slam competitions have brought great joy to audiences. Often, as a nod to the slam community, performance poets are included in these events.

The Least You Need to Know

- ◆ You know you have the desire to become a slammaster if you constantly are preoccupied with thoughts of how you would run your ideal show.

- ◆ Before becoming a slammaster, be sure you have the necessary resources: a clear vision, a strong and reliable support network, lots of time and energy, the personality of a show maker, and a certain level of insanity.

- ◆ You probably have observed enough and done enough to acquire the knowledge and talents required to be an effective slammaster.

- ◆ Anticipate problems and keep a little cash on hand for those unexpected expenses.

- ◆ You can sharpen your vision by determining what you want from your show, how it will feed your community's needs, and how it can be original.

Chapter 13

Scoping Out the Right Venue

In This Chapter

◆ Composing your venue wish list

◆ Assessing a venue's ambience

◆ Knowing when to scratch a venue off your list

◆ Striking a deal with the venue's owner or manager

◆ Breathing your vision into the venue

As slammaster, your first order of business is to find a home for this brain-child of yours—a suitable place for poets to perform and patrons to kick back. The venue can be anything from the neighborhood dive to the base-ment of the public library. It can blare bold neon or hunker down under a dim street lamp. It can have the java-juiced ambience of a coffee house or the shake, rattle, and roll of a dance club.

Whatever your target venue is, it must be the right size and shape, attract the right crowd, and have the potential to reflect the desired personality of your show. But what is the right size and shape? What is the right crowd? How do you select a venue that provides your show with the best chance of succeeding? This chapter answers all these questions and more as it shows you how to scope out the best slam poetry venue in your hood.

Composing a Venue Wish List

The fact that you enjoy hanging out at the Jumpin' Java Bean and the manager's cute does not qualify the place as a first-class slam poetry venue. It might accommodate only a couple dozen patrons, provide no stage area, or have the look and feel of a dentist's office. You might like the joint, but maybe your show would play better elsewhere. Always keep in mind that this is business—show business, but business nevertheless—and you want your business to succeed. So shove your personal likes and dislikes aside and start thinking of your slam show objectively.

Pretend you're shopping for a new set of wheels. Hardtop or convertible? Manual or automatic? Sedan or sports car? A new honey or one that's shed a little rubber? Each specific narrows the choices and reduces the time and energy you'll spend searching.

> **Dig This!**
>
> If you've never had a show, it's okay to make educated guesses. You'll learn more and more as you go along. It's like the process of writing itself. First a blank sheet, then a few scattered thoughts, and then more thoughts. Soon a direction appears and it all starts to come together and make sense.

At first, locating the right venue in a world packed with apparently endless options seems like an over-whelming task. But as you narrow your focus, you blot out the options on the periphery and make the choices much more obvious. The reality of your vision becomes tangible; when you can sniff and taste what you're looking for, when the specifics are as second nature to you as the lines you've memorized and performed a thousand times, then the choice becomes intuitive and just happens. You realize, "This is it! This is the place!"

So grab a pen and paper, and let's get specific.

Think Small—Small Enough to Create a Happening

If this is your first venue, think small. Your aim is to create a happening, and happenings spill out the door and onto the street. People drive by and see lines of anxious fans pushing to get in. "Hey, something must be happening there." Inside, people stand shoulder to shoulder and when they applaud, the roar gets physical. "It's happening, man!"

If a club is too big, it sucks the energy out of the event, leaving it a hollow shell. Cheers in a half-empty club (even if it has 300 fans scattered through an 800 seat auditorium) echo like whispers in a mausoleum. Harry Houdini could be swimming back from the dead, popping out of his upright, watertight glass tank like a spooky fish, and people would probably say, "Oh, that's nice."

Whoa!

You're moving on up. Your first venue is splitting at its seams. Thinking small isn't what you had in mind. Get a grip. The same principles apply. Estimate your potential audience and add 10 or 20 percent max. No matter how successful your current show is, it's probably a mistake to book a "moving-on-up venue" that's double the size of your old one. Starting a spin-off slam is not a guaranteed success.

For a newborn slam in a mid-size city with some sort of existing literary arts scene (either at the library or at the local book club), anticipate drawing 30 to 50 people, but don't be surprised if 80 or 100 show up. That's not unusual in the slam world. The venue you choose should feel comfortably occupied with 30 people and like a spilling-out-the-door-call-911 HAPPENING MAN! with 100.

Ambience Is Everything

It's the final round of Bout 3 at the Could-Be-You National Slam: Boston vs. LA vs. the dark horse Omaha. Michael Brown, famous slam elder and group piece strategist, needs the Boston team to score a near-perfect 30 to win the bout and move on to the semi-finals. The team is outside having a communal-hug psyche-up session. The emcee announces, "Next up. Boston! With a Group Piece!"

They squeeze through the kitchen and enter from behind the coffee counter. One of the team members gets stuck behind the manager, who is sick of this poetry stuff and won't budge. Boston finally takes the stage and starts executing its seductively searing group piece. Just then, the gurgling espresso machine blasts out its steam and grind. (The manager chuckles. This happened twice before during the first two bouts.) The performers recover and recapture the audience's attention. They're halfway through the piece, building tension, walking the razor's edge, lifting the audience to new heights. Then … bam! A frenetic wedding party blasts in through a doorway next to the stage cackling in oblivion. Stunned, they pause in front of the stage and gaze up at the performers. Poets in their faces emoting "Oh my." They scurry to the counter and titter nervously over a round of lattes.

Ambience can make or break a slam. The reading room of the district library or the conference room of the corporate center is not going to infuse the audience with a raucous, Elizabethan feel. If you're expecting your crowd to be under-thirty American hardcore rockers, a straight-ahead jazz joint ain't gonna cut it, either.

A friendly, funky place fits for most slams. Slick, shiny Las Vegas styles have worked, too (though less often). Most successful slam venues share some common traits, "specifics" that create a winning ambience:

◆ **Comfort.** You want a place where people like to hang out, regardless of whether something is happening onstage, a sit-down place with comfortable chairs, stools, or couches. It needs good sight lines so people can catch the action without leaning or moving or missing something. The place should have a down-home feel to it.

Whoa! _____

In some cases a venue can be *too* comfortable. If its ambience induces the clientele to *just* hang or chill in a too-cool pose oblivious to the performance, then nix the place. An army of your most devoted fans might be able to overcome their ambivalence, but if the rest of the crowd fails to join in, your show's sure to be a downer.

◆ **Dripping with Character.** The ideal venue has personality—oddball stuff on the walls, original art, a cheesy theme, and so on. It has to have something. Butchie, the owner of the Get Me High Jazz Club, nailed old 45s on the walls and turned the ceiling into a chalkboard for everyone to scribble on. A few slams have tried brand-name venues, franchise bookstores, coffee houses, and restaurants, but not many have survived. What works is usually home-grown, unique, Ma and Pa. Stimulating and authentic can score 10s all around.

◆ **Supportive service staff.** The servers have to be into it. They can't be taking orders and talking louder than the performers onstage. They can't be flinging empties into the bottle shoot and banging the cash register every ten seconds. On slow nights, Judy, the bartender at the Get Me High, used to lead us all in a limerick *round robin* until the audience finally poured in late.

SlamSlang _____

Round robin is a term we started using in Chicago to describe a series of very short poems performed one right after another by several poets planted at different locations in the audience. The trick was to jump on the heels of the preceding poet's last line and hold back the audience's response until all the poems had been delivered. Round robins build to a palpable tension and burst into a crowd roar on the final syllable.

◆ **Enthusiastic clientele.** The regulars are like globs of living color splashed on the walls of a venue's atmosphere. They set the tone. What they do and how they react can give your show an immediate boost or snuff it out like a wet cigarette. If they came to watch the wet t-shirt contest or Monday Night Football, the regulars might treat you and your poetry troupe as a nuisance, in which case your show is doomed before you even step onstage.

♦ **Conducive background music.** This is a concern primarily in nightclubs, coffee shops, and other venues that have a regular day and night business serving the public. The style of ambient music played through the house sound system or off the jukebox must be in tune with your vision. "Where Have All the Flowers Gone?" is not going to make it with the hip-hop crowd. Sometimes the owner and management are more than happy to set the tone you want, but sometimes they are not. On your criteria list, jot down the kind of preshow and intermittent music you desire.

♦ **Consistency.** A place can have character, but if that character changes from month to month, it will create problems. Part of the slam experience is ritual. People come because they know what to expect. They expect the unexpected, but they have faith that the furnishings will be familiar.

♦ **A supportive owner.** I have been very lucky; for nearly two decades I've worked with and for one of the finest, most honorable, and supportive owners a show maker could hope for—Dave Jemilo, owner of the Green Mill. If your personality clashes with that of the owner, hightail it out of there; it is not worth the aggravation.

Plan on having several conversations with the owner or person in charge. They're very busy people and have defense mechanisms for putting off first encounters, so don't expect them to welcome you with open arms. These people deal with a hundred personalities a day. Get through their defense mechanisms before making an assessment. If your vision clicks with their personality, you've struck gold.

Backstage Skinny

Talk to the local musicians who gig around your town. They'll fill you in on which club owners, managers, presenters, and curators of entertainment have and do not have a clue. The lousy ones are usually new to the biz. You can't have long-term success in the entertainment business unless you're good and personable.

Frame the Picture

Visualize your ideal show. What will you need for it—a big stage, or just floor space? Are there many people performing at once? Musicians? Dancers? Do you see light cues changing the mood? Is there a grand entrance of performers on roller skates throwing confetti? Now imagine a space that could accommodate your show. Draw a rough floor plan, list its specifics in your criteria notebook, or both. How will your performers maneuver through it? Where will the audience sit? A venue can have great ambience, but if your show does not function well in it, you're doomed.

Following are some physical conditions to avoid:

- Stages situated in front of big windows or some other glass barrier that allows passersby to peer in and make faces behind the performers.

- Performing areas that are neither fully joined nor completely separated from other sections of the bar or restaurant, allowing the bar noise, the hoots and hollers of the sports fanatics, or the clank and clunk of table chatter to spill over and mangle the performance.

- Restaurants in general! Spoken word performances are not background music. They require active audiences. It's hard for some people to eat spaghetti and enjoy a sonnet at the same time.

- Open areas like food courts or student union lobbies, where peripheral traffic pulls focus from the stage.

- Stages in odd places like on the top of a portable hot dog stand. (Don't laugh. I've been there, done that. And I hope I'm not going back for more.)

- Venues that have nooks and crannies where patrons can hide and talk loud.

- Oddly-shaped venues that divide the seating area so portions of the audience cannot see or hear each other.

The Necessary Services

You can't expect your audience to sit through three hours of performance poetry if they're not physically comfortable, fed and watered, and able to use the restroom occasionally. Make sure that the venue has all the services you need and expect, such as adequate restrooms, food (at least some bar nuts or potato chips), beer, cocktails, decent coffee, and/or soft drinks at reasonable prices. Also, do they accept all credit cards?

Location, Location, Location

If you open a snow cone stand in Alaska, don't expect the locals to line up for your cool, refreshing treats. Similarly, when scoping out potential venues, location should be near the top of your list. In major urban centers, it's an absolute necessity that your venue be located near convenient public transportation, easy to find, and in a fairly safe neighborhood (only a few drive-bys now and then). It's a huge plus if parking is nearby and free. Being within the cluster of a hip new neighborhood's artsy business district adds a couple points. And chalk up a couple more points for a lot of pedestrian traffic and a dynamic nightlife.

The slam qualifies as an offbeat art form, so people will travel to seek it out. That's part of the fun. But the easier you make it for the audience, the more assured you can be that they'll return week after week.

Now Write It Down

Your wish list is growing, but it's only floating around in your brain. If you're anything like I am, your brain is not the most reliable storage facility, so write it down. Save your memory for memorizing poems. Get nerdy. Make a chart. You can burn the evidence later. A criteria list in black and white is worth much more than one bouncing around in your brain like a pinball. Your list should address the following key categories, plus any other issues that you find important:

- Size
- Clientele
- Ambience
- Location
- Performance area
- Customer comforts and services
- Owner personality

Backstage Skinny

When you're heading out for a night on the town, stick a small notepad and a pen or pencil in your pocket so you can jot down information about potential slam hot spots. Sure, you might look a little geeky, but when you emerge from your drunken stupor, you'll be able to recount where you've been … assuming, of course, that you had the wherewithal to write it down.

Say Ohhmmm and Begin the Search

Now that you have a detailed list of venue criteria, crumple it up and toss it. You're a poet. Poets don't do lists. Yeah, yeah, I just told you to write things down. And that was a necessary stage in the process. But now that you've taken the rational approach, allow the irrational a chance to show you how silly lists can be. Take the Zen approach; feel the force. The place is going to find you.

Of course, if that's a little too loosey-goosy, welcome-to-the-'60s for you, dig that crumpled criteria list out of the trash, smooth the wrinkles, and use that list to create one or two additional lists of venues that show potential. The following sections explain various ways to locate prospective slam venues.

SlamSlang

The term **rag** refers to a low-cost magazine, newspaper, or newsletter.

Backstage Skinny

Many local newspapers, bookstores, TV stations, radio stations, bands, and poetry organizations have websites. Check those sites to figure out where the happenings are happenin' in your town or city.

The Finger Walking List

One of the easiest ways to spot prospective venues doesn't even require you to leave your home or apartment. You probably have some newspapers lying around—gather them up. Grab your phone book—the yellow pages. See if you have any neighborhood *rags* hidden under your bed or lying on the bathroom floor.

Now, check the entertainment sections of the newspapers and write down (or circle, if you're like me) every venue listing that seems to fit your criteria. Check the yellow pages for bookstores, nightclubs, libraries, cultural institutions, and any other places that sound promising, and jot down their names, addresses, and phone numbers.

Foot Walking List

Get out of the house. You've been cooped up too long making lists. You're a creative artist. You need fresh air, trees, moonlight. Oh! There's the library; it's still open. Lucky thing you've got your criteria notes in your pocket. Check the bulletin board. Any poetry readings or venue possibilities? Check out the basement, just in case.

Hey, wait. Don't go home yet. Get a cup of coffee at the Café Mocha Loca. It has a bulletin board, too. So do the art gallery and the theaters. And look! There's a flyer in the window of that grocery store.

Did you talk with the librarian? The coffee counter person? The cashier? Go back. Now is not the time to act shy. You're on a mission.

Okay, you're tired. Go home. But if you didn't write this all down, you're going to have to do it again tomorrow. If you did log your discoveries, you've got a good grip on what's available, and you can take a well-deserved nap.

Get Connected

Searching for and exploring venue candidates can be exhilarating, but sometimes the most efficient way to track down top venues is to pick up the phone and network. Call people you know in the arts and entertainment fields. Call your party-animal friends—the ones who go clubbing every weekend. Call people you don't know and get phone numbers of people they know. People love to help other people. You'd be surprised how helpful most people are. I get calls from strangers from all over world, asking for my advice on how to start a slam. You never know where your next lead will come from. Sometimes the person you call can't help you directly, but they know a person who can. In addition to helping you gather the information you need, talking to folks spreads the word that you're going into the slam business, and people will start contacting you.

Pick a Night

After you've hit on the right venue or narrowed your list to three or four promising candidates, pick a night for your show. For obvious reasons, Fridays and Saturdays are the best nights for attracting an audience. Unfortunately, they're also the most competitive nights for entertainment. You not only compete with regular weekly shows, but also with special concerts that come to town for weekend engagements. And there's going to be pressure from the venue owner for you to prove yourself in prime time. So which days are best? The following list can help you decide:

- **Monday:** This is down time for most bars and nightclubs, so the owner might let you try out a show—what does she have to lose? However, people might not attend your show, especially during football season when you'll be contending with Monday Night Football.

- **Tuesday:** Like Monday, Tuesday is usually an off day. Bring in a steady crowd on a Monday or Tuesday and the venue owner will kiss your poetic feet.

- **Hump Day:** Wednesday is generally a good day for poetry performances, because they usually don't become party-hardy affairs … usually. People drop in, have a couple drinks, and get home at a reasonable hour.

- **Thursday:** Like Friday and Saturday, Thursday is a night out for many people. They figure they can fake a half-day Friday no matter how frazzled they become Thursday night.

- **Friday:** Friday night is a great night with a lot of excitement, but generally too much competition. If an owner has a choice between your slam poetry show and a popular local rock band, guess who's going to win!

- ◆ **Saturday:** See Friday.

- ◆ **Sunday:** Like Monday and Tuesday, Sunday is an off night, but it is still weekend time. I've had pretty good success with my Sunday night show.

Judgment Day

You've got criteria and a list of possibilities. You're ready to let that venue find you. You're going to know without looking at your list, but grab the list anyway and take the following steps to zoom in on the perfect venue:

1. Arrange your list of potential candidates by location, from most to least desirable.

2. Check to see which venues are available on the evenings you hope to stage your show. For instance, if your plan is to have a weekly show on Mondays and the place is closed on Mondays … duh!

3. See if any other criteria eliminate venues before taking the next big step. Scratch these losers off your list, leaving no more than six prospects. (Scratch lightly; you might need that list if your top six prospects fall through.)

4. Check out the six best locations that survived your cuts.

Ideally your first visit should be on the night you'd like to hold your show. Go to the place, order something tasty, and observe. Observe the clientele, the service staff, your own feelings, and the entertainment. If the vibe feels good, find out who the manager is and/or meet the owner. If you're shy about this, join the club. It's perfectly natural. (Read Chapter 5 and work through it.) The reaction you get from the owner will tell you a lot about whether you want to stage your show there.

Dig This!

I stopped by the Get Me High Jazz Club almost a dozen times before speaking to Butchie, the owner, about doing my first show there. An obstacle to speaking to Butchie was that we didn't think he could talk. He always communicated by snapping his fingers like some Gone Hipster from the Beat Age. When he finally did speak, it shocked us, but it also opened the door to the Monday night readings.

At this point, keep in mind that you're not visiting the venue to make a decision. You're there to gather in the vibe. You can also sneak that criteria list out of your pocket and check things off while nobody's looking.

After you've looked at the top six venues, when you return home, compare the specifics of each. Is that intuition percolating? If nothing's blowing your skirt up, grab your list and highlight the next top six. If none of the possibilities pan out, pack your bags and come to Chicago.

Closing the Deal

Hopefully your skirt did fly up, and you've narrowed down your options to choice A and choice B. You've met the owners from both and maybe casually mentioned the idea you have in your head. It's time to make it happen. Choice A is way better than choice B, but B could work. So go to B first and practice. But before you're ready to talk turkey, read the fine print and iron out the details, as explained in the following sections.

Money Talk

Nowadays you don't have to beg a venue owner to allow you the use of his back rooms for your poetry show. Poetry, spoken word, and especially slams are now respected forms of entertainment. Club owners and presenters in all categories often seek out well-known slam organizers to create new and special events for them. So don't grovel—you have something of value to offer.

Here are a variety of money deals often agreed upon for club work.

- ◆ **A Cut of the Door.** This is a low-end deal. As the show-maker or slammaster, you get a percentage of the cover charged at the door. If the club owner is making money off drinks and you draw a big drinking crowd, this is a lousy deal. But if it's the best you can get, take it. It's better than you paying them to use their space, which happens more often than it should.

- ◆ **Full Door.** The cover charge goes in your pocket, and the club makes its money off the big-spending crowd you attract. This is the standard club deal and it's fair for both sides. An added expense on your part might be that the club will require you to provide a door person to collect the money, but this isn't always the case.

- ◆ **Full Door Plus.** If you attract a huge crowd, you might be able to negotiate a cut of the money that is made off of the drinks. Ask the owner to add a quarter or so to the cost of drinks during your performances. The club doesn't lose, as long as people keep buying drinks, and you pocket a little more change to pay expenses.

♦ **Guaranteed Minimum.** For special shows and one-night stands (especially touring shows), ask for a guaranteed minimum against the door charge. This means that the venue will pay you a minimum amount, say $200. If more than $200 is collected at the door, you get the full door. But if less than $200 is collected, the owner makes up the difference.

For institutional work and some club work, you negotiate a flat fee. They pay you an agreed-upon amount, you show up and do a show. This sometimes requires a contract and negotiations to nail down all the specifics: load in time, lighting and sound requirements, length of performances, lodging, travel expenses … M&Ms backstage with wine, cheese, and finger sandwiches?

You're going to have to work your way up the pay scale when selling a show for a flat fee. You might have to start out very low (for example, $500 for a two-hour show featuring a band and four slammers), but if your show gains a fine reputation in the concert circles, it's not a false illusion to dream that someday you could earn $10,000 or more for the same show—polished to perfection, of course.

Who Does What?

Everything about the 1999 NPS in Chicago was ringing bells and invoking high fives all around. We had larger audiences than could fit into the preliminary night venues. Great performances. *60 Minutes* film crews were roaming the streets to catch the fever and action. Saturday Night Finals lay ahead. I had my checklist of things to do; it was hectic, but things were getting done. Ten minutes before curtain, the stage manager for the huge historical Chicago Theater, where all the greats dating back to vaudevillian days have played, asked me where our cue caller for the lights was. "Our what?" "Your cue caller." "I gave the light guy the script." "He just throws the switch, someone on your side calls the cues." "Oh s*** …."

Luckily in a heroic slam moment, Danny Solis, famed slam elder from Albuquerque, stepped up to handle those light cues like a pro. The curtain went up and the show was magnificent.

Every detail discussed in this chapter has or should have a human being attached to it, and it's your job as slammaster or show maker to make sure the bodies are there and that they know what to do.

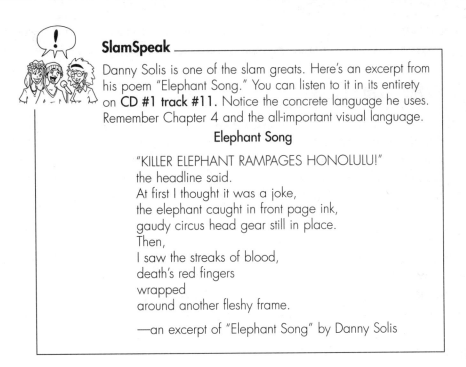

SlamSpeak

Danny Solis is one of the slam greats. Here's an excerpt from his poem "Elephant Song." You can listen to it in its entirety on **CD #1 track #11.** Notice the concrete language he uses. Remember Chapter 4 and the all-important visual language.

Elephant Song

"KILLER ELEPHANT RAMPAGES HONOLULU!"
the headline said.
At first I thought it was a joke,
the elephant caught in front page ink,
gaudy circus head gear still in place.
Then,
I saw the streaks of blood,
death's red fingers
wrapped
around another fleshy frame.

—an excerpt of "Elephant Song" by Danny Solis

Hey! I Can't Find a Venue!

"That's right, there's nothing and no place in my town! Watching the streetlights go on is the highlight of the evening. I'm doomed. I'll have to move to the big city. Peapod, Pennsylvania, is going to remain slamless."

Hold on. A few stones remain unturned.

You have an apartment, don't you? Have a house party slam. Start low key with an eye toward renting an abandoned space. There's got to be a church basement left vacant at least one night every couple weeks. Come on, did you check out the library?

When you boil it down, it's not the space that makes the slam, it's the people versifying and listening in it. If you've got people, you've got the main ingredient for a slam.

Hooray! You Did It! Now Make It Yours

Congratulations! You found the right home for your slam, with the right venue owner and manager, and you worked out a deal that made everyone happy. Now, reckon back to your vision and splash it all over your new home. Skip ahead to Chapter 19 to get a glimpse of the sizzle and spark you can add to *your* show. That's right, it's yours; now infuse it with your vision and spirit.

The Least You Need to Know

♦ A venue should be large enough to accommodate the patrons, but small enough to generate the excitement of a happening.

♦ A venue's ambience or feel is a critical element in ensuring the success of a slam poetry show.

♦ Choose a venue that's conveniently located, preferably in an artsy area where it's more likely to attract a crowd.

♦ Compose a list of criteria for the ideal venue to give yourself a way to size up the venues objectively.

♦ After you have narrowed your list of prospective venues to two or three, talk to the owners and see if you can strike a reasonable deal.

All the Slam's a Stage

In This Chapter

◆ Appreciating the importance of stage focus

◆ Examining your stage options—the good, the bad, and the ugly

◆ Tailoring your performance to fit your stage

◆ Avoiding the inevitable worst-case scenarios

From the morality pageants of medieval times to the extravaganzas of the Roman Coliseum or the outrageous spectacles of Marilyn Manson, performers, producers, directors, and slammasters have had to make clear choices concerning the creative use of spaces and stages. When you get down to the nitty-gritty of deciding how to present yourself, your show, or your slam on the stage and space you've selected—or found yourself stuck with—turn to this chapter to learn how to manage and manipulate the variables. Here, you learn about the types of stages you might encounter, their pros and cons, and what shows they best accommodate.

Rising Above the Rabble—Stage Focus

All the world might be a stage, but some parts of it get more focus than others. And that's what a stage is for—to draw focus, giving heightened importance to what takes place upon it. Sure, a single voice bellowing like a red-faced clown in the bustle of a city street can draw focus, if the voice is strong enough and the antics compelling, but performing over the assemblage of chattering humanity can be a losing battle. On the other hand, a whispered stanza at the footlights of a *proscenium* stage can hush a thousand people.

SlamSlang

A **proscenium** is the area of a modern stage between the curtain and the orchestra pit—the main area where the actors act, the dancers dance, and the slammers slam.

As a performing poet and slammaster, you'll be dealing with all kinds of stages, and—surprise—sometimes no stage at all. The following sections describe the most common setups you will encounter. Each has its purpose. Each has its problems. As a performer, you'll know what to expect, and as a slammaster, you'll be aware of your options … assuming the venue owner gives you an option.

Poet-in-a-Box: The Black Box

One of the most formal "stages" a performance poet encounters is the black box—a small, intimate, flexible theater space with three walls, a floor, and a ceiling painted black. It's sort of like those boxes used for puppet shows, only people (instead of puppets) play in them. Stadium-style seating is commonly found in the black box, but moveable chairs are often used so that the seating and performance area can be moved anywhere in the room. With the right lighting, the black box enables a performance poetry presentation to attain a mesmerizing intimacy and a subtle power unachievable in most nightclub or coffeehouse settings.

Dig This!

The history of the physical stage dates back to ancient times. The evolution and diversity of stage structures are directly related to the forms of theater presented on them and how they best serve the mobility of the players and the plot.

By its nature, the black box attaches a formality to an evening and heightens the audience's expectations. Your every word will be scrutinized like never before. Your ability to establish a back porch connection with the audience might be stymied. And if you're deadly serious, you'd better be losing blood. Success in the black box depends upon carefully selecting the texts that suit the nature of the black box, establishing (by your wily slam poet ways) an informal tone early on, and executing your serious poems with the passion and authenticity the space deserves.

If you're a slammaster assessing whether to use a black box or not, ask yourself the following questions (and answer them, too):

◆ **Does your show's vision fit the black box ambience?** If the crystal ball vision that's materializing in your head reveals poets and audience kibitzing with each other in a "Hello there! Howdy! How are ya?" revelry as slammers bump their way up to the stage and hecklers boogaloo in the aisles, a black box might not be the appropriate spot for your anything-goes scenario.

◆ **How's the seating arranged?** Remember a black box sometimes offers flexibility in seating and sometimes doesn't. However, in either situation it's always seating that focuses on one spot, the performance, not on the hottie at the end of the bar or the group of poet cronies grousing in the back row. In a black box, people sit down for one purpose, and one purpose only—to see the show. You can minimize distractions and control focus by arranging and rearranging the seating.

◆ **Are you planning to include music?** Acoustic and very laid-back amplified music can add the right touch to the black box ambience. A big brassy orchestra will blow heads off shoulders.

◆ **Is there enough room?** Black box theater spaces are small, holding 25 to 150 people max. If you're planning a "Slam Spectacular" with ten teams bussed in from around the country competing in a one-night marathon performance, look elsewhere. Very focused ensemble work and solo shows work best in a black box. And if you're hoping to sell 300 tickets, forget about it.

Above the Crowd on the Bandstand

Commonly found in most clubs and in some coffeehouses, the bandstand is the performance poet's most familiar stage setting. The stage platform is typically several inches to a few feet above floor level. Positioned high up there with the bright lights shining on your countenance might be exhilarating, but the pin-spot reality of the situation is that the higher the stage climbs, the more disconnected from the audience a performer feels. When you consider whether the bandstand is going to play well for your show, check the following:

◆ **Line of sight.** You want everyone in the venue to be able to see the performances without craning their necks or having to sit on their friends' shoulders. For a rock 'n' roll band, it doesn't matter much if the crowd can't see the bass player strumming

> **Dig This!**
>
> It is much more difficult for an audience to comprehend vocal communication when unable to see a performer's lips. For this reason, actors are always directed to speak with more volume and slightly over-emphasized enunciation when their backs are turned to the audience.

Backstage Skinny

If you're way up high onstage and begin to feel as though you're losing the audience, get off that stage and step right into the heart of the crowd or at least lean over the edge of the stage and engage them.

the melody. However, being unable to see a slam poet perform is like "watching" Shakespeare's *Macbeth* on the radio.

♦ **Level of intimacy.** The higher the performer is elevated above the crowd, the less intimate the connection. Just think about it: Do you seduce your sweetheart by yelling across the room or talking across an intimate table for two? It's a tradeoff; you want the performer to be as close to audience level as possible while still being visible to the audience.

Most bandstands come equipped with beaucoup lighting and sound capabilities and are very slammer-friendly. They can range in size from a cramped 4-by-4-foot platform to a huge platform 20 feet across and 15 feet deep, and beyond—think of the enormous stages erected in the ball parks at all those Big Time Rock Star concerts you've attended, the true American bandstands.

The Spartan Stage: Cleared Space

Many times slammers find themselves performing in bookstores, coffeehouses, and multi-purpose rooms where the stage consists of floor space cleared of the usual furniture that occupies it. Be careful that whoever reconfigures the room has at least a smidgen of theater sense and hasn't placed his idea of a-good-spot-to-perform in front of a marble staircase or in the dreariest corner of a cluttered bookstore.

Cleared space is not conducive to highly dramatic material. If you're performing in cleared space, it's best to go super-casual—try a little Billy Clinton, town-hall meeting, gift-of-gab (and grab) approach, and if you're about to go highly dramatic on them qualify it with a "Hey, hold onto your cushions—I'm going to shift gears a little and drive into performance mode now. It might be a little scary for a minute or so. Don't panic. I won't hurt you. It's just the slam."

The Great Hall

A variation on the Spartan space is the Great Hall. During the Renaissance and medieval times the King, Queen, and their court were entertained while seated at a long banquet table in a rectangular room, the Great Hall, with entrances at each of the four corners. Jugglers, dancers, jesters, and troubadours entered from the various points of the compass to gain the favor of the court with their performances.

When you're faced with staging a performance in a rather sterile meeting room or hotel conference hall, you might be able to transform a potential "poetry lecture" into a courtly banquet. Don't bring shanks of pork in, just position your poets around the room and have them feign grand entrances into the Great Hall flourishing their words and juggling their syllables. You might not want to keep this up for forty minutes, but to start the show and accent it now and then or put a befitting closer on it, it could be just the right elixir for a savory meal of acrobatic verse.

The Big-Time Stage: The Proscenium

Big-time performances, such as the championship bouts of the national slam, are almost always held on a proscenium stage. These are the stages you're accustomed to seeing when you attend a Broadway play, opera, or ballet. The stage is typically at or below the audience level with tiered theater seating facing it. In some cases, an orchestra pit stands between the stage and the audience. The great thing about the proscenium is that it typically comes equipped with great lighting and a fantastic sound system.

Bring on the Bells and Whistles

To make the big stage work, your show needs big *big* visuals. You need props, backdrops, lots of people on the boards all at once, lighting that changes moods and isolates areas, and blocking (stage movement) that makes maximum use of the space. Think of figure skating champions and how they cover the expanse of the rink, circles of light following them as they spray shaved ice to a halt in one corner and then glide gracefully across to another. When you're on the big stage, plan a big show that uses every square foot of it.

Bigger's Not Always Better

As slammaster, the proscenium might seem like the ideal arrangement for your really big show, a perfect opportunity to stage the ultimate happening. But you better back up a moment, big guy! The proscenium is often too large and too formal to generate super-charged, shoulder-to-shoulder excitement. In 1999 we held the final night of the National Slam at the massive Chicago Theater, and even though we filled the main floor with 2,500 bodies, we never attained that busting-at-the-seams, happening feel. The balcony and lobby area could have held 5,000 more. It was a great, great show, but not Woodstock revisited.

Backstage Skinny

Part of the reason that many slam poets have drifted toward using overly rhetorical language in their texts is because they often find themselves orating on proscenium stages in high school auditoriums, at universities, and on the final night of NPS competitions. It takes far more skill and experience to engage an audience with lyrical poetics from a proscenium than it does to unleash the fury of a speechmaker.

The Outdoor Stage: Help!

Sooner or later, if you've been gigging it hard year after year, you're going to end up on an outdoor stage performing at the Dawn-to-Dusk Bird & Bat Word Fest or (by the mayor's invitation) at the grand opening of the new city library. At first you're going to say "Yippee!" But hold that yip. Sure, you've been to lots of outdoor festivals and envied the rock-a-billy bands cranking it out for hordes of crazed fans who swing dance their way up to the elevated platform like they're going to see the Memphis Boy rotating his hips from the great beyond. But I guarantee that you'll have a different attitude after you've experienced the far-away feeling you get facing a crowd that seems more like a sea of cliché faces than flesh-and-blood humanity.

Speak Up, They Can't Hear Ya!

Outdoor work is tough. You're generally performing on either a permanent (concrete usually) outdoor facility, like a band shell or a gazebo, or on temporary stages erected especially for the current event. And many times there is no stage, just a tent and folding chairs, maybe a riser that elevates the performer 6 to 8 inches above the grass. In any event, expect the permanent outdoor space to suck—it might be architecturally beautiful, but acoustically it's a nightmare.

Backstage Skinny

The great outdoors swallows sound. A tree could fall onstage and nobody would hear it. Nearly every outdoor stage I've performed on chewed up my words and puked them back at everybody like cold mashed potatoes. And you can imagine how enthusiastically the audience gobbled them up.

Temporary outdoor staging can even be worse. It elevates and frames you into a proscenium picture, which is good, but the open sky above you does little to help the passersby focus on you. And if the lighting and sound fall through, you're sunk. Without sound amplification and good (colorful) lighting you're just another body on the stage. "Hey there, is that the stagehand or the sound technician? Oh, it's the poet. Sorry."

Think Big

As with the big proscenium stage, to make an outdoor situation work, your show demands big visuals, movement, music, and strong animated performances. The music draws the focus of the passing crowds, and after they're engaged, a dynamic performer in the spotlight can hold their attention ... for a while, anyway. It's best to mix in ensemble work or slammers performing with the music. If you're holding a competition as part of the show, play up the pomp and pageantry of it. Be sure the slammers dress the part. Put some giant scoreboards on the stage. Think big outside and maybe you can keep from being swallowed by that big open sky.

> **Dig This!**
>
> Many performers, musicians, and troupes are experienced in performing at outdoor festivals. And many of these have a spoken word/poetic element to them. Jugglers, acrobats, circus performers, and dada artists have all participated in slam shows I've staged in difficult open-air facilities. They know how to compel even the most scattered crowd to listen.

The Rickety Rent-A-Stage

Beware of rental stages, especially the low-rent variety. On a cheap rent-a-stage you feel like you're standing in a rowboat bobbing about on choppy seas. If you romp around on the shaky platform, everything that isn't nailed down teeters, totters, and usually falls. And if that's not enough to unnerve even the steadiest performer, the microphone picks up every audible thump and clump that sounds when you step too hard on the some-assembly-required stage. If you have an elaborate dance-the-poem routine blocked out and see that you're going to be performing it on a flimsy platform, tone it down to finger dancing and hand gestures.

> **Backstage Skinny**
>
> You can find some high-quality rental stages and seating. Just go on the web and use your favorite search engine to look for "rental stage," or grab your handy-dandy yellow pages and look under "event planning." Or talk to local festival organizers and find out what they use.

If you're a slammaster planning that big show with elephant props and giant flip-flopping word acrobats, spend a little extra bread and get high-quality equipment, or be sure that the promoter who contracted the elephantine show has lined up a solid platform.

What? No Stage?! No Cleared Space?!

When you're skipping from venue to venue on your next tour, you're likely to encounter at least one joint where you begin to think, "Why did they book me? Where am I supposed to perform? Not this again." The place has no stage, no clearing in the woods. Not even an X taped to the floor to show you where to stand. Of course, this is totally unacceptable, so your only recourse is to make it work, by making your own space:

◆ Find an area with some decent lighting and where the audience can see you, shove the tables aside, find some crates to stand on, and let 'er rip!

Or

◆ Make the whole room your stage! Whatever you do, do it in a way that's not going to rattle the owner and in a way that makes it look planned.

If you're hosting a slam, never let your performers feel as though they're an afterthought. You wouldn't invite people into your home without offering them a place to sit, so don't have performers standing around wondering where they'll be performing. Slam poets (the pros amongst them) generally adapt to any space they perform in. If you've got time, consult with them—listen to their suggestions. If your weekly or monthly venue comes with no stage, nail some 2-by-6's to the perimeters of a 4-by-4 sheet of $^3/_4$- inch plywood, paint it black, staple some carpeting to the top of it, and bingo—Broadway. You've got your own portable stage. Just make sure it'll hold a good-sized performer jumping up and down as if on a trampoline.

Whoa!

"Everything about this place is unfocused!" Don't get into an angry huff and start banging chairs and tables around. You'll get attention alright—from the owner, the bouncer, and the off-duty cop sitting at the bar.

Worse Than Nothing: Bad Scenes

Although the complete lack of a performance area is a definite bummer, other stage options that seem workable at first glance can be steel traps waiting to snap. The following list describes some setups you would be wise to avoid:

◆ **A stage behind the bar top and bartender.** That might be a safe place if you're doing a striptease, but for a poetry performance, it's like being a monkey in the zoo. And when the bartender starts shaking martinis, all is lost.

♦ **A very high proscenium with an open, unoccupied orchestra pit hugging its edge.** Again, the distance from the crowd makes this less than attractive. And there's always a chance that in the midst of a passionate stanza you'll fall in the pit.

♦ **In front of any entranceway to the outside or an adjacent room—swinging doors, revolving doors, any doors.** Every time a new patron comes in and looks up at the performer, the audience watches the unplanned drama. Even if the door never opens, the expectation that it might open can often draw more attention than your act.

♦ **Boats, football fields, ski jumps, and so on.** Unless you've reached the star status of a rock legend or a Hollywood film star, don't attempt it. On second thought, never attempt it.

> ### Dig This!
>
> The "His" and "Hers" doors at the Green Mill are adjacent to the stage and are an avoidable distraction depending on who has to use them and when. For years I've been working them into the act. Many times I've announced the next open-mike poet and they instantly and unexpectedly emerged from the restroom for their unplanned grand entrance.

The Least You Need to Know

♦ The right stage draws a room's focus to the performer, providing an essential element for the success of a performance.

♦ Different types of stages have evolved over time to accommodate different performance needs.

♦ Slammasters and performance poets should anticipate encountering a wide variety of stages and performance spaces, from the tiny black box to huge outdoor rental stages.

♦ To ensure the success of your performance, try to secure stages that best accommodate your performance style, and when that's not possible, tailor your performance to fit the space.

♦ Stages that have the potential of drawing the audience focus away from the performer can often be worse than no stage at all.

Chapter 15

Let's Get Technical

In This Chapter

- ◆ Drawing precision focus with sound and lighting
- ◆ Testing, one … two … three …; setting up and managing the sound system
- ◆ Creating an illuminating performance with the proper lighting
- ◆ Enhancing a performance with costumes, props, music, and other extras

A good stage, well-suited to a particular performance, can frame your show and focus your audience's attention in the right direction. But without proper lighting and quality sound amplification, even the best stage can seem like a vacant lot at midnight. If it's dark up there, you might try holding a flashlight beam on Sally Slammer's lovely face, but your arm is going to droop after thirty minutes. If you're running an open mike and the shyest, most inexperienced virgin virgins are eager to "do it" for the first time, you're going to need a microphone to catch their whispers and a powered mixer to send their amplified jitters through the speakers to the hecklers thirty rows back so they can hear and have at them.

If you're lucky, the venue itself will have all the required tech equipment in place when you arrive. They might even provide you or one of your cronies with a brief tutorial on how to use the equipment in case you need to fine-tune it during the show. When you're not so lucky, turn to this chapter to learn how to cope. Here, you learn how to manipulate and manage a sound system, how to deal with stage lighting, and how to introduce costumes, props, and other add-ons to your show.

Tuning In to Sound Systems—Can You Hear Me Now?

Nothing can knock the power out of a great performance faster than the piercing scream of feedback or the garbled tones of a mediocre sound system. Spoken word artists require more precise sound amplification than singers, and way better than rock groups. As a slammaster and as a performer you're going to encounter many different situations, from sound systems so complex they require professional technicians to man them, to no sound system at all requiring you to provide your own.

"Testing ... One ... Two ... Three ..."

Whether you're heading down to Barnie's Sound Amplification Emporium to rent speakers, microphones, and amplifiers for your Basketball Poetry Slam or inspecting the in-house system at the Blues Etc. nightclub, you'll need to be familiar with the following characteristics and components of a quality sound system:

- **Omni- or unidirectional microphones.** All microphones are not created equal. Unidirectional microphones reduce the *off-access sound*, sounds to the side and back of the microphone, such as audience chatter or mumbles from the performer next to you, and generally are preferable for spoken word performances. The Shure 57 is a good choice. It's the workhorse of the industry. The one drawback to the unidirectional microphone is that it tends to boost the bass sounds, causing the percussion to pop. Omni-directional microphones are better at picking up sounds from several sources. If you're in charge of the sound setup, make sure you have a stable microphone stand that's easy to adjust, and don't go cheap on the cables.

Backstage Skinny _____

A six- to eight-inch gooseneck attachment screwed onto the top of the microphone stand can be of great benefit during the open-mike session of a slam. Rather than struggling with the height adjustments of the stand itself, usually over-tightened by the last performer or broken by an aggressive musician/poet/madman with ham hands, the performers simply bend the gooseneck up or down to the desired height and emote.

◆ **4-channel mixer.** Powered mixers mix and amplify the sound received through the microphones and send it out through the speakers. Unpowered mixers require a separate amplifier to drive the speakers. It's best to have at least four channels on the mixer, one for each microphone, musical instrument, and/or other gadget you intend to plug in, plus a spare in case a channel goes dead in the middle of a performance. Each channel should have, at the very least, a dial for high-, mid-, and low-range frequencies, a dial for gain (volume), and a slide adjustment for tweaking the volume. High-end boards have lots of other buttons and switches for reverb, monitors, muting, and so on.

◆ **Graphic EQ settings.** The sound equipment in many clubs, theaters, and concert halls often includes a row of sliding levers stretched across a grid of a dozen or so sound frequencies for equalizing (EQing) the system. The function of these levers is to tune the system to the room's acoustic characteristics, but many clubs allow bands to change the Graphic EQ settings for individual performances. If something starts sounding bad no matter how carefully you adjust the channel dials for high-, mid-, and low-range frequencies, the problem could be in the Graphic EQ settings. Before messing with them yourself, ask the club manager for assistance, and pray that he knows what he's doing.

◆ **Speaker location.** Speaker location can drastically affect the tonal quality of the sound. Feedback (that awful eardrum-blowing screech) is caused by the amplified sound coming out of the speakers feeding back through the microphone—think of it as sound amplified to the infinite power. If the speakers are placed directly behind or too close to the microphones, they're going to create feedback. It's always best to situate them a little forward of the microphone and above the head of your performers. Setting the speakers on a bar stool at chest level is better than leaving them on the floor.

> **Backstage Skinny**
>
> If you're renting a system, let your needs and your budget guide your choice. A quality six-channel board, two speakers, four microphones, stands, and cords can be delivered to your show on the night of the performance for as little as $250. Of course, you can get up into the thousands if you get carried away.

> **Whoa!**
>
> Beware of in-house PA systems with speakers embedded in the ceiling—the kind you find at convention centers or in hospitals. These systems are not made to produce quality sound. They are designed to carry information, not art. Avoid using them and know that if you do use them, your performance will suffer.

◆ **Monitors.** Monitors are like audio mirrors. They sit on stage facing the performers so the performers can hear what they sound like to the audience. Monitors are not always necessary for spoken word performances, but it's good to have them available, just in case. Feeling comfortable with the sound onstage gives a performer confidence, and knowing that the sound you hear onstage is the same as what the audience hears doubles that confidence. If you've ever been bludgeoned by a voice blaring over a loudspeaker, you can bet there are no monitors on stage and the performers don't even realize how nasty loud they are.

Light 'Em if They Got 'Em

More important than a fancy stage, but somewhat less important than the audio quality, is the lighting. Lighting can create a stage that's not there. It can set a mood. It can add another creative facet to your show. The right lighting can instantly catapult your poetry event from the dimly-lit backstage of another poetry snore into the bright limelight of performance art.

However, you need to use lighting creatively and subtly in order for it to be effective. Don't run out to Ace Hardware, buy a portable floodlight, and assume that blasting your performers with a 200-watt halogen beam will make their performances shine brighter than ever before. They'll just squint through the furnace of light to find you and affix their glare to your forehead. The following sections show you how to put together a quality, low-cost lighting system and use it effectively.

Lights Up, Lights Down

Unless you're dealing with a big theatrical house or concert hall, lighting is going to be basic: lights up and lights down. The control usually consists of a rheostat that clicks on and off, and either slides or rotates to increase or decrease intensity. Sometimes the switch controls only one light. Sometimes it controls a bank of lights. If you're going to change the lighting during your show, someone, preferably a person with a great sense of timing and excellent reflexes, must work the switches.

Backstage Skinny

White light can often be too harsh for poetry performances. Yellow makes performers look jaundiced. Blue is murky. A combination of colors—white, red, blue, and amber—works best.

Before the show, check the position of the lights to be sure they're pointing to the desired locations onstage. Draft someone to stand onstage where the performers will stand and provide feedback as you climb the ladder and nudge the lights to point in the right direction. Between the two of you, you'll know when the lighting is right—when your mock performer looks properly illuminated to you, and when she stops screaming that the light is burning her eyeballs. Adjusting the lights is pretty simple if the lights are new or well maintained, but adjustments can be tricky if the lights are old and rickety.

Homespun Lighting Systems

For about $50, you can put together an adequate, portable lighting system for your show. Head over to your neighborhood hardware store and purchase four to six clamp-on work lights (which look like silver cones), a few heavy-duty extension cords of various lengths, and some 100-watt red or amber accent bulbs. For years I carried five or six of these set-ups around in the trunk of my car just in case I arrived at a gig to find poor lighting. They illuminated a dark situation on several occasions. The Green Mill stage has one theater spotlight and four of these homespun pan lights, and some of the country's top jazz groups play there every week, not to mention the most famous of the slam shows.

Dig This!
For a string of Chicago Poetry Ensemble performances, the performers were positioned in the audience amidst a network of homespun clamp-on lights. I ran extension cords equipped with on/off switches down the walls to each performer. It was a black box situation, total blackout when the house lights went down. The performers used the switched cords to pop on their do-it-yourself spotlights at the appropriate cues.

Top-Shelf Lighting

The big houses, concert halls, and proscenium theaters have complex computerized light boards that control dozens of lights, and some high class nightclubs have small spotlights that can be moved and focused mechanically with the touch of a button. These conditions almost always carry with them an experienced light technician who is accustomed to working on shows with hundreds of light cues. As elaborate as my poetry shows have been, never have they come close to the complexity of a major theater production or big-time rock concert. Trust the light technicians to handle your lighting needs; give them license to be creative, and they will always keep you and/or your performers properly illuminated. Mistreat them and you might find half your head eclipsed for most of the show.

Adding Some Glitz

A little glitz can liven up any event. Baseball teams use fireworks, get-a-bat days, and be-a-Sumo-wrestler fan bouts to get the crowd going. Football uses pass and kick competitions, gyrating cheerleaders, and roaming mascot gags to rile up the fans. Even Las Vegas energizes its already-glitzy neon image with show-stopping celebrities, circus tigers, and mesmerizing architecture. But Aristotle, whose writings have guided the evolution of drama for more than 2,000 years, considered Spectacle to be the least important of the theatrical elements present in a dramatic experience. According to Aristotle, Spectacle is ornamentation to be used sparingly.

Think of it as a Christmas tree. When you bring it home and stand it up unadorned in the parlor, it's quite a moving experience. It brings the outside in. The pine fragrance supercharges the air. Its presence changes the mood and landscape of the living room into a miracle on Thirty-Fourth Street. Deck the halls, baby!

Then Bobby, the oldest, opens the ornament box and starts pulling out strings of tangled lights, more ornaments, beads, and packets of silver garland. Bobby and the other three kids start bouncing around like SuperBalls in a frenetic sports flick sticking tin soldiers and gold spiders on the low branches, jumping up to toss reindeer near the top. Hey! Up to a point the extras enhance the natural beauty of the tree, but after too many tosses of tinsel, the magical spirit of the tree disappears under a thick coat of plastic and overdone garland. The moral of the story: There's a fine line between tasteful spectacle and gaudiness; don't cross it.

You've been creative in your hunt for a venue, creative in finding a crew, and creative in your overall show vision. Now, get creative with the technical matters that can enhance your show with tasteful spectacle. The following sections provide some guidance.

Dressing for Performance

It was laughable how my fellow performers and I sometimes dressed for those early shows at the Green Mill Uptown Poetry Slam—carnival clothes, suspenders, goofy hats. At other times it was pure magic. It made the audience feel like something mythical had come before them—poetry and pageantry.

Costumes are part of ritual experience. Think about it, every sport has a unique, identifiable uniform. At religious ceremonies, priests and priestesses don ceremonial garb. At graduations, the graduates wear long robes and funny hats. Costumes add to the mystery and meaning of the occasion. Like poetry, it's a heightened visual language.

It separates the stage experience and its main characters from everydayness. It gives it and you, the costumed person, importance. It identifies you as the person to watch, which is especially important when working inside an audience and not strictly on the stage.

Marc Smith decked out to perform "The Spirit of Xmas Expectations."

I remember a performance I did with the Bob Shakespeare Band at a local community college. We all entered in lavish black performance clothing—not backstage stuff, but in-the-spotlight-glamour, embroidered, textured, silky, lacey, sharp. A man in the audience later commented to the newspaper: "When those three poets entered, all fancied up in their black outfits, it was like three superheroes had flown into our school. My heart made a racket as soon as they appeared Zap! at the door."

The right degree of costuming adds dazzle to a show and performance. Too much can look very silly.

Dig This!

The Bob Shakespeare Band, formed in Chicago in 1988, was the original multi-voiced slam performance group. It consisted of Cin Salach, Sheila Donohue, Doug Rand, Kendall Dunkelberg, and Marc Smith. It developed multi-voice techniques that became the root of later group pieces.

Spicing It Up with a Little Music

Many slams use music to set a preshow mood or as segues between poets, or during intermissions, or as an integral part of the night's performances. DJs spin at many slams providing a backbeat for poets and a transition between performers. Live music can be a welcome break from poet after poet after poet. Singer-songwriters are kinfolk to poets and are often poets themselves. Their performances can deliver a refreshing and inspiring new perspective to a show.

Dig This!

Spectacle was a requirement at the Fat Tuesday Celebrations of the Seven Deadly Sins held at Fitzgerald's West Side Poetry Slam in Berwyn, Illinois. Seven poetry ensembles (krewes) created poetry parades modeled after those found on the streets of New Orleans during Mardi Gras. Each krewe represented and expressed sentiments of one of the deadly sins: lust, anger, greed, gluttony, envy, pride, and sloth. Without music, costumes, and spectacle, much of the fun would have been … sinless.

What's on the CD

CD #1 track #15:
The Weird Sisters performing "Forbidden Love"

SlamSlang

A **Pong Jam** is a musical/poetic jam session in which poets read or recite their poems to musical improvisation. Regretfully, I coined the term through an off-the-cuff introduction, "Pong. They're not poems. They're not songs. They're pongs." The Pong Unit Band hates the name, but its members are too busy to invent a better one.

All forms of music have been incorporated into slam shows—rock, folk, jazz, funk, you name it. The opening act at NPS 2002 in Minneapolis was a Native American drum and dance troupe that whirled and stomped and spirited us away to a pre-European wilderness. It was sensational.

A favorite musical additional to the Green Mill Uptown Poetry Slam is the Weird Sisters. The precise and surprising power of their poetic, comedic lyrics places them firmly within the slam tradition of poetry and performance.

Slide Shows

Dateline Chicago: Sunday night. May 10, 1988. Mother's Day. First they load in sound equipment, lots of sound equipment—amps, synthesizers, speakers.

SlamSpeak

"WORD UP! BE WITH THE BAND!"

Influenced by Marc Smith's Pong Jams in Chicago and New York's Words Jazz, Poetry, and Hip Hop Shows, the world's only (as far as we know it) poetry-DJ, Rayl Da P-Jay, initiated "Word up!," a music-poetry-entertainment revue at Munich's Atomic Café. Five invited global poets perform their poems together with the funky "Word up!" house band. An open-mike round gives new talents a chance. Dancers, acrobats, and magicians produce the romantic flair of a poetic circus. After the show, Rayl Da P-Jay and other DJs lead into the wonder world of rhymes, poetry, and beats. Dance the poem!

—from the "Word Up!" file

"Hey, we've already got speakers at the Green Mill."

"We need extras! The Loofah Methode have arrived."

"What the hell is a Loofah Methode? And what the hell is that?" (Referring to the procession of a 16-foot-wide movie screen, film projectors, slide projectors, drummers, and sax players, marching in through the door.)

"Oh my god! What's next?!"

What came next was a spectacular mix of music, visual projections, props, costumes, and poetry that became a staple of the avant-garde performance art scene (in Chicago) for over a decade. And it began at the slam.

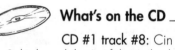

What's on the CD

CD #1 track #8: Cin Salach and the Loofah Methode performing "Blind Spots"

SlamSpeak

Loofah Methode

someone brushed away some dead skin.
held up a mirror, showed me some nerves.
my nerves, exposed, still raw, and gasping for air
like little heads, nostrils flaring, tongues lapping,
at some fresh air.

it was less than a second, less than a second,
and new skin scarred over this aggressive innocence.
less than a second, but i felt the conception take place.
now under my skin
a new life begins.

—by Cin Salach

Over almost two decades, scores of performers have used visual arts as a backdrop for their verse. One of the most famous of the early slammer/artists who decorated the stage with slides of his iconoclastic art as he punched out his poems is Tony Fitzpatrick. Tony was the first official referee at the Green Mill, where for a couple years his big Irish mug didn't take no guff from "nobody no how," especially the "art victim poets" who didn't like slammin'. Nobody dared mess with him. If you got a zero, you got a zero. "Now shut up and sit down." Here's one of his drawings and the poem that inspired it.

Setting up slide projectors at a slam is a relatively easy affair. All you need is an outlet, a table, and a light-colored wall. A well-done slideshow can instantly transform the stale ambience of a room into a snake-charming experience.

Tony Fitzpatrick's
"Snake Hand."

SlamSpeak

Hand

in the dream a jailhouse hand slid out
    with a mirror in its fist
and we locked eyes
and the mirror asked You got a cigarette

a tailor-made cigarette
for me?
and do you play chess and could we play?
and could you lay sticks and kindling at my feet
and light me up like a rocket ship?
I want to hold hands with a bomb
and learn how they sing
—from "Hard Angels" by Tony Fitzpatrick

Props and Drops

Yeah, yeah, we all know about the no-prop rule. That's okay for the national competitions, but I suggest you break the rules now and then for the sake of spectacle and stick some huge props in the room. Maybe a mannequin representing the dead poet society. Maybe a long-handle hook in the corner to put the fear of humiliation into the hearts of the more pompous open-mike poets. How about a gong?! How about a huge banner with your slam logo on the back wall? Or posters from the national competitions? Maybe drapes of poems pasted together week after week.

For years I would forget to make important announcements at the Sunday show. It became part of the ritual, part of the spectacle when I started pasting the announcement notes on the support post that occupies the center of the Green Mill. The audience would shout, "Read a note, Marc." That was a great game for the audience while it lasted. Now I can't even remember to paste up the … what was that I was supposed to do?

The Least You Need to Know

- Lighting, sound amplification, and spectacle help draw more precise focus to a performance.

- A unidirectional microphone is best for individual spoken word poetry performances, because it blocks out most background noise.

- Don't place the speakers behind or too close to the microphone, because you'll end up blowing out everybody's eardrums.

- A little subtle lighting can significantly enhance performances and influence the ambience of a room.

- Add some spectacle to liven up your show and energize the audience, but don't over-season your main course.

Chapter 16

Choosing Your Crew

In This Chapter

- ◆ Going it alone, ugh!
- ◆ Distributing responsibility through a committee
- ◆ Delegating duties—marketers, performers, and qualified assistants
- ◆ Auditioning emcees, hosts, and co-hosts
- ◆ Assembling a solid, reliable support staff

Before you fling open the doors to your show, you'd better have a reliable staff in place. Without assistants to market the show, line up performers, greet patrons, collect money, manage the sign-up sheet, work the sound system, tinker with the lights, baby-sit the virgin virgins, select and educate scorekeepers, and perform a host of other essential tasks, you're going to feel like you're playing 50 instruments in a one-man marching band.

I'm not saying it can't be done solo. I and many others have been there, done that, and even enjoyed it. In fact, going solo has some advantages: No worries of whether the help will show up; no personality conflicts; no one to blame. And when the show wails, you get all the credit. It's the perfect job for a hyperactive, workaholic control freak. At some point, however, when the show grows beyond your wildest dreams, you'll have to delegate so you can focus on the more critical aspects of the show. This chapter shows you how to delegate effectively, efficiently, and without losing control of your show.

Flying Solo—the Self-Made Slam

You are a hyperactive, workaholic control freak, and flying solo is just what you have in mind. Excellent, but you better be prepared. Jot down a checklist of everything that needs to be done and then prioritize. Put everything that can be done before the show at the top of the list: distributing flyers, hanging posters, lining up an opening act, setting up and testing the sound system, adjusting the lights, arranging the tables and chairs, setting up a ticket table, and so on. Perform those preshow tasks long before the doors open.

Backstage Skinny _____

If you're flying solo and taking on the duties of emcee, the importance of a checklist cannot be over-emphasized. When show time hits, you're going to want your mind "in the moment," reacting to and guiding the artistic aspects of the show, not trying desperately to remember what you promised to pay your performers or what announcements you wanted to make. A checklist frees your mind and saves you from embarrassing glitches like forgetting to put the mayor and his wife on the guest list.

If the venue has staff in place for collecting money, selling tickets, and seating people, cross those tasks off your list. All remaining tasks are your job: crafting the show, finding timekeepers and judges, managing the sign-up sheet, making sure the poet/performers have what they need, acting as emcee, and perhaps even performing yourself.

Organizing by Committee

Anyone who has ever sat on a committee knows the conflicts and complications that can arise. You get six opinions on how to do the most menial task, arguments over the most trivial matters, complaints without recommendations, power struggles, and personality clashes. In a creative endeavor, artistic passions can intensify these conflicts and complications to extremes. Everybody's opinion becomes valid and difficult to refute diplomatically, no matter how illogical or impractical it might be. All the opinions might be valid paths to the same goal, but which do you choose? And who does the choosing?

Despite these drawbacks, a hard-working and harmonious committee can achieve many times more than a solo slammaster can and in half the time. In addition, collaborating with creative soulmates can often trigger synergies that enrich your vision and embellish your show. If you have a cluster of slam lovers who are mature and confident enough to share your vision without diluting it or wrestling for control, you should strongly consider forming a committee. When your slam takes flight, you'll be able to celebrate together, and that's a lot more fun than celebrating alone.

Whoa!

Don't give up your leadership role just because you've formed a committee. Good committees need strong leaders to balance and focus all the talent and ideas. Learn the strengths and weaknesses of your committee members. Don't try to remake their personalities. Tap into their talents and try to keep their quirks and foibles from steering the vision too far askew from the desired goal.

The Duties to Delegate

Whether you end up creating and producing your slam solo or by committee, eventually you will divide and delegate duties to get things done efficiently, on time, and in a manner that allows you and your slam monster to grow beyond your wildest dreams. The following sections explore the four main areas you need to focus on when delegating tasks:

- Marketing
- Scouting and booking talent
- Show time assistants
- Offstage support

Marketing

You might have initiated your marketing campaign by sketching a logo, pasting up a crude flyer, running off a couple hundred copies on the sly at work, and then handing them out at poetry functions. But when you're ready to take your show to the next level (as explained in Chapters 9 and 18), you need to pump up your marketing blitz with press releases, an informative website, mass mailings, TV appearances, radio interviews, and any other marketing gimmicks you can dream up.

Unless you're a Madison Avenue marketing guru who finds every promotional task as gratifying as a cup of coffee at sunrise, be on the lookout for a marketing maven. The ideal candidate will have the following traits:

Backstage Skinny

If you're slammin' by committee, put one person in charge of marketing and advise that person to seek piecemeal help from several sources: someone to design a logo, someone to write press releases, someone to create a website, and so on. Marketing is a big domain; the more help the better.

♦ Artistic flair

♦ The ability to write clever ad copy and kick out some catchy hype

♦ A pleasant telephone voice and personality

♦ A reliable and trustworthy character

♦ A willingness to act as a go-for (go for this, go for that) every now and then

♦ A familiarity with computers, desktop publishing software, website management, and e-mail

Scouting for Talented Performers

Obviously, even when flying solo, you can't be the one and only performer. Today, slammasters are very fortunate to be able to draw from a fairly large talent pool. Performance poets and slammers travel across the country looking for new shows to fill in their tour routes. Get on the slam listserv and put out the word that your slam has openings for out-of-town slammers who are passing through. They'll start calling you and sending you *their* press packs.

Whoa!

Be sure to check an unknown performer's credentials. Ask him or her to send you a press pack and check with other slammasters—and heed their recommendations and warnings. Giving an ambitious novice a start is commendable, but not at the expense of damaging your show's reputation.

Avidly seek out the talent in your own city, both poets and variety acts. Your goal is to develop a broad audience base that extends beyond the existing poet community. Keep a talent address book or a list with each performer's contact information to jog your memory when you book the coming months. Attend other poetry events, read reviews, and ask around to get the names and numbers of who's high caliber and who has a strong following.

Trustworthy and Reliable Assistants

When you're focused on crafting a show that packs a wallop, it's easy to overlook the minor details, and there are zillions of them—from purchasing markers and scorecards to making sure the mailing lists get circulated. A dedicated assistant show manager or slammaster can be a great relief, ensuring that attention gets paid to every aspect of the show. The following list describes the duties that you can expect a competent assistant to handle before, during, and after a show:

♦ **Before the Show.** Arrange the furniture and set up the stage (mike in place, lights and sound system working). Stack and set out flyers announcing future events. Seat people and answer questions. Check to be sure the feature performers have arrived or are on their way.

♦ **During the Show.** Get open mikers lined up and on the mark. Provide hospitality to guest performers. Monitor sound and lights. Cue the emcee about announcements and what's coming next. Keep track of contact information. Handle prizes.

♦ **After the Show.** Put the furniture where the venue owner wants it. Pack your toys, including markers, index cards, mailing list, and lights. Help clean up if you and the venue owner (or manager) have an understanding that you're part of the clean-up crew. Make sure the performers aren't pacing the parking lot looking for jumper cables. Direct everyone to the after-show party place.

Emcees Wanted—Charisma Required

No one individual is more important to your slam show than its emcee, the onstage personality who will make your audience feel comfortable, bestow glamour and respect on the talent, and keep the show moving ever forward. Whether you choose to play this role yourself or delegate the job to someone more qualified, a good emcee must exhibit the following qualities:

♦ **Attractiveness:** The emcee doesn't have to be a knockout, but the emcee should be appearance-conscious (not a slob) and must have an engaging personality. Even in the slam world, appearance counts. Fortunately, in slam circles, eccentric appearance counts more than magazine fashion. Through the slam, people gain the confidence they need to express their unique selves through their appearance and dress. Look for someone who appears as though they spent some time thinking about their appearance and someone who is lively, passionate, interesting, unique, and pleasantly eccentric.

♦ **Audience Sensitivity.** A sensitive emcee has a sixth sense about what the audience is thinking and feeling about a performer or the night in general. Without audience sensitivity, a show can bomb or dissolve into chaos before the emcee realizes anything is wrong.

- **Charisma.** A charismatic emcee is magnetic, drawing the audience's focus and generating excitement in some mysterious way. Look for someone who can turn on the juice and fire up a crowd.

- **Coolness.** The ability to think quickly under pressure without becoming flustered enables the emcee to stay the course when the show falters.

- **Dedication.** The right emcee understands your vision of the slam and wants to bring it to life.

- **Flexibility.** The ability to switch directions in reaction to the audience response or lack thereof is essential.

- **Generosity.** A good emcee is generous to the poets and patrons, yet savvy enough not to be bowled over by hecklers or arrogant performers.

- **Magnanimity.** Magnanimity (or selflessness) enables an emcee to step out of the spotlight and generously welcome others into it. Magnanimous people generally are self-fulfilled; they're happy with their lives and want to celebrate other people's joy.

Backstage Skinny

If you're watching your slam show bomb and hear your brain chattering, "Why doesn't Emcee Julio do something?" or "Why can't Julio shut up and get on to the next poet?" maybe it's time for an emcee pink slip.

- **Preparedness.** A well-stocked repertoire of performance material can help bail out an emcee when the show starts to sag.

- **Resourcefulness.** A good emcee does what's required to make the show run smoothly regardless of the tasks required. If the mike needs adjusting, the emcee does it on the spot instead of calling the sound tech or slammaster.

- **Talent.** Emcees are performers, too, so they should be as (or almost as) comfortable, engaging, and entertaining onstage as the performers.

Auditioning Emcees

The best way to audition emcees is to try them out at your slam or check them out at some other performance they're participating in. Assess how they interact with the audience and analyze their performance against the traits described in the previous section. When you find a candidate or two, talk with them casually and allow the inner workings of their personalities to unravel. If you're intimidating or confrontational, they'll tighten their ropes, and nothing will unravel. Subtly work the following questions into the conversation:

◆ What do you think about different styles of poetry?

◆ What do you think about slam poetry?

◆ What are your ambitions?

If they think poetry should remain locked and chained in the ivory towers and that slam poets should be institutionalized, and their lifelong ambition is to write obituaries, you'll want to continue your search. However, if your candidate did well onstage, thinks that slam has a grand future as a performance art, and can't live without a steady diet of stage time, you might have found the perfect match to fire up your show. Just make sure your personalities click and that your potential emcee understands and supports your vision.

Relief Pitchers—Back-Up Emcees Need Charisma, Too

After you line up a dynamite emcee, shop for backups or build sub-emcees into your show by trying out different emcees in different positions. You might construct a show with a main emcee who's responsible for the overall direction of the show and a co-emcee (or co-host) who referees the slam competition or introduces guest performers. The emcee role is too important to leave to a single person; make sure you have a couple fine options in the bullpen in case the starter calls in sick, gets hurt, or just doesn't show.

SlamSlang

The terms *emcee, slam host, and slammaster* are commonly used interchangeably because the slammaster often dons all these hats. However, technically speaking, the emcee is the onstage personality who introduces the acts. The host is in charge of organizing all the details of a particular event and greeting the clientele and performers. The slammaster is the organizer who is responsible for all the events of a particular slam venue and who has a direct relationship with and responsibility to PSI (Poetry Slam, Inc.).

Mixing It Up with Different Personalities

Many slams distribute the duties of hosting and emceeing a show. At some slams, the slammaster acts as both host and emcee. At others, the slammaster might act as host by meeting, greeting, and seating the patrons, and then take the stage as emcee, while the assistant slammaster assumes the duties as host. However you set up your show, consider having two or more personalities act as host, co-host, and emcee, even if you choose to take turns. Different personalities draw different fans and can help expand your audience base. The host might be warm and welcoming, making reticent patrons feel at home, whereas the emcee might have an edgy sense of humor that appeals to the more daring, experienced clientele. Different personalities add variety to the evening and to the overall schedule. They also help promote your show through casual word-of-mouth advertising … "Hey, come by the Goose Neck Slam on Tuesday. I'm hosting it next week." Finally, this arrangement results in the training of more people and creates more leaders for the movement in general; this could possibly lead to more shows in your town.

Offstage Support

Patrons leave your show replaying the performances in their minds. That's what they came for—to escape the mundane and revel in the visions and re-creations of your performance artists. However, much of the work that goes into making any show a success goes on offstage, and people generally don't remember it unless something goes wrong. If the lighting left performers in the shadows, the sound system emitted garbled verse, or the fans had to wait in line for a half hour while the ticket-taker looked for change, they'll remember *that* and probably mention it to their friends the next day. To make sure that no offstage crisis undermines your show's onstage integrity, assemble a good crew to handle the "minor" details.

Sound and Light

Chapter 15 teaches you everything you need to know to manage a sound system and adjust the lights for your show, but consider delegating these technical tasks. As slam-master, you should act as host and perhaps as the show's emcee. If you're adjusting the lights or fiddling with the sound system, the distractions pull your attention from the show, the audience, and the performers. It's like having a dinner party and spending the entire evening in the kitchen.

Every slam family has one gifted consumer electronics whiz who loves playing with the stereo and adding mood lighting to his bedroom. If this electro-wizard isn't too far out there (strobe lights, echo chambers), give the whiz a shot at managing the technical details of your show.

Doorperson

An honest, reliable, and charming, or at least interesting (as in eccentric) doorperson is a must, especially for shows just starting out. Nightclubs and other over-twenty-one establishments sometimes insist on having their own doorperson checking IDs and collecting the cover charge. That saves you the expense of hiring someone, but it gives you no control over the money or how the patrons are greeted. Be sure you're comfortable with the doorperson, and if you have reservations about the person, express them to the owner or manager in a diplomatic way.

Backstage Skinny

An experienced doorperson can often handle several additional tasks: the sign-up sheets, passing out flyers, checking the guest list, and ordering pizzas for the after-show pig-out.

Scorekeepers/Timers

If you're not too concerned with accuracy, assign audience members to watch the clock and tally the scores. Hand him or her a digital wristwatch that bleeps out the seconds, a pen, and a pad of paper. If the slam is serious, such as a competition to determine who goes on tour with Viggo Mortensen, you might want to buy some stopwatches and calculators and appoint someone in your crew to manage these tasks. Give these scorekeepers and timers a brief lesson on their duties and instruct the emcee to watch over them and bail them out when they screw up, because they will screw up, they always do … at least once.

Merchandise Sellers

The role of merchant is a dedicated job that should be delegated only to a loyal assistant or trustworthy volunteer. It involves record keeping, money handling, pitching, and schmoozing. If you can put a couple people on this task, do it. It can get lonely and boring sitting alone at a table far from where the action's happening, and who watches the money when your merchandise person needs a break?

Judges

Usually slam judges are selected from the audience, but sometimes they're recruited ahead of time either to add a higher level of legitimacy to the competition or, in the case of slams just starting out, to be sure that someone is on hand to do the job. Skip ahead to Chapter 22 to review the judges instructions employed at the National Slams. In all cases, the judges should become part of the show, part of the ritual, and enhance the entertainment value of the night.

In-House Ensembles

You learned earlier that the Chicago Poetry Ensemble was essential to the success of the early slams at the Green Mill. Each week they injected pizzazz, spectacle, and daring poetics into the early slam atmosphere. They were the backbone entertainment, but they also doubled up on other production tasks, ranging from covering the door to acting as last-minute ringers in the slam competition when not enough poets had signed up. That's not unusual for shoestring theater and entertainment operations. Everyone pitches in to serve the cause in a variety of capacities. And this is the greatest attribute of, and reason for having, an in-house ensemble: They're an insurance policy to cover those eleventh-hour flubs and loopholes, as well as serving as a surefire staple of proven entertainment.

The Least You Need to Know

- Creating and staging a show by yourself might be rewarding, but it can become too demanding for any single person.

- A committee serves three basic purposes: to share responsibility, to distribute the workload, and to foster synergies that energize the show.

- When delegating, focus on the following four areas: marketing, scouting and booking talent, general staff, and offstage support.

- Make sure your show's emcee has a personality that clicks with yours, understands and supports your vision for the show, and has all the qualities of an outstanding host and performer.

- At show time, you need plenty of offstage hands: a sound and light technician, doorperson, scorekeeper, timer, merchandiser, and judges.

- An in-house ensemble is a valuable addition to any show, providing background music and musical accompaniment, filling in gaps in the show, and acting as ringers when poets don't show up.

Chapter
Taking Ownership of *Your* Show

In This Chapter

- ◆ Maintaining control of your show without acting like an overbearing boss

- ◆ Making your guests feel welcome

- ◆ Anticipating and dealing with undesirable poet/performer personalities

- ◆ Whipping the audience into a state of frenzied enthusiasm

- ◆ Using your show's success to market your chapbooks, CDs, and other merchandise

You're the consummate puppet master. You invented and organized a first-class show and promoted the heck out of it. You delegated the duties of doorperson, ticket-taker, emcee, sign-up secretary, scorekeeper, audio technician, and lighting expert to trusted members of your crew. You're a behind-the-scenes type, and you like it that way. Now you're ready to kick back with your favorite beverage and watch the majesty of the evening unfold before you.

Not so fast!

Whoa!

Nobody's advocating dictatorship, but you should maintain a benign authority over your show. Be open to all voices, but make the final decisions yourself. It's your canvas; hold onto the brushes and watch the paint cans.

Your pilot and crew might run the show brilliantly, but you still need to stand at the helm. Responsible and professional helpers appreciate a visible captain and usually need (or want) to demonstrate their expertise to the person in charge. You're the foundation upon which they stand. They feel secure when you're there, and they feel abandoned when you're not. In addition, you have a responsibility to make your guests feel at home, and that's essential for making any slam a success. This chapter shows you how to play your part as slammaster when show time rolls around.

Acting as Gracious Host

It's opening night. You carefully arrange the tables and chairs so everyone can see. You pull out the risers and assemble your do-it-yourself stage. You climb the ladder, focus the lights, and turn on the properly equalized sound system. You even set up a ticket table and stock it with programs and a pass-out hand stamp. Everything is in place.

But all this hard work will be for naught if people don't feel a personal connection with you. Your job as slammaster is to help your guests chill—with themselves, with you, with each other, with your crew, and with the performers. The following sections show you how to go about establishing a good rapport with the audience and foster the sense of community that really makes a show take off.

Greeting Your Guests

As the patrons begin to enter, stand by the door and say "howdy, welcome, whatup" as they come in. A few first-timers will look at you as if you're some kind of goof, but so what? By the end of the slam they'll understand that it's all part of the game. And if they don't? Que sera, sera … you'll never see them again.

After you greet the arrivals, ask them if they have a poem to perform. If they do, sign them up. If not, then say something like, "Just here to listen? Well, you're the most important part of the night." It's true; without an audience, we're just howling in a dark and lonely room. Slams are active, powered by the energy of the performance-audience interaction. By greeting folks, you're sparking the fuse that's about to blast your show wide open.

Introducing Your Guests

When you're not at the door greeting people, work the crowd. Introduce one table of veterans to a neighboring table of virgins and have them all shout "Yo!" across the room and to the visitors from France. By introducing people, you're forming a community, breaking down inhibitions, loosening tongues, and priming your audience to respond and react to what they're about to witness. The more the audience reacts, the more rewarding the show will be for all.

Acting as the Maitre d'

At the Green Mill it's almost always standing room only, so the manager and I seat people to make sure all the booths, stools, and tables are used to their capacity. This has turned into a great opportunity for us to help audience members connect to one another. Someone passes a chair or scoots over to make room, their eyes meet, they exchange a few words, and suddenly they're connected. Eighty percent of the time, a chance encounter transforms acquaintances into comrades, kind of like that wedding table of strangers that have a grand time during the reception despite the grumbling in-laws. If you have the opportunity to act as maitre d' at your show, make the most of it.

> **Dig This!**
>
> Try this experiment once, just once. Start your show without introducing people to each another. Observe how it goes and how responsive the audience is. At the first break, work the crowd and do your introductions—focus on the people you thought were particularly reserved. Start the second set and see how things change. I bet the second set will rock with more fervor than the first.

Setting a Stage, Not a Pedestal

Your stage might raise you, your emcee, and your performers above the level of the audience, but don't let it go to your head or your performers' heads. The stage is raised only so the audience can see. If the people above start to think they're better than the people below, all sorts of problems rear up and bray.

As slammaster, you will meet (and have to deal with) a host of personalities from pleasant to repulsive, from beautiful to hideous, from responsible to reckless. As time goes on, you'll weed out the arrogant and unreliable performers and cultivate a garden of fine performers you can rely on to be punctual, courteous, and brilliant onstage. Until then, be prepared to encounter a few of these less-attractive personality types:

- **The Apologizer** Late, unprepared, and generally incompetent, the apologizer is always sorry and says so as easily as saying "Hello." "Sorry I'm late." "Sorry my piece sucked so bad—next time I'll rehearse." Tell the apologizer what you think, what you expect, and that if it happens again, he might want to consider performing solo on a street corner in another town.

- **The Blamer** When something goes wrong, the blamer is never at fault. "Man, you need to work on your sound system." "If you would've given me that third slot, I'd have kicked bootie." "Your whole vision for this show is screwed up." If the blamer is right, ask for advice—you might be able to improve your show. If the complaint is unfounded, encourage the blamer to take his act elsewhere.

- **SuperSlammer** The arrogant slammer is one of the most obnoxious personalities you'll meet. This slammer thinks that you, your crew, the audience, and the club owner should bow down and pay homage to the master. Maybe Super-Slammer really is a great poet and performer, but the true greats typically are humble and treat others with respect. If you encounter a SuperSlammer who's good, a little advice on honing people skills might be useful. If he's mediocre (or lousy) and continues to treat you, your audience, or your crew disrespect-fully, show SuperSlammer the door.

- **The Interrogator** The Interrogator has no self-confidence and peppers you with questions throughout the evening just to get some attention. "When do I go on? Who's going on before me? Where can I set up my stuff? Can my friends get in free? Can you adjust the lights just so? Where's the dressing room?" Of course, many of these questions are valid, but they should have been addressed before (not during) the show. If you have several Interrogators, it might be a good sign that you need to type up an information sheet for per-formers. If the Interrogator keeps asking the same questions and follows you around like a lost puppy, shake him, fast.

- **Slam Cop** A stickler for the rules, the Slam Cop points out every digression from the official rules, no matter how miniscule the infraction. At national com-petitions this might be welcomed, to a point, but if you're trying to foster an informal atmosphere at a local club, the Slam Cop can become an annoying control freak. Explain what you're trying to do and why you're allowing rules to be bent and broken. If that doesn't make him back off, take a more direct approach—suggest that he start his own show.

Watch the Clock—Starting on Time

One of the banes of poetry readings is that they rarely start on time and usually run long. People start looking at their watches and wiggling in their seats, the readings become drawn out and watered down, and the whole experience loses its intensity. Set a starting and an ending time for your show and stick to the schedule. Everything that's going to happen tonight will happen between 8:00 and 11:00. That gives your show intensity and forces you, your emcee, and the performers to keep the show moving.

Nothing is more discouraging to an audience than a show that starts late. Think about attending a play and waiting an hour for the curtain to rise—it would be unbearable. It's a little more tolerable in a bar where you can buy a drink and play some music. But a large percentage of first-time audience members won't tolerate late starts, and the negative word-of-mouth they generate will eventually chip away at your show's reputation. A ten-minute hold is fine, occasionally, but don't make a habit of it.

Fueling Audience Frenzy

Sometimes a show just doesn't start chugging. Either the open mikers were all somber or the special guest went flat as a pep-less Dr. Pepper. No fizzle, no sizzle, no spark. Blah. You could just chalk it up to experience and try to jazz up your next show, but why let the entire evening flop? Dig down in that show-master toolbox of yours, pull out your jumper cables, and zap the seats with jump juice. Here are some suggestions for pumping life into a dying show:

♦ Have one of your more accomplished open-mike regulars stand up in the audience, unannounced, and belt out a short exclamatory poem, "Oh Thou Mighty Muse within My Mighty Pen!" Usually a loud, high-energy piece is the best for this, but tenderness has worked. Ask the poet to keep it to two minutes or less—you're looking for intensity here, short and punchy, not ponderously profound.

♦ Recruit several open mikers or your in-house ensemble to knock out a *round robin*, emoting from around the room and on the stage. Planned or impromptu, a round robin is an easy and exciting way to stoke the flames of audience interest.

> **Dig This!**
>
> The first across-the-room duet I encountered was performed by two eighth-grade students in a workshop I conducted. They stood atop the tables in the school library and delivered a poem about the struggles of their friendship. All of us were hushed and almost in tears at its end. I've used the technique successfully in shows ever since.

◆ Stage an *across-the-room duet*. Have two of your better performers with strong voices position themselves at opposite ends of the room and perform a duet. Be sure there's some lighting focused on them and that they're clearly visible. To make this stunt effective, the performers must speak and respond directly to each other, creating an intimate scene to which the audience is privy—like overhearing poets in the heavens playing out their passions and words.

◆ Initiate a *call and response*. You can do this with your in-house ensemble or with the audience. Have a poem in your repertoire that calls for the audience to respond with words or whistles or groans. You've seen this done a million times at church, at concerts, at political rallies. Invent your own call and response tricks and have them handy.

◆ Be a momentary *big mouth*. Sometimes all an audience needs to smash their inhibitions is to hear someone else get vocal. A word or three in response to a poet's offering onstage can open the door. If you think you might be too conspicuous doing it yourself, find an eager friend to serve as the ringer. It's a blast.

◆ If you have a brave soul in your ensemble, send him up to the stage to be purposely awful, to invoke the snap, the groan, and/or the feminist hiss laying the groundwork for authentic audience retaliation against the drones of a failing open mike.

Making the Most of a $lam $ituation

Genuine poets and slammasters don't like to treat their artistic creations like run-of-the mill "products" to be hawked like trinkets at a fair. Their art is as important to them as their souls. That doesn't mean they don't like to make money. As long as they remain true to their vision, many slammers and slammasters serve the patrons by offering quality *chapbooks*, anthologies, CDs, t-shirts, and other merchandise. The following sections provide ideas to help you develop your own product line.

SlamSlang

A **chapbook** is a small, typically self-published book of poems, ballads, or stories.

Preserving the History

Establish a system for preserving your show's history. If you've already staged a few shows, it's not too late to start. Keep a journal and audio recordings, and, if possible, videotape your shows. These audio and video recordings can also provide the raw materials you need to create anthologies—collections of your slam's best performances.

Of course, when you're playing the role of slammaster, you can't possibly videotape the show yourself. Find someone who loves your slam and is bubbling with the passion to record it. They're out there. Turn over the reins to them. Having a camcorder running inspires and rewards your performers and adds an aura of importance to your show.

Whoa!

Don't subject your audience to a tactless and clumsy video cameraman who gets in their way or distracts them with noisy, clumsy movements. If you videotape, make sure the equipment and operators are as inconspicuous and considerate as possible. And please, no glaring lights!

Creating Anthologies

Desktop publishing is commonplace now. With relative ease, a slammaster or someone in her crew can collect poems from the slammers and assemble them into a chapbook anthology:

1. Collect the poems you want to include and obtain written permission from the poets to use them in your anthology.

2. Work with the poets to edit the selections into an acceptable page form.

3. Assemble the selections into some kind of logical order—alphabetically by poet or subject matter, by date of performance, or according to some other system.

4. Lay out the poems in a book format (or have someone else do it). Use a computer equipped with a good desktop publishing program.

5. Find an artist to design a book cover.

6. Compile and create the incidentals: table of contents, acknowledgements, title page, graphics, forward, and so on. Check out a couple of poetry anthologies and see what incidentals they include.

7. Get some quotes from local printers and find out how they want the originals delivered. Can you submit the book electronically—on CD or via modem? Do you need to submit it in print, as *page proofs?* What size? If you're printing

Backstage Skinny

Get ready for some sloppy manuscripts (or no manuscripts at all) from some of your favorite performers. Many performers, myself included, do not actively seek publication, and their poems evolve onstage to forms that have no page equivalent. As editor, you'll be guiding some slammers through the page process.

SlamSlang

Page proofs are the final printouts of a publication that are ready to be reproduced at the printer's to created bound versions.

in color, how must you do the color separations? If you don't know anything about printing, don't try to fake it; admit your ignorance and let the printer explain things to you.

8. Put your baby into production and plan a release party, and don't forget to issue a press release announcing its birth.

Unless your anthology is being released through a major publishing house, you can offer the contributors little or no payment. (You'll be lucky to break even.) It's a labor of love; most poets realize this and are happy just to have their poems honored in print. If someone demands payment that you cannot guarantee, omit their works. Giving your contributors a set number of free copies, however, is expected, and if you should sell out of the first edition and make a cool thousand fish or so, have a party for your poets to pay them back.

Dig This!

The *Nuyorican Anthology*, which captures the performers and poems, has become a classic reference book depicting the early years of performance poetry—not only by Nuyorican poets, but also by those of us non–New Yorkers who performed there. More specific to the Slam, Gary Glazner's book *Poetry Slam* and Mark Eleveld's anthology *The Spoken Word Revolution* are being used in schools and universities throughout the world as guides to slam and performance poetry.

Compilation CDs

Almost every touring poet has two or more CDs featuring his or her performances. It's about as easy to make a CD compilation as it is to make a print anthology—probably easier, especially if you forgo including a text of the poems in the *liner notes*. Reproduction companies like Disc Makers will send you catalogues that give you the step-by-step, and sometimes a sales rep will guide you through the process. In case they don't, the following steps describe the overall process:

1. Select the recorded performances you want to include. They might come from the nightly recordings you've done of your show, from CDs already produced by others, or from recordings made by the poets themselves, or you might record poets in your or your friend's studio.

2. Arrange the recordings into some logical order.

3. Find an artist to design the cover art and lay out the *liner notes* following the file formats provided by the reproduction company. Get him or her working on it.

4. Enlist the service of or employ a professional sound engineer to mix the tracks and lay them down on a mastered disc. The sound engineer must provide certain technical information about the recordings to the reproduction company to get the job done properly, so it's best to hire a professional.

SlamSlang

Liner notes are the printed texts inside a CD case. They list the track selections, running times, and give biographical information about the performers.

5. Deliver the master disc, layout, and artwork to the reproduction company. Send in a check and wait two to six weeks for your first CD compilation disc.

Backstage Skinny

Anticipate having to make a host of production choices concerning liner notes, types of jewel cases, and artwork. You can ask and answer questions about such matters over the phone or through e-mail with a sales representative from the reproduction company. They're in business to do everything for you; pick their brains.

T-Shirts and Souvenirs

Many local slams, and every national slam event, produce t-shirts to promote and commemorate their events. And because the slam is still hovering above the grassroots level and well below super-mainstream radar, almost all of these t-shirts become collector's items. But slammers and slammasters have not stopped there—we're a very creative bunch. Here are some other kitschy options you might consider for promoting your slam (or just being goofy):

♦ **Cartoon strips and comic books.** It's been done, but it's never been taken as far as it could go. Imagine Poetic Action Heroes and the drama of their performance unfolding in each frame.

♦ **Trading cards.** Charles Ellik and the California poets started this. There's no reason why each local slam couldn't have its own deck of poet trading cards.

♦ **More stuff.** Bumper stickers. Tattoos. Pennants. Baseball caps. Bowling shirts. Poetic slippers.

Go for it. And make it fun. All these products help promote your show and create physical emblems of belonging for the slam community you're building.

Establishing Profitable Partnerships

After your slam is cruising along and you've established an audience, it's time to hook up with other literary arts organizations in your city. They might have been critical of your early efforts, but set that aside and work with them to …

- Bring in special guest performers.
- Stage special citywide shows.
- Create workshop and outreach programs.
- Share advertising expenses.

Grants and governmental funding heavily support most literary arts establishments and cultural institutions. They have the financial resources and you have, if you've followed the slam path, a strong audience base. Hook up with them and see what can happen. The point is not you vs. them, the point is poetry. To learn more about tracking down these institutions, skip ahead to Chapter 20.

Absurd Ambitions and Other Worldly Temptations

The slam has not gone mainstream, but some of its family members have capitalized on great opportunities offered to them by mainstream commercial entities. Performance poets who got a big boost from local and national slams have obtained recording contracts, TV sitcom roles, book contracts, radio show appearances, stage show roles, film options, and teaching positions at major universities. Many of these opportunities would have come their way without the slam's help, but many would not. The media attention and focus a slam or a slammer receives is often enough to catapult an individual or group of individuals into huge commercial success. Ambitions that were once absurd for a poet to think about now seem very possible. And that's okay as long as their art remains honest and as sacred as it was when there were no worldly temptations to consider.

The Least You Need to Know

- As slammaster, your job doesn't end when the doors open.

- Greet patrons at the door, introduce them to one another, and make sure they feel welcome before that first performer takes the stage.

- Be prepared to deal with a wide range of personality types, especially when dealing with temperamental performers.

- Start your show on time, end on time, and make sure that the audience stays engaged.

- You can add to your show's income and feed fan appetites by selling anthologies, compilation CDs, t-shirts, and other merchandise.

Chapter 18

Get the Word Out: Publicizing Your Show

In This Chapter

◆ Describing your show in 10 dazzling words or fewer

◆ Identifying your show's top selling points

◆ Choosing the most effective promotional materials and media for your show

◆ Guesstimating the amount of publicity required to fill the seats (and turn away a few unfortunate souls)

◆ Kicking yourself in the pants with some semi-realistic deadlines

You created it. You polished it. You wrapped it up in a tight little package. And now you're ready to deliver your show to an eager audience … Audience?! You forgot the audience?! You can have the Ringling Bros. & Barnum & Bailey Circus of slams, but if you don't promote your show, if nobody knows about it, your performers will be playing to an audience of empty seats. And nobody wants that.

You need to pound the pavement, agitate the airwaves, and let people know what they'll miss if they stay home or go to the movies. You need to figure out your show's draw, its most attractive feature, and then dangle it in front of your prospective patrons seductively enough to entice the most firmly rooted couch potato off the sofa and into a seat at your show.

Know What You're Promoting

The nature of your show, its essence, defines and drives your marketing strategy. And the best way to give your marketing strategy focus is to come up with a succinct description of it. For example, you approach a one-night-only engagement differently than a two-month run, an all-ages pop poetry concert differently than a senior citizens open mike. Is your show comedic or dramatic, or both? Is star power in the lineup? Are you planning a royal gimmick … maybe a drag queen slam competition in the final set? Asking yourself these questions helps you zero in on how to make the most of your marketing time and materials. So spend moments, even hours, getting specific with your vision. Skip ahead to Chapter 19 if you get stuck.

Angles and Selling Points

A good show is not a one-note samba. It's filled with a lot of surprises and compelling performances and is packed with variety. The Sunday night slam at the Green Mill has been described as a circus, a church, a town meeting, and a free-for-all. That's great for the show, but not necessarily for a marketing campaign. Effective marketing needs focus, an angle, a clear perspective—a selling point.

Let's say that Ralphie, the local shock jock whom everybody knows by first name and recognizes on sight, hosts your show. Ralphie's your selling point. Your goal as marketing maven is to make Ralphie's name and face synonymous with your show and tattoo the connection on the brain cells of John Q. Public. If your show features acrobatic poets versifying through back-flips, pitch that as your main event. Create an image of bodies and words cartwheeling across the stage, and drill that image into the hearts and minds of your prospective audience.

> **Whoa!**
>
> If you do hire some back-flipping poets, you might want to look into some event insurance or check with the venue to be sure it has liability coverage. It's one thing to get smacked by a metaphor, but quite another to be flattened by a flipper.

There are dozens and dozens of angles to consider when trying to find the hot selling point for your show. The following questions can jump-start your brain to discover your show's main draw:

- Is your show brand-new? Is it the longest running slam in the world?

- Is it focused on a specific theme or does it showcase a particular style? The Hip Hop Slam? The Dog Slam?

- Will your special guests appeal to a certain demographic? Is it naughty? Is it educational?

- Does your slam feature music? Costumes? Ensemble work? Rivalries between local poet heroes?

- What's the lowdown on the performers? Any big names?

Discover your show's strongest selling points and use them to guide you as you prepare your marketing materials.

Marketing Materials: Forms That Fit

A plethora of marketing materials and media are available for promoting your show; you just need to choose the form that will hit your target audience and effectively communicate your show's top selling points. If your slam vision is a Punch and Judy Puppet Poetry Hour at the local library, special invitations sent to grade school teachers accompanied by colorful posters to hang in the halls is going to do more than a mass mailing to your nightclub regulars. A midnight Raise the Dead Slam might demand a psychedelic print ad in the *Weed* newsletter. The following sections provide some ideas to stimulate your own creative strategies.

Making a Name (and Logo) for Yourself

"Bongo the Bootmaker." "Trolley Times." "Mouth of America." Everything has a brand name these days and a logo to go with it. And because you're competing in the marketplace of entertainment and arts galore, it'll help if you have one, too. (I came up with a catchy name, "Slam Poetry," and look what happened.) A captivating name pins a memorable mental image on the audience members' foreheads, making it nearly impossible for them to forget about your show. One way to invent a catchy name is to think of words and phrases that communicate vital information about your event:

Location: "Uptown Poetry Slam" or "Horseshoe Bend Poetry Slam"

Day, Date, or Time: "Blue Monday Poetry Scam Slam" or "Hump Day Poetry Slam"

Show Name: "Fat Tuesday Celebration of the Seven Deadly Sins" or "Gong Slam"

Add to that a little sliver of mystery to get folks curious about what's up and spur them to make an effort to find out more by reading the fine print or asking the counter kid "What's up?" Following are examples from real slam shows:

Slam Dunk Poetry Day. "What the heck is that? Poets stuffing words through hoops?"

Battle of Bay. "Who's battling whom? Over what? Poetry! You gotta be kidding me."

Backstage Skinny

Go to www.poetryslam. com/nps/history. htm and take a gander at the different logos host cities have designed for the NPS (National Poetry Slam) over the years.

After you have a name, transform it into a show logo by blowing up the letters BIGGIE & Clever in a EYECatchy font, or by strong-arming a design student in love with slammin' and giving him the poetic license to ink one out for you. Your logo/show name needs to visually SHOUT the news of your event from flyers, posters, websites, letterheads, t-shirts, and an assortment of other marketing materials you haven't even thought of yet.

Cheap, but Effective: Flyers and Postcards

Throughout your life, you probably have seen thousands of flyers, postcards, and handbills. They're pasted on walls, tacked to bulletin boards, stuffed in your mailbox, and buried under mounds of clutter. Some you don't notice at all. Some you pick up and throw away. Some you keep in your pocket or hang on the fridge for months. Why do you hold on to a particular flyer? Like all effective advertisements, eye-catching artwork and brain-gripping words are key, but the advertisement probably has some information you need, as well. While you're making your flyers and other marketing materials look sassy and seductive, be sure you include the essential information:

Backstage Skinny

The battle for attention on the flyer walls is intense. When someone comes up with a new color combination or size or shape that stands out, everyone copies it. The new and effective style soon becomes commonplace until the next new idea jumps off the wall.

- ◆ Date of the event
- ◆ Venue address (and directions if the show is at a remote site)
- ◆ A description of the show (what's happening)
- ◆ Starting time
- ◆ Cover charge or ticket price
- ◆ A phone number to call for more information

Postcards must be rectangular; at least 3.5-by-5 inches and .007 inch thick; and no larger than 4.25-by-6 inches and .016 inch thick to qualify for the lower postcard rate. Flyers and handbills range in size from 8.5-by-11 inches to business card size, but you can make them whatever size or shape you want. It might be hot to pass out a circular flyer, but it might also cost a chunk of change to produce. You make the call. Remember that golden rule of advertising: What would *stop you* and say, "Look at me?"

Not as Cheap, but Very Effective: Posters

Quality posters give your show an air of success. They are larger and pricier than flyers, but people notice them. They place your show on a level above the rookie, homebrew status. Coffee shops, storefronts, taverns, and restaurants, libraries, and cultural centers often allow promoters to display larger posters in their windows and on their bulletin boards.

The key to postering is to approach the owners and managers with humility and grace. If you're out there beating the pavement, they might admire your dedication and hard work. In most cases, they eagerly support your efforts to add something valuable to the community. If they don't know anything about you, visit them and make their acquaintance. Strike a deal to put their menu in your newsletter or plan a post-show party at their bar. Use good manners. Ask before you put something up, don't cover up other people's stuff, and bring your own tape and pushpins.

Garnering Some Free Press

Chapter 9 teaches you how to create press releases and generate articles about yourself as a performance poet. Apply these same principles to your show, and remember that you're not just a slammaster, you're a spokesperson for a worldwide social/literary arts movement growing and blossoming right there in your fair city. Maybe that's a little over the top, but not to a newspaper. Slam is a natural for the press. It's new; it's different; it appeals to a general audience; it maintains a certain "hipness"; and because it involves writing, performance, entrepreneurial efforts, local talent, and local venues, it can find its way into the Arts Section, the

Backstage Skinny

Most daily and weekly entertainment and arts sections have free listings. They look like classified ads. You type up the details of your event and e-mail them to the listings editor on or before the deadline, and the editor prints it under an appropriate heading free of charge.

Business Pages, the Weekend Insert, and even the front page—why not?! Get those press releases out and see how many photographers come by to snap you mid-stanza.

Managing Mailing (and E-Mailing) Lists

Begin developing a mailing list today. Start with your personal address book. Get some user-friendly software and type in all the names and numbers you know.

♦ Plan to have a mailing list sign-up sheet at every event, and make sure it gets passed around and returned to you at the end of the night.

Whoa!

If you do too much mass e-mailing, your online service or Internet service provider might suspect you of spamming and put you on probation or cancel your account altogether. Read your provider's rules on spam before you start e-mailing with wild abandon.

♦ Take the list home and add the names to your database.

♦ Send out simple e-mail messages informing everyone of your events.

♦ Create a monthly newsletter to inform your fans of your long-range plans, fun gossip, and how they can get more deeply involved in your slam and the slam family.

♦ Update your list on a regular basis by removing invalid addresses and records of people requesting to be removed from the list.

Some slam fans don't have computers or e-mail accounts (or just don't want to hand out their e-mail addresses). In such cases, you might need to snail-mail a hardcopy of your flyer. Snail mail costs a little more, but for mailing a handful of flyers, it's well worth the postage. (You might also consider mailing hardcopy if you have a dazzling flyer; sending a hundred flyers at 37 cents apiece would cost 37 bucks, but if it helps you build a loyal fan base, it's worth it.)

Paid Ads

Promoters with deep pockets take out full-page color ads in the major dailies and thousands of readers see them. What an enviable luxury! If your pockets aren't so deep, consider some alternatives. In most midsize cities, at least three or four neighborhood or trade papers are published daily or weekly. Major metropolitan areas have many more than that. Choose a paper that fits your audience and your budget, take out an ad, and see what happens.

Backstage Skinny _____

The best marketing tool of all time is a *great review*. People follow what the "experts" say, and when it comes to slam, the critics are the "experts." If they praise your show, the masses will flock to it. If they pan it, the masses will scamper away. And if a radio or newspaper critic says your show is "dazzling," incorporate that praise into your marketing materials:

Dazzling!

—Codger and Eggbert of the *Chicago Sometimes*

Such praise should be blazoned on every flyer, poster, and shred of paper you send out. And the only honest way to achieve that elusive *great review* is to produce a *really* great show.

Cool Calls

Some people break out in a cold sweat when they think of phoning people out of the blue. There's a reason for this—calling people out of the blue stinks. You catch people offguard or in the middle of work or dinner, if you catch them at all. With cell phones and caller ID, if the person you're calling doesn't recognize the number, he or she will usually choose to not pick up the phone.

Who can blame them? Phone solicitation is rapidly becoming a thing of the past, but the reason it's still done from time to time is simple: If you get an interested party on the other end, you're in. All the flyers in the world can be tossed in the garbage, but a human voice, given the chance, can produce interest and even commit to your project. If you're seriously concerned that the word isn't getting out about a particular event, pick up the phone and start dialing. Ask your close buddies to do the same.

Whoa! _____

Don't call strangers. Reminding friends and fans that an event is around the corner sometimes puts folks on the spot, but it is often a welcome nudge to the memory. Calling strangers is just plain rude, and it might even get you into trouble with the law if the person is on a no-call list.

Website Appeal

All roads lead to the Internet. And most slams arrived there sooner rather than later. The Internet gives you space to elaborate. You can lay down biographies, schedules, photos, audio and video clips, stories, live journals, letters to the slammaster, and anything else you can imagine and convert into digital media. Post your logo on your home page and build from there. And when your site is up and running, make sure you promote it on all of those promotional materials you created earlier. Just add those four magic words, "Check out our website!" and type your website address. If your public takes your advice, they can get all the little bits of information they missed and learn more about you and your show.

Backstage Skinny

Several websites, including Yahoo!, offer free web-hosting and provide the tools you need to create your own website online. However, they usually post ads on your site that annoy your visitors. Check with your Internet service provider to see if your account includes web-hosting and if they provide web page creation and management tools. You can find plenty of shareware for designing and editing your pages on the web—go to www.tucows.com and follow the trail of links to the HTML Editors.

Radio and TV

Obviously, television is the most effective marketing medium on the planet. Manufacturers use it to peddle their products and services, politicians use it to promote their platforms, and nonprofits use it to attract new members and solicit contributions. Many people watch a lot of TV, so you hit an enormous crowd every time your spot plays. That doesn't make it cheap; even a brief local TV spot comes in at anywhere from $350 to $50,000!

Radio is the slammaster's medium of choice. It's verbal, relatively affordable, and it typically plays to the target audience—people who like to listen to music and experience the community's night life. Radio is the medium that best informs us about what's happening in and around town.

Backstage Skinny

Paying for TV ads might be out of your reach, but persuading local TV news and arts programming to cover it is not—especially when it is a major event such as a regional or national slam. Call the producers and pitch them an exciting image and angle, and there's a good chance they'll show up. TV is a hungry beast that needs constant feeding.

Never Underestimate Word-of-Mouth

You can spend thousands of dollars on the slickest, glossiest, and most eye-popping ad materials a sugar-mommy can buy and raise the curtain on your big night only to find *nobody* in the audience! On the other hand, Louie down the street has been cooking up a night of erotica poetry that has such a reputation that Louie doesn't make one phone call to tell anybody about it. They just come because they heard "from Joanie, who heard from Bill that Bobby the harp player read a poem about Margaret, you remember Margaret, and that time she … Yeah! Out Loud! At Louie's! The Erotica Thing."

Almost anyone in the entertainment industry will testify that getting the buzz going out-distances any other form of advertisement by miles and dollars. How you get the buzz going is a combination of luck, persistence, and staging an impeccable show, week-in and week-out.

Whoa! _____

Don't confuse word-of-mouth with hype. Hype is what mega-entertainment moguls pour millions into to convince a gullible public that something unseen and untested is going to be the most sensational and rewarding experience of their lives. Sometimes it is, but usually it's not. Word-of-mouth is generated by people who have actually witnessed something sensational and rewarding and feel an uncontrollable urge to pass it on—word-of-mouth doesn't cost a cent.

To Whom Are You Promoting?

Munich slammasters Rayl Patzak and Ko Bylanzky know that one of the mainstays of their monthly slam at the Substanz nightclub is the student body at Munich University. So during the week preceding their Sunday show they spend hours placing hundreds of flyers on desktops in dozens of classrooms and standing in the hallways between classes passing out handbills. They know their target market, and they hit it hard. They also know that a percentage of their audience comes from the general population, so they seize every opportunity they can to score an article or interview in the daily or weekly newspaper, magazine, or radio show.

How Many People Do You Need to Reach?

Your marketing needs vary according to the number of seats available. If your show is in a 20-seat theatre and you're running three shows total, posters, word of mouth, and e-mailing should be sufficient. But follow this crucial rule of thumb: *Always overestimate*. If you think putting up 50 posters will do the trick, put up 75 or 100. Turning away a few disappointed fans at the door is better than having a few empty seats. Besides, that'll teach them to show up early for the next show.

Dig This!

Since the late '90s, virgin slams in midsize and smaller cities have been reporting initial audiences ranging from 50 to 150 people. A good rule of thumb for a slam show starting up is to plan on an average of 50 people per show, and be jolly when 200 cram through the doors. Don't commit to packing a three-hundred-seat house every Friday for six months if this is your first slam.

Calculating the Break-Even Point

Your marketing budget is limited by the amount of money you realistically expect your show to net. Determine the full capacity of your show (a packed house) and estimate a high and low number of paying patrons. Multiply the low number by the cover charge or ticket price (or the percentage the venue is letting you keep). Subtract all your expenses: sound system rental, venue rental, performer fees, drinks for the reporters, and every other expense you can think of. Subtract some extra for unexpected expenses, as well. What's left is your marketing budget. Use it, but use it wisely. Spending $300 for a $1/2$ -page print ad in the alternative newspaper could possibly reach thousands, but will it be as effective as:

Backstage Skinny

Many literary events, including slams, are subsidized by grants and funding that allow them to create high-quality high-class marketing tools and campaigns. This is great! But if it doesn't fill the house or it becomes life support for poor programming, these events run counter to one of the slam's strongest points—poetry shows should pay their own way by attracting and entertaining huge audiences.

- ◆ 40 posters displayed in every café and storefront in the hip neighborhood surrounding your venue?

- ◆ 200 postcards mailed out to your tried-and-true fans?

- ◆ 600 handbills placed in the grip of poets at the other six readings in town?

- ◆ A $1/8$ -page print ad in the same paper?

Don't squander your money, and don't spend more than you expect to take in. A glitzy marketing campaign might fill the house every week, but at what expense? Is your show's popularity worth your having to take out a second mortgage?

Motivating Yourself with Deadlines

Deadlines are a necessary evil. You know them, you hate them, you avoid them, and you test their limits. Perhaps you simply need to look at them differently. Deadlines are your friends. They motivate you, keep you focused, and can actually free your procrastinating mind from having to think about performing a task. Look at a calendar and set deadlines/goals for your project's marketing plan. Here are some examples of marketing deadlines you might see on a marketing whiz kid's calendar:

- Design logo for new show
- Create flyers and postcards with logo
- Take flyer and postcard copy to printer
- Start composing press release
- Pick up flyers and postcards at printer
- Finalize press release
- Mail out postcards
- Start distributing flyers
- Mail out press releases
- Continue distributing flyers
- Make follow-up calls to press contacts

By not setting deadlines (and meeting them) you're working without a time frame and are therefore under no pressure. For an independent project such as organizing a slam, you probably don't have to answer to anyone. No one's going to nag you to mail the postcards or punish you if the flyers aren't passed out. That doesn't mean there aren't consequences—the thought of an empty house on opening night should be punishment enough. To ensure that you have all the marketing materials you need when you need them and that all necessary tasks are accomplished, jot down a checklist and assign a deadline to every item on your list. Use the deadlines to kick yourself in the pants; nobody else is going to do it for you.

The Push

The push is the exciting homestretch—the time when you're working as a full-time/over-time/self-made marketing guru sending out press releases and postcards, papering the bulletin boards, scooting back and forth across the city handing out paper, paper, and more paper, e-mailing, phone calling, and spilling your passions in interviews. After you push yourself into the push, it'll take over.

> ### Whoa!
>
> Don't do it alone if you can help it. Ask for help. During The Great Push (a week of heavy flyering, e-mailing, and so on, three or four weeks before your event), recruit some helping hands. Ask for an hour or two of someone's time to help stuff envelopes or hang posters. Offer them free tickets to the show or a pizza and some beer. Let them know that their help means a lot to you (it should) and that you want to compensate them for their efforts.
>
> If you have a college or university nearby, consider taking on an intern. The English, performing arts, social services, and marketing departments all have creative students who are willing to work for a little on-the-job training and the prospect of establishing professional contacts.

Thank You and Goodnight

It's over. You had record-setting ticket sales and you're now a cult classic, thanks to your infallible marketing blitzkrieg. You've got a pocketful of money and lots of opportunities are now banging on your door. Now what?

- **Say Thank You.** It would be impossible to send thank-you notes to every person who came to see your show, but you can certainly thank the people who made the extra effort to help. You can also use your e-mail list to send one general thank you. Make an extra effort to slobber thanks on your crew.

- **Update the mailing lists.** The sign-up list you set up in the lobby is no doubt full of new signatures. Add them to your database. They already did what you wanted them to do—and they'll do it again (assuming you put on a good show).

- **Follow up with the reporters.** Thank the reporters who wrote up your show before show time and let them know of your show's success. They might just do a follow-up story (if they haven't already). Use the success of this show to generate interest in future shows.

The Least You Need to Know

- Before you start generating marketing materials, describe your show with a dynamic phrase of 10 words or fewer.

- Every show has one or more solid selling points that you can use to focus your marketing efforts.

- Choose marketing materials and media that will be most effective in reaching your target audience and inspiring their enthusiasm.

- Great reviews and word-of-mouth advertising are your two most effective marketing tools—and they're free!

- To calculate your marketing budget, subtract your expenses from a low to mid estimate of your show's gross income.

- Don't forget to follow up after the show, thanking those who helped, updating your mailing list, and connecting with any reporters who helped spread the word.

Chapter

19

It's Showtime!

In This Chapter

- ◆ Developing a framework on which to hang your show's vision and substance

- ◆ Establishing a pace and then breaking stride with a carefully orchestrated surprise or two

- ◆ Jazzing up your show with a musical accompaniment and other variations on the theme

- ◆ Exploring the main components of your show—from open-mike performers to the all-important emcee

- ◆ Laying out a spread on which the audience can feast and still hunger for more

Opening Night! The adrenaline's up, and the novelty of a new slam happening has audience members bouncing up and down in their seats. All your homies have come out to support you. The owner's excited because it looks like something is finally going to fill the coffers on that dark, dead Tuesday. Opening night of your first slam might glide to success on this alone.

But don't count on it.

The excited anticipation has drawn the multitudes, but it has also inflated their expectations. Now, you must deliver. To guarantee that your show satisfies the anxious patrons, you must create a framework for your show, flesh it out with a variety of entertaining performances, and refine the individual components that can make or break your show. This chapter is your guide.

Finding Form in Your Vision

Like a successful solo performance, your show must be a unified and entertaining whole, not a discordant hodgepodge of poetry, music, drama, comedy, and whatever else anyone wants to throw in the mix. You're the maestro and the conductor, and as such, your job is to orchestrate a show that plays like a concerto consisting of several movements … lifting and dropping the audience's emotions, raising its consciousness, and eliciting its most lurid dreams.

> **Dig This!**
>
> Even the most haphazard show has form—bad form, but form nonetheless. The early shows at the Green Mill seemed off-the-cuff, even approaching chaotic, but they were actually planned out at five-minute intervals. That was overkill, but even that rudimentary and choppy structure worked. Start with a basic formula and don't be afraid to adjust it.

A show's structure is not (or should not be) mechanical; it should evolve organically. In other words, no cookie-cutter approach works for every show. The structure must fit the show's style and accommodate the physical nature of the venue—the stage and the access to the stage, the lighting and sound capabilities, the seating arrangement, and so on. Just as you allowed your vision to guide your choice of venues, now the venue's physical realities influence the specifics of your show. You cannot write elaborate costume changes into the script if you do not have a backstage. And you cannot have a troupe of tap-dancing poets on a 4-by-4-foot plywood stage with one spotlight.

Drawing Up a Slam Itinerary

Think of your slam show as an adventure, a journey with fascinating stops and intriguing detours along the way. As slammaster, you need to draw up an itinerary for your slam journey. Begin with the departure and arrival times. When will your show start? When will it end? Your talks with the venue owner might have determined this. She might have made it clear that her full wait staff does not come in until 7:00 P.M. and that they need a good hour to set up before they're ready to handle heavy crowds. Your slam can't start before 8:00 P.M., but it can run until midnight if you want it to. Do you want it to go that long? It's your choice, but I suggest that you tune the length of your show to one of these two entertainment models:

- **Theater productions.** One-act plays with no intermission run from one to one and a half hours. The common time frame for a two- or three-act play with a fifteen-minute intermission is two hours, plus or minus a few minutes. On occasion a play will run three hours or more with two or three intermissions, but it had better be outstanding.

- **Nightclub acts.** Club time is divided into sets, not acts. The duration of the sets vary from a brief thirty-minute set to a very long one-hour-and-fifteen-minute set. Between sets are intermissions that range from ten to twenty minutes. A three-hour show consisting of three fifty-minute sets and two twenty-minute intermissions is standard, and it goes up and down from there. It's very rare for people to come out for an evening of only one forty-minute set, and if they do, they can easily feel cheated if that forty minutes doesn't contain something extraordinary.

> **Whoa!**
> Don't let the physical nature of the venue and stage limit you without a fight. At the Green Mill we've done costume changes in the restrooms and we've moved the tables back and had dancers hoof to the verse. Push the limitations as far as you can, but know your limits.

A Sample Slam Journey

Let's create a sample slam show itinerary. Our show begins at 9:00 P.M. on Tuesday night and runs until the clock strikes 12:00 A.M. We're going to design it to hold two and a half hours of antics, reserving a half hour for late arrivals and run-over time. The owner has asked us to include two fifteen-minute intermissions for selling drinks; this helps to keep the servers subdued during the performances, especially if the poets and patrons tip well. Our model starts out looking like this:

9:00	**Opening Set**
9:45	Intermission
10:00	**Middle Set**
10:45	Intermission
11:00	**Closing Set**

The Main Station Stops

Now that we know how much travel time we have, the next step in creating our slam itinerary is to mark on our map the types of sites we want our travelers to visit. In drama, we call these sites *plot points*—episodes where the action takes a turn, a glide, or a spin and arrives at a new destination and a new departure point. The following sections describe the most familiar and rock-solid station stops on a slam journey.

Greetings

The slam experience begins as soon as someone walks through the door. How you meet, greet, and treat people as they enter influences their interactions throughout the night. If the patrons are shy and fail to meet someone right away, they're likely to be meek or aloof throughout the evening, making even the liveliest of shows a dreary affair. Before things get rolling onstage, seize the opportunity to set the mood with some ceremony and ritual:

- **Introduce people to one another.** Make a game of it. Appoint an audience member as each week's meet-and-greet-person or have your assistant handle the greetings.

- **Season your event with preshow music or antics.** Encourage people to sign up for the open-mike set. Lead create-a-poem sessions. Pass around a photo album. Have each table compose a group poem to be performed later. Try a round robin from table to table. Any activity that introduces people to one another is game.

- **Open your show with a bang.** Stage a grand entrance of performers, a parade through the venue. Add a little emcee spiel. Initiate the virgin virgins who signed up for the open mike. Slot a wild and crazy performer for the opening act. Surprise everyone with a spontaneous, in-audience ensemble round robin ending with the emcee center stage behind the microphone to say "Welcome."

Open Mike

Stick your open-mike session at the beginning of your show and keep it relatively brief—eight to ten poets performing one poem each. The open-mike session provides a good warm-up for the rest of the show, gives aspiring slammers an opportunity to perform, allows the emcee to get a feel for the audience's mood and disposition, and provides a buffer zone for late-arriving patrons and feature poets. And, unless one of your open mikers rocks the house with a stellar performance, the open mike establishes a well-grounded platform (baseline) from which you can launch the rest of the show. It's your opening act.

To quiet the grumblings and retain control over the number of participants in the open mike, draw names from a fish bowl or hat to determine who gets stage time. Always provide space for the virgin virgins and newcomers, but stick the names of those who have been to the show more than a few times into the bowl or hat and let fate (and your cunning handiwork) determine who speaks and who doesn't.

Take liberties with the order. If the open mike has become a funeral march of pain and you know that Josie's got a steamy poem that will end the torture, get Josie on-stage immediately, whether she's last on the list or not on the list at all. Pull names out of the fishbowl that aren't even in the fishbowl. Your job is to create a good show and entertain the audience, not to be a slave to poet etiquette and protocol.

Backstage Skinny _____

As a slammaster, you will without a doubt encounter *repeat offenders*, open-mike cronies who travel from show to show and bore audiences with the same laborious poems and styles. If you are too generous with them they'll return week after week, overstaying their welcome and killing the excitement and spirit of your show. Don't let them do it. Put their names at the bottom of the list and bear no guilt if you forget to call them, "Oh, I'm sorry, Bob, not enough time tonight."

Special Acts and Guest Performers

To ensure that your show's journey includes a guaranteed worthwhile site to visit and an experience to treasure, scout out, find, and book guest performers and specialty acts that you know will rock the rafters. Place these acts at strategic points along the trail to raise the stakes and hit a peak. Select acts that offer a new flavor, sound, or visual component that counters what precedes them.

The guest spot is the place to experiment with different styles of spoken word entertainment. It's less of a risk because you've scouted these acts and seen them succeed on other stages, or you have received good reports about them from other slammasters. Now you're giving them a go on your stage to see if they click with your audience. If they do, you've found a sweet destination to visit again and again.

Dig This!

I've found that a fifteen- to twenty-minute set for guest performers is optimum. I usually ask them to have a couple encores ready in case the crowd screams for more. I've witnessed a few great performers hold the stage for forty minutes and still leave the crowd wanting more, but only a few.

The Competition

For most slams, the competition is the show within the show—the main course. Everything leading up to this point—the emcee chatter, the open mikers, the guest performer, acted as hors d'oeuvres. The competition is the dance festival regaling in the plaza at the end of the tour, the jousting match on the queen's lawn, the duel duked out on a foggy wharf while the sailors and writers and lovers huddled in the tavern doorway watch with glimmering eyes. It has structure, suspense, conflict, and characters. It also has a …

- **Beginning.** This includes the emcee spiel, the introduction of judges and naming of contestants, the announcement of the prizes, and the explanation of the rules.

- **Middle.** This covers the bout structure of preliminary rounds, the poets stepping on and off the stage, the scoring, the personalities, the performances, the emcee's behavior, the crowd's reactions, and the poems themselves.

- **End.** This is the final round, the playoff between competitors, the audience's bias informed by the earlier rounds, the informed attitude toward the early judging, the final scoring, the determination of the winner, and the awarding of the prize.

It's a natural drama. It hardly ever determines who's really the best poet/performer, but who cares? It entertains. And because it has such an obvious end to it (someone wins and others lose), it's best to insert your slam competition at the end of your show so its finish coincides with the climatic finish of your entire event.

Putting the full competition (its beginning, middle, and end) at the start of your show can make everything that follows feel anti-climatic. Dividing the competition into segments spread throughout the evening squeezed in between other acts works … sometimes, but it can disrupt the unity and cohesiveness and diminish the dramatic effect and suspense, especially if patrons are coming and going.

Expanding Our Sample Itinerary

The slam competition is our final destination, our show's climax and denouement, so we'll devote the major portion of our itinerary to it. We'll limit the open-mike session to weed out the windbags and provide stage time for a limited number of newcomers who really have something fresh to say. We've recruited a local singer/songwriter to play blues instrumentals for fifteen minutes during the preshow segment as the host signs up poets and greets people. Our itinerary is beginning to tighten up:

8:45	Preshow music and greetings
9:00	**Open Mike**
9:40	**Specialty Act**
9:50	Intermission
10:00	**Slam Competition**
	Rounds 1 & 2
10:50	Intermission
11:10	**Slam Competition**
	Final round

Detailing Your Trip Tick

So far we've been viewing our slam adventure map from a balloon floating above the landscape, zoomed out to look at the overall structure and at primary departures and destinations. That's a good way to start the planning process, but eventually you must swoop down on the "details" of your adventure—the special flavors, customs, activities, and planned happenstance that elevate your show from mediocre to magnificent. As you proceed through the rest of this chapter, jot down any ideas that pop into your head to detail the twists and turns of your slam and any detours to special roadside attractions. You're about to take your audience on a guided tour of your artistic vision. Start by considering the elements described in the following sections.

Adding Ceremony and Ritual

All planned human events have ceremony and ritual. At birthday parties we turn out the lights, bring in the cake aglow with burning candles, and sing off-key. At sporting events we stand and choir the national anthem, toss a coin, face-off, or shout "Play ball!" Ceremony and ritual frame an event, giving the audience familiar guideposts that get them involved and pique and fulfill their expectations. The more imaginative you are when creating rituals and ceremony for your slam, the more hooked your audience will become.

We've already touched upon and described many slam rituals: treating newcomers as virgin virgins; the snapping, stomping, and groaning of disapproval; greeting people at the door when they arrive; selecting and introducing judges; and drawing names out of a fish bowl. Here are a few more examples of rituals used at the national events and various slams across the world:

♦ **The emcee spiel.** Almost every long-running slam has developed certain house rules that the emcee explains at the beginning of the show. "All heckles must be more intelligent than the poem heckled." "If a poet dedicates a poem to someone in the audience, that person must come onstage during the performance of the poem." The spiel gets repeated every week and provides a blueprint for performers and the audience, advising them how they should behave and what they can expect.

♦ **The group initiation.** Many slams have a ceremony to shine the spotlight on first-time audience members. They could all be brought to the stage to compose an *exquisite corpse* poem or just be asked to stand and name their favorite poet. Acknowledging and identifying newcomers helps fold them into the tribe and usually doesn't require any bloodletting … usually, anyway.

SlamSlang

An **exquisite corpse** is a poem that many poets (often everyone in the room) construct by adding a line to a preceding line, having seen only the preceding line.

Backstage Skinny

When developing rituals, consider your audience. What will they find fun and engaging? Should the audience members tap their feet when a performance starts to fade? Should the emcee ask an audience member to choose the next open-mike performer? Should performers call out challenges to one another? Should the judges be brought onstage to explain their scoring?

♦ **Counting out the dollars.** Slams that pay cash prizes sometimes have the emcee and audience count out the prize money dollar by dollar. Some slams provide several prizes from which to choose, and the audience watches with interest to see whether the winning poet chooses the red bikini underpants or the "I'm a Poet, Too!" t-shirt.

♦ **Speak along.** A few slams have community poems they recite en masse each week, sort of like a church hymn or the national anthem, which expresses the commonality and purpose of everyone there.

The ritual and ceremony you pack into your slam provide an underpinning of structure and entertainment that can save it from disaster should your guest performers and/or slam competitors bomb. The booing ritual has saved many a home team loss from becoming a total waste of an afternoon at the ballpark. Ask any Cubs fan.

Bring It On—Heckles, Jekylls, and Hydes

Some slams and poetry circles discourage hecklers and any negative reactions from the audience. Others not only allow it, but also make a point of informing the audience that they have a moral obligation to voice their opinions, positive or negative. Aggressive audience participation is a foundation of the slam. It's what set slam apart from the failing traditional readings of the late '70s and early '80s. It also created an atmosphere of honest feedback that forced the early slammers to develop better performance skills and more accessible texts. Of course, it's your show, and the choice is yours, but I strongly encourage you to at least consider giving patrons the license to express their displeasure over a poem or performance. Give careful thought to finding the best spot in your show to introduce such activity.

Jacks in the Box

A tedious drive through the flatland fields of corn and soybeans can be the adventure of a lifetime if you bump into colorful characters along the way, or know that your sexy sweetheart is awaiting your arrival. Likewise, your slam should provide some unexpected pleasures, some titillating surprises, and enough roadside attractions to break up the scenery along the way.

Here are a few suggestions for building suspense at your slam:

◆ Introduce the competing slammers as longtime rivals facing off for blood and honor. Add a few dollars to the prize pot and pass the hat around prodding the audience to kick in a few bucks to sweeten the pot and heighten the stakes for the grudge match.

◆ Initiate impromptu collaborations between guest performers and audience members. For instance, if your friend Barry the Blues Harmonica is in the audience, instruct Emcee Joan Anne to pull him up onstage to perform a duet with HeAmHe, your guest performer from New Jersey. Audiences love spontaneous collaborations, even when they crash and burn.

◆ Have your in-house ensemble stage an argument (about poetry, of course) that breaks into a verse dialogue across the bar.

Backstage Skinny

As slammaster, you must build suspense—inflate expectations for the upcoming performances without lifting the curtain too high and revealing too much. If you cultivate no expectations, if the audience doesn't think that there's something ahead that is worth waiting for, they're going to bolt at the first dull performance or set.

♦ Jump up onto the bar and kick out a poem while dancing between drinks. Shut out all the lights and have everyone whisper a poem into the ear of the person next to them.

Ready to Run Our Sample Slam Journey

To boost attendance we lined up a local literary hero to make a cameo appearance, and our in-house ensemble is ready to try out some new material. So let's work those elements and a few more into our itinerary and round out our journey.

8:45	Preshow music and greetings
9:00	**Open Mike**
	Emcee: short, funny, in-audience poem
	Emcee: greeting and slam spiel
	Open-mike poets 1, 2, and 3
	Cameo poet performs poem
	Open-mike poets 4 and 5
9:40	**Specialty Act**
	Emcee does short call-and-response poem to conjure and introduce the in-house ensemble
	In-house ensemble performs costumed group piece
9:50	Intermission
10:00	**Slam Competition**
	Emcee: Ritualized introduction of judges
	Ritual: Reading of the rules by unsuspecting audience member
	Emcee: Contestants are announced by name and rush to stage in mock rivalry bumping heads and shoulders.
	Rounds 1 & 2 (6 contestants in each round)
10:50	Intermission

11:10	**Slam Competition—Final round**
	Emcee recites the Bloody Battle Final Round call-and-response poem
	Round 3 (4 contestants)
	Round 4 (2 contestants)
	Emcee counts out cash to the winner
	Encore poem by winner and/or Cameo poet
	Ensemble, Emcee, and Cameo poet do a high-energy collaboration to close show

Competition as a Theatrical Device

People who take themselves too seriously are bores; they usually end up talking to themselves or being mocked snidely. Overly serious slam competitions can produce the same effect on an entire audience. Use the competition to heighten your show's drama, not deaden it. Generate excitement and entertainment by creating rituals and ceremonies that answer the following questions: Who's going to judge? How? What are the rules? How many bouts? How are contestants chosen? What do they win? The following sections will help guide you.

Signing 'Em Up

Most slams sign up contestants on a first come, first serve basis. At the Green Mill, the doorman handles the sign-up board, which consists of 6 to 10 slips of blank paper taped to posterboard. Sign your name on one of them and you're in the slam. Some slams sign up contestants weeks in advance on tournament charts that safeguard against repeat offenders. Some charge a nominal entry fee to discourage those darn repeat offenders.

Picking the Judges

Slam hosts traditionally pick three or five judges randomly from the audience, give them cards and markers, and instruct them to score each poem/performance from 1 to 10, paying equal attention to text and presentation. Variations on this method

Backstage Skinny

Adding three scores takes just the right amount of time to clear the palate between slammers. When you use five judges, you usually knock out the high and low score, but it slows the pace of the show. Waiting for more than five judges to hold up their cards and scoring more than five numbers can drag the slam to a halt.

are abundant. Feel free to modify it as you wish, with the goal of generating more fun, surprise, and suspense. But be careful not to slow the pace of the show by making the process overly complicated. Here are some do's and don'ts:

- **Do keep the judges in clear view of the scorekeepers and emcees** for speedy retrieval of the numbers, but *don't* seat the judges close together. Spread them out across the front of the room in prominent positions near the stage so the audience can watch and react to their scoring. "*Oh my gosh!* I can't believe that guy gave my little sister a minus four!"

- **Do get the judges' bios.** When introducing the judges, have the emcee turn it into a ritual by gathering and embellishing on biographical information about the judges. Where is he from? Is it his first time at the slam? What does he do for a living? Is he here just because he heard that smart chicks like slam? Judges are characters in the slam play. Flesh out those characters and make them colorful.

- **Do use celebrity judges—maybe.** If they're truly celebrities and have playful, charismatic personalities, they can spark things up quite a bit. But if they take their judging roles too seriously or are just plain drips, beware! A barfly who gets booed for his bogus scoring provides more action than prissy judges doing a "proper" job.

SlamSpeak

California's Evolving Slam Scene

As slam spread across North America, it evolved into many different forms. These changes depended on the organizers and their agendas for using the slam format. San Francisco, for example, had a free-wheeling "performative" slam with few rules. Costumes were encouraged! In Southern California, we wanted to draw together large audiences from the scattered suburbs, so it was important to create simple but strict rules and a level playing field for suspicious strangers. We offered big prizes, and used "expert" judges to legitimize the competition.

Sometimes these different approaches led to conflicts in how rules should be interpreted. (Just what *is* a costume?) The first time I featured a San Francisco team in Long Beach, they thought we took the rules too seriously. Because we used "expert" judges, I had asked the SF team to judge and they responded by pulling down their pants and *mooning* the competitors! Repeatedly!

—Charles Ellik, Berkley slammaster

◆ **Do judge by committee—if it works.** Judging by committee can result in too much consultation and dead air while you wait for the consensus score. If you can hustle them to deliver in a timely fashion, it can be great. Give a table of judges a name and personality. "Okay. And now the score from the Budweiser Table! And where's the score from Wino Professors?" If a committee takes too long, ignore their score, or set a time limit—"Committees have 30 seconds to come up with a number, or they'll need to rise and deliver a group apology— in iambic pentameter!"

Alternative Styles of Judging

The more the audience participates, the more memorable the evening is for them. And it's important that everybody sees what's going on, so visual judging stunts make for a good show. Here are some examples:

◆ **Rose battle.** In Bonn, Germany, everyone in the barroom receives a rose when they arrive. At the conclusion of the first round of slammers they hold the rose over their heads when their favorite poet's name is announced. The raised roses are counted and the poets with the three highest counts go on to the final round. After the poems have been presented in the final round, the poets are brought up to the stage one by one, and the audience tosses the roses to their desired champion. The slammer with the biggest bouquet is declared the Rose Winner.

◆ **Applause-o-meter.** When judging by audience applause, emcees often turn themselves into human sound-sensing machines, using their arms like the pointers on a gas gauge to display for all to see the levels of applause they're hearing. Some slammasters have gone as far as purchasing actual sound-sensitive devices and jury-rigging them into slam meters with flashing lights that respond to the hoots, hollers, and claps. Unfortunately, these machines register all audio feedback—cheers and boos—equally.

◆ **Pass the bucket.** As a supplement to numerical judging, several slams pass buckets with the names of the competitors pasted on them to collect tribute from the patrons who place bucks in the buckets for the slammers they think deserve their support. It doesn't determine the official winner, but a bucketful of cash always generates a little excitement.

When devising an alternative judging style, be sure that it has a simple structure, a light-hearted nature, and some visual element that the entire audience can watch and enjoy.

> **Dig This!**
>
> In Northern California, organizers use many different formats: haiku, limerick, freestyle battles. In the dreaded "Canadian Bucket Match," two poets perform while two buckets are passed around. The audience votes by pitching money into their favorite poet's bucket. The poet with the most money wins. Other changes in rules include ballots instead of scores, themed slams, different time limits, even returning to the head-to-head bout format from which slam originated.
>
> —Charles Ellik, Berkley slammaster

To Spin or Not to Spin?

Onstage, DJs behind a table spinning and scratching tunes before, after, and during slams are now a common sight and sound, especially at shows that cater to the younger crowds. Done with style and a sense of the diversity that slams seek to encourage, a DJ can add an exciting background to an evening. However, in the wrong hands, spinning can burden your show with tedium and alienate many wavelengths of the broad slam audience spectrum. A DJ who spins a narrow selection of beats engineers the music to be more important than the words, or inspires each and every poet to be a rapper might be better suited for a hip-hop showcase. On the flip side, if your show is a bit sleepy and you can't afford to hire live musicians, a DJ might be just the needle you need to scratch the groove.

Pace

A good show keeps rolling forward under its own momentum, pinching the audience's attention as it proceeds. This seemingly "natural" momentum is usually due to the creative elements you've sown into it, the maneuverings of a competent emcee, and a surprise or two that recaptivates the audience. And the pacing of all of it has to be right. Your show should move forward and upward as a series of crescendos that rise and plateau, rise and plateau, each time to a higher level. The peaks should rise to an ultimate climax very close to the last syllable of the show.

If you were to draw a graph of a finely constructed show, it would look like a mountain range rising from foothills to mid-size mountains to High Sierras to snowcaps to Mt. Everest to a lover's leap drop-off at the end, with folks floating on clouds gently down to sea level as they put on their coats to leave. When structuring your show, make it Bing-Bang-Boom interesting out of the starting blocks, but make sure it crosses the finish line with a *Blast!!!* that rumbles and roars.

Leave 'Em Wanting More Effect

Touch them and they'll stick with you through the mediocrity. Overburden them, even with great stuff, and they'll stay away for years. All audiences have a saturation point; end your show before it reaches that point. An astute emcee can sense when the "that's enough" line approaches. If you, as the host or emcee, are unsure of whether the audience wants more or not, just ask them, "Have you had enough yet?" They might be polite and say "No" when they really mean "Yes," but if the screams for more are sincere, you've got clear approval to slam on.

The Least You Need to Know

- ◆ Establish an overall structure for your show to give it form and direction.

- ◆ Your show should be engaging from start to finish, rising in intensity and quality as the evening progresses.

- ◆ Focus on the fundamentals of your show: the emcee, the open-mike performers, the feature artists, the in-house ensemble, and the ever-unpredictable audience.

- ◆ Use slam's competitive aspect to generate energy for your show. Decide on a system of scoring that engages and entertains the audience.

- ◆ Don't feed your audience any more than they can swallow. Your show should exceed their expectations, but leave them hungry for more.

Chapter 20

Expanding Your Market: Special Shows

In This Chapter

 ◆ Taking your show outside the bars, theaters, and coffeehouses

 ◆ Earning your cut of that sweet corporate cash

 ◆ Giving back by performing at benefits and gaining some valuable contacts in return

 ◆ Creating special shows for niche markets—samples and examples

Taverns, coffeehouses, nightclubs, and other small venues are the slam family's bread and butter. They give the slammaster a space to create a happening and a laboratory in which to experiment with different shows and performers. They provide new talent with open-mike opportunities and old talent with chances to polish the old and test the new. They expose thousands of potential slam fans to the beauty and intensity of spoken word performance poetry. And they ensure a steady flow of cash ... hopefully.

However, these small venues represent only one slice of the slam earnings pie. Granted, it's a big slice, but it's still not the whole pie. Other lucrative markets are out there, waiting to be tapped. This chapter shows you where to look for them, how to approach their gatekeepers, what to do to re-figure your show to suit their special needs, and how to keep your foot in the door, and it provides plenty of ideas to get your creative juices flowing.

Courting the Institutions

Large institutions are always looking for new and exciting programming, especially in the literary arts department. Your slam can offer these institutions what they long for: entertaining, compelling, and accessible spoken word presentations that appeal to the general public. That's the key with large institutions—appealing to general audiences. Most institutions cater to the broad spectrum of the population. Their target audience is everybody, and so is slam's.

Fortunately, most large institutions have the money to make it happen—budgets fattened by big donors, access to government funding, and foundations set up to keep them in operation. Fees for creating and producing exciting poetry shows for large institutions can range from a few hundred to thousands of dollars. After you've established a sound reputation and staged a successful show, arrange it into a fresh bouquet and knock on an institution's door.

Types of Institutions

Don't limit your courtships. Slammin' at the Northwest Cattle Breeders Association? Why not? I've done poetry gigs for Commonwealth Edison and Kraft Foods. These large corporations can get pretty boring. They need creative employees. What better way to shake things up than with a poetry slam?

How do you find these gigs? Where do you start looking? Here are some obvious choices. Use them as a starting point, not an end:

- **Associations** such as the National Association of Speech Therapists or the National Association of Librarians, … Psychologists, … Bookbinders, you name it, all hold annual conventions and are always seeking out fun and thoughtful activities for their members to enjoy.

- **Cultural arts centers** can be found in almost every mid-size city and in all major metropolitan areas. They're in the business of creating arts programming and are usually struggling to fill their calendars with the required number of literary arts events.

- **Libraries** usually have programs once or twice a year that are linked to some national, state, or locally designated day or month, such as Dogpatch Days or National Fried Steak Week. April is National Poetry month and it's a big time for library events and the performance poets that work them. They have smaller budgets than museums, but bigger libraries can sometimes put on big shows. After you've done a good job, it almost always leads to repeat engagements.

- **Museums,** big and small, have programming throughout the year connected to different themes and exhibits. If you can shape a slam event to fit one of their themes, you're in. Museums typically pay well and provide high-profile exposure through their elaborate advertising campaigns. An added benefit is that your show will probably play to a new audience of potential slam converts. If you do a good job, you'll get asked back for their next special event and possibly draw a few converts to your venue.

Getting Your Foot in the Door

The downside of seeking institutional work is that it's a who-you-know situation. Unless your name or your slam has been splashed across the front page of the Arts section of the newspaper for several weeks running, securing a gig on a cold call is iffy. Sending a press pack and a query letter is little more than a shot in the dark. But do it anyway; it's the first step. And if you are met with no response, try some of these tactics:

- Find out who the director of your city's cultural art center is and send her a letter of introduction.

- Volunteer your services to the institution you're courting. Give them a taste of who you are and what you can do. Get to know who does what and how it gets done. Under the right circumstances, it will lead to future opportunities for you and your show.

- Invite program directors to attend your slam events and give them the red carpet treatment. Heck, invite the whole department and give them candy poems.

- Serve on programming boards. As a slammaster, you come in contact with lots of talent and you're connected to a big family of performers across the country through PSI (Poetry Slam, Inc.). You're a valuable resource to the programming folks. And if you're involved with their project planning, it's as easy as pulling off an inside job.

Once you're on the inside, be ready to fit your show (for a fair price) into one of the institution's programming slots. If it turns out to be a smashing success, it almost always turns into repeat engagements. But don't rest on your laurels; as soon as the institution's administration changes, you'll find yourself on the outside again.

Backstage Skinny

In the spring of 1990, I offered to manage a citywide slam tournament to support Chicago's new Sister Cities program, the Poem for Osaka Award. This donation of time and effort was rewarded later that year when Lois Weisberg, commissioner of Chicago Cultural Affairs, suggested (and paid for) a team of Chicago slammers to fly to San Francisco and compete in the first national slam competition. Over the years, I've been contracted to do more than a hundred events at the Cultural Center and have donated back an equal amount of time. Give to your local arts associations and you—as well as your community—shall truly receive.

Book Fairs and Festivals

As the slam has grown and gained more international visibility, book fairs and literary festivals have sought it out to add some spark to their events. Because slammers and slammasters know how to organize, they bring a readymade arts and entertainment package, which is an easy-to-plug-in, low-maintenance addition to such fairs and festivals. Participating in these events can be a great opportunity to expose a large audience to slam and to your show.

If you do a book fair or festival gig, be sure to have a lot of flyers on hand to promote your weekly or monthly events. Get that mailing list out and gather names and addresses. Sell t-shirts and CDs. These fairs and festivals are open marketplaces. Make the best of them.

Backstage Skinny

Specialty acts such as jugglers and magicians work the corporate circuit extensively. If you have a friend in that line of work, ask your pal for the inside scoop.

Corporate Conventions and Corporate Programming

Similar to associations, large corporations hold conventions and need fun activities for their conventioneers to participate in when the day's meetings are over. Sometimes they're enlightened enough to seek out something other than a stand-up comedian spewing dirty jokes and golf anecdotes. Slam provides an entertaining, intellectually stimulating alternative.

Benefits and Their Paybacks

Sometimes it's better to give than to receive, but you'll find that giving often lead to receiving. By volunteering your services and performances at a benefit you can make contacts and gain exposure that lead to opportunities for your own work and shows—and you help a needy organization in the process. Many times these organizations grow into major cultural institutions, and they often remember and reward your early assistance. It's very easy to get involved—show up at the door, give the benefit planners a call, and offer your services. Believe me, you won't be turned away.

> **Whoa!**
>
> Be careful when donating your time, talents, and energy to an organization. Some benefits are bogus, poorly run, and are sometimes fronts for lining some crook's pockets. Check the organization's credentials before lending your aid.

Shaping Your Show for a Special Gig

You just got off the phone with the president of the local chapter of the Harley Hogs. You got the gig. Now what? Should you tweak your Save the Whales Slam show? That might not work at the biker bar. You'd better go back to the drawing board and draw up something fresh. Don't freak out, and never despair. This is an opportunity to be creative and dig up artistic treasures you never knew were buried deep below the surface of your soul. Start with the basic slam as a foundation and build from there, using the theme of the particular event as your guide. The following sections give you an idea how the basic slam structure can be reshaped to create exciting programming for special institutions.

Motorcycle Slam

Chicago's Field Museum of Natural History, January 1999. A portable stage is erected on the main floor. Streams of Midwestern humanity climb up and down the huge marble staircases at each end of the Grand Hall. Nuns, Boy Scouts, Indiana State Young Republicans, truck-drivin' daddies with strings of kids, and truck-drivin' mamas with teenaged daughters—they're all here. On the stage a band of experimental musicians fills the hall with rhythms emanating from drums, guitars, and homemade instruments that resemble bicycle wheels. Between each tune I apologize to the audience for the late start, "Sorry, folks, the biker poets aren't here yet. You know how bikers are—very independent, big, and scary. We're hoping they'll show up." After the third apology, an air horn blasts on the Grand Staircase and into the Grand Hall. Under the bones of a dinosaur's neck, a crew of slammers clad in black leather, chains, and Harley Davidson emblems clank their way through the open-mouthed crowd. Another blast from the air horn and they start blaring poetry over their hand-held bull horns.

That was the beginning of the Spoke 'N Word Poetry Slam, a special program to augment the Guggenheim Museum's traveling exhibit "Art of the Motor Cycle." The afternoon included ensemble performances by slam pros and an impromptu fill-in-the-blank open-mike competition by audience members. A twelve-year-old soon-to-be-biker won the prize. His power poem is long lost in the exhaust fumes, but you can try creating one yourself.

> **SlamSpeak**
>
> **The Power Poem**
> To each and every life there comes
> An hour when timidity no longer rules.
> And when that time arrives at last
>
> Give me power to _____
> And power to _____
> Power that _____(adv.) _____(verb)
> Every _____ (noun) that ever _____(verb)
> Oh yes, Power is the goddess! Power is the king!
> Give me that _____
> (lots of adjectives) Powerful thing!

Celebrity Slam

For several years I helped create and produce a benefit for The Three Arts Club of Chicago, an institution that supports female artists and performers. The centerpiece of these nights of food and entertainment were celebrity slams. We recruited radio personalities to create poems for the SOUND BITE SLAM. Here's how it worked: Each of six radio personalities composed a 30-second, 60-second, and 120-second poem about the benefit's theme and performed their poems in a three-round slam bout. Judges were chosen from the audience and were very excited to be in such close proximity to their local radio heroes.

You might think that convincing a world-renowned slammer or a local celebrity to perform at your show would be a monumental task, but many big-name performers need you just as much as you need them. Many slam poets have achieved great notoriety through their slam and mass media appearances and can often be recruited for benefits to participate in an All-Star Slammer night. If your All-Star show is fantastic and the All Star names draw a crowd, you've created a winner. Don't assume that your city's mayor, the local football coach, Cher, or Bill Gates wouldn't be interested in a slam-off. Call them. You'd be surprised at how many closet poets are out there. After their names are on the roster, you can bet on a standing-room-only house. I haven't heard of Madonna getting in on the slam *yet*, but she obviously doesn't know what she's missing.

> ### Dig This!
>
> Former Philadelphia Eagles running back Cecil Martin organized and participated in (as a poet, not a running back) a slam benefit for the Evanston, Illinois YWCA. Ray Suarez of National Public Radio fame hosted a kids vs. pros (U.S. Poet Laureate Robert Hass, Nikki Giovanni, and a few others) slam in Washington, D.C. to benefit The Writers Corporation. Viggo Mortensen, film star of *Lord of the Rings*, unveiled his art and poetry at a slam-related event to benefit San Francisco-based Youth Speaks. All these big names donated their time for poetry and a good cause.

Slam Dunk Poetry Day

An ensemble of local and national slam poets assembled in Chicago for a day-long event to celebrate a traveling poetry and photo exhibit based upon John Huet and Jimmy Smith's book *Soul of the Game*. The day culminated in a slam competition between two teams of slam greats performing solos, duets, and trios. A team would "shoot" by performing a poem. The opposing team could then try to "block the shot" by performing a short improvisational verse based on the same theme and gaining the crowd's approval by applause. Judges held up cards that read "Slam Dunk" 3 points, "Score" 2 points, or "Stuff" 1 point, and, of course, if your poem was blocked by audience applause, 0 points.

A Poetry Slam is a lively poetry performance judged by audience members. Native Chicagoan Marc Smith, a former construction worker, first coined the term "slam" in July 1986 to describe the poetry/vaudeville show he started at Chicago's Green Mill Cocktail Lounge. Since its beginning, the slam concept has spread to over 100 cities worldwide. The most distinctive feature of slam poetry is its competitive spirit. Poets face off with one another in a half serious, half comedic confrontation of words judged by audience members who rate the poems 1 to 10 (and sometimes into the minus numbers). Somehow through the excitement, a champion emerges. **Our Slam Dunk Poetry Slam** is a variation on the traditional slam competition. Two teams composed of champion "slammers" from around the country perform solo poems, duets, and trios. The two hour show promises to break down the preconceptions of poetry as a reserved art form. [Main Stage, Stanley Field Hall - 2 p.m.]

Booksigning: 11:00 - 11:45 a.m.
One of the poets featured in the "Soul of the Game" exhibit, **Gerald Quickley**, will sign copies of the book *Soul of the Game* adjacent to the exhibit. [Purchase books at the Dino Store, 2nd floor.]

Poetry Activities: 11:00 a.m. - 1:30 p.m.
Explore your poetic side through ongoing activities.
[Families at Work, East Balcony, 2nd floor]

Environmental Poetry - E. Donald Two-Rivers/Broeffle

Rules of the Game, Traditional Forms, Meter and Rhyming in Poetry - John Biederman

Giant-sized Magnetic Poetry Board - Daniel Ferri & Charlie Rossiter

Poetry Readings:
Hear a variety of poetry styles read by locally and nationally known poets.

11:30 a.m.	**Daniel Ferri** [East Balcony]
12:00 p.m.	**Gerald Quickley** [Main Stage, Stanley Field Hall]
12:30 p.m.	**E. Donald Two-Rivers/Broeffle** [East Balcony]
1:00 p.m.	**Charlie Rossiter** [East Balcony]

Performances:

1:00 p.m.   **Duncan YMCA Chernin's Center for the Arts – "Homer G. & the Rhapsodies":** a collection of sketches, musings & improvised "rap talkin" about the sport of the gods, otherwise known as b-ball, hoops or "The Game." [Black Box Theater—Sea Mammals, Ground Floor]

1:00 p.m.   **Preschool Alert! Focus on Poetry:** Relax and enjoy learning new songs and stories and have fun creating art work. Today we feature the rhyming book *How to Hide a Polar Bear & Other Mammals*. [Place for Wonder, 1st Floor]

2:00 p.m.   **Slam Dunk Poetry Slam** [Main Stage, Stanley Field Hall]

A program from the Slam Dunk event.

Other Twists

Your slam is successful—or at least everyone involved, including the audience, thinks it's grand, but something seems to be missing. It just doesn't snap and sizzle for you anymore. You're in a rut. Your slam needs a good old-fashioned cold shower—a special night to rejuvenate it, wash the cobwebs from your brain, and draw some fresh faces to the crowd. This is a good sign that you need to juice up your weekly slam with a special event or a different set of rules. Think of this one-shot show as a holiday special or a two-hour episode of your favorite TV show. Everyone will tune in because they want to see something new and different infused with the energy of your innovative mind. The following sections can help inspire you.

The Youth Slam

Youth slams are hot. The next generation of poets are already starting slams coast to coast and creating communities of unique, fresh voices. Slam is taught in workshops in high school and junior high school, in libraries, and in after-school programs as an effective means to get kids talking, creating, and sharing their thoughts and feelings.

Every year the National Youth Slam is held in a different city in America. When they say "youth," they mean it—unless you're between 13 and 19 years old, you're not qualified. The venues are in coffeehouses and other non-drinking, non-smoking venues, of course, and the slams are just as exciting as any other slams. You'll keep asking yourself, "Why wasn't I doing this when I was their age?" Borrow on the youth idea to create a special ages show at your event.

> **Dig This!**
>
> The national youth slam was the brainchild of Connecticut slammer Elizabeth Thomas. It's more than five years old and travels under the name of Brave New Voices. For more information, check out www.upwordspoetry.com/brave_new_voices.htm.

The Music + Poetry + Slam Slam

What do you get when you make a poet use music in his piece? Occasionally, you get a train wreck. Many times, though, you get a lovely marriage of spoken word and music that no one (including you) ever expected. Holding an "All Poets Must Groove with the Band" Slam might not be an option for some venues—many slams these days use a DJ to supply tunes or simply throw a few CDs in the blender and hit "play." However, some venues have live musicians in-house and if you have the chance to host a slam with a band or the opportunity to perform with one, do it. Do you have a sad, melancholy poem? Ask the band to play "My Funny Valentine." Got an angry, "give-me-my-stuff-back" poem? Sex Pistols. You'll be surprised about what transpires. The best part about a Band Slam is that it adds a new element of competition— maybe your poem is great, and maybe your performance is good, but can you play well with others?

Bah! Humbug! The Holiday Slam

Just when you couldn't stand any more holiday cheer, you see that your favorite poetry venue is holding a Holiday Slam. What can you do? Go home and dust off that punk version of *A Christmas Carol* you scratched onto a piece of dark metal one bitter winter night or compose a verse explaining what the Easter Bunny should do with those eggs. A lot of slam venues hold special Holiday Slams and donate the funds raised to local charities. Often the cover charge for this event is a nonperishable food item or a pair of mittens. If there is a cover charge, some slammasters donate the proceeds to a good cause—during the holidays, people are better about remembering those less fortunate, and you can help out by participating.

From Nothing Something Slams

Perceiving and filling a need is a basic business concept that applies to creating new slam shows as well. A particular section of the community yearns for a slam that focuses more on their sensibilities and creates the "We Read Off The Paper—Nonmemorized Slam" or the "Politics Are Not Our Game Slam" or the "West Side Slam." The need could be related to an untapped resource; for instance, a large community of short story writers with no place to speak their works—"The North Shore Story Slam." Recognizing a potential or need takes a keen eye—an ability to step back and see what others are missing. Of course, I can't give you specifics on what your community needs, but take a look at the real-life examples described in the following sections.

Fat Tuesday Celebration of the Seven Deadly Sins

For some time I had been running a second slam in the western suburbs of Chicago. I wanted to create a special show to boost my weekly Tuesday night show. I reasoned that people love to celebrate special occasions, so I started to think about calendar dates and holidays. Birthday slams? Christmas slam? But everyone has a special Christmas show, and the same was true for Halloween. Good Friday/Easter weekend was another obvious choice. How 'bout the Dog Days of August Slam? Wait a minute! Mardi Gras! Fat Tuesday! That's it!

When I created the Fat Tuesday Celebration of the Seven Deadly Sins there were absolutely no high-profile Fat Tuesday celebrations in Chicago. It was a big gaping hole, an unperceived need that has since filled up with numerous Fat Tuesday events after the Sin Slam paved the way.

> **What's on the CD**
>
> **CD #1 track #20:** Charles Ellik performing "Little Green Peas"
>
> **CD #1 track #21:** Marcel Murphy performing "23 Chromosomes"

> **Backstage Skinny**
>
> The newspapers love to cover special events. They might be reluctant to cover your weekly slam, even if it's the best matching of local poets ever. But make it a special occasion, and give it an event angle—"Poet Titans meet Poet Godzillas for the First Time"—and the press will do it up right.

Chi Town Classic

Krystal Ashe, who for years produced one of Chicago's spin-off slams, recognized the potential of creating a grand slam event on the Thursday preceding the annual slammasters meeting in Chicago. She reasoned quite correctly that all this great talent from across the country would be in town for the meetings, so why not schedule a performance and use it as a benefit to PSI? That's how the Chi Town Classic began. At the Chi Town Classic, Chicago slammers pair off against slammers and slammasters from around the country for a king-of-the-hill slam extravaganza. Listen to Berkley slammaster Charles Ellik performing his poem, "Little Green Peas," and Houston's Marcel Murphy performing his poem, "23 Chromosomes," at the 2002 Chi Town Classic.

A flyer explaining the rules for Fat Tuesday.

YOU AND YOUR FRIENDS CAN ENTER
THE 7TH ANNUAL POETRY PARADE
COMPETITION

HERE ARE THE OFFCIAL UNOFFICIAL RULES OF MISRULE
FOR ENTRY INTO THE POETRY PARADE COMPETITION

1)   Only seven groups will be allowed to enter, one for each of the seven deadly sins: (*PRIDE has already been taken*), *AVARICE, LUST, ENVY, GLUTTONY, ANGER, AND   SLOTH.*

2)   Each "krewe" must have at least 3 members and no more than 5.

3)   The poetry parade performance must include some kind of promenade around the audience and up to the stage. It should be a minimum of eight (8) minutes (promenade and performance) but should not exceed fifteen (15) minutes in total lenght. You'll be sorry, maybe, if it did. Think of the poems as floats in a parade -- let your imaginations get outrageous. Remember Fat Tuesday is the day of Misrule.

4) $716 in prizes will be awarded. $232 for the Grand Mardi Gras King Rex Prize. $77 for 2nd place. $34 for 3rd. Plus a $61 prize for best costume. $52 for best poem of the night. An an assortment of other cash prizes adding up to $716. The judges, as is traditional, will be chosen from the audience and their word will be final. In the past, the poets have been judged on techinique, content, audacity, performance, costume, and spectacle.

IF YOU WISH TO ENTER, SELECT A SIN AND
CALL:
MARC SMITH 708-484-2009

Slammin' Across America

Gary Glazner, the passion and promotion behind the First National Slam, provided the business savvy to create and ramrod the 2000 Slam America Tour. Over 100 poets participated in this Ken Kesey-style bus tour (minus most of the drugs), which covered over 8000 miles, 32 cities, and 36 readings in 30 days. Grand Marnier sponsored the tour through PSI along with support from Manic D Press, publisher of Gary's book, *Poetry Slam, The Competitive Art of Performance Poetry*. Slam America showcases the performance aspect of Slam Poetry and reduces emphasis on the competition, inspiring the following events:

♦ **The Haiku Death Match** evolved from Gary's hosting of Haiku Slams at the Nationals. It is a fast-paced exchange of haiku punctuated with audience chants of "HI-KU, HI-KU, HI-KU." At the end, one of the poets would feign committing hari-kari.

♦ **The Yo Mama Samurai Skits** are based on the old Japanese Samurai movies where the voices were out of sync. Two poets offstage using microphones provide the dialog, and two poets onstage act out the scene and try to keep up with the words. If it is done well, the audience has a hard time telling who is speaking.

> **Dig This!**
>
> The television, radio, and print media coverage of the tour reached over 5 million people; and bus driver, Paul Cavendish, started speaking haiku about halfway through the tour.

The Slam America Tour was a huge success. It played down the competition and played up the theatrics of performance, dispelling the image of poetry as a dry and dusty art.

Your Overall Strategy

Whether you're pitching your slam to the board members of your local public library system, the CEO of a large corporation, or the programming director of the cultural arts center, your strategy is the same: Provoke their imagination and then implant your vision in their brains. You want the vision of your slam playing like a movie on the inner wall of their skulls. Then, after you've hooked them, make them believe that you can pull it off.

Programming people want to be inspired and then leave it all to you. Take charge. Don't expect the institution director or her assistants to tell you what to do or how to do it. They're providing you with time and space in their schedule, and backup support. And sometimes that support doesn't include all the cash needed, so part of your job might be finding supplemental financing or a least a scheme of how to make ends meet. Get to work. Attend to every last detail or delegate tasks to people you trust, making sure that whomever you've delegated a duty to has done it. A hassle-free night of fine art entertainment will keep you in the slam-producing business for a long time.

The Least You Need to Know

◆ Although the small venues are your meat and potatoes, special shows, benefits, and appearances at institutions can benefit you greatly.

◆ Look to museums, libraries, associations, and your town's cultural arts center for opportunities to stage your show.

◆ Corporations are always looking for entertaining, imaginative, illuminating presentations to refresh and inspire their employees.

◆ For most institutional presentations, you must tailor your show to appeal specifically to the institution's audience or to a particular event or situation.

◆ You can breathe new life into your weekly show by staging a holiday show or one-time special that changes your slam's focus or follows a different set of rules.

Part 5

We Are Slamily: The Slam Family

Poetry slam reaches far beyond the front and back cover of this book, beyond the walls of your local slam venue, beyond the city limits, over the state line, and across the oceans to the international community. Yet the slam community remains as close as family.

This part provides an overview of the ever-expanding national and international slam community and their various events and programs, and shows you how to become an active member of this vital personal network.

Chapter 21

Take It from the Top: PSI, the National Organization

In This Chapter

- ◆ Becoming an official PSI member
- ◆ Playing an active role by volunteering your time and talents
- ◆ Understanding PSI's noncorporate, nonprofit structure
- ◆ Recognizing the role of PSI's Executive Council! (EC)

Slam infected the poetry scene like a virulent virus. Slam's founders had no master plan for global domination, no desire to commercialize and profit from its popularity, and no organizational chart to enthrone themselves in a crystal tower. Slam spread not by following a success strategy, but through its own inherent merits and the passion, integrity, and energy of its devoted artists and organizers.

So why did the slam community sell out and create a (dare I say it?) "organization"? What's this PSI (Poetry Slam, Inc.) all about? Is anarchy dead? This chapter answers these questions, explains why the organization is necessary, and shows you how you can get involved in PSI as both a member and volunteer.

Incorporation—A Necessary Evil

By incorporating as a national nonprofit, the Slam Movement evolved from a purely ragtag tribe of rebellious free spirits to a ragtag *institution* of rebellious free spirits. Many of us vociferously resisted the transition. We had grown to be an internationally recognized art form by the seat of our pants, so why couldn't we keep growing by the seat of our pants? After all, we wanted to be bottom heavy! We wanted to freely pass our discoveries and experiences from city to city, poet to poet, and generation to generation as a gift.

Unfortunately, much of the world operates under the impetus of unbridled greed. We came to realize that unscrupulous individuals and organizations, sensing the commercial value of our grassroots movement, were increasingly hunting for opportunities to exploit our name, network, and reputation for their own capital gain. For years the slam elders had held the exploiters at bay, dissuading them from using our name and reputation without some payback and approval. "Listen," we'd tell them, "Slam belongs to thousands of devotees who have put their sweat and souls into it. It wouldn't be right for you to use its name for your slick TV show or your goofy board game." We all shoved our thumbs into the dike and held our collective breath, but the pressure became frightening.

> ### Dig This!
>
> A firm in North Carolina did create a word game called Poetry Slam. They were unaware of PSI, the slam family, or the reputation upon which they were infringing. As the result of some friendly negotiations, they revised their promotional copy and the game's instructions to include a description and history of the slam movement, and fed back a percentage of the small profits to PSI. The game never took off. If you have one, it could be a collector's item.

In 1997 we succumbed to the pressure and started the process of incorporating as a national nonprofit group. After we were incorporated, we were no longer a simple tribe, no longer a scattered extended family. Now we had a hierarchy, bylaws, an executive council, petty political in-fighting, bureaucratic nightmares, forms to file, miscommunications, disputed decisions, official votes, mandatory approvals, and power struggles. Ugh!

> ### Dig This!
>
> PSI is structured as a pure democracy, a from-the-bottom-up organization … never without conflict, but always with a passionate drive forward.

But it might have all been worth it. PSI is emerging as a powerful national nonprofit arts institution. It survived the recession years following the 9/11 tragedy when other long-standing nonprofits disappeared due to lack of funds. It did so because of its dedicated audience base and membership.

Connecting to the National Scene

The absolute best way to dive into the slam family gene pool is to attend its two major events: the NPS (National Poetry Slam) and IWPS (Individual World Poetry Slam). At these events, you can make all-important contacts, see first-hand what this slam thing is all about, and witness how slam competitions are run. Another way is to take a trip to Chicago for the annual spring slammasters meeting. Even if you're not a slammaster, you're welcome to attend and watch the proceedings. A third way is to jump on the Internet, visit slam websites, and drink in the information. Then make contact. Start at www.poetryslam.com and surf. Become a PSI member, as discussed in the next section, and exchange ideas and opinions in PSI's members' chat room. After checking out the scene, read through the following sections to learn how to become more involved.

Whoa!

"You mean I gotta be a *paid* member to communicate? What kind of open democracy is that? Besides, I'm broke." Nope. Anyone can get on the informal slam family listserv. Send an e-mail to poetry_slam@yahoogroups.com. The rules are pretty loose, but you're not allowed to post poetry on the list, and troublemakers do get kicked off. But living in abject poverty does not prevent you from connecting.

Becoming a PSI Member

Anyone with a credit card that's not maxed out or a checking account with a few bucks in it has all the qualifications required to become a PSI member. You don't need to be a slammaster, volunteer, organizer, poet, or even a member of the audience. You can join just to support a good cause. So grab your credit card, go to www.poetryslam.com, follow the trail of links to the membership form, and sign up. If you don't have plastic (I know a few of you are out there), copy the following form, fill it out, and send the completed form and your check (made out to Poetry Slam, Inc.) to the following address:

> PSI c/o Steve Marsh
> 11462 East Lane
> Whitmore Lake, MI 48189

The PSI membership form.

PSi Poetry Slam, Inc.
Poetry Slam, Inc.
www.poetryslam.com

Membership Application Form

Make check or money order payable to Poetry Slam, Inc. Please mail membership application to: PSI c/o Steve Marsh, 11462 East Lane, Whitmore Lake, MI 48189

New Member [_]   Renewal [_] Name:_____

Date:_____

Address:_____

City:_____   State:_____   Zip   Code: _____

Phone:_____

E-mail Address:_____

Name of venue: _____

Membership level: If paid on line, indicate date. _____

___ Basic ($15) ___Associate ($35) ___Booster ($50) ___Sustainer ($100) ___

Patron ($500) ___ Benefactor ($1000)

Poetic License Information (New Members Only)

Date   of   Birth: _____

Endorsements:_____

Restrictions:_____

Gender:_____ Height:_____ Poetic Foot Size:_____

[_] Photo enclosed. Send a tiny photo (1"x1") if you want your photo on your license.
for office use only

Paid: ___ cash ___check #_____ membership #_____

What do you receive for your generous donation? A feeling of generosity and the knowledge that you are now an official patron of the arts. Okay, you also receive a handful of goodies, depending on how much you donate:

- **$15 NPS Participant**   This level allows you to participate in the National Poetry Slam and gives you voting rights. Your generosity is rewarded with a novelty (frame-able) Poetic License and Certificate of Slambership.

- **$35 PSI Associate**   For thirty-five bucks, you get everything a participant receives, plus a tri-annual newsletter, an opportunity to sell your products on PSI's website (at a low consignment rate), and your name listed on the website.

- ◆ **$50 PSI Booster** As a Booster, you get everything a PSI Associate receives, plus a poetry.slam e-mail address and access to poetryslam.com's Boosters page.

- ◆ **$100 PSI Sustainer** For a single Ben Franklin, you receive all the goodies due to a PSI Booster, plus your very own annual slam poetry anthology.

- ◆ **$500 PSI Patron** As a Patron, you receive everything a sustainer receives, plus one free all-access pass to NPS and your name printed in the tri-annual newsletter.

- ◆ **$1,000 PSI Benefactor** For a fraction of the cost of a new Jaguar, you can become a PSI Benefactor. You get everything a Patron receives, plus a second pass to the NPS (for your date) and your name (but not your date's) in the NPS program for the same year you donated.

Help Wanted: Volunteers

After you've joined PSI, checked out the NPS, and seen the energy and community spirit it fosters, you undoubtedly will want to become more involved in the organization. Following is a list of various ways you can help:

- ◆ **Contribute to the newsletter as an editor or reporter.** You like to write, don't you? Be a reporter for your local slam or help proofread and edit copy. It'll introduce you to writers around the country and around the world.

- ◆ **Help your local slammaster.** You can move the furniture and set up the stage, collect the money at the door, hang posters, pass out fliers, or drive the celebrity slammers in from the airport.

- ◆ **Help maintain local histories of slam and add to the national slam archive.** The archive consists of an ever-growing collection of poems, competition records, collections of fliers and NPS logos, promotional artwork, and anecdotes that color the history. All these keep the roots and principles from being lost. As a volunteer in the archive department, you serve an important role in their preservation.

Backstage Skinny _____

If you're a budding historian, you should be getting excited right now. Reconstructing slam history is like an archeological dig. So much of it is in boxes waiting to be uncovered. Some of us have neglected to bring to light so much of what went down in the early days. For the Green Mill show alone there are dozens of boxes of recordings, videos, fliers, poems, and documents that might someday be a treasure chest to some clever historian who uncovers them long after the original elders have passed into poet heaven.

- **Help with record keeping.** PSI must keep track of all sorts of records, from membership rolls to meeting minutes to e-store accounts. As we get more systematic in our approach to these duties, volunteers are becoming more essential.

- **Copyedit for anthologies and other PSI print materials.** PSI is producing more copy as the movement spreads, and all of this printed material must be checked and rechecked for grammar, accuracy, and spelling.

- **Write grants for national and local slam chapters.** Some groups support the arts by providing grants, but PSI won't get the money unless it asks for it by submitting a grant proposal. If you're a writer, you can help.

- **Design work for brochures, anthologies, CD coverage, and other marketing and promotional materials.** Whether you're a graphics designer or an expert doodler, you can help design and print eye-catching illustrations, logos, and other much-needed images.

- **Work national events.** During the NPS, PSI is always in need of organizers, emcees, ticket-takers, door-openers, equipment-toters, and an army of volunteers.

Staying in the Loop with the Listserv

You'll get a good taste of the democracy that has propelled the slam forward, sideways, and in circles by viewing the official listservs. At times the listserv discussion gets ugly; it can be free speech at its best and worst. But it is our greatest communication tool. Famed slammer Beau Sia first established his identity on the listserv. Long before anyone outside a small circle in New York City had even seen or heard any of his legendary slam performances, we knew of a young, prolific Beau Sia by his ponderous posts on the listserv.

> **Dig This!**
>
> Beau Sia appeared in the film documentary *SlamNation* and later in the commercial film *Slam*. He went on to star in the NYC theatrical production *Def Jam On Broadway*. For more information, check out www.defpoetryjam. com.

Open Lines of Communication

From the top to the bottom, most of the slam family is accessible to the inquiring public. Few of us have gatekeepers safeguarding us from those who are interested in the movement. Teachers, aspiring poets, students, reporters, and mothers looking to place their children in a literary environment are only a phone call, letter, or e-mail away from the pulse of our grassroots movement.

PSI's Noncorporate, Nonprofit Structure

Since its inception, Poetry Slam, Inc. has faced an ongoing struggle to overcome a serious identity crisis. It wanted to be like a family or tribe, but reality often demanded that it function more like a government or corporation. Hence, its structure and by-laws are constantly evolving. The net result is an organization that functions in various ways at various times: Sometimes it interacts with the ritual, honor, and ceremony of a tribe; at other times, with the closeness and tension of a passionate family; and some-times, with the political manglings of a government agency, complete with deadlines, red tape, and forms. It experiences moments of golden clarity inspired by selfless co-operation and times when all communication and compromise break down.

This functional dysfunctional beast named PSI has three distinct bodies: the slam family, the SlamMasters' Council, and the Executive Council. The following sections describe these groups in detail so you can begin to appreciate the various facets of this beast.

The Slam Family

"Poetry is the heart of the people, and the People is everyone …." Everybody. The slam family includes everybody: audience members, board members, slammasters, slammers, and people passing by the slam's open doorway looking in and enjoying themselves. Anyone who has an interest in performance poetry is part of our family. Of course, to be official and have a vote, you must become a member. But to attend the slam family meetings and add your voice, all you have to do is be present. (Of course, if you get loud, long-winded, and feisty, all the paid members are going to lean into your face and say, "Pay up or shut up.")

All PSI members share an equal status, one vote apiece, nobody better than the next. An annual meeting of the family is held each August during the NPS. Members dis-cuss, debate, vote on, and eventually approve the general direction of the slam family and the principles behind it. PSI members propose and vote on future projects and discuss rules and procedures. Many heated arguments have peppered the slam family meetings over the years as the organization struggled with the meaning of democracy in its fledgling movement. The interactions resulting from these conflicts have created an informal cabinet of strong leaders called *elders*. The elders use their memories of prior debates to steer the family around roadblocks that were already encountered years ago. The family is a blend of experience and new vision.

During the year, members communicate informally via e-mail and telephone. Online discussions and debates occur through the slam family listserv. Soon (cross your fingers and hope to die) PSI will have an online voting system that will allow members to cast critical slam family votes throughout the year.

SlamSlang _____

The term **elder** was first used at the NPS 1992 slam family meeting in San Francisco. There were many new faces at that meeting and, rather than have the old guard dominate, the elders were asked to remain tacitly present in the background. A few of those elders were only thirty years old. They listened and observed, and interjected their wisdom and experience only when discussions went far askew of "slam truth."

The slam family provides the general vision of how PSI should proceed. It provides input and criticism concerning projects and management. It's the mass voice—the voice of the people.

The SlamMasters' Council

The SlamMasters' Council is the strongest and most important body in the PSI structure. Ironically, council members are not elected. If you create a slam and register it with PSI, you earn the right to sit on the SlamMasters' Council. (Of course, you have to be a PSI member to do that.) The SlamMasters' Council meets at least twice a year, once at the NPS and once in Chicago during the now traditional slammasters week.

SlamSpeak _____

In 2001, April Ardito (Worcester Slam member, associate level) won the first Spirit of the Slam award for her efforts in coordinating the first (and only) 24-hour open mike at NPS in Seattle. In 2002, Ms. Spelt won in Minneapolis and is now chair of the Spirit of Slam Committee.

The duties and responsibilities of the SlamMasters' Council include the following:

- Considering and approving bids for the NPS, IWPS, and other annual projects

- Considering and approving proposals brought to the council via the slam family and/or the Executive Council (EC)

- Nominating and electing members to the EC board

- Proposing and approving new projects

- Managing all changes in NPS and IWPS rules

- Forming subcommittees to discuss and debate issues and projects

◆ Formulating and modifying rules and regulations concerning certification and registration of slam venues

◆ Establishing a selection committee

◆ Bestowing the *Spirit of Slam* award

How to Register and Certify Your Slam

You've got a slam happening. Each week, more people come, and more poets perform. It's the bomb. Now it's time to register your slam. Why? Because of the following benefits:

◆ The right to submit an application to have your team considered for entry in the National Poetry Slam

◆ The right to submit an application to have a representative of your venue considered for entry in the Individual World Poetry Slam

◆ The right to participate in the SlamMasters' listserv, in which you can access the best promotional and organizational minds in PSI

◆ The right to use the "Certified" or "Registered" PSI seal of approval in your ads or fliers

◆ The right to attend and vote in the official business meetings of the SlamMasters' Council and be a voice in determining the PSI policies and projects

◆ The right to establish a *GrantBack* account to aid in the fundraising efforts of your venue

SlamSlang

The PSI **GrantBack** Program allows a slam organization that does not have a nonprofit status to use the PSI nonprofit status to obtain funding and grants that would not otherwise be available to it. Go to www.poetryslam.com for the details.

Certification and Registration—What's the Difference?

All venues that are run by a slammaster who is a current member of PSI, has signed the Equal Opportunity Statement, and has paid the registration fee (currently $45), are considered "Registered." Registration gives your venue all of the benefits of official affiliation with PSI *except* the right to send representatives to the Individual World Poetry Slam or the National Poetry Slam, or to make a bid to host a future national- or world-level poetry Slam event.

"Certified" venues are poetry slams that have demonstrated through at least six separate pieces of evidence that they meet the minimum criteria. They must:

◆ Be a part of an ongoing poetry reading series and hold at least six slams per year.

◆ Have an audience base that averages at least 30 members.

◆ Have a slammaster attend the Spring SlamMasters' Council meeting each year (or send a voting proxy).

What Is Certification "Evidence"?

Generally anything that shows the ongoing nature of your poetry slam is considered evidence. Evidence can take the form of copies of articles in the local press, fliers you use to promote your show, a website URL, or copies of advertisements. We have even received copies of videotapes of events and used them as evidence in the past.

Dig This!

To begin the certification process go to www.poetryslam.com/eosform.htm, read the equal opportunity statement, fill in the requested information, click the I Agree button, and then proceed to the online store, as instructed, to pay the certification fee.

How Long Does Certification or Registration Last?

Any poetry slam may register or certify at any time. That process is good through the next National Poetry Slam and is renewable before January 1 after that NPS. New registrations and certifications are good for at least one year. Renewals are available at a reduced fee. Renewals after January 1 are subject to the higher fee.

The Closest Thing to a Corporate Structure: The Executive Council

The Executive Council (EC) is the only elected body in PSI, and its members are the servants to the slammasters' and the family itself. Any PSI member can be nominated and elected to serve on the EC. Each EC member serves a two-year term. Terms are staggered so that only half the council comes up for election in any one year. Elections are held at the Spring slammasters meeting. Currently seven people are on the EC board. They are responsible for getting things done—for turning the visions of the slammasters and slam family into reality. The following list describes some of the projects and responsibilities that lie under their domain:

- ◆ **NPS & IWPS**   After the slammasters approve a host city for the NPS and IWPS, it's the EC's duty to create and negotiate the details of the host city contracts. This is no small task. Considerations include managing and financing publicity for the event, considering what kinds of venues will be selected for the event, determining what side events they will stage, and deciding what kind of funding the host city will bring to the table.

- ◆ **The Membership Slam**   As a means of recruiting members at the local level, the EC manages the Membership Slam each year. PSI pays for NPS entry fees, travel expenses, and lodging for the venue that has the most new PSI members by a set deadline in spring.

- ◆ **Cross Training Poetry Camp**   If you yearn for some face-to-face instruction, CTPC (initiated in the summer of 2004) is a workshop retreat that guides the participants through every aspect of slam poetry. (See Chapter 23 for more about the PSI Summer Camp.)

- ◆ **Fundraising**   The main task of the EC is finding the funds to make all of PSI's projects happen and then managing those funds so they don't slip away. Keeping those purse strings tied tight can be a challenge.

Professional and Volunteer Staff

The day-to-day business of PSI is carried on by a very small professional staff assisted by a handful of dedicated volunteers. Steve Marsh, one of PSI's most important slam elders, has served as Executive Director since 1999. The professional and volunteer staff attends to the following:

- ◆ **Accounting and Taxes**   The numbers! PSI is always broke, but Uncle Sam needs to know just how broke PSI is.

- ◆ **Fundraising**   Our development director assists the EC in finding corporate sponsorship for events and grant funding for PSI operations. Like any other nonprofit organization, PSI needs financial support and therefore a vigilant staff to pan for gold.

- ◆ **Legal Affairs**   When someone outside the family starts to infringe upon slam territory uninvited, the professional staff goes after them. They also check amendments to the bylaws, the host city contracts, and any other legal beagles that come sniffing around.

- ◆ **Poet Gallery**   The Poet Gallery is an online resumé service for PSI members pursuing full- or part-time careers as performance poets. You can view it on the www.poetryslam.com website.

- ◆ **PSI Newsletter** PSI's tri-annual newsletter keeps the general membership informed of activities and controversy brewing in the slam family.

- ◆ **The E Store** On the website you can visit the e-store and browse the electronic shelves for books, audio recordings, videos, t-shirts, and virtually all merchandise the slam membership has to offer.

- ◆ **Venue and Membership Certifications and Records** Forms, forms, and more forms. These poor people are the ones that have to keep track of all the paper-work. Good grief.

- ◆ **Website** The website is PSI's most powerful tool for communication and record keeping. The best way to see what it offers is to visit www.poetryslam.com.

Subcommittees

Of course, the work and issues bubble up and trickle down from the slam family mem-bership. Formal, informal, and pro- and anti-subcommittees are formed to debate, decide, and activate regional slams, membership perks, corporate funding, NPS pro-cedures, touring, world affairs, and any other matters that require attention. Like everything slam, if something must be done and nobody and no resources are available, somebody will step up, find some help, secure the required resources, and get it done.

The Least You Need to Know

- ◆ PSI is the formal organization that handles legal and financial issues and provides members with the direction, services, and resources they need to move slam for-ward.

- ◆ The slam family reluctantly incorporated to prevent the money-grubbers from exploiting slam for their own capital gain.

- ◆ To become an active slam family member, visit www.poetryslam.com often, pay your dues, volunteer, and stay connected through the PSI listserv.

- ◆ PSI is comprised of three main bodies—the family, the SlamMasters' Council, and the Executive Council.

- ◆ PSI's professional and volunteer staff consists of paid and unpaid members who do most of the grunt work, including promoting, defending, and serving PSI and its members.

22

NPS-IWPS: The National Competitions

In This Chapter

- ◆ Tracing the brief history of NPS's offspring—the Individual World Poetry Slam (IWPS)

- ◆ Spending a week at Nationals … vicariously, of course

- ◆ Boning up on the National Poetry Slam rules and regulations

- ◆ Entering a team or flying solo at Nationals

- ◆ Meeting the entrance requirements and the all-important deadlines

Every summer dozens of four-person teams from North America and Europe celebrate a week of poetic activities that run from morning to midnight at the NPS (National Poetry Slam). In February, individual competitors rock the poetry world at the IWPS (Individual World Poetry Slam). And at each event, poets and audience members record in their journals that they had the time of their lives. This chapter takes you backstage to reveal the history, rituals, rules, and regulations that structure these events, and shows you how you can become involved.

A Brief History Lesson

Chapters 1 and 3 related the NPS history and background, but the other national slam competition, the IWPS, has barely been mentioned. That's because the IWPS is still in diapers. The NPS grew fat with success, and the slam family realized that it needed another event, one to accommodate individual performers and allow the parent NPS to refocus attention back on the teams, where it properly belonged.

Backstage Skinny

For a quick and easy glance at the National Slam's lengthy history go to www.poetryslam.com/nps/history.htm. For the latest on the IWPS, go to www.worldpoetrychampionship.com.

During the writing of this book, the first screams of an IWPS event were about to crack the southern atmosphere. The event was scheduled to take place in Greenville, South Carolina, February 2004. Slammaster Kimberly Sims opened the tournament to 50 performance poets from certified slams. In its first year, the IWPS hoped to attract close to one thousand people and make the slam family's second official annual event a long-lasting success.

Tournament Rites and Rituals

Like the activities leading up to a wedded couple's first kiss, the rites of passage and the excitement at the NPS and IWPS build as the time draws near. Ritual plays an important role in how folks prepare and participate, and how the events themselves are structured.

The following sections take you on a road trip to the Nationals and describe the overall structure of the NPS event. When you finally witness it for yourself, don't be surprised to find some of the rites and rituals missing and some new ones in their place. The glorious part about the NPS is that it is an organic art form—it's not about to ossify into a marble Venus museum piece. The slam is a hot-blooded mama ready to swing its booty (and yours) around the dance floor.

Preshow Tuesday

Have you signed the video-release form? Did you pick up your poet bag with all the goodies—CDs, maps, coupons for a free poet dog? Hey, it's registration time, and most experienced slam teams know they must take care of business the day before kick-off. NPS is big. It takes a substantial amount of coordination and systematic form checking to be sure that everybody who's expected shows up. Have all your team members paid their annual membership dues?

In addition to mundane organizational matters, this day includes the Rookie Open Mike, the first chance for first-time attendees to proclaim their existence and gain special focus from the family. And sometimes someone in the host city cooks up a barbecue or plans a late-evening kegger. Always, after early registration closes, there's a pretournament party/performance at a local club. It's a time to connect with old friends and kick back with new acquaintances before the competitive tension gets thick. Got an idea for preshow Tuesday? Do it. Don't ask for official permission, but don't step on other people's events, either; that's contrary to the spirit of this movement.

Opening Day

The slam community is a savvy marketing machine. It understands the need for shameless self-promotion, especially when it comes to the Nationals. And, because the audience is such a critical component of our art form, we're determined to have our venues bursting at the seams. And we love to be creative. Therefore, when the NPS kicks off, we do it with pomp and pageantry and a huge dose of anarchy.

> ### Dig This!
>
> In Chicago 1999, on opening day, NPS held an open mike on the steps of the Chicago Cultural Center. Rants, rap, and couplets bounced down the stone and steel canyons of the Loop via loud speakers, attracting shoppers, vagrants, and Chicago's finest, the boys in blue, who wanted to know, "Just what's dis dat yous folks are doin' on the steps dere?" "Poetry, officer! Poetry."
>
> In Minneapolis 2002, the opening day of the NPS kicked off with team piece limericks in a public park followed by free-style dancing to the sweet sounds of a local poetry band. Old man Marc even danced—it's true, there's even a picture to prove it.

It's All About Bouts

The tournament structure currently allows 64 teams to enter the competition. On Wednesday and Thursday, each team competes in one of the 16 four-team preliminary *bouts*. On Friday, the 16 top-rated teams move on to the semi-finals. On Saturday, the final four compete for the championship title in front of one, two, or three thousand people.

SlamSlang

A **bout** is a competition between two or more slam poets or between two or more slam teams. The winner of a bout typically advances to the next bout to compete with other teams.

Sideshows and Other Roadside Attractions

The daytime and late-evening events have become some of the most important parts of the NPS tournament/festival, and they're open to all. Each year an inquiry goes out to the slam family asking what kind of side events they want. An informal balloting is done, and suggestions are made to the host city. Here are some of the sideshows and happenings you can expect at the NPS:

- **Cover slam**   Pay homage to the masters by performing their work instead of your own. Rub elbows with the likes of Bill Shakespeare, Bob Frost, T.S. Eliot, Wallace Stevens, Charles Bukowski, and Patricia Smith.

- **Erotica slam**   Adults-only, this bawdy, titillating slam is intended to appeal to your more sensual side.

- **Head-to-Head Haiku**   Conceived and perfected by Daniel Ferri, Head-to-Head Haiku pits one sage against the other and lets them duke it out, Eastern-style:

  Precise words battle!
  On the landscape of a stage.
  Sl … AM victorious!

- **Hip-hop slam**   If inner-city spoken word is what you're after, check out the hip-hop slam, and learn that it was around long before the movie *8 Mile*.

- **Poetry and performance workshops**   Developing as a performance poet is a lifelong pursuit, and the slam community knows it. The Nationals feature workshops to help you hone your skills.

- **Prop slam**   No props are allowed in the official competitions, so if you just gotta have a prop for one of your poems, do it here.

- **Slam Speaks Out**   You'll find plenty of political rants in the main competitions, but Slam Speaks Out focuses exclusively on political slam. Topics include war, environment, race, feminism, and other controversial themes.

Meetings and Other Formalities

The NPS is the one time during the year when the slam community can be together en masse and settle its most important business matters—budgets, project proposals, rule changes, the Slam Spirit Award, and a host of other issues. In a few stolen hours during an already slam-packed week, we handle more business than some local governments crawl through in a year … well, maybe a month. Following is a list of the various groups that meet at Nationals:

◆ **The EC (Executive Council)** acts as the NPS tournament committee at Nationals. It meets daily to address any unforeseen problems, monitor the host city's efforts, and ensure that the tournament is fair and fulfilling for all.

◆ **The SlamMasters' Council** meets once, usually on Friday morning, to discuss, debate, and vote on issues ranging from revisions to the nonprofit bylaws to the election of EC members.

◆ **The slam family** members gather on Saturday morning to voice their vision of slam's future and sometimes to air their concerns about how things have gone down at Nationals.

The slam family meeting has given rise to many famous, spirited debates concerning tournament rules and rituals. The film documentary *SlamNation*, which you can purchase online at the PSI e-store, contains an excerpt from one of the most passionate family meetings.

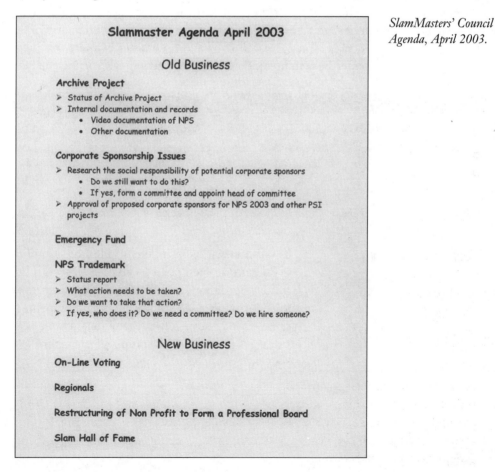

Slammaster Agenda April 2003

Old Business

Archive Project
➢ Status of Archive Project
➢ Internal documentation and records
  • Video documentation of NPS
  • Other documentation

Corporate Sponsorship Issues
➢ Research the social responsibility of potential corporate sponsors
  • Do we still want to do this?
  • If yes, form a committee and appoint head of committee
➢ Approval of proposed corporate sponsors for NPS 2003 and other PSI projects

Emergency Fund

NPS Trademark
➢ Status report
➢ What action needs to be taken?
➢ Do we want to take that action?
➢ If yes, who does it? Do we need a committee? Do we hire someone?

New Business

On-Line Voting

Regionals

Restructuring of Non Profit to Form a Professional Board

Slam Hall of Fame

SlamMasters' Council Agenda, April 2003.

Hey, We Have Fun, Too

Don't let the talk of meetings and more meetings scare you off. The Nationals also host a picnic and softball game, and possibly a bowling "round robin" (if my dreams come true). Each year the host city tries to invent new ways to pull the family together, ensure that it stays interconnected and continues to grow, and keeps participants from getting too caught up in the fever of competitive poetics. So far, the model has worked quite well.

It's Official—The PSI Rule Book

Given the fact that the slam community welcomes anarchy, you might think that the Nationals would encourage an anything-goes battle royale. But, as with most competitions, the national event enforces several rules to keep the event from dissolving into a chaotic brawl and to ensure a level playing field for the competitors. Realizing the need for rules, slam elder and notorious rule-bender Taylor Mali put together the first standardized version of slam rules. Taylor, one of the most highly competitive slammers in the history of this crazy "sport," is well known as the master exploiter of the gray areas. Who knows better how to break the rules than the guy who wrote the book?

Dig This!

It's rumored that Taylor has kept statistics of every national bout since he began slamming in 1992—every score, every title, every poet. Despite his over-attention to competition, Taylor has been one of the stalwarts of the slam family, a devoted servant and mentor to many newcomers. His poem "How To Write a Political Poem" will give you a deeper look into the heart of the notorious rule-master Taylor Mali.

What's on the CD

CD #2 track #4: Taylor Mali performing "How To Write a Political Poem"

CD #2 track #5: Taylor Mali performing "Playground Love"

You can view the entire unabridged version of the NPS rules at www.poetryslam.com/nps/rules.htm. The following sections provide the *Reader's Digest* version, salt-and-peppered with my running commentary. (You see, we never stop getting opinionated about the rules. It's part of the slam fun and our unbridled free speech.)

Backstage Skinny _____

These rules have been revised and tweaked at every SlamMasters meeting since the first Chicago National Poetry Slam in 1990. Some debates have been ongoing for more than a decade. Loopholes have continually been closed, and many gray areas have been made either black or white. In the process, new loopholes and gray areas were probably created. But the rulebook was never intended to put an end to the healthy controversy that has always been an integral part of the slam. It will always be an attempt to agree on the wording (if not the spirit) of the rules of the National Poetry Slam, as well as the consequences and penalties for breaking those rules. All we can hope for is to make the playing field as level as our trust in one another will allow.

—from the Official NPS Rule Book

Three Basic Rules

The NPS has established the following three basic rules (as stated in the rule book):

1. Poems can be any subject and in any style.

2. Each poet must perform work that s/he has created.

3. No props.

The first two rules need no clarification: You can perform any type of poem you want just as long as you wrote it. The prop rule was never easy. It has been at the center of many heated debates, one of which involved the rule-master himself, Taylor Mali. It was kind of a nutty clash of family members deeply invested in their own points-of-view that spun out of control; but when you live in a world of nuclear warheads and global terrorists, arguing over props is a whole lot safer. Here's how Taylor and the rules committee cleared up the controversy over the props issue:

> Generally, poets are allowed to use [as if they were props, but please don't call them that] their given environment and the accoutrements it offers—microphones, mic stands, the stage itself, chairs onstage, a table or bar top, the aisle—as long as these accoutrements are available to other competitors as well. The rule concerning props is not intended to squelch the spontaneity, unpredictability, or on-the-fly choreography that people love about the slam; its intent is to keep the focus on the words rather than objects.

NPS has established several other "basic" rules that have generated some controversy, though less than the prop rule. The following list introduces these rules and some of the discussion they've inspired:

- **No costumes.** No exceptions, no excuses, no further clarification.

- **No musical instruments or pre-recorded music.** This includes harmonicas, jaw harps, and those little plastic things you stick in your mouth to make bird-calls.

- **No plagiarism.** You can play off ("signify on" or "sample") another poet's lines for effect, but you cannot steal another poet's lines. This rule is meant to reiterate and clarify the rule about performing your own work.

- **The No Repeat rule.** You can perform a poem "once during the preliminary and semifinal rounds and once again on the night of the finals (in either the team finals or individual finals), but not both."

The Three-Minute Rule

The three-minute rule bugaboo has haunted us for years. It began in 1991 at the NPS. A three-minute timing mechanism was being used throughout the tournament. It flashed lights to warn the poet that the final thirty seconds of the three minutes was at hand. At two minutes fifty seconds a beeper counted down the last ten seconds. At three minutes a buzzer sounded. Of course, the poets hated this intrusive nuisance. During the final night of the 1991 competition, the audience and poets, annoyed by the presence of the clock, screamed for its removal. I tried to auction it off as a piece of postindustrial decorative art, but no luck. Its big, blue, buzzing nose is staring at me as I write this.

Here's how we finally (we hope) resolved the three-minute rule:

> No performance should last longer than three minutes. The time begins when the performance begins, which may well be before the first utterance is made. A poet is certainly allowed several full seconds to adjust the microphone and get settled & ready, but as soon as s/he makes a connection with the audience ("Hey look, she's been standing there for 10 seconds and hasn't even moved"), the timekeeper can start the clock. The poet does not have an unlimited amount of "mime time." Poets with ambiguous beginnings & endings to their performances should seek out the timekeeper at each venue to settle on a starting & ending time. After three minutes, there is a ten-second grace period (up to and including 3:10.00). Starting at 3:10.01, a penalty is automatically deducted from each poet's overall score according to the following schedule:

3:10 and under	no penalty
3:10.01–3:20	–0.5
3:20.01–3:30	–1.0
3:30.01–3:40	–1.5
3:40.01–3:50	–2.0
and so on	–0.5 for every 10 seconds over 3:10

Team Pieces

Duos, trios, and quartets are allowed, even encouraged. In the spirit of collaboration and to carry on the tradition laid down in Chicago by the Chicago Poetry Ensemble, the constantly evolving team pieces have been an exciting and important part of the national event. In 2003, the Los Angeles Slam team secured its first-place position with a team piece. When done well, team pieces provide an exciting diversion in a night of solo poets. When they haven't been well-conceived or adequately rehearsed, they can be awful.

Several complex, convoluted rules govern the creation and performance of a team piece:

- The *primary author(s)* of the poem must perform the poem. In other words, a poet cannot write a team piece and then sit in the audience and watch his teammates perform it.

- The poet/performer who gives up her individual performance slot for the team piece must be one of the primary authors of the team piece, and hence be one of its performers.

- A team piece composed by only one primary author must be performed in that author's individual slot. A team piece composed by multiple primary authors can be performed in any one of the primary author's individual slots in the course of a competition.

- A team piece can be performed at subsequent NPS competitions, but all of its primary authors must be present and on the same team.

Whoa! _____

By giving up his or her individual slot for the sake of a team piece, a slammer sacrifices his or her opportunity to be included in the Individual Championship portion of the NPS tournament, which many do!

SlamSlang

A **primary author** is a poet who contributed significantly enough to the composition of a group piece to be considered an equal owner of that piece.

♦ The team piece score is assigned to the team, not to the individual who gave up her individual slot.

♦ The team can decide to perform a team piece in place of an individual piece for any and all team members. In other words, a team could use up to four team pieces in a bout and have no team members perform as individuals.

Scoring

At the national tournaments scoring is serious, even though "points are not the point." Each bout has an official volunteer scorekeeper and a timer. The judges are instructed to rate poems from 0 to 10, with 10 being the highest or "perfect" score. (Minus scores are not allowed at the national events, although some judges have tried.) The rulebook encourages judges "to use one decimal place in order to preclude the likelihood of a tie. Each poem gets five scores. The high and the low scores are dropped and the remaining three scores are added together [so the highest score is a 30, even if a performance gets five 10's]. Team scores are displayed or otherwise publicly available during the bout."

Judges

At the national events, organizers try to select five impartial judges—judges who have no personal relationship with any of the competing performers. According to the rulebook: "Once chosen, the judges: (1) are given a set of printed instructions on how to judge a poetry slam (see below for an example), (2) have a private, verbal crash course by the emcee or house manager on the do's and don'ts of poetry slam judging, and (3) hear the standardized Official Emcee Spiel (rewritten and tweaked each year by the host city of the national competition), which, among other things, will apprise the audience of their own responsibilities as well as remind the judges of theirs."

If you're fortunate enough to be chosen to judge at the Nationals (it's a blast), here's a rendition of the instructions you're likely to hear:

> You have been enlisted in the service of poetry. This is supposed to be fun, and we don't expect you to be an expert, but we can offer certain guidelines that might help to make this more fun for everyone involved, especially you:

- We use the word *poem* to include text and performance. Some say you should assign a certain number of points for a poem's literary merit and a certain number of points for the poet's performance. Others feel that you are experiencing the poem only through the performance, and it may be impossible to separate the two. You will give each poem only one score.

- Trust your gut, and give the better poem the better score.

- Be fair. We all have our personal prejudices, but try to suspend yours for the duration of the slam. On the other hand, it's okay to have a prejudice that favors the true and the beautiful over the mundane and superficial, the fascinating and enchanting over the boring and pedestrian.

- The audience may boo you, that's their prerogative; as long as the better poem gets the better score, you're doing your job well.

- Be consistent with yourself. If you give the first poem a seven and the other judges give it a nine, that doesn't mean you should give the second poem a nine—unless it's a lot better than the first poem. In fact, if it's not as good as the first poem, we count on you to give it a lower score.

- Although the high and low scores will be thrown out, don't ever make a joke out of your score thinking that it doesn't really matter. A poem about geometry does not automatically deserve 3.14 as a score. Nor does one about failing a breathalyzer test deserve a 0.08.

- Your scores may rise as the night progresses. That's called 'Score Creep.' As long as you stay consistent, you're doing your job well.

The poets have worked hard to get here; treat them with respect. They are the show, not you (although there could be no show without you). All of us thank you for having the courage to put your opinions on the line."

Sending a Team

Teams at the NPS represent certified slams. (See Chapter 21 for the criteria of a certified slam.) Four people in their basement can't decide that they want to be a team and enter. The whole purpose of the NPS is to encourage the growth of slam shows across the world. And it has succeeded beyond our wildest dreams. During the writing of this book there were 101 certified PSI slams representing venues in the United States and Canada and another 200 affiliated slam venues in Switzerland, Germany, France, UK, and Italy. That's quite an accomplishment for the ragtag tribe that we are.

Team Selection Process

To discourage discrimination and nepotism, NPS has developed guidelines for selecting team members based on talent and performance rather than race, sexual preference, beliefs, social standing, economic status, or anything else that doesn't really matter. Here's a statement of the NPS guidelines:

> Teams must be chosen from an ongoing slam or reading series open to all poets regardless of age, sex, race, ability, appearance, or sexual orientation. All certified/registered venues are expected to uphold the Equal Opportunity Statement. Team members must be chosen through some form of competition; how that competition is structured is up to the local venue or slammaster so long as anyone who considers him/herself to be a part of the community fielding the slam team has the competitive opportunity to join it.

To apply to have your slam team considered for the next NPS, go to www.poetryslam.com/npsform.htm and fill out the application form. It should take you less than ten minutes.

Who Gets To Go?

The number of teams invited to participate at the Nationals has grown from 8 in 1991 to 64 in 2004. Up until 2002, if you were an alert slammaster and got your act together you were assured a spot at the NPS. In 2003 that changed—the 56 spots filled up within hours of the opening of registration. The host city added seven more slots to accommodate teams that missed the cut, but several teams still had to be omitted.

Debate about how to handle this expansion has been heated. Some factions of the family want to create official regional tournaments that feed their winners to the Nationals. Some are in favor of stretching the national tournament to a five- or six-day event, thus accommodating over a hundred teams. Some have devised a point system that takes into account the service work and outreach programs local slams have initiated to support their communities. In the past a lottery system has been the method of choice for selecting participants. A certain number of slots have always been reserved for brand new slams so that new blood would always be included. To find out which system is currently in use, visit the PSI website at www.poetryslam.com.

Dig This!

Teams that are not selected to compete at Nationals often attend the Nationals anyway to enjoy the camaraderie, network, and participate in the sideshows.

Competing as an Individual

Poetry Slam, Inc. encourages both individual performers and teams to compete locally and nationally. NPS focuses more on team competition (though it does provide a stage for individual performers), whereas IWPS focuses on individual performers. Read through the following sections for additional details on individual competitions at both NPS and IWPS.

Storm Poets at NPS

At the NPS, 16 individuals not affiliated with any team are allowed to compete as *Storm poets*, as long as some condition beyond the control of the poet prevents the poet from participating in a local tournament to get on a team. Some acceptable reasons are …

◆ The poet lives farther than one hundred miles (or a two-hour drive) from a PSI-certified slam.

◆ A medical condition prohibits the individual from competing at a local tournament.

◆ The poet is not old enough to be admitted to the local venues where the PSI certified slams are held; for example, the poet is 18, but all the slams are held at bars where you need to be 21 years old or older to get in.

Having lost your bid to get on a team by one tenth of a point or missing the local tournament because you were off touring in Istanbul does not qualify you to be a Storm poet.

> **SlamSlang**
>
> The term **Storm poet** refers to individual competitors unaffiliated with any team competing at NPS. It honors deceased slam elder Pat Storm who brought slam to many schools and cities in the southeastern United States. His heart and mind glowed red with the blood passion of words and performance.

Flying Solo at IWPS

Because IWPS focuses on individual poet/performers, it has many more slots open for individuals (50 in 2004). The criteria and rules for the IWPS are still in their embryonic stage, but several rules and deadlines are already in place. Here's how it works:

◆ Registration opens on October 1.

◆ 40 certified PSI slam venues register to send 40 of the participating poets. A venue can register prior to knowing who their competing poets will be.

♦ Each venue must hold a slam-off to determine who will represent it at IWPS. You can't just pick yourself or your lover to go.

Backstage Skinny

For more information about IWPS, go to www.worldpoetry championship.com.

♦ Up to 10 Storm poets will be accepted. Storm poets must be PSI members. Priority is given to poets who have limited access to a certified venue due to distance. Because this is an international event, slammers from all around the world are invited.

♦ Registration acceptance is based on a first come, first serve process.

Attending as a Volunteer

What's that? You're not a poet, not a performer; you just like to listen? Great. Show up, grab a drink, and hang out with some of the greatest people you'll ever meet. Soak in the scene and share the joy and inspiration of performance poetry. Better yet, get involved … volunteer! Many, many people travel to the NPS and IWPS to serve as volunteers, and the slam community needs as much help as it can get. Following is a short list of the many available positions:

♦ Backstage hospitality (bring the stars their water)

♦ Bag-stuffers and ushers and flyer-hander-outters

♦ Equipment-luggers (there's lots to carry in and out)

♦ Go-fors (go for whatever's needed)

♦ Sales clerks (to manage merchandise)

♦ Scorekeepers

♦ Sound system techies (if you've worked a sound system it helps)

♦ Timekeepers

Hosting a National Competition

If you get to the point at which you're crazy enough to want to host the NPS, contact PSI's Executive Council first thing, and ask them for the "If You Want To Host Nationals" guidelines. This is a very detailed description of what you should expect to encounter and what will be expected of you. Using these guidelines, you should form a planning committee, find some money, and go to counseling to check your sanity.

Slam organizers from potential host cities bring proposals to the annual SlamMasters' Council meeting, the organizational meeting held each Spring in Chicago. This meeting brings PSI's Executive Council and the coalition of slam organizers together to debate rules, vote on PSI bylaws, and discuss new projects intended to cultivate a wider interest in slam poetry. Potential host cities make presentations highlighting their visions of Nationals, including venues, side events, publicity plans, and budgets.

The Least You Need to Know

♦ The slam community has two big official annual events: NPS for team competition, and IWPS for individual competition.

♦ NPS has several rites and rituals to give the national competition some structure and help slam poets hone their poetry and performance skills.

♦ The rules that govern the national competitions are not intended to stifle creativity; they're there to create a level playing field for the performers.

♦ Team members must be selected based on the quality of their performances in fair competition rather than on their power, influence, or drop-dead good looks.

♦ If you're interested in hosting a national competition, contact PSI to obtain the "If You Want To Host Nationals" guidelines, and then go have your head examined.

23

More Eventful Events (and How to Get Involved)

In This Chapter

◆ Experiencing the many incarnations of slam

◆ Spreading the word with ACUI College Slam, Slam Summer Retreat, and other educational and outreach programs

◆ Tasting the assorted flavors of regional slams

◆ Tuning in to the cacophony of slam spin-offs and wannabes

Sure, the slam community has an organization and it even has a rulebook (for the NPS), but slam has successfully resisted any attempts to fix it, stamp it, and shrink-wrap it into a neat little package delivered to slam start-ups around the world. Instead, slam spreads by manifesting itself in diverse geographical areas, communities, and cultures to form unique incarnations of itself.

This chapter reveals some of the more interesting incarnations of slam and shows how slam continues to spread through educational and outreach programs and the innovations of artists inside and outside the slam family. Here, you go past the pages of the PSI rulebook and outside the NPS to Slammin' @ Your Library, the Southern Fried Poetry Slam, the Battle of the Bay, and a host of other slam competitions and celebrations. Prepare yourself to feast on a smorgasbord of slam.

PSI Educational and Outreach Programs

The friction between academia and the slam community is dying a quick and thankful death. Both sides realize that they have common goals and can help raise the level of each other's art. Not a school day goes by that some slammer somewhere isn't inspiring a classroom of students to embrace poetry as a vital part of their lives. And not a day goes by that some literature professor doesn't help a performance poet fine-tune her poetic ear.

Year-round, slam clubs and slam events take place in hundreds, maybe even thousands, of schools and libraries across the country. It is now impossible to keep track of them. The following sections give you just a small sampling of the ways that PSI, the slam family, and outside organizations are using performance poetry as an educational tool.

Slam Graduates: ACUI College Slam

The first ACUI/PSI College Unions Poetry Slam Invitational (CUPSI) occurred on April 14 and 15, 2001, at the University of Michigan, Ann Arbor. Seven colleges competed: the University of California-Berkeley, Case Western Reserve University, Eastern Michigan University, Yale University, Louisiana State University, Southern University, and the host school, the University of Michigan. The event is modeled after PSI's National Poetry Slam tournament.

SlamSpeak

In the summer of 2000, Robb Thibault, a program coordinator at the University of Michigan, Ann Arbor, set the dates and booked the slammers for the first U-Club Poetry Slam in the Michigan Union. On September 21, 2000, more than 220 people attended the slam. This caught his supervisor's attention and immediately a bi-weekly show was initiated, drawing an average crowd of more than 200 students, professors, and others. In late October, Robb gained the support of his programming office to organize what he dubbed the College Unions Poetry Slam Invitational (CUPSI). Working with Steve Marsh (Executive Director of PSI) and Tony Ellis (ACUI, Association of College Unions International), Robb developed an agreement with the two organizations to act as co-sponsors of the event. The CUPSI is held during the month of April as a way to honor National Poetry Month.

Here are some of the ideas that formed Robb Thibault's vision of slam as a vital multicultural campus program and convinced him that the events should play in college unions or student center buildings:

- The college poetry slam is the "Varsity Sport of the Soul." If Brown University can have a varsity chess team and offer chess scholarships, why not varsity slam teams and scholarships for that, too! How about the "NCAA Poetry Slam"?

- The slam is a direct and contemporary link to the origins of the college union and its celebration of freedom of public expression. It is the place where people gather and build an open community. The slam breathes life into this literary club.

Backstage Skinny

Wanna get involved? Contact Robb Thibault at thibaurr@oneonnta. edu or (607) 436-3013 or go directly to www.poetryslam.com to register your campus slam with PSI, and check out the ACUI webpage and the poetry slam section at www.acuiweb.org.

- The college slam encourages all students and employees of the college community to participate. Professors from all fields, secretaries, electricians, plumbers, and students should all feel free to experience the gift of slam.

- Many slammers have earned advanced degrees and now teach at colleges. Combining that with the efforts of campus activity staff and college unions, doors have been opened to slam performances, workshops, and classes on the campus, increasing academia's acceptance and appreciation of performance poetry as a credible art form.

Slam Summer Camp

One of the most important components of PSI's mission is education. Its goal is to expose audiences to the excitement and poignancy of performance poetry and encourage people to compose and perform their own works. PSI has done much over the years to advance the performance side of the slam definition; now it's time to reinforce the slam text and pass on the expertise its members have accumulated in all things slam.

As an outgrowth of workshops at national and local events, PSI developed a full-blown writing and performance retreat called "Poetry Slam, Inc. Cross Training Poetry Camp."

The camp consists of three days of workshops, panel discussions, open mikes, feature performances and, of course, poetry slam competitions.

Dig This!

Slam greats including Taylor Mali, Patricia Smith, Gayle Danley, Sara Holbrook, and Regie Gibson teach and perform at the summer training camp. It's a great opportunity to meet and learn from the people directly responsible for the movement's success.

The program is called "cross training" because the focus is threefold—writing, performance, and promotion. You think you have the performance portion of your game down? Come hone your writing skills. Looking to set up a tour, publish your verse, or promote your reading series? Sign up to learn from the slammin' pros. If you are a writer, performer, or educator, the camp offers important information and teaches you slam skills on all levels.

Pumping Poetic Iron at the United States Scholar-Athlete Games

Who says poetry slamming isn't "real" poetry? For over 10 years, the Institute for International Sport has held the United States Scholar-Athlete Games at the University of Rhode Island for precocious youth. Starting in 2003, the committee added slamming to their "scholar-writers" program. Boston Slam elder Michael Brown formed the relationship with USSAG and continues to act as our informal PSI liaison. During the opening and closing ceremonies, a PSI banner hangs in a prominent position as tribute and acknowledgement to the slam family! If you are a smart, poetry-writing kid between the ages of 15 and 19 (or if you know one), check out www. internationalsport.com for more information on the United States Scholar-Athlete Games.

Slammin' @ Your Library

Each year, the American Library Association's Young Adult Library Services Association chooses a different theme for Teen Read Week in October. In 2003 they chose Slammin' @ Your Library in an effort to connect more young people with performance poetry and libraries. To see their rockin' website and its resources (including an explanation of slam adapted from PSI's site), go to http://www.ala.org/ala/yalsa/teenreading/trw/slamminyour.htm.

SlamSpeak

Here's the word from me, Marc (So What!) Smith: Take any or all of the information, exercises, and classroom activities in this book and start a slam workshop in your school or community. Accept the gift and pass it on.

New York SCORES Annual Poetry

If you want to do a good deed and strengthen your community, there's no shortage of people who could use your help. Poetry slam has proven to be an effective social service tool for all sorts of community organizations. One shining example is New York

SCORES, a youth program that combines creative writing and the thrill of soccer to get Washington Heights kids off the streets and into the game. What better way to combine sport and poetry than by holding a slam? This program held its third annual youth slam in 2003. For more information about New York SCORES and programs like it, and to learn how to start a slam like this in your own community, check out www.newyorkscores.org.

Sowing the Seeds of Slam

PSI is involved in schools at all grade levels across the country. Our membership presents workshops, lectures, and performances to hundreds of classes every year in every academic setting—from elementary schools to universities. Slammers have established a presence at major educator conferences such as the National Conference of Teachers of English, the American Library Association, and The Writer's Corps in our ongoing effort to spread the gospel of the spoken word. We're sowing the seeds of slam today, so we can harvest a bumper crop of performance poets tomorrow.

Closer to Home: Regional Slams

The National Poetry Slam is indeed the Grand Poobah of slams in America—at least for now. But if you can't make it to the Nationals for one reason or another, look closer to home. Performance poets are addicts, and after they start slamming (and winning) they want to slam all the time. In order to feed their addiction, many smaller versions of the Nationals, called regionals, have sprouted up across the country. Regional slams are slams that provide opportunities for a specific area of the country to gather its finest poets and compete in what is often regarded as pre-national events.

Backstage Skinny

Regional slams are as diverse as local slams. Some are big, some are small, some are invitational, and some are open to all. Some are one-day events. Some are extended weekend affairs.

New regional slams are being created all the time, and you should look into your slam scene to see who's doing what where. The following sections explore a handful of successful regional slams to give you a sense of what you can expect.

Southern Fried Poetry Slam

Getcher' coveralls on and a bottle of RC Cola—we're goin' to meetin'! The Southern Fried Regional Poetry Slam has reigned for more than a decade as one of the most popular slam events in existence. This slam is the oldest ongoing regional slam in the country, and for a good reason—it's a fabulous event run well by people who care about cultivating slam in their part of the U.S.A., the beautiful South. Allan Wolfe (remember, the author of "the points are not the point") and the folks at *Poetry Alive* gave birth to this southern belle. The following list provides more specifics about the event:

Who? The SFPS is open to both teams and individuals. A registration fee is required. Information about past SFPSs can be found by entering *Southern Fried Poetry Slam* into your favorite search engine and poking around for articles, photos, scoreboards, and testimonials. The organizers of the event list their contact information, making it ridiculously easy to get involved and obtain information. That's southern hospitality for you.

What? Think Moon Pies (Moon Pie was one of the event's official sponsors in 2003): sweet and a whole lotta love. The general consensus is that SFPS is one of the more laid-back and enjoyable poetry events around. Not to say that this slam isn't competitive and heated, but it's summertime and the livin' is easy. The prize money has gone up steadily every year and is now over $1,000 for teams and $500 for indies, but so what!

When? Summertime. Specific dates vary each year.

Where? The Southern Fried Poetry Slam takes place in a different Southern city every year— New Orleans in 2003, Miami in 2004.

Why? Slam poetry, southern accents, fried chicken, and mint juleps. What more could you ask for?

SlamSlang

Poetry Alive is an educational organization founded in Asheville, North Carolina, by Bob Falls. It sends troupes of performance poets to high schools across the country to expose students to the passion of performed poetry. Hook up with them at www.poetryalive.com.

Rust Belt Slam

In 2000, a group of dedicated poets led by Bill Abbott got together in Dayton, Ohio (a city virtually unknown in the slam community at the time) to create the Rust Belt competition. Running for more than five years now, the Rust Belt is drawing more and more respect and attention:

Who? In past years six teams have been allowed into the RBS, and a limited number of indie participants are able to register. For more information, search the web for "Rust Belt Slam," and if you still have questions, contact Scott Woods at sewoods1@yahoo.com.

What?   Similar to the Southern Fried Poetry Slam, the Rust Belt event is a fun, "rejuvenating" experience. Poets from the upper Midwest to as far east as New Jersey gather for this weekend event. Bouts on Friday and Saturday nights usually end in a party atmosphere, and poets crash on couches and futons. The events are incredibly well-attended and completely rust-free.

When?   Late Spring, early Summer.

Where?   The RBS is held in a different city every year. The "Rust Belt," in case you didn't know, is the region comprising Pennsylvania, Ohio, Michigan, Illinois, and Indiana. (The Rust Belt Slam also includes Pennsylvania's neighbor, New Jersey.) You can bet whichever city the organizers choose to hold the slam in will be in one of these six states.

Why?   Aside from helping this important event grow, you'll be meeting a lot of poets you might not meet at Nationals (yet) or at your hometown venues. Besides, "Hang On Sloopy" is the RBS's (and Ohio's) official rock song. Do you need another reason?

Western Regional Slam at Big Sur

California is a big state with a vibrant, ever-expanding slam scene. From L.A. to San Francisco, from Berkley to San Jose, there's a lot of poetic ground to cover in the Golden State. The Western Regional competition focuses on bouts between many of Cali's own teams and the surrounding states, as well—Washington, Oregon, Vancouver, B.C.—but the competition is open to any team in the country.

Since 1998, this event has been popular for teams going to the National Poetry Slam later in that same year, but the Western Regionals allow for "Straw Teams" (teams not participating at the Nationals). This big party of a weekend features a campout on the second night of competition and draws veterans and rookies alike to shoot it out in the Wild West.

Who?   Open to all. Garland Thompson has been the organizer of the WRS for years. E-mail him at garland@westcoastslam.com.

What?   This is the only regional competition that can boast that it's held among the Redwoods. It's an outside event, and poets who have attended recall seeing big butterflies and hearing birds calling overhead. The winners take home a $1,000 prize.

When?   Sometime in July.

Where?   Big Sur, California.

Why? California's slam scene is a force to be reckoned with—you can choose from hundreds of open mikes and dozens of slams across the state. You could learn a lot and, more important, you get to camp on the beaches of Big Sur. Not bad.

Slam Spin-Offs

Although slam's borders encompass a wide variety of official and unofficial slams all around the world, it does not encompass everything related to spoken word poetry or even performance poetry. Other poets and poetry aficionados (many inspired by the slam movement and some not) have created their own poetry festivals and competitions to cater to the unique needs and character of their communities. The following sections describe a small selection of slam-inspired offshoots.

Midwest Poetry Slam League

In an effort to mix things up a bit, slammasters in the Midwest got together to form the Midwest Poetry Slam League. The league consists of seven teams competing in three-team bouts. Each team participates in no less than seven competitions over a six-month period starting in January. Home teams find floor space/couches/beds for the visiting teams to crash on. Teams pay their own traveling expenses.

> The MPSL has the spirit of regular slams, but twists the form here and there for comic and crafty effect, bringing it solidly in line with its roots as a bridge between poets and audiences who may not be hip to or even like poetry. Extra rounds were added and time limits vary within a bout. One piece involving more than one poet onstage at a time (a "team piece") is required. A free-for-all round—in which music, props or costumes may be used—was added, and team sizes were expanded substantially. Each team has a roster of up to 13 poets, any number of which may participate in a poem in a bout, as opposed to the national standard of 4.
>
> —From the MPSL website
> www.blackair.coolfreepages.com/MIDWEST_Front.htm

Here are the official rules:

> **Rounds and Scoring** Bouts will be six rounds judged by three judges selected from the audience using a three-color scoring system. Judges will be asked to show one of three colored cards at the end of each round after hearing all of the poems from that round: red for favorite team that round, white for second favorite, and blue for least favorite—hey, use other colors if you want to.

Time Limits   Time limits for the six rounds vary as follows:

One four-minute round
Two three-minute rounds
Two two-minute rounds
One one-minute round

A whistle will sound to stop the round. No points will be deducted, but the poets do have to stop with the whistle.

Required Rounds   One round in each bout must utilize a team piece (duets, trios, quartets, sextets, septets, octets, and so on).

One round can be a free-for-all—costumes, props, music. All add-ons must be portable (carried to the stage by the performer) and require no advance set-up. This is totally optional.

In the event of ties, a two-minute sudden-death round judged by audience applause will determine the winner.

Three team members must show up for the sudden-death round (in or out of town) or that team has to default while the other two teams go on doing their things.

The Dough   Prize money will come out of the door. It's usually something like ...

First place: $100
Second place: $60
Third place: $40

All teams understand that if there isn't enough money from the door, prize money might be less. The money should ideally pay for travel expenses and be put into a team fund rather than paying off individuals, but this is up to the team.

The MPSL has been a great success thanks to the enthusiasm of the Midwest slam-masters and Scott Woods, the slammaster from Columbus, Ohio, who is its chief coordinator.

The New Word Series

The New Word Series doesn't have the illustrious history of baseball's World Series (yet), but it has definitely come out swinging. Held in Berkeley, California, in October of 2003, this event was sponsored by Youth Speaks and NorCal Spoken Word as part of the Living Word Festival. The organizers of this spoken word extravaganza are interested in seeing spoken-word artists push the envelope of the art form. In 2003, there were multi-media artists, musicians, and dancers who combined their art with spoken word to create a new kind of art. That's not to say there weren't a few "regular" poets at the big slam. 40 individual poets competed for a whopping $1,000 in prize money. Visit www.newwordseries.com for details.

SlamSpeak

Oakland and San Francisco both have adopted a head-to-head bout system using flags instead of scores, with no time penalty. Instead of each poet having an individual time limit or an individual score, teams of four poets win or lose based on the cumulative total of flags earned by all their poets over five rounds, including a one-minute round. The whole team is limited to fourteen minutes for the entire bout, instead of three minutes per poem.

Organizers hope that the flag system will remove the sting of low scores, de-emphasize the competition by removing score creep, and encourage a more committed kind of listening.

—Charles Ellik, Berkley Slammaster

Battle of the Bay

When it comes to poetry slam and spoken word, the Bay Area is hot stuff. In 1999, San Jose and San Francisco tied for first at the Nationals; and in 2003, L.A. took the trophy. These West coast poets are definitely contenders. They've got dozens of slams and hundreds of slammers, as well as a huge public following. The Battle of the Bay pits the five most prominent Bay Area teams (in 2003: Oakland, San Francisco, San Jose, Berkeley, and Sacramento) against one another to duke it out in front of a huge crowd. All the proceeds from the events go to finance the respective teams' trips to the NPS. Check out www.norcalslam.com for more information on the Battle of the Bay and slamming in California.

Dig This!

The Taos Poetry Circus is a competitive predecessor to the slam. The first World Heavyweight Championship Poetry Bout between Terry Jacobus and Gregory Corso was quite a spectacle, and quite controversial. Alan Ginsburg was involved in the fray. Listen to Terry's account of that occasion in Mark Eleveld's *The Spoken Word Revolution* published by Sourcebooks.

Taos Poetry Circus

The Taos Poetry Circus is one of the nation's premiere poetry events which annually features the work of locally, nationally, and internationally known poets in a unique and exciting week-long performance series that includes open readings, panel seminars, individual and group competitions (including poetry slams), and the famous Main Event—the World Heavyweight Championship Poetry Bout. It comes to life each June at a variety of venues throughout Taos, New Mexico.

The Canadian Spoken Word Olympics

In 2004, Canada hosts the Spoken Word Olympics in Ottawa. Forty-eight poets (Canadian and international) compete in this three-day event. This event focuses heavily on the team and indie competitions, but there are a slew of showcases and lots of side events to get everyone involved. With over 80 total performers set to take to the mike, this event is definitely catching some buzz. Go to www.wordolympics. com for more information.

Russell Simmons's Def Poetry Jam

It's glitzy and glamorous and heavy on the hip-hop ... it's Russell Simmons's Def Poetry Jam®. Famed producer and media mogul Russell Simmons set out to tap the grassroots slam and spoken word movement and has succeeded well in commercializing spoken word poetry. Many poets who competed in the early years of the NPS have been able to build their fan base through this popular show. To learn more about this event, check out www.defpoetryjam.com.

> **Dig This!**
>
> Def Poetry Jam® is more of a franchise these days, with a television show, a book, and a Broadway revue.

The Least You Need to Know

- PSI directly and indirectly supports several educational and outreach programs, such as the ACUI College Slam and New York's SCORES program, to encourage people to write and perform poetry.

- Regional slams enable slam teams from several neighboring states to compete and celebrate performance poetry.

- A regional slam typically has a theme that's unique to its geographical location and culture.

- Although slam does not encompass the whole of spoken word and performance poetry, it has inspired countless spin-offs and offshoots that add to the diversity of the movement.

Chapter 24

Slam the World Over: The Global Community

In This Chapter

- ◆ Following slam's migration from the United States to Europe and beyond
- ◆ Identifying the similarities of slam's development in all regions of the world
- ◆ Witnessing slam's explosive growth in Germany (with words from the two guys who made it happen)
- ◆ Exploring slam's spread to Denmark, Switzerland, and France
- ◆ Sailing to Singapore, where East meets West

Everything slam offers is universally appealing—poetry, drama, comedy, competition, camaraderie, spectacle. It brings people together, keeps them entertained, and challenges them to understand and experience life more fully. It knows no borders. It's a cosmopolitan spirit on a world tour, equally at home in Chicago's Green Mill, Germany's Substanz, and Singapore's Zouk. It speaks to men, women, and children, drop-outs and professors, the poor and the wealthy, and people of every race and culture.

To witness slam's universal appeal firsthand, you'd have to travel to a half a dozen countries and visit slams in dozens of cities. That could get expensive. This chapter acts as a cheap substitute, taking you on a nickel tour of various cities around the world where slammasters have popularized slam and driven its growth.

Dig This!

How big is this slam thing? Nobody really knows. What we do know, however, is that the slam movement is constantly growing and spreading. Every day, some slammaster somewhere in the world is hatching a plan for a new show or devising a strategy to move the current show to a larger venue. And nobody expects slam's growth to plateau anytime soon.

Exploring Slam's Growth Pattern

As you explore the growth and development of slams across the country and around the world, you begin to notice that they all follow the same general pattern, starting with a conflict between establishment and performance poets and eventually settling down to become a democratic community of dedicated poets, fans, and organizers. It's as though conflict and resolution define the cycles of each slam's history. Here's a blow-by-blow account of the pattern that most slams follow:

- A slammaster, with or without assistants, begins a slam in a slam-free town or city.

- The slam encounters resistance from establishment poetry circles and is criticized for trying to pass off false poetry as the real (sacred) stuff. It's just too entertaining to be poetry.

- A few scabs from the establishment cross the picket lines, and some of their colleagues follow when they begin to realize that the perceived threat was more menacing than the reality. Some even begin to see slam as having a positive influence. What's not to like?

- Slams attract larger, more diverse audiences than ever thought possible. It seems that everyone is attracted to poetry if it's presented in an entertaining fashion.

- Organizers become zealots who act as missionaries to help spread slam to other cities.

- Poets, audience members, and organizers working together to support slam's growth form a slam community and become more organized.

- As the slam succeeds, conflicts arise between members of the newly formed community, which spawns a need for some kind of democratic organization to settle disputes. This in turn fuels another growth spurt.

- The slam begins to inspire local educators to teach poetry in a new, dynamic way, encouraging students to compose and perform their poems.

- As enthusiasm grows, the slam begins to attract more and more media attention. The establishment becomes more accepting of the slam as part of the community's fabric.

- The slam begins to chip away at the walls separating races and cultures; this inspires tolerance and cooperation. The slam's base broadens.

Whoa! _____

Though the positive aspects of slam far outweigh the negatives, slam does have a downside common in all countries. Slam tends to ignite and fuel egos. Poets and organizers frequently begin to take the competition too seriously. Outside entities and individuals try to capitalize on its success. Of course, heated conflicts arise in all creative endeavors, because no two people share an identical vision, but when people who are adept with language begin to argue, watch out!

Slam in Germany

The early history of slam in Germany is a little foggy. A German television crew in 1988 taped a segment of the slam at the Green Mill for broadcast on a continental arts and travel show. Around the same time, several German print journalists on assignment in America posted stories about the Green Mill slam. Whether this media attention inspired future German slammasters, we don't know, but word reached Germany sometime in the late '80s or early '90s.

As far as we can determine, the first German slam was held in Berlin during the summer of 1993. Others might have preceded it, but there is no known solid evidence of them. Slammasters Patricia B. and Rik Maverik organized this first German slam, and a descendant of the slam continues to this day under the leadership of Wolfgang Hogekamp at a club called the Bastard.

Dig This!

Here's a great example of where some nonperforming slam enthusiast could make a mark uncovering the accurate history of slam's migration to Germany, where it now thrives.

Boris Preckwitz of Hamburg (and later Berlin) came to the United States in 1997 to experience the American slam scene and the NPS held in Connecticut. With assistance from Boston slammaster Michael Brown, Boris brought back to Germany vital information and slam experience that fertilized areas and prepared the soil for the astounding growth to follow.

SlamSlang

Slamily is the name for the German Slam Newsgroup similar to the American slam family listserv. German slams are more regionally influenced. The slamily has its mashes and clashes, but like slams around the world, they work through conflicts to points of compromise and cooperation.

Germany is now filled with many astonishingly talented slam performers and organizers. Like their American counterparts, they all contribute and support their community, their *slamily*. Without their support, the slam movement wouldn't be flowering and re-flowering at its current rapid pace. From my perspective, the two most virile pollinators of the German slam scene, the two men who have devoted their souls, energies, time, and all of their resources (to the point of being broke more often than the slam gods should allow), are Rayl Patzak and Ko Bylanzky, slammaster zealots of Munich.

Slammin' at the Substanz

The first slam in Munich occurred in 1994. It was an unusual blend of traditional reading and literary competition organized by a radio journalist who was influenced by articles about slam, but who had not actually experienced a slam (at least to my knowledge). They had a chair and a table onstage and invited mostly traditional, published authors to read but not perform. It was more of a gimmicky stunt than a serious attempt at carrying the traditional slam spirit and principles forward. The serious attempt was to come a couple years later.

In February, 1996, Rayl Patzak and his crew began slammin' at a music club called the Substanz. Five poets selected from an open-mike list competed in two rounds of competition with a popular band playing a set between rounds and DJs spinning before and after the show. Ko Bylanzky joined the crew midyear and became Rayl's partner and equal in energy, zeal, and devotion. The Substanz slam plays monthly to the largest and most consistent slam audience of all the local German slams—300 people inside and sometimes a couple hundred more lined up outside waiting to get in.

The History of the German International Poetry Slam

The German International Poetry Slam (GIPS) started small but has developed into a spectacular show drawing thousands of fans. Similar to the American NPS, the

German Nationals are held once a year and invite slam poets from Germany, Austria, and Switzerland to come together in friendly competition to determine the best German-speaking performance poetry team of the year. For seven years GIPS has been an adventure in organizing and art made possible by the endless hours of work by large committees of slammasters and volunteers.

SlamSpeak

I asked Ko how many slams he, Rayl, and their crew helped start. Here's his reply:

> It's hard to say who we influenced to start slams. The slam in Munich is by far the biggest in Germany; a lot of people have seen it. Maybe it has fortified their plans to start a slam, who knows. I'll just name a few cities we helped out, showing up with a car full of poets and slam mania: Augsburg, Passau, Stuttgart, Konstanz, Landshut, Erlangen, Kempten (with Michael Brown), Ulm, and St. Gallen where I have hosted shows on several occasions. We are the official slammasters for shows in Regensburg and Landsberg, and help run slams in Freising, Steinebach, and Heidelberg.

> My arms are wide open. I help and encourage everyone to start a slam. But when I see someone exploiting the idea of slam, disrespecting the poets who are making a show for him, and using the slam as a self-display for himself, he can't count on me anymore.

—Ko Bylanzky, Munich slammaster

GIPS has grown to be more than just a big poetry event. It's a grand festival with a party atmosphere. It has a strong print component and offers merchandise collections, festival books, and other memorabilia. Unlike NPS, GIPS separates individual and team competition. Each slam sends a team of four poets along with two individual competitors. Teams perform in blocks of time with all the members performing solo or in ensemble. Teams receive one score for the entire team performance.

Here's the short history of the GIPS as told by Rayl Patzak:

Berlin, October 1997   Four cities compete in the first GIPS held at Berlin's "Ex 'n' Pop" club. The competition runs two evenings and functions as the first annual meeting of the German slam scene. Berlin, Munich, Hamburg, and Duesseldorf battle for the title in front of 200 spectators. Rap poet Bastian Böttcher (Bremen) becomes the first individual champion. Hamburg becomes the first team champ.

Munich, November 1998   500 people witness two nights of slammin' at Munich's Kunstpark Ost Club and become part of a national slam in which 11 teams and 20 individuals compete for the German international title. Marc (So What!) Smith is the honored patron of the festival and opens each evening with a special showcase performance. The Cologne team wins first place, and Michael Lentz (Munich) becomes the indie champion. Five years later, Lentz will win the Ingeborg Bachmann Prize, Germany's most important Literature Award. Paul Devlin's film documentary Slam Nation makes its German film debut as part of the festival.

Weimar, October 1999   600 people witness two nights of slammin' Nationals. 30 individuals and 13 teams participate. Tracy Splinter wins for Hamburg. Tuübingen takes the team title.

Duesseldorf, September/October 2000   Sixteen teams and fifty individual poets compete. Because of the growing number of poets, qualification bouts are held for the first time. The Nationals run four nights. Each finals night has around 600 people. Jan Off wins for Braunschweig. Aachen wins the team competition. First-time delegations from Austria and Switzerland compete.

Hamburg, November 2001   Slam booms in Switzerland and Austria bring tons of Swiss teams and audience members to the Nationals, inspiring a change in the event's title from "German National Poetry Slam" (NPS) to "German International Poetry Slam" (GIPS), a yearly festival for German-speaking slam poets. The indie champ is Sebastian Kraemer (Berlin), and the team champ is Winterthur (Switzerland). Around 900 spectators attend each night's competition.

Bern, Switzerland, September 2002   For the first time the event takes place outside Germany. With only two years exposure to slam-mania, Switzerland mobilizes the largest slam audience to date for the GIPS, attracting news coverage from all major Swiss television networks and print media. Lasse Samström wins the individual title for Bonn; and the team prize, huge circles of Swiss cheese, goes to Wuppertal. The show sells out with over 1,000 people each night. And for the second time Marc (So What!) Smith performs at GIPS.

Darmstadt and Frankfurt, October 2003   Darmstadt and Frankfurt, twin cities connected by subway, hold the Nationals together. Shuttle busses transport poets and audiences between the two cities. One thousand people watch the team finals in Frank-furt. Over 1,200 people attend the indie finals in Darmstadt. Both finals nights are sold out weeks in advance. Twenty-four teams and over one hundred individual poets compete. Sebastian Kraemer (Berlin) is the first two-time indie champ. Passau wins the team title. Stormy parties make the Nationals a 48-hour event that exposes both cities to the slamily and inspires organizers for the years to come.

The future of the GIPS is very strong. Planning for future events is already underway. Stuttgart holds the GIPS in 2004, Leipzig in 2005, and Munich in 2006. The spirit and zeal of the slam movement in Germany mirrors the early years of the slam movement in the United States, and surpasses it in organization, media attention, print support, and documentation.

Poetry Slam in Denmark

Frederik Bjerre A. of Denmark gives this account of the slam community in his country:

> Poetry slam migrated to Denmark from the United States hand in hand with Michael Lee Burgess. In cooperation with Danish poets Janus Kodahl and Adam Drewes, he arranged the first slams in Copenhagen, the capital of Denmark, in 1999. Since then, almost every spring has seen the blossoming of new slams and slam organizers within the Copenhagen community. In the summer of 2002, touring groups of Danish underground poets spread the word of poetry slam all over the country.

> Besides the scene at the Kulkaféen in the heart of Copenhagen, a continual poetry slam has been established in Denmark's second-biggest town, Aarhus. Danish championships were held in September 2003 and performed to an audience of 200. Teams from Odense, Aarhus, and Copenhagen participated. Northern Europe's biggest music event, The Roskilde Festival, features four poetry slams, one per night.

> In general, the Danish poetry slam scene experiences the same childhood diseases as the American scene. Traditional and academic-minded poets picture the poetry slam as facile and devastating for a "serious" occupation with The Poetic. Some also see it as bad influence from the United States, like the Coca Cola of poetry. When it comes to the themes of the slam poetry itself, the Danish slam audience shuns direct political messages, preferring everyday issues, wordplay, and comical angles over serious matters. You can hardly prevent it; poetry slam is to some extent what the audience wants it to be.

Slam in Switzerland

The Swiss slam scene started with two slam tours, organized by *Verlag Der gesunde Menschenversand* and performed throughout Switzerland in 1999/2000. Journalist Matthias Burki and Yves Thomi, "founder" of Verlag Der gesunde Menschenversand, brought to life the tour, which featured joint performances by German and Swiss poets. The German influence on Swiss slammers is extensive, and cultural exchange between the two countries continues. Swiss poets travel and tour in Germany as Germans do in Switzerland. About 20 to 25 slammers perform regularly in Switzerland, supporting a number of ongoing slams.

Matthias Burki reports that:

> As a result of the slam tours, the movement inspired organizers, including Martin Otzenberger (Zürich), to establish regular weekly and monthly slams in their cities. In 2002, for the first time, the German International Poetry Slam was held outside Germany. Organized by the Verlag Der gesunde Menschenversand, the Berne GIPS attracted slammers from Germany, Austria, and Switzerland.

The Swiss slam scene remains a fragile buiding whose existence hinges on the devotion of a few key people. For example, Lukas Hofstetter and Etrit Hasler, members of the St. Galler team, keep interest alive by performing at festivals that reach 200, 400, and sometimes thousands of people.

Slam in Switzerland, as elsewhere, sometimes remains quarantined from the "normal" literary arts institutions. Established Swiss writers approach slam with an innate skepticism inspired by slam's emergence from an apparent subculture imported from the United States via Germany. However, it's astonishing to note that cultural institutions, governmental arts agencies, and private arts donors have supported the Swiss slam scene from its inception. They might be skeptical, but they haven't been stingy.

> **Dig This!**
>
> If you're fluent in Swiss German, track down Matthias's academic account of poetry slam: *Der Dichter und sein Publikum— Poetry Slam zwischen sozialer und theatraler Performance* (Bern, 2003).

> **Dig This!**
>
> In 2003 I had the pleasure of working with the Swiss Consulate based in Chicago. With its help we instituted the first official PSI-sponsored Slam Exchange between Switzerland and North America.

Slam in France

Slam is going mad in France! The fever is fresh and contagious. Rival slam organizers are hustling to see who can bring the most focus to their slam communities. Pilote le Hot of Paris is the maniac zealot of the French slam scene. Let's let him start the story:

> In February 1995, in a happening Parisian bar called le Club-Club in Pigalle district near le Moulin Rouge a girl named Samira whom we called Samourai tripping from New York City organized a performance poetry evening loosely based

on the slam poetry format and rules. (You sign up, no censure, no music, one poem, three-minute limit, and a free drink after you perform, but no jury.) In France, the competition between poets trying to get recognized was already strong enough. With or without a jury, people flocked to see the performances. Newspapers talked about it and the little Club-Club was as full as an egg every Tuesday evening from 22h to 00h.

Pilote le Hot and his associate Ben Vistros were a couple of the underground poets who came every Tuesday to meet the public and other poets. Ben Vistros began his performances by displaying a piece of wood engraved with his name and saying "Hello Ladies and Gentlemen! My name is Ben Vistros." And ending it by clapping for himself and shouting, "Bravo, Ben Vistros!" Pilote le Hot was a street performer hawking his poetry in the subway. At le Club-Club he found an audience to shout and spit his poetry to and a stage where he could be noticed by journalists and recognized by the public as a living "un academist," an authentic street poet. His performances are not about interpretation, they're about energy. Even the people who like his poetry say they would understand better if he didn't shout so much into the microphone.

After a few months, Ben Vistros and Samourai left le Club-Club and turned the slam over to Pilote le Hot. When le Club-Club closed, Pilote le Hot and the poets moved to another bar called les Lucioles in Paris ménilmontant to continue the Tuesday evening event. Around about 1998 the French press and media became very interested in slam poetry as a result of the attention given to Saul Williams and the movie *Slam* at the Cannes Film Festival.

Pilote le Hot and other slam activists of the time (Paul Cash, a specialist of comedic verse stories, and Angel Pastor, an aging Spanish Anarchist poet) created an association called Slam Productions. They established a "slam cultural institution" similar to PSI that gave their movement a website, press communication, a financial budget, and a contact network for venues. They felt they needed to organize their efforts into a unified force to counter "the fantasies that a few French journalists [were] concocting under the influence of a certain major recording company that slam was a form of music poetry and an outgrowth of hip-hop culture."

Very quickly they received the support of cultural institutions and the public in general. They were invited to conduct "Slam Poetry Sessions" at arts centers and schools, and they soon educated the press about the authentic roots of slam in France and the United States.

The French slam family has more than 300 poets performing in small venues or at national theatres. Since 2001, Slam Productions has been in association with PSI and other slam communities in Europe. In 2002, Slam Productions organized a European slam poetry session, which included performance poets from nine countries. In September 2003, they created the French Federation of Slam. Now 20 slam venues hold shows in Paris and surrounding communities. June 2004 ushers in the First Grand National French Slam Poetry Festival involving 15 teams from across the country.

Slam in Singapore

On May 27, 2003, the first officially registered poetry slam venue in an Asian country was launched in Singapore by Word Forward Limited, a nonprofit arts company dedicated to promoting Spoken Word in the region. Chris Mooney-Singh is the program director of the new arts company. He is also an accomplished poet-musician and showman. In April 2003, he received funding from the Singapore National Arts Council and visited the United States; he traveled from Texas to Chicago visiting slams along the way and studying the movement firsthand.

Singapore's 2003 opening season was an unqualified success, exposing over 2,000 people to performance poetry. As a result of the generous coverage by local newspapers, radio, and mainstream magazines (including *Harpers Bazaar*) and *Word Forward*'s extensive advertising campaign distributing color posters at arts venues, flyers at the universities, and abundant e-publicity, the words "poetry slam" have now been heard and read by over 150,000 residents of southeast Asia.

SlamSpeak

Previously, the Singaporean poetry reading scene was very modest with only one monthly English-speaking poetry event, which usually attracted a few specialized poets and their supporters. By contrast, the first Poetry Slam Cabaret pulled a general audience of almost 200 people who also broke with tradition and paid a cover charge of $10, which put to death the myth that Singaporeans won't pay for poetry events.

—Singapore slammaster, Chris Mooney-Singe

Chris has incorporated the idea of "cabaret" art that originated in 1890s Parisian café culture into Singapore slam as a way of exposing the literary arts to a wider audience. On the last Tuesday of the month the poetry slam competition becomes part of a cross-arts event at Zouk, Singapore's premier nightclub. Audiences enjoy live world music, singers, short experimental films, movement ensembles, belly dancing, mime, stand-up comedy, and even unicycle juggling acts, along with theme programs like Dead Poet and Halloween Gothic Slams. Group pieces for seasonal holidays such as the Chinese Moon Cake Festival have been staged, and a pantoum slam was held on Muslim Hari Raya Day to celebrate the origins of the Malay literary form.

Word Forward understands the educational value of the slam and has already taken steps to introduce slam to schools in Singapore. In October 2003 it staged a slam event in one of Singapore's leading secondary institutions. About 500 highly charged students from Singapore Chinese Girls School cheered their peers as they performed on the slam stage. The school elders hailed it as one of the most entertaining arts education programs ever presented, and it is now a part of the National Arts and Education Program funding, enabling both privileged and under-privileged schools to participate in slam competitions and workshops offered by Word Forward.

According to Chris,

> Singapore, long known as a gateway to Asia, is an ideal launching pad for the slam movement to spread further to Asia, and to truly make it an international movement, not just a Western one. Being from a multi-cultural and multi-lingual society where English, Mandarin, Malay, Tamil, and other North Indian languages are all spoken, I'm certain that the slam culture will start to resonate in a variety of languages here in Singapore. Also, the original spoken word traditions, though languishing, are still prevalent in Eastern culture, and thus contemporary oral poetry can feed back and nourish the local literary bloodstream.

> We have been officially invited to stage and host the first Hong Kong poetry slam event during the Hong Kong Literary Festival in March 2004 and are now working steadily to develop an Asian Slam League that will plug directly into the international slam community activities. In doing so, we want to make it viable for international poets to visit Asia and for our Asian talents to also travel the world in the name of poetry.

As you can see from Chris's own words, slam is now alive and well in the Eastern hemisphere.

Other Slam Importers

It would take several volumes to do justice to the efforts of hundreds of international organizers and performance poets promoting and creating slams around the globe. Slam movements are blossoming in Italy, the UK, Poland, Israel, Sweden, and Norway. They're springing up in high schools and universities. Some communities that have no idea where slam came from are slamming. Even young poets who weren't born when the movement began are slamming. Egad! Am I that old?!

I guess there's a slam being born somewhere on the planet every week, or at least every other week, and they all began with me and a handful of ill-bred poets at a far-out jazz club in Chicago called the Get Me High Jazz Club. (So What!)

The Least You Need to Know

♦ Through movies, media outlets, word of mouth, and the effort of slam organizers and poets, slam has traveled around the world to become an international movement.

♦ The evolution of local slams follows a fairly predictable pattern that eventually establishes each slam as a democratic community.

♦ Rayl Patzak and Ko Bylanzky, slammaster zealots of Munich, are largely responsible for slam's popularity in Germany and surrounding countries.

♦ Slam is alive and thriving in France, where it has given the traditional street poets a more formal stage on which to spout their verse.

♦ Singapore's opening slam extravaganza exposed more than 2,000 people to the beauty and power of slam poetry and has introduced this Western art form to the East.

Reference Material

Concerning Slam, Writing, and Performance

To learn more about the slam and about writing and performing poetry, check out the books and other reference material in this section. Although some of the books are out of print, you can still track down copies at libraries and used-book stores.

Bonney, Jo. ed. *Extreme Exposure: An Anthology of Solo Texts from the Twentieth Century*. New York: Theatre Communications Group, 2000.

Devlin, Paul director. *SlamNation*. Slammin' Entertainment, 1998.

Eleveld, Mark. ed. *The Spoken Word Revolution*. Naperville, Illinois: Sourcebooks, 2002.

Foley, John Miles. *How to Read an Oral Poem*. Urbana, Illinois: University of Illinois Press.

Glazner, Gary Mex, ed. *Poetry Slam: The Competitive Art of Performance Poetry*. San Francisco: Manic D Press, 2000.

———. *Ears On Fire: Snapshot Essays In a World of Poets*. Albuquerque, New Mexico: La Alamedia Press, 2002.

Jerome, Judson. *The Poet's Handbook*. Cincinnati, Ohio: Writer's Digest Books, 1980.

Jesse, Anita. *Let the Part Play You: A Practical Approach to the Actor's Creative Process.* Burbank, California: Wolf Creek Press, 1994.

Lee, Charotte I. and Frank Galati. *Oral Interpretation.* Boston: Houghton Mifflin Company, 1977.

Lessac, Arthur. *The Use and Training of the Human Voice: A Practical Approach to Speech and Voice Dynamics.* Mountain View, California: Mayfield Publishing Company, 1973.

Moustaki, Nikki. *The Complete Idiot's Guide to Writing Poetry.* Indianapolis: Alpha Books, 2001.

Oliver, Mary. *Rules for the Dance: A Handbook for Writing and Reading Metrical Verse.* New York: Houghton Mifflin Company, 1998.

Stanton, Victoria, and Vincent Tinguely. *Impure: Reinventing the Word.* Montreal, Quebec, Canada: Conundrum Press, 2001.

Turco, Lewis. *The New Book of Forms: A Handbook of Poetics.* Hanover, New Hampshire: University Press of New England, 1986.

Other Sources for Slam Poetry

Still hungry for slam? Then track down the nearest slam in your area and plan to experience a fine night of entertainment. You can probably even pick up a chapbook or two. Still not enough? Then check out the anthologies, books, and videos cited in the following sections.

Algarin, Miguel and Bob Holman ed. *ALOUD: Voices from the Nuyorican Poets Café.* New York: Henry Holt and Company, LLC 1994.

Blum, Joshua and Bob Holman, co-creators; Mark Pellington, director; Joshua Blum and Bob Holman and Anne Mullen, producers, *The United States of Poetry.* PBS 1996.

Blum, Joshua and Bob Holman and Mark Pellington ed. *The United States of Poetry.* New York: H. N. Abrams, 1996.

Bylanzky, Ko, and Rayl Patsak. *Poetry Slam: Was Die Mikrofone Halten.* Munich, Germany: Posie fur dasneue Jahrtausend. Ariel-Verlag, 2000.

Kaufman, Alan. ed. *The Outlaw Bible of American Poetry.* New York: Thunder's Mouth Press, 1999.

By Slammers in This Book

Acey, Taalam. *Eyes Free*. USA: Word Supremacy Press, 2003.

Avery, CR. *Goner 4 Honor*. East-Side Eternity Records.

Barnidge, Mary Shen. *Piano Player at the Dionysia*. Chicago: Thompson Hill Publishing, 1984.

Buscani, Lisa. *Jangle*. Chicago: Tia Chucha Press, 1992.

Fitzpatrick, Tony. *Hard Angels*. Philadelphia, PA: Janet Fleisher Gallery, 1988.

Gibson, Regie. *Storms Beneath the Skin*. Joilet: EM Press, 2001.

Gillette, Ron. *Hardware & Variety, a Collection of Poems*. Oak Park, Illinois: Erie Street Press, 1984.

Holman, Bob. *A Collect Call of the Wild*. New York: Holt, 1995.

———. *In with the Out Crowd*. New York: MouthAlmighty/Mercury, 1998.

Mali, Taylor. *What Learning Leaves*. Hanover Press: Newtown CT, 2002.

McCarthy, Jack. *Say Goodnight, Grace Notes: New and Corrected Poems*. Joilet: EM Press, 2003.

Salach, Cin. *Looking for a Soft Place to Land*. Chicago: Tia Chucha Press, 1996.

Salinger, Michael. *Neon*. Huron, Ohio: Bottom Dog Press – Firelands College, 2002.

Smith, Marc Kelly. *Crowdpleaser*. Chicago: Collage Press, 1996.

Smith, Patricia. *Life According to Motown*. Chicago: Tia Chucha Press, 1991.

———. *Big Towns, Big Talk*. Chicago: Tia Chucha Press, 1992.

———. *Close to Death*. Chicago: Tia Chucha Press, 1993.

———. *Africans in America*. New York: Harcourt Brace, 1998.

Thibault, Robb. *A Crack in the Rock*. Ann Arbor: Wordsmith Press, 2004.

Publishers of Slam Poetry

EM Press
24041 S. Navajo Drive
Channahon, Il 60410
Tel: 1-815-723-3184
Website: www.em-press.com

Manic D Press
Box 410804
San Francisco, CA 94141
E-mail: info@manicdpress.com
Website: www.manicdpress.com

Tia Chucha Press
Chicago Distribution Center
11030 South Langley Avenue
Chicago, IL 60628
Tel: 1-800-621-2736 or 312-568-1550
Fax: 1-800-621-8476 or 312-660-2235
Website: www.guildcomplex.com/tiachucha/

Wordsmith Press
11462 East Lane
Whitmore Lake, MI 48189
Tel: 810-231-8129
Website: www.wordsmith.com

Slammin' Websites

No doubt this book contains everything you need to know to become a world-class slam poet and host, but you can find even more information about slam and details about the National and International Poetry Slams on the information superhighway—the Internet. The following list highlights the best slam websites and provides a brief description of each site.

Albuquerque Poetry Slam

www.abqpoetryslam.org

To check out the slam scene in Albuquerque and Santa Fe, New Mexico, visit the home site of the Albuquerque Poetry Slam. Here you'll find schedules of events, information about team Albuquerque, a list of venues (with a description of each venue), slam statistics, photos, and contact information. Some video footage is also included.

Ann Arbor Poetry Slam

www.a2slam.com

This website is the home of the Ann Arbor Poetry Slam, "the longest continuously running poetry series in Ann Arbor, and the Second organized Slam in the known universe!" Along with the standard schedule of events you'll find at most sites, this site includes information about slam and the people who helped it evolve, about the poets who continue to raise the bar, and the resulting poetry, which is what this site is really all about.

Austin Poetry Slam

www.austinslam.com

Austin, Texas, has a rich and growing slam tradition, and you can visit this site to learn all about it. Check out Austin's venue, its poets, its teams, and a timeline of its history. Here, you can also listen to some audio clips of selected poetry performances, order books and CDs online, chat with other slam fans and poets, or gather some basic information about the rules and regulations that govern the Austin Poetry Slam.

Bristol Poetry Slam

www.bristol2008.com/171.asp

The Bristol Poetry Slam has been doing its thing since 1994 and hosted the first ever UK Slam Championship in 1998. Their belief is that slams help spread the love of poetry and introduce the art form to new audiences. Big Bristol slams are held at the historic Old Vic Theatre every year and are known for their workshop and outreach programs.

ChicagoPoetry.com

www.chicagopoetry.com

As this site proves, Chicago's poetry scene is alive and well, and you can check it out online. Here, you'll find the latest news regarding various poetry events in the Chicago area, along with a poet of the month, anthology of poems, a gossip department, a photo gallery, and much more. This site features links to plenty of poet websites, online poetry magazines, and other poetry resources, as well.

Classic Cleveland Poetry Slam

my.en.com/68/CB/mgsal/classic/

Visit the electronic home of the Classic Cleveland Poetry Slam, which started in 1998, to learn more about the group, its poets, and its teams. This site includes a schedule of shows, links to classes and workshops that can help you develop your own poetic voice, and some good background information about slam and about the evolution of the Classic Cleveland Poetry Slam. If you live in the Cleveland area, check out the list of local venues that feature open-mike performances.

EM Press

www.em-press.com

EM Press is a fairly new publishing house, but one that already has an impressive list of published poets. Regie Gibson, Mike Kadela, and Jack McCarthy all have books published by EM, and more authors are on the way. This two-man operation seeks to publish writers that are pushing the literary envelope and challenging the bounds of ordinary poetry, fiction, and essay.

Festival della Parola

www.romapoesia.org

Poetry slam is big and getting bigger in Italy. Every year this "Festival of Words" is held by Roma Poesia in, you guessed it, Rome. Guest poets and speakers from all corners of the globe come to be a part of this lively event, and audience members will see everything from deejayed poetry sets to round-table discussions with poets and writers. Ciao, bella! By the way, the site is in Italian, of course.

Backstage Skinny

If you cannot read the Italian language, go to Google (www.google.com), type the website address (www.romapoesia.org) in the search box, and press **Enter**. This brings up a link to the site along with a **Translate this page** link. Click **Translate this page** to get a rough translation of the site. It's not the best, but it'll help you get around. This works for most foreign language sites.

GotPoetry.com

www.gotpoetry.com

This website acts as a sort of commune for spoken word poets. As a visitor to the site, you can read reports about past or upcoming events, listen to audio clips posted by registered members, watch video clips of performances, read poems, check out the poet pages, or just hang out and do nothing. If you register, you can log in and then post announcements or submit articles, reviews, photos, and anything else you want to appear on the site. Assuming your submission passes the review process, it appears on the site in a matter of days. It's a great place to market your work on the web!

Incomplete History of Slam

www.e-poets.net/library/slam/

If you enjoyed the brief history of slam provided in Chapter 1 of this book and are interested in learning a little more, check out "An Incomplete History of Slam" by Kurt Heintz (principal photography by Jeannine Deubel). Kurt spent quite a bit of time interviewing the key players in the slam movement and assembling this intriguing history.

Northern California

www.norcalslam.com

Northern California and the Bay Area are home to some of the most thriving and innovative slam and spoken word communities. Check out this website for information about the New Word Series, Living Word Festival, Youth Speaks, and the Battle of the Bay.

Nuyorican Poets Cafe

www.nuyorican.org

The Nuyorican Poets Cafe bills itself as the "Town Hall in New York's Theatre District." It has served as a stage for theatre, spoken word poetry, hip-hop, live music, film, and other art forms for more than 30 years. This site provides a complete schedule of upcoming events along with a bookstore and information about the various performers scheduled for the weekly poetry slams. The Nuyorican Poetry Slam team has a long tradition of being a top contender in the National contest.

Poetry International Rotterdam

www.poetry.nl or www.poetry.nl/general_new/home.php (English version)

Poetry International has been hosting international poetry festivals for more than 30 years. This website is divided into two sections: Activities and Archives. The Activities section features dates, times, and locations of upcoming events. The Archives section provides a well-stocked library of poems, photos, letters, audio and video clips, translations, and other stuff from past events. The digital archive is still under construction, but it's well worth a visit.

Poetry Slam Erlangen, Nürnberg, Fürth

www.e-poetry.de

Are you interested in the evolution of slam in Europe, particularly in Germany? Then check out this slam poetry site. Here, you can find general information about slam, the rules and regulations that govern this particular slam competition, and contact information. If you're organizing a slam and need some ideas for designing your flyers, this site has an archive that exhibits some very cool designs. Oh, by the way, the site is in German, of course.

PoetrySlam.com

www.poetryslam.com

If you visit only one slam site, this is the site you want to hit—the official site of Poetry Slam, Inc. Here you'll find a Slam FAQs (frequently asked questions), information about the current year's National Poetry Slam, a list of poetry slam venues around the country, free audio and video clips of top performers, discussion forums, chat rooms, and much more. You can even shop online for slam CDs, books, t-shirts, and other paraphernalia.

Rubber Chicken Poetry Slam

www.rubberchickenpoetry.com

For a humor break, complete with coffee, check out The Rubber Chicken Poetry Slam's website. If you're planning your own show and need some ideas for what to award the winning performers, you can find an interesting idea here—cash for first place, a gift certificate for second, and for third … a rubber chicken! Of course, the site offers more than that, including a description of the venue, a schedule of shows, a list of rules, and brief biographies of featured poets.

SlamNation

www.slamnation.com

SlamNation is a documentary, by Paul Devlin, about the 1996 National Poetry Slam, held in Portland, Oregon, during which 27 teams competed. This site provides information about the documentary and other videos, including *Slammin'* and *2000 National Poetry Slam Finals*. Here, you can download movie trailers, read reviews, check out still photos from the videos, view video clips of some brilliant poetry performances, and order the videos online. This site also includes a bulletin board where you can connect with other fans and performance poets.

slampapi.com

www.slampapi.com

This is the official digital hangout of yours truly, Marc Smith. Here you can check out information about upcoming events at the Green Mill, read a selection of my poems, learn about slam shows and other performance poetry events around the country, submit an article for publication on the site, or contact me personally. This site provides a good feel for the family nature of the poetry slam and its commitment to allowing people to voice their opinions, even if those opinions are highly critical of slam.

Stone Circle

www.expage.com/page/stonecircle

"Located on a narrow strip of land between Lake Michigan and Torch Lake, the Stone Circle is a triple ring of 88 large boulders capturing the atmosphere of ancient cultures that gathered in family and community groups to entertain and exchange stories of everyday life and lore." Founder and poet Terry Wooten began his Stone Circle tradition several years ago and has created a strong following for the event. Although the Stone Circle doesn't hold slams, in this outdoor venue your poetry will compete with Mother Nature, the toughest competition I can think of.

Swiss Slams

Slam has taken off in Switzerland and has spread not only across the country but also across the Internet. If you're planning a trip to Switzerland in the near future or simply want to learn more about slam's manifestation in this beautiful country, check out the following websites organized by the names of the cities that the various slams call home:

> **Bern and Lucern:** www.menschenversand.ch
>
> **Frauenfeld:** www.offkultur.ch (organized by Mathias Frei)
>
> **St. Gallen:** www.gapevents.ch (organized by Lukas Hofstetter and Etrit Hasler)
>
> **Winterthur:** www.kraftfeld.ch (organized by Manuel Lehmann)

SWOT: Spoken Word Of Tulsa

www.swot.org

As I was writing this book, SWOT's website was under construction, but it holds forth the promise of eventually containing background information about SWOT, a schedule of shows, and an online store where you can purchase chapbooks and other stuff.

Urbana Poetry Series

www.bowerypoetry.com

One of the hottest slams in the country is held at The Bowery Poetry Club in New York City every Thursday. Founded in 1998 under the keen eye of Bob Holman, this show found its home at CBGB's. Several years ago, the group renovated the building at 308 Bowery and turned it into a state-of-the-art poetry venue. There's a bar with great coffee and cheap beer, a back room for intimate readings, and lots of art up on the walls. The open mike is vibrant, the slam is hot, and you can be sure that the featured poet at Urbana will be among the best poets in the country.

Volume Project Poetry

www.nocommentweb.com

Ann Arbor Michigan has developed an after-school creative writing project for teen-agers, and this is its dynamic website. Here, you can learn more about the program, read a schedule of events, check out featured poets, scan the postings in the forum, chat live with other young poets, buy merchandise online to support the group, and much more. If you're a K–12 teacher looking for another way to encourage students to read, write, and perform poetry, check out this site for ideas.

World of Poetry

www.worldofpoetry.org

Billing itself as "the first digital poetry anthology," The World of Poetry is a project that's designed to pick up where *The United States of Poetry* left off. The project pairs up filmmakers with poets from across the country and around the world to record poets composing, performing, and teaching their art. The ultimate goal is to create a digital video library of hundreds of the best, most original contemporary poets. Selected clips, along with narration, will be compiled into a one-hour PBS special called *World of Poetry*. Here you can learn more about the project and access the official website for *The United States of Poetry*.

World Poetry Bout Association

www.poetrycircus.org

The World Poetry Bout Association (WPBA) has been promoting performance poetry for more than 20 years through its annual Taos Poetry Circus, "the nation's premier poetry festival." Here you can find news about the most recent competition, upcoming bouts, and top poet/performers who have competed at this event. You can also purchase merchandise online.

SlamSlang

As you read through this book and begin your own exploration of slam, you might feel as though you've been captured by Australian Aborigines who talk primarily by making curious clicking sounds or by double-talkers who are giving your language strange new meanings. How do you interpret this strange, sub-cultural language? How do you make sense of all the cryptic terms of the slam underground? Where can you get translations for the most common insider talk?

Well, you've come to the right place. Although this limited glossary can't possibly cover all the gobbledygook and reinvention you'll encounter in the world of slam, it does define enough basic terms, rules, and concepts to get you through your first slam.

accompaniment   Music or other media that's designed to add another facet to a poet's performance. The National Poetry Slam does not allow accompaniment.

accoutrement   Anything on or around the stage that's accessible to all performers and is not a prop. Accoutrements include the microphone, chairs, tables, and other furniture, and the aisles between the tables.

alternate   A replacement member of a slam team who can fill in for another team member only in the event of an emergency.

articulation   The time value a performer assigns to each syllable during the performance of a poem.

audience   One of the most essential components of a slam poetry event, the people who witness the event and provide feedback to the performance poets.

backbeat   Sounds produced by the human voice to provide a basic 4-beat rhythmic pattern behind verses laid down by rappers.

block   A theater term for the process of mapping out the various actors' positions and movements onstage during a scene.

blog   A publicly accessible personal journal on the web that enables an individual to voice his or her opinions and insights or keep an online record of experiences.

bout   A competition between two or more slam poets or between two or more slam teams. A bout consists of one or more rounds (see *round*). The winner of a bout typically advances to the next bout to compete with other teams.

calibration poet   The first slam poet of the event who is offered up to the audience and judges as a sacrificial lamb before the actual competition begins. Calibration poets help the judges warm up and give the slam poets some idea of what to expect from the judges. The calibration poet typically does not take part in the competition.

call and response   A theatrical device that encourages the audience to become part of the performance by saying a particular word or phrase on the performer's queue. For example, the performer might instruct the audience to holler "Top!" whenever she says "… up to the …." When the poet says, "I'm goin' up to the …" the audience yells "Top!"

call time   A theater term that designates the hour and minute when you're expected to arrive at the theater for the night's performance.

chapbook   A small, typically self-published book of poems, ballads, or stories.

competition   A theatrical device essential to slam poetry that's designed to rev up the audience and raise the level of the art—both the poetry and the performance.

concrete poem   Verse that's arranged on the page in a way that forms a visual image that supports or embellishes its message.

disclaimer   A statement, typically recited before a slam event, in which the emcee introduces the event, briefly describes the type of competition the audience is about to witness, explains some of the rules and regulations, and undercuts the seriousness of what's about to take place.

duo   Two poets performing a piece together as a team slam.

elders—Seasoned slammasters who often are called upon to settle disputes and provide guidance at slam family meetings.

emcee   The master of ceremonies at a slam show. The emcee is expected to be impartial (or at least act impartial), keep the show moving at a steady clip, make sure the judges behave themselves (hold up their scores at the same time), and keep the audience engaged between performances.

Executive Council   The steering committee of Poetry Slam, Inc. devoted to promoting slam, managing slam family business, and preserving the slam tradition. Members of the Executive Council are elected by the SlamMasters' Council of Poetry Slam, Inc.

exquisite corpse   A poem constructed by a number of poets (often everyone in the room) adding a line to a preceding line having seen only the preceding line.

feet   The basic units of measure in a line of poetry that are determined by different combinations of stressed and unstressed syllables.

format   The structure that directs the proceedings at a poetry slam. In most cases, poetry slams consist of several bouts in which individuals and/or teams compete for a chance to advance to the next round until one person or team ultimately beats out the others.

free-stylers   Improv rappers who duel poetically onstage or in circled groups on street corners over vocally or instrumentally produced rhythms called *backbeats*. Free-styling has extended into the slam world and even into more traditional poetry realms.

gag rule   Teammates of the individual performing poet must not coach the audience to respond in a particular way to the performance. In other words, if you're performing a particular piece, your teammates can't cheer or call out words or phrases in the hopes that the audience will follow their lead.

Grant Back   A PSI Program that allows a slam organization without nonprofit status to use the PSI nonprofit status to obtain funding and grants that would not otherwise be available to them.

group piece   *See* team piece.

host   (1) Another term for emcee (*see* emcee). (2) The person who meets, greets, and seats the patrons as they enter the venue.

host city   The city selected by the slammasters and contracted by PSI for the staging of the IWPS and/or the NPS.

Individual World Poetry Slam (IWPS)   The annual slam competition for individual competitors started in February 2004.

influence rule   Performers may not attempt, directly or indirectly, to win the audience's favor before the competition begins. The performers may strike up casual conversations with friends or audience members before the competition begins, but they may not hand out free t-shirts, do stand-up comedy outside the front door, or do anything else to give themselves an edge over their competition.

judge   An impartial (not necessarily well-qualified) member of the audience who is chosen by one of the slam organizers to score the poems and the performances of those poems (usually on a scale of 0 to 10).

judging   The process of watching, listening to, and rating the performances of the various poets and/or teams during a poetry slam.

liner notes   The printed texts inside a CD case. They list the track selections and running times, and give biographical information about the performers.

listserv   An automated mailing list on the Internet. Poetry listservs contain the names and e-mail addresses of people who want to receive up-to-date news, announcements, and information about poetry and poetry events. When you send an announcement to a listserv, the listserv automatically broadcasts it, via e-mail, to everyone on the list.

maximum time   *See* time limit.

mixing   The process of combining and layering audio clips to produce a final recording.

National Poetry Slam   The annual official slam event organized by Poetry Slam, Inc. The National Poetry Slam attracts more than 60 slam teams from all across North America.

no-repeat rule   A poem can only be performed once during the preliminary or semi-final rounds and once in the finals.

NPS   *See* National Poetry Slam.

NPS code of honor   A statement of proper behavior that slammers agree to adhere to during the National Poetry Slam. The code of honor basically states that you should respect others (and their rights), be a good sport, follow the rules, work for the greater glory of poetry, and not act like a jerk.

open mike   A portion of a typical slam event that provides an opportunity for anyone in the audience to perform a poem.

pantoum   A Malayan form of accentual-syllabic verse that consists of an indefinite number of quatrain stanzas with the specific restriction that lines two and four of each stanza be repeated in lines one and three of the following stanza.

performance   The dramatic recitation and acting out of a poem. Slam poets use voice, gesture, eye contact, and other dramatic tools to engage the audience and communicate their poems as effectively as possible.

Poetry Alive   An educational organization founded in Asheville, North Carolina, by Bob Falls. It sends troupes of performance poets to high schools across the country to expose students to the passion of performed poetry.

poetry slam   The actual performance poetry event that usually culminates in figurative battle between slam poets.

Poetry Slam Rule Book   The stone tablet that contains the laws and bylaws that poets and teams must follow when competing in the National Poetry Slam.

Poetry Slam, Inc.   The official organization that tries to provide some semblance of order to the general chaos that slam embraces.

points   A number, typically between 0 and 10, applied by judges to a particular poetry performance in an attempt to assign some objective value to the poem and the performance of it.

Pong Jam   A musical/poetic jam session in which poets read or recite their poems to musical improvisation.

praise poets   South African poets, also known as Imbongi, who have influenced their local politics for time immemorial by creating and maintaining the reputation of tribal chiefs. To this day praise poets, through oral poetry, declaim the political climate and social injustices around them.

press pack   A collection of documents, photos, audio clips, video clips, and anything else that represents your work designed to be sent to club owners, organizers, slammasters, and others to convince them to book you for a performance. Press packs are commonly sent to newspaper reporters or magazine writers to provide them with the information they need to compose an article.

primary author   A poet who contributed significantly enough to the composition of a group piece to be considered an equal owner of that piece.

prop   Any object (other than an accoutrement) that a performer uses during a performance for dramatic effect. This includes necklaces, earrings, pocket change, walking sticks, beer bottles, you name it.

proscenium   The area of a modern stage between the curtain and the orchestra pit—the main area where the actors act, the dancers dance, and the slammers slam.

protest A formal complaint filed by one team against another team pointing out a suspected rule infraction during a bout at the National Poetry Slam. Protests are submitted to the Protest Committee, which reviews the complaint and issues its verdict.

quartet Four poets (the maximum number allowed at a National Poetry Slam) performing a team slam.

rhymation The tedious and sometimes nonsensical practice of rhyming a long, long series of –tion and -sion words. It also applies to common word endings of –ize, -ism, -ary, -etic, -ation, and a dozen others.

rotation The order in which poets on a particular team perform—who goes first, second, third, and fourth. The team captain, with input from the team members, usually decides on the rotation. There are many "rotation" strategies for maximizing a team's points.

round A set of performances in which one or more members of each competing team gets a chance to perform. The standard time limit for each team in a round is three minutes, but some competitions include one-minute rounds, four-minute rounds, and even fifteen-minute rounds.

round robin A term we started using in Chicago to describe a series of very short poems performed one right after another by several poets planted at different locations in the audience.

sampling The incorporation of another poet's words into a poem. Slam poets commonly play off another poet's words, and this is acceptable. However, stealing the words outright is disdainful, not to mention criminal.

scan To determine the kind and number of feet in each poetic line. See also *feet*.

score card The device held up by the judges to display their scores to the audience, poets, and emcee. Score cards at a slam range from reusable wooden paddles that have numbered cards on rings that judges flip over to form a score to cocktail napkins marked up with ink pens.

score creep The tendency of scores to rise as a competition progresses.

score tracking The process by which judges record the scores of the various performances. In most cases, the judges write the scores on a paper form given to them before the competition starts. The tracking sheet is used to verify the official scores.

scoring The ridiculous practice of assigning a numerical value to a poetry performance. Traditional slams call for scores between 0 and 10 or down to negative infinity.

scout   To scan the audience for impartial, not necessarily well-qualified, judges. Organizers and emcees scout for judges who are not affiliated with any of the performers in the competition.

show   All the components and events that comprise a particular poetry slam. The organizer of a slam is its visionary.

slam   (n) (1) A term that describes a type of performance poetry show that usually culminates in a poetic competition. (2) A performance poetry competition.

slam   (v) To perform a poem in front of a live audience and quite often in a competitive arena.

slam family   The entire membership of Poetry Slam, Inc. (PSI) and anyone else who wants to hang around slams and slammers.

slam poetry   A term that describes any spoken word poetry composed and rehearsed for presentation in front of a live audience and quite often in a competitive arena.

slammaster   A person who organizes a local slam community and tries to keep the slam going. On the national level, the slammaster contacts Poetry Slam, Inc. to enter the slam's team in the National Poetry Slam.

SlamMasters' Council   This strongest and most important body in the PSI structure is comprised of slammasters who run the various certified slams around the country. The SlamMasters' Council meets twice a year to set rules, resolve conflicts, and define the future course of slam.

SlamMasters' Council meetings   Biannual gatherings of slammasters from around the country to discuss issues relating to the rules of slam, its current condition, and its future evolution.

So What!   Marc Smith's handle, which reminds all involved, including Marc Smith himself, that slam is a level playing field on which everyone is equally important.

Spirit of Slam Award   An honor bestowed upon a performer or slammaster at the Nationals who has done something exceptional to promote the spirit of slam poetry.

spoken-word poetry   Verse that's composed primarily to be recited or performed rather than read in silence, even though it might be excellent in print, as well.

Storm poet   A performance poet not affiliated with any team who competes individually at a National Poetry Slam. Storm poets are named after well-known Asheville slammer, Pat Storm, who has passed on from the material world.

team   A group of slam poets who compete at a slam event against other teams. At the National Poetry Slam, each team has four members plus an alternate. *See also* alternate.

team piece   A poem performed by two, three, or all four members of a slam team.

three-minute rule   A limitation at the National Poetry Slam and most local slams that prevents a performance from running past the amount of time that most of the audience can tolerate. Poets are allowed to run over by 10 seconds, but beyond that, a half point is deducted for every 10 seconds the performance runs over.

time limit   A restriction on the amount of time a poet's performance can last. *See also* three-minute rule.

venue   A place where a performance takes place; for example, a specific tavern, club, or concerthall.

virgin virgin   A person who has never performed his or her poetry onstage in front of a live audience.

youth slam   A performance poetry competition for young performance poets, typically between the ages of 13 and 19 years old.

Index

Number

"23 Chromosomes" (Murphy, Marcel), 269

A

abstract language, 48-51
 oblique literary references, 51
 versus concrete language, 50-51
accommodations, tour preparations, 134
across-the-room duets, 222
actions, storytelling, 58
ACUI (Association of College Unions International), 304
"Adman" (Gillette, Ron), 39
advertisements, paid, 234. See also marketing strategies, promotions, publicizing shows
affecting the audience, 77
agents (booking), roles, 137-138
alcohol use, coping with stage fright, 68

alliterations (sonic devices), 53
ambiance, venue selection criteria, 173-175
ambition, 226
antanagoge (rhetorical device), 56
anthologies, creating, 223
antiphrasis (rhetorical device), 56
apologizers (personality types), 220
aporia (rhetorical device), 56
apostrophes (rhetorical device), 56
applause-o-meter judging method, 255
approach techniques, 150
art forms, 76
articulation, 81
artistic elements, 249-253
 ceremonies and rituals, 249-250
  emcee spiels, 250
  group initiations, 250
  speak alongs, 250
 hecklers, 251
 suspense, 251-252

Ashe, Krystal, 268
assistants, delegation of duties, 210-211
Association of College Unions International. See ACUI
assonances (sonic devices), 53
audiences
 affecting, 77
 engagement of, 76
 entertainment, 77
 estimating size, 237
 etiquette rules, 113
 fueling frenzy, 221-222
 participation, 23
 respect, 151
 serving, 22
audio recordings
 do-it-yourself methods, 120
 editing and productions, 122
 preparations, 121
 professional recordings, 121
auditions, emcees, 212-213

B

backbeats, 48
balancing performance sets, 94
band slams, 267
bandstands, 187
Barnidge, Mary Shen ("Dionysia" poem), 31
Barrett, Mike, 12
Battle of the Bay, 312
beatniks, spoken word poetry traditions, 6
"Beethoven" (Koyczan, Shane), 49
benefit shows, 263
Berry, Wendell, 8
"Bicycle Jockey" (Smith, Marc), 58
Big John Scam, 12
biographies (press packages), 119
black box stages, 186-187
blamers (personality types), 220
blocks, 148
blogs, 124
body movement exercises, 83-85
  dance movements, 85
  imagine the stone, 84
  motions to avoid, 84
  paint exercise, 85
  walk the talk, 84
bombasts (rhetorical device), 56
book fair shows, 262
booking agents, roles, 137-138
booking shows, 133
bookstores, locating performance opportunities, 109
bouts, NPS rituals, 289
brand names (marketing tool), 231
breaths, performance techniques, 82
Brown, Anna, 12
budgets, marketing, 238
bulletin boards, locating venues, 178
bulls-eyes, storytelling, 59
Burgess, Michael Lee, 321
Burki, Matthias, 322
Buscani, Lisa, 49
Bylanzky, Ko, 318

C

cacophony, 53
call and response, 222
call times, 139
camaraderie, 25-26
Canadian Spoken Word Olympics, 313
CDs, compilation, 224
celebrity judges, 254
celebrity slams, 264
ceremonies. See rituals
certifications
  evidence, 284
  renewal, 284
certifying slam versus registering slam, 283-284
chapbooks, 71
characters, storytelling, 57
cheerleading (etiquette rules), 145-146
Chi Town Classic, 268
Chicago Poetry Ensemble, 11-12
chick slams, 168
children, youth slams, 266
Chmara, Joel, 69
cleared spaces as stages, 188
clichés to avoid, 99
clientele, venue selection criteria, 174-175
closers, structuring performance sets, 97
closing deals
  determining roles, 182
  money issues, 181-182
clothes. See dress suggestions
club managers, roles, 136
club owners, roles, 136
Club-Club (France), 322
cohesion, structuring performance sets, 94
College Unions Poetry Slam Invitational (CUPSI). See CUPSI
colleges
  ACUI (Association of College Unions International), 304
  CUPSI (College Unions Poetry Slam Invitational), 304
comedic elements, structuring performance sets, 95
comfort of venues, 174
committees
  judges, 255
  organizing shows, 208

community needs, vision-focusing process, 167-168
competitions. *See also* performances, shows
as a theatrical device
contestant sign-ups, 253
judging methods, 255
selection of judges, 253
camaraderie and compromise, 25-26
CUPSI (College Unions Poetry Slam Invitational), 304
famous disclaimers
Holman, Bob, 35
NPS (National Poetry Slam), 37
Smith, Marc, 36-37
first slam competitions, 31-32
formats
Cover Slam, 39
Pong Jam Slam, 40
Prop Slam, 40
Relay Slam, 39-40
Theme Slam, 38
Unseen Slam, 37-38
goals, 20
history of slam poetry, 5-6, 9-10, 16
IWPS (Individual World Poetry Slam), 287-300
history, 288
rituals, 288-292
rules and regulations, 292-297

local slam laws, 41-42
NPS (National Poetry Slam)
first competition, 14-16
history, 288
individuals, 299
qualifying criteria, 42
rituals, 288-292
rules and regulations, 292-297
second and third competitions, 16
team competitions, 297-298
volunteers, 300
purpose, 30-31
regional slams
Rust Belt competition, 308-309
Southern Fried Regional Poetry Slam, 307
Western Regional competition, 309-310
relearning the art of listening, 21
rules and regulations, 32-35
no props rule, 33
performing your own work, 33
scoring rules, 34-35
time limits, 33
show itineraries, 248
World Poetry Bout Association, 5
compilation CDs, 224

Complete Idiot's Guide to Writing Poetry, The, 48
compositions, poetic devices, 47-56
abstract language, 48-50
concrete language, 48-49
rhetorical devices, 55-56
rhymes, 54-55
rhythmic patterns, 51
sonic devices, 53
compromises, 25-26
concert halls, role of staff members, 138
concrete language, 48-49
concrete poems, 61-62
Confessions of a Virgin Slammaster, 158
conflicts
history of slam poetry, 9
storytelling, 58
consonances (sonic devices), 53
contacts
booking agents, 137-138
club owners and managers, 136
concert hall staff, 138
slammasters, 136
contestants, signing up for slams, 253
Cooper, Dave, 12
cops (slam), 220
corporate convention shows, 262
costumes, 200
counterpoints, 94
Cover Slams, 39, 290

crew members
committees, 208
delegation of duties
assistants, 210-211
marketing, 209
scouting and booking,
210
emcees
auditioning, 212-213
personalities, 213-214
qualifications, 211
relief emcees, 213
in-house ensembles, 216
offstage support
doorperson, 214
judges, 215
merchandise sellers,
215
scorekeepers and
timers, 215
sound and light, 214
crisis storytelling, 59
critiques, rehearsals, 73
Cross Rhymes, 54
Cross Training Poetry
Camp, 305
CUPSI (College Unions
Poetry Slam Invitational),
304
customer service offerings
(venues), 176

D

dance movements (body
movement exercises), 85
dance slams, 168

deadlines, marketing, 239
delegation of duties
assistants, 210-211
marketing, 209
scouting and booking
talent, 210
democracy, 26
Denmark slam, 321
"Dionysia" poem (Barnidge,
Mary Shen), 31
Direct Approach eye
contact, 86
disclaimers (famous slam
disclaimers)
Holman, Bob, 35
NPS (National Poetry
Slam), 37
Smith, Marc, 36-37
discrimination, breaking
down racial and socio-
economic barriers, 23
do-it-yourself venues, 111
Dodge Poetry Festival, 123
donation levels, PSI mem-
berships, 278-279
doorperson, 214
drama slams, 168
dress suggestions, 151-152,
200
Drewes, Adam, 321
drug use, coping with stage
fright, 68
duties, delegation of
assistants, 210-211
marketing, 209
scouting and booking
talent, 210

E

e-mail, mailing lists, 234
e-store website, 286
ecphonesis (rhetorical
device), 56-57
Eddy Two Rivers, 25
Edge, The, 96-97
editing audio recordings, 122
educational programs,
304-307
ACUI (Association of
College Unions
International), 304
New York SCORES, 306
Slammin' @ Your Library,
306
summer camps, 305
United States Scholar-
Athlete Games, 306
elders, 282
"Elephant Song" (Solis,
Danny), 183
Ellik, Charles, 254, 269
emcees
auditioning, 212-213
personality styles, 213-214
qualifications, 211
relief emcees, 213
encoding process (memorization), 100
ending shows, 244-245
engagement of audiences,
performance goals, 76
entertainment
performance goals, 77
performance techniques
articulation, 81

body movements, 83-85

breaths and pauses, 82

eye contact, 85-86

moods, 87-88

personas, 87-88

tempo variations, 80

volume variations, 78-80

epiphonemas (rhetorical device), 57

erotica slam, 290

etiquette rules, 114

audiences, 113

poets and performers, 111-113

professional performers, 144-147

cheerleading, 145-146

foul language, 147

negativity, 146

scowling during performances, 145

vocal commotion, 145

euphony, 53

Executive Council, 284-285, 291

exercises

coping with stage fright

relaxation exercises, 66

tension release exercises, 67-68

memorization, 102

relaxation exercises, 149-150

expenses

marketing budgets, 238

press packages, 124

slammasters, 165

exquisite corpses, 250

eye contact techniques, 85-86

Direct Approach, 86

Imaginary Friend Routine, 86

Speechmaker's Shift technique, 86

Wall Focus, 86

F

famous slam disclaimers

Holman, Bob, 35

NPS (National Poetry Slam), 37

Smith, Marc, 36-37

Fat Tuesday celebrations, 268

fears, coping with stage fright

accumulation of stage time, 70-71

alcohol and drug use, 68

being prepared, 65

determining the cause, 64-65

Jobbers, 65

practice, 66

relaxation exercises, 66

Reluctant Martyrs, 65

shifting focus, 66

Shy Guys, 65

tension release exercises, 67-68

Total Avoiders, 65

tricks of the trade, 68

virgin virgin slammers, 69

visualizing success, 66

feet (poetic), 83

festival shows, 262

first slam competition, 31-32

flaccid phrasing, 50-51

flyers (marketing tool), 232

focus, coping with stage fright, 66

follow-ups, marketing strategies, 240

formats

Cover Slam, 39

Pong Jam Slam, 40

Prop Slam, 40

Relay Slam, 39-40

Theme Slam, 38

Unseen Slam, 37-38

forms, poetic, 99

foul language, etiquette rules, 147

four-channel mixers (sound systems), 197

free press, generating, 233

Free-styler poets, 48

French slam, 322, 324

Friday night performances, 179

fundraising, PSI (Poetry Slam, Inc.), 285

funny poems as openers, 92

G

German International Poetry Slam. *See* GIPS

German slam, 317

GIPS (German International Poetry Slam), 318, 321

Substanz, 318

Get Me High Jazz Club, 11
Gillette, Ron, 12, 39
GIPS (German International Poetry Slam), 318, 321
Glazer, Gary, 15-16
globalization, 326
  Denmark, 321
  France, 322-324
  Germany, 317
    GIPS (German International Poetry Slam), 318, 321
    Substanz, 318
  growth and development patterns, 315-316
  history of slam poetry, 16
  Singapore, 324-325
  Switzerland, 321
goals
  competitions, 20
  performances
    affecting the audience, 77
    engagement of audiences, 76
    entertainment, 77
    virgin virgin slammers, 69
GrantBack Program, 283
Graphic EQ settings (sound systems), 197
Great Halls, 188-189
Green Mill Cocktail Lounge, Uptown Poetry Slam, 12
greetings
  guests, 218
  show itineraries, 246

group initiations, 250
growth and development patterns, 315-316
guests
  greeting, 218
  introductions, 219
  performers, 247

H

haikus
  Haiku Death Match, 270
  head-to-head haikus, 290
hall stages, 188-189
head-to-head haikus, 290
hecklers, 251
hidden alliterations (sonic devices), 53
hip-hop slam, 6-7, 290
hippies, spoken word poetry traditions, 6
history of slam poetry
  Chicago Poetry Ensemble, 11-12
  competitions, 9-10
  conflicts and synergies, 9
  defining characteristics, 8-9
  first slam competition, 31-32
  Get Me High Jazz Club, 7-8, 11
  international slam, 16
  IWPS (Individual World Poetry Slam), 288
  literary movement, 17-18

NPS (National Poetry Slam), 288
  first competition, 14-16
  second and third competitions, 16
performances, 9
preserving your show's history, 222-223
"slam elders," 13
spoken word poetry traditions, 4-7
  beatniks and hippies, 6
  competitions, 5-6
  Hip-Hop traditions, 6-7
  New Criticisms interpretations, 6-7
  Uptown Poetry Slam, 12
  venues, 13
holiday slams, 267
Holman, Bob, slam disclaimers, 35
homespun lighting systems, 199
house party slams, 183
Howard, Jean, 12
humor, structuring performance sets, 95

I

ideas. *See* topics
Imaginary Friend Routine technique (eye contact), 86
imagine the stone (body movement exercise), 84

Imbongi (South African praise poets), 48
improv slams, 168
in-house ensembles, 216
incorporation, PSI (Poetry Slam, Inc.), 276
individual competitions
    IWPS (Individual World Poetry Slam), 287-297
        history, 288
        rituals, 288-292
        rules and regulations, 292-297
    NPS (National Poetry Slam), 299
Individual World Poetry Slam. *See* IWPS
institutions
    contact tactics, 261
    locating, 260-261
Interlaced Rhymes, 54
Internal Rhymes, 54
international slam, 16
Internet
    as a marketing tool, 235
    creating a website
        benefits, 124
        promotions, 126
        structuring websites, 125
    listserv mailing lists, 135
interrogators (personality types), 220
introducing guests, 219
inventorying readiness (slammasters), 158-163
    self-centered individuals, 159-160

show-maker abilities, 162
support networks, 160
time and energy obligations, 161-162
visions, 160
itineraries (show itineraries)
    competitions, 248
    examples, 245, 248-249
    greetings, 246
    nightclub acts, 245
    open-mike sessions, 246
    plot points, 246-249
    special acts and guest performers, 247
    start and end times, 244
    theater productions, 245
    visions, 244
IWPS (Individual World Poetry Slam), 287-297
    history, 288
    rituals, 288-292
    rules and regulations, 292-297

J

Jobbers, 65
judges
    celebrity, 254
    committees, 255
    NPS rules, 296-297
    roles, 215
    selection processes, 253
    styles of judging
        applause-o-meter, 255
        pass the bucket, 255
        rose battles, 255

K

Kodahl, Janus, 321
Koyczan, Shane, 49

L

language
    abstract, 48-50
    concrete, 48-49
    foul (etiquette rules), 147
late-night theaters, locating performance opportunities, 110
layering rehearsals, 71-72
le Hot, Pilote, 323
lighting systems
    do-it-yourself, 199
    lights-up and lights-down concept, 198-199
    offstage support, 214
    top-shelf, 199
Linked Rhymes, 54
listening, relearning the art of, 21
listserv mailing lists, 135, 280
"Little Green Peas" (Ellik, Charles), 269
local slam laws, 41-42
location issues
    speakers, 197
    storytelling, 58
    tour routes, 132
    venue selection process, 176-177
logos (marketing tool), 231

M

MacDougal, Al, 31
mailing lists
  listserv, 135
  marketing tools, 234
maitre d', slammaster's roles,
  219
managers (club), roles, 136
marketing strategies. *See also*
  advertisements, promo-
  tions, publicizing shows
  angles and selling points,
    230-231
  creating a website
    benefits, 124
    promotions, 126
    structuring, 125
  deadlines, 239
  delegation of duties, 209
  development of, 118
  follow-ups, 240
  press packages, 118-124
    audio recordings,
      120-122
    biographies, 119
    expenses, 124
    photographs, 119
    resumés, 119
    reviews, 119
    sample poems, 120
    video recordings,
      123-124
  press releases, 126-129
    radio and television
      stations, 129

sending, 127
working your angle,
  128
writing, 127
publicizing shows, 230
target markets
  calculating marketing
    budgets, 238
  estimating audience
    size, 237
the push, 239
tools
  brand names and
    logos, 231
  flyers and postcards,
    232
  generating free press,
    233
  mailing lists, 234
  paid advertisements,
    234
  posters, 233
  radio, 236
  telephone solicitation,
    235
  television, 236
  websites, 235
tours, 135
word-of-mouth, 237
media
  generating free press, 233
  press releases, 126-129
    radio and television
      stations, 129
    sending, 127
    working your angle,
      128
    writing, 127

memberships, PSI (Poetry
  Slam, Inc.)
  donation levels, 278-279
  qualifications, 277-279
memorizing poems
  benefits, 100
  encoding process, 100
  exercises, 102
  "memorization curve,"
    101-102
  recall process, 101
merchandise
  options
    anthologies, 223
    compilation CDs, 224
    partnerships, 226
    preserving your show's
      history, 222-223
    t-shirts and souvenirs,
      225-226
  role of seller, 215
  selling, 152
microphones, unidirectional
  microphones, 196
Midwest Poetry Slam
  League, 310-311
misconceptions, poem
  topics, 61-62
"Mitch" (Salinger, Michael),
  24
mixers, four-channel, 197
mixing, 121
Monday night perform-
  ances, 179
money issues
  closing deals, 181-182
  marketing budgets, 238
  slammasters, 165

monitors (sound systems), 198

monthly shows, 108

moods, performance techniques, 87-88

Mooney-Singh, Chris, 324

"Motor Red, Motor White, Motor Blue" (West, Phil), 52

motorcycle slams, 263

Murphy, Marcel ("23 Chromosomes"), 269

music
  band slams, 267
  music slams, 168
  Pong Jams, 202
  spectacles, 202
  spinning, 256
  structuring performance sets, 96
  venue selection criteria, 175

N

Nanak, Guru, 17

narratives, storytelling components, 57-59

Near Rhymes, 54

negativity (etiquette rules), 146

nervousness, performance tips, 150

networking, locating venues, 179

New Criticism, 6-7

New Word Series, 311

New York SCORES, 306

nightclubs
  locating performance opportunities, 109
  show itineraries, 245

no props rule, 33

noncorporate structures, PSI (Poetry Slam, Inc.)
  slam family, 281-282
  SlamMasters' Council, 282

NPS (National Poetry Slam), 26
  first competition
    Gary Glazer's recollections of, 15-16
    Marc Smith's accounts of, 14
  history, 288
  individual competitions, 299
  qualifying criteria, 42
  rituals, 288-292
    bouts, 289
    meetings, 290
    opening days, 289
    preshow Tuesday, 288-289
    sideshows, 290
  rules and regulations, 292-297
    judges, 296-297
    scoring, 296
    team pieces, 295
    three-minute rule, 294-295
  second and third competitions, 16

slam disclaimers, 37

team competitions, 297-298
  availability of slots, 298
  selection process, 298

volunteers, 300

Nuyorican Anthology, 224

Nystrom, Karen, 12

O

oblique literary references, 51

obstacles
  jealousy, 164-165
  money issues, 165
  pettiness and social hostilities, 166
  unforeseen changes, 165

Off-Rhymes, 54

offstage support
  doorperson, 214
  judges, 215
  merchandise sellers, 215
  scorekeepers and timers, 215
  sound and light, 214

onomatopoeias (sonic devices), 53

openers
  funny poems, 92
  NPS rituals, 289
  participation poems, 93
  self-effacing patter, 92
  series of short poems, 93

open-mike nights
  locating performance opportunities, 106-108
  show itineraries, 246

organizations, PSI (Poetry Slam, Inc.)
 certifications, 283-284
 communication lines, 280
 Executive Council, 284-285
 GrantBack Program, 283
 incorporation, 276
 listserv connections, 280
 memberships, 277-279
 noncorporate structures, 281-282
 registering slam, 283-284
 staff members, 285-286
 subcommittees, 286
 volunteers, 279-280
organizing shows
 assessing talents and resources, 163-164
 committees, 208
 delegation of duties
  assistants, 210-211
  marketing, 209
  scouting and booking talent, 210
 emcees
  auditioning, 212-213
  personality styles, 213-214
  qualifications, 211
  relief, 213
 in-house ensembles, 216
 inventorying readiness, 158-163
  self-centered individuals, 159-160

show-maker abilities, 162
 support networks, 160
 time and energy obligations, 161-162
 visions, 160
obstacles, 164-166
 money issues, 165
 pettiness and social hostilities, 166
 unforeseen changes, 165
offstage support
 doorperson, 214
 judges, 215
 merchandise sellers, 215
 scorekeepers and timers, 215
 sound and light, 214
self-made slams, 208
vision-focusing process
 community needs, 167-168
 personal needs, 167
 spin-offs, 168
outdoor stages, 190
outreach programs, 304-307
 ACUI (Association of College Unions International), 304
 New York SCORES, 306
 Slammin' @ Your Library, 306
 summer camps, 305
 United States Scholar-Athlete Games, 306

P

P-Jay, Rayl Da, "Word Up," 203
pace
 shows, 256
 structuring performance sets, 94
page proofs, 224
paid advertisements, 234
paint exercise (body movement), 85
pantoums, 41
participation
 audiences, 23
 poems, 93
partnerships, merchandising options, 226
pass-the-bucket judging, 255
patter
 self-effacing patter, 92
 structuring performance sets, 97
Patzak, Rayl, 318
pauses, performance techniques, 82
payment arrangements
 performances, 140-142
 closing deals, 181-182
performances. *See also* competitions, shows
 as an art form, 76
 audience considerations
  affecting the audience, 77
  engagement of, 76
  entertainment, 77

participation, 23
respect, 151
serving the audience, 22
audio recordings
do-it-yourself methods, 120
editing and productions, 122
preparations, 121
professional recordings, 121
booking shows, 133
concert halls, 138
coping with stage fright
accumulation of stage time, 70-71
alcohol and drug use, 68
being prepared, 65
determining the cause, 64-65
Jobbers, 65
practice, 66
relaxation exercises, 66
Reluctant Martyrs, 65
shifting focus, 66
Shy Guys, 65
tension release exercises, 67-68
Total Avoiders, 65
tricks of the trade, 68
virgin virgin slammers, 69
visualizing success, 66
dress suggestions, 151-152

entering the zone, 102-103
etiquette rules, 114
audiences, 113
poets and performers, 111-113
professional performers, 144-147
famous slam disclaimers
Holman, Bob, 35
NPS (National Poetry Slam), 37
Smith, Marc, 36-37
first slam competition, 31-32
formats
Cover Slam, 39
Pong Jam Slam, 40
Prop Slam, 40
Relay Slam, 39-40
Theme Slam, 38
Unseen Slam, 37-38
fueling audience frenzy, 221-222
goals, 20
affecting the audience, 77
engagement of audiences, 76
entertainment, 77
lighting systems
do-it-yourself systems, 199
lights-up and lights-down concept, 198-199
top-shelf lighting, 199

local slam laws, 41-42
locating performance opportunities
bookstores, 109
do-it-yourself venues, 111
late-night theaters, 110
nightclubs, 109
open-mike nights, 106-108
performance venues, 110
schools, 110
slams, 110-111
weekly and monthly shows, 108
marketing strategies
creating a website, 124-126
development of, 118
press packages, 118-124
press releases, 126-129
memorization
benefits, 100
encoding process, 100
exercises, 102
"memorization curve," 101-102
recall process, 101
NPS (National Poetry Slam). *See* NPS
organizing shows
by committees, 208
delegation of duties, 209-211
emcees, 211-214

in-house ensembles, 216

offstage support, 214-215

self-made slams, 208

payment arrangements, 140-142

poetic devices, 47-59
  abstract language, 48-50
  concrete language, 48-49
  rhetorical devices, 55-57
  rhymes, 54-55
  rhythmic patterns, 51-52
  sonic devices, 53
  storytelling, 57-59

preparations, 148-150

purpose of competitions, 30-31

rehearsals. *See* rehearsals

relearning the art of listening, 21

rules and regulations
  no props rule, 33
  performing your own work, 33
  scoring rules, 34-35
  time limits, 33

selecting a night to perform, 179-180

selling merchandise, 152

sound systems
  four-channel mixers, 197
  Graphic EQ settings, 197

location of speakers, 197

monitors, 198

unidirectional microphones, 196

spectacles
  costumes, 200
  music, 202
  props, 205
  slide shows, 202, 204

stages. *See* stages

starting shows on time, 221

structuring sets
  balance, 94
  clichés to avoid, 99
  closers, 97
  cohesion, 94
  comedic elements, 95
  content and style, 98-99
  musical accompaniment, 96
  openers, 92-93
  pace, 94
  patter, 97
  sound effects, 96
  spectacle and visual accessories, 96
  suspense and surprise elements, 95
  The Edge, 96-97
  unity, 94
  variety, 95, 97

techniques
  articulation, 81
  body movements, 83-85

breaths and pauses, 82
  eye contact, 85-86
  moods, 87-88
  personas, 87-88
  tempo variations, 80
  volume variations, 78-80

tips
  approach techniques, 150
  nervousness, 150
  taking the mike, 151

topics, 59-62
  concrete poems, 61-62
  misconceptions, 61-62
  persona poems, 60
  political poems, 60
  pop poems, 60

tours. *See* tours

venues, 108

video recordings
  DVD transfers, 124
  professional recordings, 123

performers. *See also* poets
  dealing with different personality types, 219-220

professional performers
  dress suggestions, 151-152
  etiquette rules, 144-147
  performance tips, 150-151
  preparations, 148-150
  respecting audiences, 151
  selling merchandise, 152

"slam elders," 13
virgin virgins, 13
persona poems, 60
personalities, 219
  apologizers, 220
  blamers, 220
  emcees, 213-214
  interrogators, 220
  slam cops, 220
  superslammers, 220
personas, performance
  techniques, 87-88
photographs (press
  packages), 119
pitching show ideas, 270
plot points, 246-249
poems
  exquisite corpses, 250
  funny poems, 92
  including sample poems
    in press packages, 120
  memorization
    benefits, 100
    encoding process, 100
    exercises, 102
    "memorization curve,"
      101-102
    recall process, 101
  participation poems, 93
  poetic devices, 47-59
    abstract language,
      48-50
    concrete language,
      48-49
    rhetorical devices,
      55-57
    rhymes, 54-55

rhythmic patterns,
  51-52
sonic devices, 53
storytelling, 57-59
poetic forms, 99
rengas, 5
scanning, 83
short poems, 93
structuring performance
  sets
  balance, 94
  clichés to avoid, 99
  closers, 97
  cohesion, 94
  comedic elements, 95
  content and style,
    98-99
  musical accompani-
    ment, 96
  openers, 92-93
  pace, 94
  patter, 97
  sound effects, 96
  spectacle and visual
    accessories, 96
  suspense and surprise
    elements, 95
  The Edge, 96-97
  unity, 94
  variety, 95, 97
topics, 59-62
  concrete poems, 61-62
  misconceptions, 61-62
  persona poems, 60
  political poems, 60
  pop poems, 60
Poet Gallery, 285

poetic devices, 47-59
  abstract language, 48-50
  concrete language, 48-49
  rhetorical devices, 55-57
  rhymes, 54-55
  rhythmic patterns, 51-52
  sonic devices, 53
  storytelling, 57-59
poetic feet, 83
Poetry Alive, 308
Poetry Slam, Inc. *See* PSI
poets. *See also* performers
  ambitions, 226
  etiquette rules, 111-113
  free-stylers, 48
  praise poets, 48
  serving the audience, 22
  "slam elders," 13
  Storm poets, 299
  virgin virgins, 13, 69
point of views, storytelling,
  58-59
political poems
  rhetorical devices, 55-57
  topic ideas, 60
Pong Jams, 40, 202
pop poems, 60
postcards (marketing tool),
  232
posters (marketing tool),
  233
practice, coping with stage
  fright, 66
praise poets, 48
preparations
  audio recordings, 121
  coping with stage fright,
    65

professional performers
    planning sets, 148
    rehearsals, 149
    relaxation exercises,
        149-150
rehearsals
    layering, 71-72
    mirrors, 72-73
    recruiting critiques, 73
    schedules, 71
    tape-recorded replays,
        73
tours
    accommodations, 134
    booking shows, 133
    marketing strategies,
        135
    routes, 132
    transportation, 134
preshow Tuesday (National
Poetry Slam), 288-289
press packages (marketing
strategies), 118-124
    audio recordings
        do-it-yourself
            methods, 120
        editing and produc-
            tions, 122
        preparations, 121
        professional record-
            ings, 121
    biographies, 119
    expenses, 124
    photographs, 119
    resumés, 119
    sample poems, 120
    video recordings
        DVD transfers, 124
        professional record-
            ings, 123

press releases, 126-129
    generating free press, 233
    radio and television sta-
        tions, 129
    sending, 127
    working your angle, 128
    writing, 127
primary authors, 296
productions, audio record-
    ings, 122
professional performers
    dress suggestions,
        151-152
    etiquette rules, 144-147
        cheerleading, 145-146
        foul language, 147
        negativity, 146
        scowling during
            performances, 145
        vocal commotion, 145
    performance tips
        approach techniques,
            150
        nervousness, 150
        taking the mike, 151
    preparations
        planning sets, 148
        rehearsals, 149
        relaxation exercises,
            149-150
    respecting audiences, 151
    selling merchandise, 152
professional recordings
    audio, 121
    video, 123
programs, educational and
    outreach, 304-307

ACUI (Association of
    College Unions
    International), 304
New York SCORES, 306
Slammin' @ Your Library,
    306
summer camps, 305
United States Scholar-
    Athlete Games, 306
promotions. *See also* adver-
    tisements, marketing
    strategies, publicizing
    shows
    angles and selling points,
        230-231
    follow-ups, 240
    marketing deadlines, 239
    marketing tools
        brand names and
            logos, 231
        flyers and postcards,
            232
        generating free press,
            233
        mailing lists, 234
        paid advertisements,
            234
        posters, 233
        radio, 236
        telephone solicitation,
            235
        television, 236
        websites, 235
    publicizing shows, 230
    target markets
        calculating marketing
            budgets, 238
        estimating audience
            size, 237

the push, 239
websites, 126
word-of-mouth, 237
props
no props rule, 33
Prop Slam, 40
spectacles, 205
proscenium stages, 186, 189
PSI (Poetry Slam, Inc.), 20, 27
certifications, 283-284
evidence, 284
renewals, 284
communication lines, 280
educational and outreach programs, 304-307
ACUI (Association of College Unions International), 304
New York SCORES, 306
Slammin' @ Your Library, 306
summer camps, 305
United States Scholar-Athlete Games, 306
Executive Council, 284-285
GrantBack Program, 283
incorporation, 276
listserv connections, 280
memberships
donation levels, 278-279
qualifications, 277-279
noncorporate structures
slam family, 281-282
SlamMasters' Council, 282

registering slam
benefits, 283-284
renewals, 284
staff members, 285-286
subcommittees, 286
volunteers, 279-280
publicizing shows. *See also* advertisements, marketing strategies, promotions
angles and selling points, 230-231
description of shows, 230
follow-ups, 240
marketing deadlines, 239
marketing tools
brand names and logos, 231
flyers and postcards, 232
generating free press, 233
mailing lists, 234
paid advertisements, 234
posters, 233
radio, 236
telephone solicitation, 235
television, 236
websites, 235
target markets
calculating marketing budgets, 238
estimating audience size, 237
the push, 239
word-of-mouth, 237

publicizing shows, 239
push, the (marketing plans), 239

Q-R

qualifications
National Poetry Slam competitions, 42
PSI memberships, 277-279

racial barriers, 23
radio
as a marketing tool, 236
press releases, 129
rags (low-cost magazine), 178
rainbow coalition, 23
recall process (memorization), 101
recordings
audio recordings
do-it-yourself methods, 120
editing and productions, 122
preparations, 121
professional recordings, 121
mixing, 121
video recordings
DVD transfer, 124
professional, 123
regional slams
Rust Belt competition, 308-309

Southern Fried Regional Poetry Slam, 307
Western Regional competition, 309-310
registering slam
  benefits, 283
  renewals, 284
  versus certifying slam, 283-284
rehearsals
  coping with stage fright, 66
  layering, 71-72
  mirrors, 72-73
  professional performers, 149
  recruiting critiques, 73
  schedules, 71
  tape-recorded replays, 73
relaxation exercises
  coping with stage fright, 66
  professional performers, 149-150
Relay Slam, 39-40
relief emcees, 213
Reluctant Martyrs, 65
renewals
  certifications, 284
  registrations, 284
renga, 5
rental stages, 191
repetition of parallel constructions, 52
replaying rehearsals, 73
resources
  locating venues, 177-179
    bulletin boards, 178
    networking, 179

newspapers and yellow pages, 178
  slammasters, 163-164
respecting audiences, 151
resumés (press packages), 119
reviews (press packages), 119
rhetorical devices, 55-57
  antanagoges, 56
  antiphrasis, 56
  aporias, 56
  apostrophes, 56
  bombasts, 56
  ecphonesis, 56-57
  epiphonemas, 57
rhymes
  Cross Rhymes, 54
  Interlaced Rhymes, 54
  Internal Rhymes, 54
  Linked Rhymes, 54
  rhymation, 55
  Slant Rhyme, 54
  Wrenched Rhymes, 55
rhythmic patterns
  exercises, 53
  repetition of parallel constructions, 52
  syntax, 51
rituals
  NPS (National Poetry Slam), 288-292
    bouts, 289
    meetings, 290
    opening days, 289
    preshow Tuesday, 288-289
    sideshows, 290

shows, 249-250
  emcee spiels, 250
  group initiations, 250
  speak-alongs, 250
roles
  booking agents, 137-138
  closing deals, 182
  club owners and managers, 136
  concert hall staff, 138
  contacts, 136
  slammasters, 136
    greeting guests, 218
    introducing guests, 219
    maitre d', 219
rose battles (judging method), 255
round robins, 174
routes, tours, 132
rules and regulations
  etiquette rules, 114
    audiences, 113
    poets and performers, 111-113
    professional performers, 144-147
  local slam laws, 41-42
  NPS (National Poetry Slam), 292, 294
    judges, 296-297
    scoring, 296
    team pieces, 295
    three-minute rule, 294-295
  slam competitions, 32-35
    no props rule, 33
    performing your own work, 33
    scoring rules, 34-35
    time limits, 33

Russell Simmons's Def Poetry Jam, 313
Rust Belt competition, 308-309

S

salaries, closing deals, 181-182
sales, merchandise, 152
Sandburg, Carl, 8
Saturday night performances, 180
scanning poems, 83
schedules, rehearsal, 71
schools, locating performance opportunities, 110
scorekeepers, 215
scoring rules
    NPS, 296
    slam competitions, 34-35
scouting talented performers, 210
scowling during performances (etiquette rules), 145
"Sea Drift" (Whitman, Walt), 52
selecting process
    judges, 253
    team competitions, 298
    venues
        ambiance, 173-175
        closing the deal, 181-182
        customer service offerings, 176

final selection stage, 180-181
house party slams, 183
location issues, 176-177
resources, 177-179
selecting a night to perform, 179-180
set-up of performance areas, 175-176
size concerns, 172-173
written list of criteria, 177
self-effacing patter, 92
self-made slams, 208
selling points, publicizing shows, 230-231
service staff, 174
services, customer service offerings, 176
sets (performance), structuring
    balance, 94
    clichés to avoid, 99
    closers, 97
    cohesion, 94
    comedic elements, 95
    content and style, 98-99
    musical accompaniment, 96
    openers, 92-93
    pace, 94
    patter, 97
    sound effects, 96
    spectacle and visual accessories, 96
    suspense and surprise elements, 95

The Edge, 96-97
unity, 94
variety, 95, 97
short poems, 93
show-makers, 162
shows. See also competitions, performances
    adding artistic elements to, 249-253
        ceremonies and rituals, 249-250
        hecklers, 251
        suspense-building ideas, 251-252
    booking, 133
    competitive aspects of
        contestant sign-ups, 253
        judging methods, 255
        selection of judges, 253
    fueling audience frenzy, 221-222
    itineraries
        competitions, 248
        examples, 245, 248-249
        greetings, 246
        nightclub acts, 245
        open-mike sessions, 246
        plot points, 246-249
        special acts and guest performers, 247
        start and end times, 244-245
        theater productions, 245
        visions, 244

marketing plans
  angles and selling
    points, 230-231
  deadlines, 239
  follow-ups, 240
  target markets,
    237-238
  the push, 239
  tools, 231-236
  word-of-mouth, 237
merchandising options
  anthologies, 223
  compilation CDs, 224
  partnerships, 226
  preserving your show's
    history, 222-223
  t-shirts and souvenirs,
    225-226
organizing
  assessing talents and
    resources, 163-164
  by committees, 208
  delegation of duties,
    209-211
  emcees, 211-214
  in-house ensembles,
    216
  inventorying readiness,
    158-162
  obstacles, 164-166
  offstage support,
    214-215
  self-made slams, 208
  vision-focusing
    process, 167-168
pacing, 256
payment arrangements,
  140-142
publicizing shows, 230

role of slammasters
  greeting guests, 218
  introducing guests, 219
  maitre d', 219
sideshows (NPS rituals),
  290
special shows
  band slams, 267
  benefits, 263
  book fairs and festivals,
    262
  celebrity slams, 264
  Chi Town Classic, 268
  corporate conventions,
    262
  Fat Tuesday celebra-
    tions, 268
  holiday slams, 267
  institutions, 260-261
  motorcycle slams, 263
  pitching ideas, 270
  Slam America Tour,
    269
  Slam Dunk events, 265
  youth slams, 266
spinning, 256
start times, 221
Shy Guys, 65
Sia, Beau, 280
sideshows (NPS rituals), 290
Singapore slam, 324-325
"Sirens at the Mill"
  (Buscani, Lisa), 49
size concerns, venue selection criteria, 172-173
slam
  certifications
    evidence, 284

renewals, 284
  versus registrations,
    283-284
defining characteristics, 4,
  8-9
families, 281-282
famous disclaimers
  Holman, Bob, 35
  NPS (National Poetry
    Slam), 37
  Smith, Marc, 36-37
formats
  Cover Slam, 39
  Pong Jam Slam, 40
  Prop Slam, 40
  Relay Slam, 39-40
  Theme Slam, 38
  Unseen Slam, 37-38
globalization, 326
  Denmark, 321
  France, 322-324
  Germany, 317-318,
    321
  growth and develop-
    ment patterns, 316
  Singapore, 324-325
  Switzerland, 321
local slam laws, 41-42
locating performance
  opportunities, 110-111
registering
  benefits, 283
  renewals, 284
  versus certifying slam,
    283-284
self-made slams, 208
slam cops (personality
  type), 220

spin-offs
Battle of the Bay, 312
Canadian Spoken
Word Olympics, 313
chick slams, 168
drama slams, 168
improv slams, 168
Midwest Poetry Slam
League, 310-311
music and dance slams,
168
New Word Series, 311
Russell Simmons's Def
Poetry Jam, 313
Taos Poetry Circus,
312
venues. *See* venues
Slam America Tour, 269
Slam Dunk events, 265
Slamily, 318
slammasters
adding artistic elements
to shows, 249-253
ceremonies and rituals,
249-250
hecklers, 251
suspense building
ideas, 251-252
assessing talents and
resources, 163-164
Confessions of a Virgin
Slammaster, 158
dealing with different
personality types,
219-220
apologizers, 220
blamers, 220
interrogators, 220

slam cops, 220
superslammers, 220
developing show itiner-
aries
competitions, 248
examples, 245,
248-249
greetings, 246
nightclub acts, 245
open-mike sessions,
246
plot points, 246-249
special acts and guest
performers, 247
start and end times,
244-245
theater productions,
245
visions, 244
fueling audience frenzy,
221-222
inventorying readiness,
158-163
self-centered individu-
als, 159-160
show-maker abilities,
162
support networks, 160
time and energy obli-
gations, 161-162
visions, 160
merchandising options
anthologies, 223
compilation CDs, 224
partnerships, 226
preserving your show's
history, 222-223
t-shirts and souvenirs,
225-226

obstacles
jealousy, 164-165
money issues, 165
pettiness and social
hostilities, 166
unforeseen changes,
165
organizing shows
by committees, 208
delegation of duties,
209-211
emcees, 211-214
in-house ensembles,
216
offstage support,
214-215
self-made slams, 208
pacing shows, 256
roles, 136
greeting guests, 218
introducing guests, 219
maitre d', 219
special shows
band slams, 267
benefits, 263
book fairs and festivals,
262
celebrity slams, 264
Chi Town Classic, 268
corporate conventions,
262
Fat Tuesday celebra-
tions, 268
holiday slams, 267
institutions, 260-261
motorcycle slams, 263
pitching ideas, 270
Slam America Tour,
269

Slam Dunk events, 265
youth slams, 266
starting shows on time,
221
venue selection process
ambiance, 173-175
closing the deal,
181-182
customer service
offerings, 176
final selection stage,
180-181
house party slams, 183
location issues,
176-177
resources, 177-179
selecting a night to
perform, 179-180
set-up of performance
areas, 175-176
size concerns, 172-173
written list of criteria,
177
vision-focusing process
community needs,
167-168
personal needs, 167
spin-offs, 168
SlamMasters' Council, 282,
291
Slammin' @ Your Library,
306
SlamNation, 280
Slant Rhymes, 54
slide shows, 202-204
Smith, Marc
accounts of first National
Poetry Slam, 14

"Bicycle Jockey," 58
history of slam poetry, 11
slam disclaimers, 36-37
"So What!" handle, 11
social hostilities, 166
socio-economic barriers, 23
Solis, Danny, 183
sonic devices
alliterations, 53
assonances, 53
cacophony, 53
consonances, 53
euphony, 53
hidden alliterations, 53
onomatopoeias, 53
rhymes
Cross Rhymes, 54
Interlaced Rhymes, 54
Internal Rhymes, 54
Linked Rhymes, 54
rhymation, 55
Slant Rhymes, 54
Wrenched Rhymes, 55
sound
sonic devices. *See* sonic
devices
sound systems
four-channel mixers,
197
Graphic EQ settings,
197
location of speakers,
197
monitors, 198
offstage support, 214
unidirectional micro-
phones, 196

structuring performance
sets, 96
volume variations, 78-80
South African praise poets
(Imbongi), 48
Southern Fried Regional
Poetry Slam, 307
souvenirs, merchandising
options, 225-226
speak alongs, 250
speakers, location of, 197
special shows
band slams, 267
benefit shows, 263
book fairs and festivals,
262
celebrity slams, 264
Chi Town Classic, 268
corporate conventions,
262
Fat Tuesday celebrations,
268
holiday slams, 267
itineraries, 247
motorcycle slams, 263
pitching ideas, 270
Slam America Tour, 269
Slam Dunk events, 265
youth slams, 266
spectacles
costumes, 200
music, 202
props, 205
slide shows, 202-204
structuring performance
sets, 96
Speechmaker's Shift tech-
nique (eye contact), 86

spin-offs
band slams, 267
Battle of the Bay, 312
Canadian Spoken Word
Olympics, 313
celebrity slams, 264
Chi Town Classic, 268
chick slams, 168
drama slams, 168
Fat Tuesday celebrations,
268
holiday slams, 267
improv slams, 168
Midwest Poetry Slam
League, 310-311
motorcycle slams, 263
music and dance slams,
168
New Word Series, 311
pitching ideas, 270
Russell Simmons's Def
Poetry Jam, 313
Slam America Tour, 269
Slam Dunk events, 265
Taos Poetry Circus, 312
youth slams, 266
spinning, 256
spoken word poetry tradi-
tions, 4-7
beatniks and hippies, 6
competitions, 5-6
Hip Hop traditions, 6-7
New Criticisms interpre-
tations, 6-7
staff members, PSI (Poetry
Slam, Inc.), 285-286

stage fright
coping mechanisms
accumulation of stage
time, 70-71
alcohol and drug use,
68
being prepared, 65
determining the cause,
64-65
Jobbers, 65
practice, 66
relaxation exercises, 66
Reluctant Martyrs, 65
shifting focus, 66
Shy Guys, 65
tension release
exercises, 67-68
Total Avoiders, 65
tricks of the trade, 68
visualizing success, 66
virgin virgin slammers, 69
stage time, 70-71
stages, 185
bandstands, 187
black boxes, 186-187
cleared spaces, 188
do-it-yourself stages, 192
Great Halls, 188-189
lighting systems
do-it-yourself systems,
199
lights-up and lights-
down concept,
198-199
top-shelf lighting, 199
outdoor stages, 190
pitfalls to avoid, 192-193

proscenium stages, 186,
189
rental stages, 191
sound systems
four-channel mixers,
197
Graphic EQ settings,
197
location of speakers,
197
monitors, 198
unidirectional micro-
phones, 196
start times, show itineraries,
244-245
stones, imagine the stone
exercise, 84
Storm poets, 299
storytelling components
actions, 58
bulls-eyes, 59
characters, 57
conflicts, 58
crisis, 59
point of views, 58-59
time and place, 58
subcommittees, PSI (Poetry
Slam, Inc.), 286
subjects. See topics
Substanz, 318
summer camps, 305
Sunday night performances,
180
superslammers (personality
type), 220
support networks, 160
support service staff, 174
surprise elements, 95

suspense elements
  adding to shows, 251-252
  structuring performance
    sets, 95
Switzerland slam, 321
syntax, 51

T

t-shirts, merchandising
  options, 225-226
talent
  scouting performers, 210
  slammasters, 163-164
Taos Poetry Circus, 5, 312
tape recording rehearsals, 73
target markets (promotions)
  calculating marketing
    budgets, 238
  estimating audience size,
    237
team competitions
  NPS (National Poetry
    Slam), 295-298
    availability of slots, 298
    rules, 295
    selection process, 298
  primary authors, 296
techniques (performance)
  articulation, 81
  body movements, 83-85
  breaths and pauses, 82
  eye contact, 85-86
  moods, 87-88
  personas, 87-88
  tempo variations, 80
  volume variations, 78-80
telephone solicitation (mar-

keting tool), 235
television
  as a marketing tool, 236
  press releases, 129
tempo variations, 80
tension release exercises,
  67-68
theaters
  locating performance
    opportunities, 110
  show itineraries, 245
theatrical devices
  competitions
    contestant sign-ups,
      253
    judging methods, 255
    selection of judges, 253
  costumes, 200
  lighting systems, 198-199
  music, 202
  props, 205
  slide shows, 202-204
  sound systems, 196-198
Theme Slam, 38
Thibault, Robb, 158
Thomas, Elizabeth, 267
three-minute rule, 33,
  294-295
Thursday night perform-
  ances, 179
time limits
  slam competitions, 33
  three-minute rule, 33,
    294-295
timers, 215
tools (marketing)
  brand names and logos,
    231

flyers and postcards, 232
  posters, 233
top-shelf lighting systems,
  199
topics, 59
  concrete poems, 61-62
  misconceptions, 61-62
  persona poems, 60
  political poems, 60
  pop poems, 60
  structuring performance
    sets
      clichés to avoid, 99
      content and style,
        98-99
Total Avoiders, 65
tours
  accommodations, 134
  booking shows, 133
  marketing strategies, 135
  payment arrangements,
    140-142
  pitfalls to avoid, 139-140
  role of contacts
    booking agents,
      137-138
    club owners and
      managers, 136
    concert hall staff, 138
    slammasters, 136
  routes, 132
  Slam America Tour, 269
  transportation, 134
transportation, 134
Tuesday night perform-
  ances, 179
Twinkie prize, 12

U

unidirectional microphones, 196
United States Scholar-Athlete Games, 306
unity, structuring performance sets, 94
Unseen Slam, 37-38
Uptown Poetry Slam, 12

V

variety, structuring performance sets, 95-97
Veeck, Bill, 162
venues, 108
  benefit shows, 263
  book fairs and festivals, 262
  corporate conventions, 262
  history of slam poetry, 13
  institutions
    contact tactics, 261
    locating, 260-261
  lighting systems
    do-it-yourself systems, 199
    lights-up and lights-down concept, 198-199
    top-shelf lighting, 199
  locating performance opportunities
    bookstores, 109
    do-it-yourself venues, 111
    late-night theaters, 110
    nightclubs, 109
    performance venues, 110

schools, 110
slams, 110-111
organizing shows. *See* organizing shows
selection process
  ambiance, 173-175
  closing the deal, 181-182
  customer service offerings, 176
  final selection stage, 180-181
  house party slams, 183
  location issues, 176-177
  resources, 177-179
  selecting a night to perform, 179-180
  set-up of performance areas, 175-176
  size concerns, 172-173
  written list of criteria, 177
sound systems
  four-channel mixers, 197
  Graphic EQ settings, 197
  location of speakers, 197
  monitors, 198
  unidirectional microphones, 196
stages. *See* stages
video recordings
  DVD transfers, 124
  professional recordings, 123
virgin virgin performers, 13, 69

visions
  show itineraries, 244
  slammasters
    inventorying readiness, 160
    vision-focusing process, 167-168
Vistros, Ben, 323
visual accessories, 96
visualization, coping with stage fright, 66
vocal exercises, 149
volume variations, 78-80
volunteers
  IWPS (Individual World Poetry Slam), 300
  NPS (National Poetry Slam), 300
  PSI (Poetry Slam, Inc.), 279-280

W–X

walk the talk (body movement exercise), 84
Wall Focus technique (eye contact), 86
websites
  as a marketing tool, 235
  creating
    benefits, 124
    promotions, 126
    structuring websites, 125
  e-store, 286
Wednesday night performances, 179
weekly shows, locating performance opportunities, 108

West, Phil, 52
Western Regional competition, 309-310
Whitman, Walt, 52
"Word Up" (P-Jay, Rayl Da), 203
word-of-mouth publicity, 237
World Poetry Association. *See* WPA
World Poetry Bout Association, 5
WPA (World Poetry Association), 5
Wrenched Rhymes, 55

Y–Z

yellow pages, locating venues, 178
Yo Mama Samurai Skits, 270
youth slams, 266

zones, entering, 102-103
Zouk (Singapore nightclub), 324

Do Not Check In Without 2 CDs

CD Track List

CD #1

#1 "Singapore Slam Song"—Chris Mooney Singe

#2 "Disclaimer"—Bob Holman

#3 "Open Mouths"—Cin Salach, engineering by Seth Green

#4 "Adman"—Ron Gillette

#5 "Careful What You Ask For"—Jack McCarthy

#6 C. R. Avery performing Tom Waits' "I'm Big in Japan"

#7 "Blind Spots"—Cin Salach and the Loofah Methode

#8 "Money"—Marc Smith and the Pong Unit

#9 "Sirens at the Mill"—Lisa Buscani

#10 "Beethoven"—Shane Korycen

#11 "Elephant Song"—Danny Solis

#12 "Medusa"—Patricia Smith, percussion by Michael Zerang, engineering by Seth Green

#13 "Television"—Todd Alcott (copyright 1990 Todd Alcott)

#14 "Nightbound"—Marc Smith and the Pong Unit Band

#15 "Forbidden Love"—The Weird Sisters

#16 "Belated Valentine"—Steve Marsh

#17 "Its Journey"—Christina Springer

#18 "For My Itchy Brother"—Joel Chmara

#19 "So Young"—Mary Fons

#20 "Little Green Peas"—Charles Ellik

#21 "23 Chromosomes"—Marcell Murphy

CD #2

#1 "The Bigger Jigger"—Dean Hacker with Rick Fazio

#2 "Black Poets on Death's Corner"—Tyehimba Jess

#3 "I Am Noise"—Yun Wei

#4 "How to Write a Political Poem"—Taylor Mali

#5 "Playground Love"—Taylor Mali

#6 "I Have A Message"—Kimberly Brazwell

#7 Marvin Bell's "Being in Love" performed by Marc Smith

#8 Paul Laurence Dunbar's "We Were the Mask" performed by Marc Smith

#9 "Pull the Next One Up"—Marc Smith and the Pong Unit

The following tracks contain language that may be unsuitable for younger audiences.

#10 Introduction to this portion of the CD

#11 "Hillbilly Girl"—Dean Hacker, engineering by Seth Green

#12 "Dionysia"—Mary Shen Barnidge

#13 "Blues Resurgence/Code Blue"—Taalam Acey

#14 "Letter My Dad Never Gave Me"—Corbet Dean (copyright 2000 Corbet Dean)

#15 "Bicycle Jockey"—Marc Smith and the Pong Unit Band

#16 "Saul William's Balls"—Kimberly Brazwell

#17 "All Praises Due"—Regie Gibson